BREAKING IN®

OVER 100 PRODUCT DESIGNERS REVEAL HOW TO BUILD
A PORTFOLIO THAT WILL GET YOU HIRED

Interviews by
Amina Horozić

TUK TUK PRESS

Breaking In® Over 100 Product Designers Reveal How to Build a Portfolio That Will Get You Hired

Interviews by Amina Horozić

TABLE OF CONTENTS

INTRODUCTION
AMINA HOROZIC
INTERVIEWER
BREAKING IN®
PRODUCT DESIGN

What's this all about?

This book is a collection of interviews with the top creative leadership of the industrial design world about how to land a job as a designer and maintain this fulfilling and fun career. Over 100 creatives share how you should prepare yourself, and your portfolio, in order to land your dream job. Industrial design is a broad field, and within these pages you will find interviews with product, furniture, footwear, and automotive designers working in-house, as freelancers, consultants, and everything in between. Wondering how to land that dream job as an industrial designer? Curious as to what the global industrial design leadership thinks about the future of the field? Want to learn how some of your heroes got their head start? Well then, read on.

It says product design on the cover, but you and the interviewees often mention industrial design…I'm confused!

"Industrial design" is still an overarching term used to define the specialities of product, automotive, and furniture design (and other micro-specialities). The term is often interchangeable with "product design," which has, over the years, evolved to include service, software, and physical product design. There are quite a few debates going on about the proper naming of the field. For our purposes, think of both terms as synonymous.

And who are you exactly?

In 2004, I started my career as an automotive designer for Chrysler. In 2009, I moved to San Francisco to pursue graduate school and work as an industrial designer for frog design and Aether Things. Currently, I am a lead industrial designer at fuseproject. I have a BFA in Industrial Design from College for Creative Studies and an MBA in Design Strategy from California College of the Arts. I was born and raised in Sarajevo, Bosnia and Herzegovina, but feel at home just about anywhere under the sun.

Why did you decide to do this?

I have been through this process myself, more than once. When I graduated from college I spent about five months sending my portfolio out to anyone and everyone, thinking that the same content would resonate equally in every car studio. It didn't. Later, when I was leaving the auto industry for a consulting gig, I had to revamp my portfolio yet again. Work that impressed my bosses at Chrysler did not have the same effect at consulting firms that dealt with consumer electronics clients. I would have loved to have had the information in this book as a guide. Understanding what the creative leadership is looking for in each organization is the key to getting your foot in the door.

Who is this book for?

Anyone considering a career in product design or who just wants insight into how the best minds in the industry think.

What if I find a typo or mistake in the book?

Please let me know and we'll fix it:
updates@breaking.in

I'm a well-respected industrial design creative, creative director, or creative recruiter. Why aren't I in here?

Well, my apologies for the oversight. I would love to hear from you. Let's talk: updates@breaking.in

Anything else?

Thanks to William Burks Spencer for giving me the opportunity (and patience) to complete this book, and Catherine Sun for forwarding me his email and saying, "You'd be perfect for this."

Of course, a huge "thank you" to every designer in this book who took time out of their extremely busy schedules to impart their wisdom and advice to the next generation of designers. And naturally, one big, giant "hvala" to my parents and my big brother for always supporting my every ricochet.

It's true, the work is never over. Keep up the hustle. BI

ALFONSO ALBAISA
EXECUTIVE DESIGN
DIRECTOR
INFINITI
ATSUGI, JAPAN

Interviewed while Mr. Albaisa was the Design Director for Global Passenger Vehicles and Electric Vehicles at Nissan Design America in San Diego.

What kinds of portfolios get your attention these days? What brings in an industrial designer for an interview?

There is not a shortage of portfolios out there; what there is a shortage of is individual risk. They're all starting to look very similar. What we look for, because we don't hire that often, is someone who's bucking those tendencies and looking for their own ground. Just technical expertise is not so critical, because what we find is that the portfolios are very professional. Then everyone who comes in actually drops in skill for the first half a year. It's very strange. Maybe because suddenly they're with all these number ones from previous years, and they're not the top person, so there's kind of a shock. For us, instead of a technically impressive portfolio, it's more about really clever individual ideas.

Has there been a portfolio recently that embodies what you just mentioned, and can you talk about it?

We haven't really been that inspired in the last four years or so. There is such a saturation, unfortunately. I would more say that there are regions that are interesting. The Russian schools have some really interesting vibes, probably because of the aggressiveness—those schools really want to make a name for themselves. They encourage the students to be a little bit more rebellious. The culture of Russia is also somewhat provocative and artistic, so I find it very interesting to look at their portfolios. Coming up strong is Brazil, and Koreans continue to have very nice portfolios. Those are the ones where you can kind of feel the passion of design.

How is "passion of design" translated in portfolios?

There is a sense of labor, like when a portfolio seems very spontaneous but with simple gestures. Effortlessness of the line-work, but with strong impact. It doesn't seem to be so tightly considered. You just immediately get the sense that this personality is exploding out on this document. It wasn't so contrived where every line was considered, or use of color was scientific. Mixing watercolor with other media, the seeping of color, the drama of perspective...when you can get that it's quite inspiring. That kind of spontaneity with power is usually a good sign of a student's portfolio that's going to come into the company and inspire the other members. At the end of the day, it's what I need. I hire so that my team can maintain a level of inspiration. In our spare time, even our most superstar exterior or interior designer is working on some sculptures for me. Right now we are making a sculpture for a gallery opening, and that helps keep the designer loose in the brain. We were doing scooters, we just did a sailboat and it's not divided between disciplines. We mix it all up.

Once you do bring a designer in for an interview, what do you expect to learn from them then?

If we are interviewing someone it's because there was a level of impressiveness. Personally, I enjoy finding out about the motivation—where this young person found inspiration to do something unique. I like the dialogue to be mostly contextual, to understand what the daily thinking is, what inspired the shapes they are creating and stuff like that. Then, just naturally from those conversations, you start to understand if this is a repeated thing, how random it is. This is a person that you're going to live with for hopefully 20 years, and because it's a long-term relationship, you want to make sure that it's a fit that is long term. We lose very few people at NDA [Nissan Design America]. I've worked with some people for over 20 years now. You're getting married, basically. It's a good polygamist situation.

What characteristics or qualities are necessary for a designer to be successful long term in this day and age?

A very flexible mind. You don't have to be flexible in personality, you can be as hard as a rock, but your mind has to be able to come up with countermeasures constantly. A car is a complex thing and there are very ambitious engineers and product planners so your little idea is being bombarded by many real things. When you fall in love with some aspect of your design, you also need to consciously and constantly have an escape route for the next big engineering hit. To be successful over a long time, your mind has to be incredibly agile to respond to new technologies. For example, electric cars are fundamentally different.

"YOU MUST BE CURIOUS TO LEARN NEW THINGS AND BE A LITTLE SKEPTICAL ABOUT YOURSELF. IF YOU'RE TOO MUCH IN LOVE WITH YOURSELF, YOU WILL PROBABLY NOT BE SO CURIOUS. JUST BE AGGRESSIVE."

You must be curious to learn new things and be a little skeptical about yourself. If you're too much in love with yourself, you will probably not be so curious. Just be aggressive. Usually the ones that go a long way are workaholics. For me, it's the curiosity, persistence and agility of mind.

How did you break into the industry?

My father was an architect and when I was a little boy I wanted to be an architect, too. I would go to his office after school, every day, and I would draw in the lobby. One day I heard this sound and I looked outside. There was a black Jaguar convertible pulling into the driveway of my dad's office, and this is 1972 more or less. And I see this black Jag with a black top on a beautiful Miami day. Honestly, from that moment I started drawing cars. I fell in love.

I started college in the mid-80s and I went to Pratt University, then I heard about a school in Detroit and I transferred there. But in the mid-80s the Big

Three were very conservative and during that time I used to dress like Napoleon. I used to wear duct tape for shoes and half of my hair was white and the other half was my natural brown hair. I had so many problems at that school that I went back to New York. I returned to Pratt and started working on small one-off projects in the city, and was a drawing assistant in the department. Just by chance, the school asked me if I could show Nissan my portfolio and talk about the curriculum. By then I was halfway through my senior year. It didn't look like an interview to me. I thought it was going to be about the school. After the presentation was over they left. I went back to my life in New York, which I was in love with, and a month later I get a call from them saying to come to California, we want to make you an offer. I was shocked. I had no interest in the West Coast, I was an East Coast kid. So I came and the studio was so cool. I remember thinking, "Oh my God, this is the coolest place in the world." I thought, "Wow, this is not a corporate life, this is the life that I couldn't imagine, a life less ordinary." So I gave them a try. Twenty-three years later and I'm still here.

If you were starting out now, what advice would you give to yourself?

Don't assume so much. I was fairly black and white. I was a little bit of a punk rocker and was very impulsive. If I didn't like something I'd leave. That's probably why I transferred schools so often. My parents didn't really like how I left scholarships behind. I was probably just a little bit too radical in my intolerance of corporate structures. That's the biggest lesson I've learned: within the very defined rules there are a million freedoms. You just have to look for those. Through my life at Nissan I've designed yachts, I've designed buildings, I've designed cars. It was nothing that I expected. Maybe I would say to myself "buy some shoes." Those duct tape shoes were really quite annoying.

Where do you see the future of transportation or industrial design going?

There's no question that technology will change the life of a designer. The consumers are expecting new cars all the time, quickly, quickly. At the same time, science is coming up with some clever solutions. As the motors go inside the wheels and as the bodies get lighter and lighter and lighter, the expectations of the customer of buying an automobile and moving around in the future are getting higher. Today, it's mostly about style and performance. I think we need something different and, for me, it's science...the mixing of art and science. That's the part I'm curious about. We can be staring at a million realities, but our mind wants to not look at it. Our mind wants to deny it and seek some alternative to it. That's what's going to save us and what will make our jobs interesting.

Anything you'd like to add that we haven't talked about? Any final words of wisdom?

The most powerful organization is the one that focuses on helping the person next to you discover their dream. When a group has everyone focusing on their own talent level, the inspiration slowly spirals downward. Usually, in design you have a top-down structure, an amazing director or president that everyone follows. I think the future has directors focusing on the creative level of individuals and the team. Organically, greatness comes from that kind of organization. I doubt there's any wisdom in that, but that's just the way I choose to live my life. BI

To see Alfonso Albaisa's work, please visit http://breaking.in

GADI AMIT
FOUNDER
NEWDEALDESIGN
SAN FRANCISCO

What kinds of portfolios get your attention these days? What brings in an industrial designer for an interview?

This is a very interesting topic because I pay more attention to the character of the person rather than the portfolio. However, the portfolio should show the creative abilities as well as the character of the person.

I look for a certain type of visual intelligence that comes through either sketching or through the type of objects that the student or the young designer often deals with: the model, the process, and obviously the end result.

The interesting thing is that I do have some big turnoffs. Super slick renderings—they are not a turnoff by themselves—but actually I'm trying to figure out if this person is a CAD jockey who has the phenomenal abilities with rendering but is possibly short on the other sides, or is the slick rendering hiding a weak object? That's one big turnoff. The other big turnoff is the hyper-realistic end sketches. I think there must be some looseness in the thinking and that must be there for great designers to grow. That looseness is characterized by being imperfect, showing sometimes the not-so-nice sketches; the hectic nature of the sketching page is what I'm looking for. So, that is on the more visual side.

I also pay attention to the opening letter or the few words that people tell me about themselves. It shouldn't be too long, but it should be somewhat personable and meaningful.

It sounds like, to you, the sketchbooks may be more important than the portfolio.

To some degree you are right. I'm not looking for a sketchbook per se, I'm looking for pages of form development and the thought development behind an object or an idea. It is very telling about the visual intelligence of the person, their ability to analyze contradicting factors of objects, and so on. To me it's the most telling of all, of what kind of a designer this person would be. There are a lot of people who want to present their cerebral process, the research, that's something that I look at very briefly just to frame the problem and the possible solution. The real design work is when the thoughts resonate with the form or the visual on the paper, where you see how their hand reacts to these conflicts, and how the mind is reacting to the hand, misinterpreting issues—it's a very interesting dialogue that happens with these doodles on a piece of paper. I mean, I think doodles are more the right word than sketches.

Have you seen a portfolio recently that resonated with you, and what about it stood out?

I cannot say, Amina. I haven't been hiring in a while, so it's been a while since I've looked at a portfolio. I can say that we had a young designer that came to us, highly recommended, with exceptional recommendations and cerebral abilities but then this person had difficulties developing forms or ideas, had a little bit of an attitude, and was a little bit difficult to work with. So we switched to somebody who was a lot less arguable and had more of a classic visual intelligence that we've discussed.

If an industrial design student came up to you and asked, "What should my portfolio be like? What do I need to show you in order to work with you?", what would you tell them?

I'd like to see thought process about cultural and aesthetic topics, so it's more about the development of ideas—design ideas—than the analysis of the problem. I also would like to see the end results: models, mock-ups, renderings. Lastly, if possible or relevant, any insights into the process of maturing the object into production, any negotiations or modifications made through that process.

I'm curious, with more than 100 design awards behind you, what characteristics or qualities are necessary to be a successful designer?

It's a very, very complex topic. In the past few years I started paying a lot more attention to character. The quality that is a combination of drive, humility and intelligence that really allows people to grow intellectually and understand their talents: absorbing, internalizing concepts from their surroundings, from their peers, from their superiors, and so on. That is a very unique personality trait that I find to be the number one driver for success. There is a process that I would say probably takes about 10 years, from school out, where you're continuously learning different layers of the design profession, starting from understanding an object or a project, going through more strategic sides of object and project creating, technical aspects, eventually management aspects, and so on. It's very difficult to have and prescribe a philosophical body around it without absorbing it from your surroundings.

In order to do that, to really internalize and come up with your own concepts about what you've observed,

you need to be both intelligent and have humility. You need to have a positive attitude and be a driven person. That's what I'm looking for in young designers if I want to take them on for a long time, and I do. A lot of my crew has been with us for many years and I really emphasize that quality. Actually, I would say loyalty is a quality that's really important because that level of dialogue between the young designer and their surroundings, and between the young designer and herself or himself, is a very important quality. So, I don't know, it's a long answer and I know that even that long answer is somewhat obtuse, so it's a matter of a long, long discussion.

How did you break into this business?

Well, first of all I grew up in Israel and I went to school there and there were not a lot of opportunities there. I started my career essentially as an assistant/model maker in a small industrial design team in a high-tech company. I was very fortunate to work with two incredible people, who I'm still very good friends with. I consider these two guys my really good friends. Through the first year, year and a half, it wasn't clear whether I would have a position there, so I was basically an intern. The arrangement that was developed there was that I'd be doing their models and then after-hours or later in the day I would be doing my designs. I think at some point my talent was actually quite apparent, and my first breakthrough was some computer that we were doing. My design won and moved forward. But still, it took a long time to get recognized within that company. And then I started working with frog design, flying to California, and enjoying the incredible environment of frog design in the early '90s—the tail end of their work with NeXT, only a few years after their work with Apple—which was an incredible experience. I joined the company in '93 and I grew there a lot both professionally and personally. And then I started my own studio. Yet again, it's a completely new beginning, a new level; you learn a lot of things about yourself and about design and the business of design as well.

I would definitely describe the career journey of a designer as a very long one, until you find your stride. That's something that probably takes 10 years on the short side.

What motivated you to open your own design studio?

Well, I don't know how to describe it. I was basically doing it all my life. I was born to a couple of architects and I've more or less always been around architectural or design practices, so I cannot think of anything else I would've done. Even though I must say that industrial design is something that I got to know only at about age 20. I was always tinkering in between building all sorts of mechanical models, all sorts of cranes, things like that, playing with model airplanes and LEGOS. I spent a lot of time in my dad's architectural practice studio, so that's either in my genes or really close to my heart.

"THE REAL DESIGN WORK IS WHEN THE THOUGHTS RESONATE WITH THE FORM OR THE VISUAL ON THE PAPER, WHERE YOU SEE HOW THEIR HAND REACTS TO THESE CONFLICTS, AND HOW THE MIND IS REACTING TO THE HAND, MISINTERPRETING ISSUES..."

I remember one thing in my early 20s, when I had to figure out what I wanted to study. I remember that I made a decision one year that I was going to an exceptionally good design school in Jerusalem; it was very tough to get in there. I had other opportunities like engineering and so on, and I remember that this was the first decision that I made that was kind of dramatic: I decided that I was going to apply only for that school, and for nothing but design. One application, one school. When they asked me, "What would you do if you don't get in?", and I said, "You guys are my number one, two, and three options, I have no other options. That's all," that was the first decision that I made in my dedication to design.

I still think it's a really tough profession. It's non-traditional, it doesn't have a very clear career path. It doesn't have establishment, so to speak. You need to have somewhat of a dogmatic, strong-willed drive in order to find your way in this business. It's not an easy business.

If you were just starting out now, what advice would you give yourself?

I kind of got 12 out of 10 of my wishes. I consider myself really lucky. In hindsight, I don't know, some level of humility, intelligence, and drive must be there. I think [it's important] to be very positive about really tough moments. Designers, especially the really young ones, have a lot of tough moments where their creation is actually being discarded or being modified or mutilated even. There's got to be some strong balance between fighting for your idea, as well as accepting defeat. That's part of the job. I think being a team player is very, very important at the beginning. You learn a lot from the team members around you, whether it's your peers or your superiors.

I think it's very important for young designers to work in environments of high design. There are very few spots like that and honestly I would recommend that young designers take a spot, even for just half a day, in such an environment. Because of the lack of establishment and the weakness of the design profession in general, there are so very few spots that have really good high-design quality and high-design culture. This is a very important environment in order to frame your personality within design.

There are so many bad opportunities, and these are the things that will affect you for many years to come. I do think that the classic design studio is kind of a formation of a design persona. I don't think there's any other opportunity than that. It doesn't mean that the classic design studio cannot be within a corporation, or within a larger design agency, but it is very important in my opinion to avoid becoming the single designer in some medium-sized corporation or a corporation that doesn't have a good design culture around it or a design agency that is based on a very cerebral process. I think that's really important for a designer. Those formative years in the first five years of the designer's career are basically an extension of school, and sometimes more important than school. Not sometimes, always more important than school.

It's almost like a foundation for the rest of one's career.

Yeah, for me, I would consider those to be the most formative years of my career. Talking to my peers I think that just about everyone agrees. It's always the first or second job placement they had that was so formative and they always talk very fondly about the works of their managers, their principles, and you definitely feel how they learned so much from those early experiences.

They had mentors and somebody to look up to, to learn from.

Definitely. I think mentorship is extremely important and there's some misconception about how it comes. Mentorship comes not necessarily by spending hours over a glass of wine or drinking coffee together; it's sometimes anecdotal. It's around a foam model or five minutes of interesting discussion during a client presentation. These are very valuable lessons and sometimes they just happen naturally. If you're on a project, and there's a moment with a principal who's been in the business for 20 to 30 years and has seen a lot, you're the young designer who suddenly gets insights that very few people would have and probably none of your school teachers even experienced. I was fortunate enough that I had true mentors early in my career and that's been very important for me.

You mentioned earlier a designer dealing with their designs being changed, or even mutilated. How do you suggest a young designer deal with this reality that their initial idea will go through many phases and changes before it hits the market? How should they retain the integrity of their initial design?

Well maybe the initial integrity of their design shouldn't be retained. It's a very strong topic obviously, very visceral reactions. Young people especially are full of emotion and convictions about their designs. It's very tough to say something anecdotal here. Essentially, there are a great deal of instances where you were wrong and that's part of the learning process, understanding that your initial idea was good to share and to get to some other aesthetic. That's a tough lesson.

The other tough lesson is that sometimes you need to lose a small battle in order to win the big war. Sometimes giving away something is actually an art that can help a bigger object or idea to survive. There's no consoling statement that I can make. It's a tough process. It's tough internally—people usually invest in their first ideas heavily, emotionally and physically. The work is taxing in many ways. It's a learning process on yourself to kind of get more concise and get more polished and so on. I still see a lot of young designers in my studio struggling with that.

I think it's also, on some levels, a weakness in the educational system in terms of critique. It happened to me more than once where I felt that I was giving—for the first time—a serious, negative critique of an idea to a student. Many of the young designers are coming out of the system where they have been pampered for years, to feel that they're good. Then they get to a point where somebody will say to them good is not good enough, it needs to be great. A new idea needs to be great and that's a difficult position to find oneself in. Maybe here I'm digressing to a different topic. I just want to state that there are many angles to the same story here.

Where do you see the future of industrial design going as it evolves further in the 21st century?

Prophecy is kind of a fool's job. It's very tough to be a prophet here. I think though that industrial designers have a very unique capacity to form logic or outline structures and organizations from very complex sets of factors, or very complex problems. I think that ability, whether it's on an ideas level or actually a physical organization around many components of technology, is a very unique capacity. I actually don't think that anyone, including engineering, comes close to that. I think that the overall capacity of designers to form solutions out of multifaceted, multilayered wicked problems is something that will be propelling this profession forward and hopefully society and industry towards recognizing it for its capacity.

I'm seeing a major shift in the breadth and depth of the assignments that designers get, and the big challenge for designers through this change of becoming architects of ideas, or architects of products or architects of information, is not to lose that capacity. I do think that's an interesting challenge because a lot of the solutions that we prescribe within the design industry are actually being thrown by the wayside, like the artistic, non-cerebral capacities of design that made them so intelligent about creating these superstructures. I think designers should be very mindful of what got them here before they throw it by the wayside and replace the methodologies with, let's say, MBA or economic methodologies and so on. Then they will lose the uniqueness of their intellectual capacity. I hope this gives you an answer. I think there's huge opportunity, but I think there's also a huge risk of losing the soul of design through the process of capitalizing on that opportunity.

Anything we didn't cover that you would like to add? Any final words of wisdom?

It's an incredibly enriching profession. I come to work every day wired and happy. I call these the white moments where there is an idea that you had that comes to life—that's an incredible moment. In a human experience I think there are very few moments like that. Designers have that capacity. Very few people have that, very few professions have that.

On a personal note, I'm about to go into a meeting with a company that just announced this incredible new camera that uses this new technology called light-field technology and I remember the moment where I made a gesture with my hand, as if you hold a kaleidoscope to your eye, and that actually drove the design of the object. It was later developed by my team, but the point is that you see this idea come to fruition; it gets support from management and the board of directors and comes to market with a bang and people are admiring the design. I call this a white moment. Pure happiness, pure joy, and I think designers who have a really, really hard time being respected, even within their family, within their relationships, they cherish these moments because they are really unique to design. Maybe musicians have that, these indelible moments that cannot be forgotten.

I think that the long and hard journey is compensated by these beautiful moments. It's something that should really be talked about and cherished by young designers because they will have a lot of hard moments through their career. [BI]

To see the work of Gadi Amit, please visit http://breaking.in

ROBERT ARKO PRINCIPAL A+O SAN FRANCISCO

Interviewed while Mr. Arko was the VP and Creative Director at Coalesse, in San Francisco.

What kinds of portfolios get your attention these days, and what brings in a product designer for an interview?

There's always the random portfolio that's really inspiring based on a philosophical view of design. Designers work across a broad spectrum and you see that in portfolios. People can be strong in methodology or strong in a skill or strong in a vertical. Furniture design is one vertical. It's one type of product and in a scope of that vertical one of the things that sets furniture design apart from some other forms of product design is the complete integration of engineering and expression. You cannot separate the two. It's not a packaging exercise, it's closer to architecture than other forms of product design. Then there's our focus on human-centered design, so people who have strong methodology or background in user-centered practices, where they are taking insights from the real world and translating them, stand in contrast to more formalistic design activities. Of course, they're both important but I'm looking for that breadth of methodology and experience.

Another aspect that's really important in the realm of furniture design is spatial competencies. Not every designer has those. An understanding or an actual practice in interior design, or architectural or environmental design, where they are relating how users in a spatial context are interacting. That's what furniture is, it's different than doing a device that has a user interaction emphasis to it. It's more of a spatial interaction.

Lastly I would say sustainability, it's important across the board of anyone practicing design in any field, but it's particularly important in the built world, so a perspective on that, a familiarity with the concepts on that topic, is useful and a growing necessity.

Have you seen a portfolio recently that really stood out? What about it caught your eye?

There's some incredible talent out there. When I look at the practices we are used to in the design world, compared to my colleagues in engineering or marketing where they are limited to a résumé and a conversation, while we have this portfolio tradition which offers up so much more perspective on an individual's background and how they think. When you couple that with a personal interview and the résumé to give context to depth of experience, it's just...I'm just so glad I don't have to make hires outside of the creative world because without that portfolio I'd feel really stunted.

"TALENT IS SOMETHING THAT GOES BEYOND WHAT CAN BE EASILY CAPTURED IN A RÉSUMÉ AND IT COMES THROUGH IN A PORTFOLIO."

Talent is something that goes beyond what can be easily captured in a résumé and it comes through in a portfolio. People who are curious, people who have the ability to translate ideas in remarkable ways, I can see that in a variety of ways. Design has this multiplicity of dimensions, so it could be shown through design thinking, which is a more process-based inspiration, or it could be something that's incredibly poetic—this ability to translate a conceptual idea into an actual proposition, or there's somebody who is coming more from the making side, a craft or technical perspective. All of those things can be incredible points of departure for a designer. When I see that I just want to meet them, even if I don't have a position open, because these are fascinating people.

What do you expect to learn from a designer during an interview?

I've spent nearly 30 years in this profession and as a designer and I'm looking at portfolios from a rich perspective, so I can get a lot out of a portfolio and it helps me with the filtering process. I have a strong philosophy about the hiring process and I take it super seriously, so I will make sure that we're looking at the right spectrum. I follow it up first with a phone interview and that is to talk through issues, hear the person articulate the white space in between the sentences, to talk about intent of the projects. To get a familiarity on how mature they are in their design practice.

Then there's the fit—how the person will fit within our group is vitally important. Face-to-face interviews are incredibly important and I believe in at least two of those, one with me first and then another with my team and my peers. My philosophy is if you make great hires, so many problems take care of themselves. Design business is hard enough and you want to be really careful there. We're looking for people that are high impact, that ideally can make a career out of the position.

What kinds of characteristics or qualities are necessary for the designer to have in order to succeed?

There are so many things, but the bottom line is you got to have talent. Like in any creative field––if you're a chef, or an actor, singer or musician, writer––talent is the unquantifiable thing. The intersection of talent and experience is fundamental. There's another thing about personality types that is huge. I really value curiosity. If there is one thing that I'm looking for it's people that are curious and act on it. It's a stance on life. Not everybody has that, and that applies to an engineer or a marketing person, any field. I'm looking for people that have that and it comes through the work and the conversation.

How did you break into this business?

I'm a Midwesterner so I didn't grow up in a culture of design. I had to find and discover design. I didn't know it existed. I didn't even know how to articulate it. I found industrial design to be a perfect expression of my need to be involved in a creative pursuit, but also it satisfied my more analytical, engineering side where I was interested in solving problems in a pragmatic sense. I also worked very hard. There's no question that in a creative field you need to be competitive because it's challenging, there are a lot more people who want positions than there are positions available. I had a lot of luck, but I made a lot of my own luck. If you don't take things for granted and have passion—in combination with hard work—things will tend to align for you and it will be easier for things to fall into place.

If you were just starting out now, what advice would you give yourself?

I learned really early how important the sequence of choices are to a career path. Any given position sets the framework for the next position—the next possible adjacency idea. You are, in a sense, what you were doing last. It's not saying it's impossible to make a 180-degree turn, but it tends to set a context for the next position. Designers should really think about that. There's a time in your life to be exploratory, to go for it, but ultimately to get to a career path you need to start making some decisions.

I moved to San Francisco with just a couple hundred dollars, so money was important, but never dominant. I came to understand that you get paid in variety of ways. You get paid in experience, and you get paid in notoriety. So make sure you intern for the right person, for the right experience and if they are noticed in the world, that will mean something to you, too. You can have a right job monetarily but a poor level of experience that's not going to get you very far.

Where do you see the future of industrial design going as it evolves further in the 21st century?

I think it's really clear that across the spectrum of creative activities there's a democratization happening. The networked economy allows us to have a different kind of communication and foster these kinds of communities—just think of vehicles like Etsy and Kickstarter. The notion of what we think of as professional endeavors will be challenged. I don't think a degree is necessarily the goal. The goal is great design, no matter how that happens. If the broader world is involved in that, it probably makes the people who are doing professionally even better as the conversation gets even richer and richer. When the culture embraces something, the bar raises in terms of sophistication, in terms of what people perceive, value and desire. If the culture demands great design because it's having richer conversations, this is better for people who are doing it professionally. Instead of

pushing onto marketplace, they're being challenged by the marketplace. I think that's a pretty good dynamic.

I also believe that design should be taught right along the level of reading, writing, and arithmetic because we are all consumers and critical thinking about the material and experiential world would make us into better consumers. You see that now in the food industry; we're challenging the kinds of things we put in our bodies and asking to be served by smarter, more conscious, and responsible suppliers. The more knowledgeable we are as consumers, the better all our industries will be.

Anything you'd like to add that we haven't talked about? Any final words of wisdom?

Having heart while doing this kind of work is really important. Having heart no matter what you're going to make as a career choice. It's a journey. I love the concept of vocation more than job. Figure out what you want to do with your life to make it fulfilling. Design is one of those fields that can be fulfilling for a variety of people. Don't go into design thinking it's going to be just a cool job—you're not going to be very successful.

Design is a philosophy and lifestyle, and a way of perceiving and acting in the world. ⊞

To see the work of Robert Arko and Coalesse, please visit http://breaking.in

MAARTEN BAAS
FOUNDER
STUDIO MAARTEN BAAS
'S-HERTOGENBOSCH,
NETHERLANDS

Your work blurs the line between art and design. Can you discuss your approach and share an example of challenges that you face in designing for a very niche market?

I don't design for a niche market. Some products end up in a niche market, and that's quite a difference. Since I don't design for a specific market, there are also no specific challenges. This "limited edition" design world is something quite funny. It seems there's not enough trust or appreciation for things that are defined to be "design," so the prices often don't cover the high costs that it takes to create them. I think it's ridiculous how people stick so much to only a definition.

"THE HANDICAP OF DESIGN IS THAT A CHAIR IS ALWAYS COMPARED TO A CHAIR, WHICH IS NOT ALWAYS FAIR. ONE WOULDN'T EVER COMPLAIN THAT A CERTAIN MICHELIN STARRED RESTAURANT IS EXPENSIVE COMPARED TO MCDONALD'S."

Personally, I like to be a sidekick in this circus, by making a limited-edition grandfather clock, as well as an iPhone app of the same thing available for 99 cents. It's strategy. It's the most stupid thing to do, but artistically, the only thing I want, because both clocks needed to be executed in that way.

Since design is published much more often than art, there's a kind of glamour aspect to it, which takes away the exclusivity of it. I once designed a unique piece that had been published a lot. A potential client wanted to buy the piece, but then said: "No, it's everywhere, so I'm not interested anymore." It's a strange mechanism of how things seem to work. It's a two-faced market. People have unreal reasons to appreciate something. It's not so much about the thing itself, or even the effort that has been put in it or the material, but it's about the marketing. The economic crisis helps a lot in putting people back on the ground again.

The handicap of design is that a chair is always compared to a chair, which is not always fair. One wouldn't ever complain that a certain Michelin starred restaurant is expensive compared to McDonald's. Everybody understands the price difference, and everybody knows that the chef doesn't get rich by his margins on food. Still, in design, unconsciously people compare IKEA with a handmade piece in experimental materials. That's something that would be nice to change.

What characteristics or qualities are necessary to be a successful industrial designer?

There are so many different designers with different characteristics that I don't see one characteristic that "makes" a good designer. One thing that is probably important is that I don't know many designers who are purely good designers. Most of them have a few other good qualities that help them to realize their designs, either in commercial thinking or in communication or in technique. It also depends on how you would interpret the word "success." I don't think the best designers are the most successful ones.

What motivated you to open your own design studio?

I didn't really think of it. It just happened since Smoke was such a success from the very beginning. Actually, right after my exams, Studio Job approached me to work for them. I considered it, but when Smoke did so well I chose to do that, and after I continued with other collections. I always went full on for what I believed. I didn't just want to make "another product," I wanted a total new concept that would open our eyes. As long as I keep on doing that, I go on. I know the moment will come when I will have the feeling that I don't have anything to add anymore. When I met Bas den Herder—now owner of Den Herder Production House—things went much faster all of a sudden. I could focus more on design and development because he took care of all practical things. That collaboration has been very important.

How do you manage the non-design aspects of running a studio?

There are much more non-design things than design things to do. On one hand, it's very important to be universal, to know a bit of business, a bit of technique, a bit of presentation, a bit of marketing, and so on. On the other hand, it's difficult that none of these aspects is my specialty. Partly I like them, and partly I'm trying to reduce them. I'm helped very much by others, mainly Bas den Herder, who is the co-owner of the studio. This year he opened Den Herder Production House [DHPH]. Apart from producing designs for me, he works for other designers as well, such as Bertjan Pot. He makes products that are in the same category as clay furniture: handmade, accessible, possible to be custom-made, and so on. DHPH is not really a mass-producer, but more a studio that reproduces certain nice products. I think that's a very interesting way of making things. The collaboration with me went very well and I'm glad he can do it with other designers now, too.

What advice would you give to a young designer who wishes to start their own practice?

Never believe in one-liners.

Where do you see the future of industrial design going as it evolves further in the 21st century?

I'm not so interested in industrial design. It should have a human scale. Someone makes the product, finishes the product, sells the product. That's much more natural than big machines and anonymous people assembling products. I've always strived to keep it small, and I think that's what industrial design should aim for as well. It's not needed anymore to make the cheapest chair again and again. People will see that impersonal design is just crap and doesn't add anything to our world. I believe much more in smaller series that are made with personal attention. Probably more expensive than a normal chair, but much nicer to have. 〔BI〕

To see Maarten Baas's work, please visit http://breaking.in

PAUL BACKETT
PARTNER
EVOLVE COLLABORATIVE
& SOHRAB VOSSOUGHI
FOUNDER, PRESIDENT AND
CHIEF CREATIVE DIRECTOR
ZIBA
PORTLAND

Interviewed while Mr. Backett was the Industrial Design Director at Ziba.

What kinds of portfolios get your attention these days? What brings in an industrial designer for an interview?

PB: I think one of the key things for us when we're looking at portfolios is designers who are storytellers. We are looking for designers who aren't just showing the same process over again, we are looking for designers who can tell different types of stories in their portfolios. That can be lots of different things. It could be the journey of the project or the theory. It could be a beautiful consumer story that resonates with the target they've chosen. What catches our eye is when they have different tastes, when they've explored different things. That the designer is aware of the multiple stories they're telling while also telling a story about themselves.

SV: I look for someone who can define and articulate a problem very clearly. What gets me is when somebody talks for a half an hour about a problem that's so simple. That usually means they don't know what it is. So, what is the problem? What is the solution, and how did you get there? I want to look at the thinking process and how you solved the problem. Framing the problem and having the ability to solve it. People show me their portfolios all the time and ask me if it's good or not, and I say "There's no good or bad design, there's only right design," meaning it's the right solution to the problem.

PB: I think that's a really important subject. We are not as interested in the final product. Of course it has to be beautiful and appropriate and right, but what's more important is how they got there. What was the journey? That can tell us way more about the designer than the final product.

SV: Skills can be taught. Of course, you have to have potential. We look at potential. We look at potential and thought process. The real learning starts after school.

Have you seen a portfolio lately that resonated with you? What about it made it stand out?

PB: We occasionally do see them. There are big schools out there that teach the kids these core skills of storytelling and [they] are producing some interesting portfolios. The good ones always capture our eye, and then we get them in to get to know them better as people. There are some interesting portfolios that don't follow the norm and describe different types of processes and approaches, the ones that aren't afraid to talk about the unfamiliar.

SV: I can't think of one either, but another thing we look for is craftsmen. Craftsmen not just in the sense of model-making, but craft in the sense of mindset. The care, the engagement in the work, the attention to details...it's really, really important.

So if an industrial design student came up to you and asked, "What should my portfolio be like? What do I need to show you in order to work with you?", what would you tell them?

SV: Only show me your best work. Show me one, preferably your best, project from start (problem definition) to end (the solution). The presentation should be very clear, articulate, and to-the-point. The solution should be smart, simple, elegant, relevant, and beautiful. This rule applies to everything you show me.

Once you do bring in a designer for an interview, what do you expect to learn from them at that one-on-one meeting?

PB: One of the key things is actually how articulate they are. Can they sit in a room and talk to a bunch of people they've never met before? Can they talk about their design? About their process and their beliefs? Their passions? Their feelings? That's a really key thing for us. We have to be able to talk about what we do

and explain it to our clients, so it's a really key thing. We are looking to get really curious people. We have a really particular person that fits here at Ziba. It's really nice to get to know them as people and try to understand if they're going to fit. We look for people who are humble, who will make things better.

SV: Being articulate is very important. As a designer, your design is as good as your presentation. It's as good as your storytelling. If you're not articulate, you cannot talk about your work, and then your work doesn't mean anything. It is so important to be able to tell a story and be articulate. There are some designers whose work is not that good from the visual point of view, but the way they present it, the way they articulate it, is amazing. The other thing is about culture fit. We definitely do not hire egos. Everyone has egos, but we try to truly collaborate here. If you have an ego, it doesn't work. You just won't fit in here. I'm not saying that people with egos are bad or good, they just won't fit in here. It's all about the work, rather than the person.

PB: Being open and able to work with a team is essential.

What characteristics or qualities are necessary to be a successful designer?

SV: Having an open mind and trying to go broad at the same time that you go deep. Too much specialization is not going to work out. Maybe at the beginning, but this whole work of design is so broad these days—there are no boundaries between disciplines. We are looking for people who like to stretch themselves. There are places for specialists, but it limits their growth. I would say that ability to see what they present is not just renderings and drawings, but the depth too. The thinking process: that's the biggest thing you should come out with from the design school. The thinking process, not the skills. At the end of the day, design is about business and helping business to be successful. The combination of business and design is really, really important, especially these days. If you don't want to be pigeonholed, you really have to go broad and extend yourself. Have confidence to be able to know where you are and confidence to stretch yourself.

PB: I think curiosity is really, really, really important. We don't expect you to be masters of multiple disciplines. Especially as industrial designers, we know they have the mastery of their craft, but then they have that curiosity of outside areas. The real education begins in the real world, once you start working. We have a lot of staff in broad areas where designers coming from college can learn a lot, so we expect them to be curious, to ask questions, and we can really help adapt best to that curiosity. Another key thing is really passion. We look for people who really love what they do. We are looking for people who get excited when they are talking about work. We want those kinds of people to be in front of our clients. We want people to show how much they love being here.

SV: Again, having that combination of craft-mentality and passion. When you're a craftsman, you love what you do and you are excited about it. We like that very much.

How did you break into this business, and what motivated you to open your own design studio?

PB: I was really lucky the way I broke into this business, and it was by having great teachers. I had great teachers in high school who inspired me to study industrial design, then I had a great professor in grad school who really pushed me and told me to challenge myself, to learn and develop further. It was through his generosity that I got my first professional break. He called up a contact he had at Seymourpowell in London and said that they had to take me on for an internship. They did and two months later [they] gave me a permanent position. He really was a great teacher that allowed me to get my break.

SV: I began at a time when industrial design was really not that popular. When I went to school in 1974, I didn't know there was industrial design. It was mostly practiced in corporations. When I went to school I wanted to study something that was creative and also I wanted to invent stuff, so I looked into architecture and took some courses. I felt limited that it was constrained to just spaces, and the only thing that I liked and had to do with making stuff and inventing was mechanical engineering. Then I was looking for a class in the industrial crafts building and I stumbled into this class and asked, "What is this?" It was industrial design. It was my destiny. I changed my major the next day and studied design. It was all I wanted to do.

Then I was working for Hewlett Packard for couple of years and I didn't like designing the same thing over

and over again. At that time a product would take three years to hit the market. That felt like a lifetime. I always had this fascination with things and I started a few projects with friends, inventing different things. It motivated us to see if we could just go ahead and do it, so I decided to start Ziba. I freelanced and moonlighted until I could get enough jobs to just quit HP and do Ziba in 1984.

If you were starting out now, what advice would you give yourself?

SV: I wouldn't do anything different. I was lucky to find out what I love and what I don't really early in my career. I was able to find teammates and colleagues to build Ziba together. As designers we think we can do everything, but we all have our unique capabilities. I would urge everyone to truly find out not what you think you are, but what you really are. I wouldn't do anything else. Everything has been a learning experience. Go after your heart. Go after your passion.

"WE ARE NOT AS INTERESTED IN THE FINAL PRODUCT. OF COURSE IT HAS TO BE BEAUTIFUL AND APPROPRIATE AND RIGHT, BUT WHAT'S MORE IMPORTANT IS HOW THEY GOT THERE. WHAT WAS THE JOURNEY?"

PB: Be curious and explore more. Have the heart to do better and love what you do.

SV: It's all about the work and not about the money. Money is a byproduct of good work. Most entrepreneurs are doing what they do because they love what they do. This is a business of passion. You won't make that much money as a designer. As a designer it's the love of creation that drives us, not the love of money. If you want to make money you should go into real estate or hedge funds.

PB: Maybe not these days.

SV: Yeah, maybe not these days. But design is a business of passion and love.

Where do you see the future of industrial design going as it evolves further in the 21st century?

PB: We really believe in experiences. Crossing physical, digital, and environmental and pushing them closer and closer and closer together. We believe that the consumers are going to demand seamless experiences. The future of industrial design, and really all design disciplines, will be in how they work together. It's something we've been doing here for a long time, but we have to push further and harder. We have to understand differences between the areas of design so they can truly live together and relate to each other.

SV: Industrial design is probably one of the broadest design disciplines. It's a great foundation to get into any other area of design. I think that's the strength of industrial design: the broad foundation it creates. It's very technical and also very visual. I hope that the educational system doesn't pigeonhole itself in creating these researchers, in creating these renderers or whatever. Keep the discipline broad.

Anything you would like to add that we haven't talked about? Any final words of wisdom?

SV: You want to go first?

PB: You're the one with the wisdom.

SV: [Laughs.]

PB: I just talked to a class at University of Oregon and I really encouraged them to break rules, to brainstorm with each other, share ideas, to not be afraid of failing. Push yourself so hard that you may fall apart but you'll learn something from that. You can turn that story into something as valuable and as beautiful as an object. Learn from your peers. That's the key thing. Your teachers are important but your peers are even more important. Those are people to whom you'll be connected for the rest of your life.

SV: Students are too focused on the object. They need to start to think of what they're creating as an experience. To understand a human being is so

important; it's really, really important. They should take courses in social science and put more tools in that toolbox and really understand human beings. At the end, you're designing an experience and not an object. That's so important. Sometimes designers design for themselves or design something cool and they don't understand how it goes beyond the focus on the object. So make connections between things that are much broader in the sea of education or areas outside of school. ⊞

To see the work of Paul Backett, Sohrab Vossoughi, and Ziba, please visit http://breaking.in

ACHIM BADSTUEBNER
HEAD OF EXTERIOR DESIGN
MERCEDES-BENZ
SINDELFINGEN, GERMANY

Interviewed while Mr. Badstuebner was Head of Exterior Design at Audi in Ingolstadt, Germany.

What portfolios get your attention these days? What brings in an industrial designer for an interview?

I don't want a person who is only into automotive. They should have some other interests and somehow project it in their portfolios. I like to hire personalities—that's really important. They should have a strong background in another area. Another field. Something unexpected. That always gets my attention. We like artistic portfolios: people who have unexpected artwork, who add to their portfolios some architectural drawings and such. It's always interesting to talk to them to get a feeling of what kind of talent they are.

It's also important to have a very strong Audi feeling. When we see your portfolio we want to see Audi projects, someone who is really into Audi. A portfolio that has a lean towards our brand is definitely more eye-catching than a standard portfolio that gets sent to everyone. Of course, it's always good to have a little bit of professional background, to know how the business works, to have had some internships. Audi is not one dimensional; it's more about team achievement. You have to be very individual and strong in your own standpoint, but you have to be able to achieve. We accept your identity but our team is like a puzzle—you have a different shape but you complete the picture.

Sounds like what you're looking for is a combination of passion for design and the brand with a diverse life experience.

Lot of times I've seen candidates who know every single car in the world and where they've been built. That's nice but it's not important. Everybody has their own perspectives on things. One of our employees didn't have a driver's license but was really into Audis, which is interesting. He brings in a completely different aspect. He grew up in Russia where he mostly took public transportation to get around. He looks at cars completely differently than we would.

So if an industrial design student came up to you and asked, "What should my portfolio be like? What do I need to show you in order to work with you?", what would you tell them?

Their portfolio should be very creative, with great sketching skills and fresh ideas.

What qualities or characteristics are necessary to be a successful designer?

Again, because our language is in sketches, it means that talking about design is through sketches. If you can talk through a picture, you're communicating. It's very important in the automotive business to be able to communicate through your sketches. You have to communicate with external departments like engineering and it's always important if you can communicate with them through your mother tongue, through sketching. It's very important.

Next, you need to have a good technical background, especially at Audi. We are very technically driven. It helps to understand complex, technical parameters because in our work a designer needs to understand the technical drawing so he can draw over it. You need to have an ability to work on your own model at least in the first phase, to build CAD models that can be milled, to make almost a CAD sketch. It's not 100%

necessary but it's definitely helpful. We've hired a lot of young people who have this skill, compared to my generation who can't do this despite being talented. It's definitely an advantage if you have CAD experience.

"IF YOU CAN TALK THROUGH A PICTURE, YOU'RE COMMUNICATING. IT'S VERY IMPORTANT IN THE AUTOMOTIVE BUSINESS TO BE ABLE TO COMMUNICATE THROUGH YOUR SKETCHES."

The most important thing, as I said at the beginning, is that you have to have a very strong character. I want leaders. I don't want followers. Most of the people are followers. You tell them what you want and they just execute it very well. You'll never get a strong character in car design if you have perfect craftsmanship, if you have perfect CAD. You need individual people who are very strong in their mind.

I love the fact that you called sketches the mother tongue of designers. Can you talk a bit more about the importance of sketching in design?

There are two very interesting aspects of sketching. The first is that you can only talk with the words you know. For example, my English vocabulary is limited, so in my mind I could tell you more in my language than I am able to now. It's the same with sketching capability. You have to be able to get on the paper what's on your mind. It's a circle. You can only grow when you see what's on the paper. That's a really interesting aspect of design work. If you hang up sketches people will see them or talk about them, sketch over them. They'll do overlays or do their own interpretations. You have to be technically capable of doing this and be able in your mind to understand what you want. There's a certain level of pretentious to it. The biggest creativity pool we have at Audi is that people communicate through sketches about their ideas and this generates new ideas. If you have a one-man show, a design superstar, and this car is dedicated to him and he holds the entire design line, that will not be successful. We don't do that. Design is always stronger with a team. You have to have very strong puzzle pieces and then you'll get a full picture of design.

How did you break into this industry?

I consider myself an atypical car designer. A lot of people knew at the beginning they wanted to be a car designer. They went to school, got an internship. In Germany you basically study or go for an apprenticeship and you train in a profession. I went to be a model-maker and went to school very late. I studied at Pforzheim and then I went to Bertone in Italy. It was my first experience with Italian design. Their work was very technical, and the designer had to be able to construct technical drawings instead of sketching as we know it. They worked from side views, very strict side views, and front views. After that I went to Opel, which was a completely different school, very Swedish, so it was interesting to me. It gave me a message to stretch your design ideas and develop your design skills. Here at Audi it is quite a different situation as well. It's very strategic.

If you were starting out now, what advice would you give yourself?

I learned sketching very late, so my biggest advantage was my model-making ability and understanding of forms. We are working on sculptures, on 3D objects. It's very important next to sketching to know what you can finally achieve in 3D. My advice would be to have a good understanding of what's feasible in 3D, to know how far you can take the brand. What's the core value of the brand? I've always said automotive design is non-verbal communication. If you see a car parked on the road, you can see if the team had fun doing it, if it was a good project or if it was really hard to do. It all reflects on our products when they're on the road. You can see the passion of the team. That would be my advice: to trust yourself, to believe in yourself, to dare to bring this out to the team. That will be the piece of the sculpture that ends up on the road. We're really having a ball. It's fantastic. We are working very hard, very competitively, but it's a team achievement in the end. We reflect the Audi soul. The product gets donated a soul by people who are

working on it: from the guy on the assembly line who puts on the front bumper to the designer who gives it shape. In the end, it's a complete product from people on the Audi cloud. You feel this. You feel that every screw is Audi in a way.

It's passion. Recently we had a young kid send us a letter with a sketch saying, "Hi Audi, I love your cars and here's what I see the next Audi looking like. Please keep on working because I'd like to apply for a job there in 10 years." I gave this letter to my designers and everybody did drawings for him and we sent him a big poster and told him to keep in touch. Once in a while, he sends us sketches. It's a very open spirit that we like to support. He might not come to Audi or might not ever become a car designer, but it's fun to have these friends of the brand. We are friends of the brand and our work should communicate this to the outside. This little guy reflected how we work and how we feel, and he became important to us.

Where do you see the future of transportation design going as it evolves further in the 21st century?

Automotive design is like a dream, and we get this dream before you can touch it, before it's on the road. Everybody has this dream of transportation, of freedom, and I think this will change dramatically. Cars will become more individual. Individualization of cars will be the next renaissance. I'm not talking about different color of the carpet or steering wheel, but low volume productions. Very niche market. The type of car that focuses on very specific transportation solutions for individual people. How can we realize very individual cars for people with very different needs? It's a little bit like a wedding ring. You can buy one off the catalog that is mass-produced in China or you can go to a jewelry designer to design your own ring. It's something unique that only you have. So there has to be something in between.

Anything you'd like to add that we didn't talk about? Any final words of wisdom?

It's all about the culture. It's about strong visions. BI

To see the work of Achim Badstuebner, please visit http:// breaking.in

CURT BAILEY
PRESIDENT
SUNDBERG-FERAR, INC.
WALLED LAKE, MICHIGAN

What kinds of portfolios get your attention these days? What brings in an industrial designer for an interview?

I get tons of résumés by email—I'd say 10 to 20 a week, particularly this time of the year around graduation. I try to look at all of the résumés and I do my best to respond to everyone, but I usually get busy on something else and stop responding as they pile up. The good ones I keep on file, the rest I trash.

There are a couple of things that I look for in a portfolio. First of all, there seems to be a rash of irrational aspect ratios in portfolios. What I mean by that is that they are not sized to fit on my computer screen. Instead they are tall and skinny or wide and flat. Consequently, I'm constantly zooming in and out and sliding back and forth. Frankly if I get one of those I usually just trash it right off the bat. Occasionally, I want to print a portfolio so it needs to fit nicely on letter-sized paper.

Secondly, I'm a little old school, but I am still looking for great sketching abilities. I've seen people who can't sketch but do generate beautiful designs via 3D computer data and rendering software; however, I still want to hire somebody who can draw well. I think it's important to be able to stand up at the white board and quickly and artistically put things in perspective.

Beyond just pure artistic talent, I like to see evidence of good judgment. I'll see a page of sketches in a project and then I'll see the one that the designer chose to pursue and sometimes it doesn't make any sense to me. Often there were some better ideas that they should've chosen from their big page of thumbnails. So I wonder how they chose. There are a lot of talented people out there who are naturally, artistically talented. Eventually though, I have to winnow out from that set of people the ones who have the potential to be successful and who I'd

be interested in hiring. One of those first cuts is if they have good judgment. Did they pick the design that has the best potential? And is there a clearly illustrated reason as to why they picked the idea they picked to pursue, other than something arbitrary?

The last thing I'll say about design portfolios is that I don't like to see team projects. Sometimes I'll get three portfolios from three different people and they all have exactly the same projects. And I don't know who did what. Listen, everyone participates in team projects and if that's your choice, I think the only thing you should put in your portfolio is what you did on the team. It should be clearly marked as that. It should be explained that it was a team project and that everything on this page was your work.

So, as I said, I get about 20 of these portfolios a week via email and I probably get, over the course of the year, only about three or four actual phone calls. Every one of those people who call me on the phone gets an interview (assuming their portfolio is decent). I'm a consultant and in a consulting world, if you can't get on the phone and talk to somebody and talk confidently and articulately, then you're not going to make it. There are a lot of talented designers who are uncomfortable talking, or they are shy. I think there's a place for those people but not in a consulting firm, at least not in ours. Or if you're super-talented and introverted, there might be a place for you, but where you can go will be somewhat limited. I put a ton of emphasis on people being confident and articulate on the telephone, and the fact that they even had the guts to call you in the first place. It's easy to send out a blanket of emails, it's more difficult to get ahold of somebody over the phone. It takes stick-to-itiveness, it takes some confidence and guts, and that's one of the rough cuts for me.

You mentioned sketching as an invaluable skill for an industrial designer. What is it about having a great sketching ability that's so important for our field?

It's an interesting thing. There are people who have good judgment and a good sense of design who aren't great sketchers. Still, I put emphasis on it. I somehow believe that there is a correlation between sketching ability and talent and judgment. If you know where to put a line, versus where not to put a line, then maybe you know where to position a product. I think there's an aesthetic decision-making process with sketching that's congruent with making good product development decisions. Beyond that, I also think that being able to stand up at a whiteboard or sit in front of a customer as they are describing something and interpret it visually with a really cool sketch that's worthy of being shown around is very desirable. It can get some legs and go viral within a small community. That's super-important versus chicken scratch. It's just a powerful tool; it's really nice to have. It's nice to have in meetings from a communication perspective, and it's a signal that the person has some aesthetic judgment.

What do you expect to learn from the designer during an interview?

The prerequisite becomes that your portfolio and phone call got you in the door, so it's clear that you have some talent. It's a must-have. The nice-to-haves, the way you get vetted further, are things like genuine and palpable passion for what you're doing. A verbal and visual manifestation in the way you talk, the way your body language is, of that passion. If a candidate comes in with a beautiful portfolio but lackluster attitude, it's not going to work out for our consulting firm where you need to be able to interact with a lot of people.

Beyond that I put a huge amount of emphasis on debating skills. I was a talented designer but I think the best class I have ever taken for the advancement of my design career, in any grade or school, was high school debate. A standard assignment was that our teacher would give you a topic but he wouldn't tell you which side of the topic you would argue for until you showed up in class. So you had to prepare both cases, and what that does is, it makes you empathetic to the other argument. It makes you consider the alternative. You do a mental game with yourself and you argue it the other way. I think that's one of the things that make a great designer. It forces you to think: why this way? Why not another way? Of these alternatives, which one is the best and why? I think it's a terrific habit to develop when you're making design decisions and dealing with people in general.

I think some people call it arguing and I have no objection to calling it arguing. There was an article

in Fast Company a couple of weeks ago about arguing and how it's an important component to brainstorming, and the idea of "there's no bad ideas" is not a good idea. I think that's really cool. If the candidate has this outward manifestation of passion and some humility and some empathy for the other side of the equation, and maybe a little bit of a self-deprecating stance, I think that's super powerful in a designer. I think a lot of designers don't have this, and part of the reason is that many design schools are trade schools. They teach you how to be a designer but not how to be a well-rounded individual.

I went to University of Illinois where, at the time, the design program was lacking compared to Art Center or CCS or Cranbrook, but what I got was a liberal arts education. I was in a fraternity and lived the campus life, so I was interacting with a whole bunch of people who weren't designers. I think that's really important because when you're a designer, you can be a designer for other designers, but that's limiting. What you really want to be is a designer for business leaders. You have to be a business leader yourself and think like a business leader, be comfortable with business leaders, and talk business language in the context of design.

If you're good at all at that you're probably going to be a natural sales person, and that's important in a consulting firm. While you're doing a project, you're looking for other opportunities. You're creating opportunities for the firm to continue to help the client.

If you have a talent with personality traits, there's no stopping you. You probably know Ralph Gilles at Chrysler. The guy is an industrial designer, and he's the president of Dodge. He's kicking ass! And if you've ever met the guy, he's very charismatic, very nice and friendly, self-deprecating. It's not just his design talent—it goes beyond that.

Sounds like the Ralph I know. I'd love to hear your story and how you broke into this business.

I'm not sure I broke in. The joke I tell people is that, when I was in high school I had three favorite classes and they were art, auto shop, and debate. My guidance counselor thought that I'd be good at haggling over the price of my paintings in front of a gas station.

The truth was that I was tired of school and didn't want to go to college right away. I wanted to be an auto mechanic or auto painter or hot rod builder and I got a job in a limousine factory where we cut Lincolns in half, added 40 inches to the wheelbase, and put new interiors in. It was a factory job but kind of fun. I did that for about six to eight months when my girlfriend, who at the time was going to University of Illinois, sent me a curriculum book and dog-eared a page with a description of industrial design. I read this paragraph and that was it, I made my decision.

"I STILL WANT TO HIRE SOMEBODY WHO CAN DRAW WELL. I THINK IT'S IMPORTANT..."

I graduated in 1982, and it was a terrible economy not unlike this one, so I had a hard time finding a job. I wanted to work in a consulting firm but my portfolio was from University of Illinois, it wasn't from Art Center—I didn't even know about Art Center or CCS. I didn't know that there were better schools. I was a big fish in a small pond. I had a hard time getting a job. I went to San Francisco and I interviewed with all of those guys, they were almost as young as me, and I couldn't land anything. I finally got a job in Indianapolis at RCA doing television sets. I was engaged to be married at the time, and my fiancé ended up with a job in Detroit. I followed her, and there was one consulting firm in Detroit: Sundberg-Ferar. I was fortunate enough to get a job. I wouldn't call that breaking into the business, it was more like I wedged a foot in the door here and there and worked my way in—but the Sundberg-Ferar thing worked out really well.

If you were starting out just now, what advice would you give yourself?

I had a student call me and ask me that, and I said whatever job you get or whatever job you take, pretend like you own the place. Pretend like it's your own company. I wish someone had told me that when

I was at RCA because what happened there is that I went into it with an attitude of "this is a stepping-stone," and in hindsight, that was a mistake. I was going to build my portfolio so I could get the hell out of there. That was unfair to my employer, and in the long run, unfair to myself. I think I realized that about a year into it. Instead of sharing the nice work I'd done, I was hoarding it and building a portfolio, making sure I could use everything. I wasn't thinking like an owner of RCA would think, and that was a mistake.

So I pledged to myself that whatever job I got next that I was going to give it three years, be completely selfless, pretend it's my company, act like everything I did was with my own money. I did that at Sundberg-Ferar. I was there for about 14 months and they asked me to be a partner. I was 24 years old.

I've watched talented kids come through here who have looked at our place as a stepping-stone. It's so disappointing to me because you can tell that they're just deliberately staying a little bit disengaged because they know they're going to be leaving. They know what they're doing is building a portfolio and they are doing themselves and us a disservice. Some of them never change their attitude, they don't realize that their attitude is holding them back. Treat every job like you own the place.

Where do you see the future of industrial design going as it evolves further in the 21st century?

You probably heard the same stuff from some other people as design leaders talk about this a lot, but from our firm's perspective there are two paths. One is tactical and one is strategic. What I see happening is that there are a lot of talented design firms out there. Any firm with over 20 people probably has a really nice portfolio, everyone has talent. The difference comes not when clients need us to design the product, but when we design their product, they need the product to be unique and compelling. They don't have the internal capability to do marketing or communication plans or launch strategies that are in concert with the product. They want us to help them out with that and advise them on strategically where they should be going next.

My whole take is that this whole "new normal economy" is unforgiving. You can't strategically try to be all things to all people. You can't aim at the proverbial broad side of the barn when you're shot-gunning your approach with a product design because you'll end up becoming a price-sensitive commodity. So how do you go about choosing what to do next? Again, the prerequisites are still talent, the ability to sketch, etc. But us designers need to talk to business leaders about how they should make strategic product design decisions in such a way that they can have a unique selling proposition. We can use design to help turn them into something other than a commodity producer. Keep them from joining the cost-cutting race to the bottom with everybody else. I just see the field becoming much more strategic.

It's not just about the product, it's about the entire ecosystem.

Exactly, and we are designing experiences. We can't lose sight of that. The best products are surrounded by great experiences. The product and the marketing and the experience all sing from the same song sheet—they're in harmony. The whole is bigger than the sum of the parts. That's where this stuff happens. Apple is a tremendous example of that, or Mini Cooper. It's not just the product but everything that surrounds the product and the product itself. I think product designers are uniquely positioned to contribute to this effort and possibly even lead that initiative.

You've already shared so many bits of wisdom, but is there anything we didn't cover that you'd like to add? Any parting words?

Design is fun. So many people are envious of what I do. We are just lucky and blessed to be able to do what we do. [BI]

To see the work of Curt Bailey and Sundberg-Ferar, please visit http://breaking.in

CHRIS BANGLE
FOUNDER
CHRIS BANGLE ASSOCIATES
CLAVESANA, ITALY

What kind of portfolio catches your eye? What would bring an industrial designer in for an interview?

I personally am very artwork oriented; if there's good artwork you get grabbed. By that I mean the kind of artwork you'd want on your wall. I like to be impressed, to come away with the feeling I'd want to blow your drawings up big, print a huge poster of something to hang behind my desk. All design directors have this feeling that they need to fill the empty space behind them on the wall. They always want to do it with an amazing rendering or a fantastic sketch. Often the ones they appreciate most are the ones that are very, very simple. Not complex or colorful or overly rendered or photorealistic or anything like that. Just attention-getting and extremely skillful in execution.

Is there an example you can give me of a really memorable portfolio that you've come across recently?

There was a kid from Art Center who's doing an internship up the road at Bertone who sent me his portfolio recently. It had 80 pages in it and he managed them without being too repetitive. It was an impressive collection quantity-wise, which generally I shy away from. I don't like people to overload my inbox, but this guy's work was of really good quality. In fact, my team dropped their jaws when they had a look, saying, "This guy is an animal." Lots of ideas showing a real dedication, a mass volume of quality. There was once a story I heard that when Syd Mead was at Art Center he did every assignment twice. That's what they say anyway. He just out produced everybody else and got those famous 10,000 hours of incredibly important quality time in very early, so the visualization of his ideas flowed wonderfully. That's what a lot of the design is: a visualization of your ideas.

This is not the same thing as saying people can get

away with just drawing rabbits, although in reality some people send portfolios of just that. A new designer needs to demonstrate that they can draw new ideas, things you haven't seen before. It's a combination of artwork skill with some ideas behind it. Although, having said that, almost every portfolio that grabs your attention has a part dedicated to life drawing, even a part dedicated to drawing rabbits. It shows that the person is all around interested in art and life, and not just blowing one note on their horn. The more sides of a person that can come through in a more subtle manner, the better. Their drawing ability is one aspect of it.

Another feature I look for in a portfolio is the joy of "intelligent abandonment." On one side you want to be impressed by something you wouldn't have thought of that they did, a clever designer. But when there's kind of an abandonment evident, where the person takes their idea and goes beyond the pale. They go beyond the first or second barriers, which might inhibit somebody else, to try something new, to see where it takes them—that's when a portfolio gets to be impressive. Not just to be destructive, or to be expressive in a juvenile manner, but to be incredibly explorative beyond where you yourself may have taken it. Their theme. When you see that happening, it grabs your attention in a most amazing manner.

I think people who review portfolios do take time to take a look at things. They are arrested by the artwork, of course. They don't like to read tons of text but, if they can see something happening there, something that unfolds before their eyes in a manner that explains that person, then it becomes quite impressive.

So if an industrial design student came up to you and asked, "What should my portfolio be like? What do I need to show you in order to work with you?", what would you tell them?

I would recommend a good mix of complete projects and artwork done for other reasons, even if it was for the joy of it all. Don't draw women in your sketches if you can't do it really well. I prefer simple stick figures with clear gestures to get the ideas across. Color and graphics are important, as are handwriting skills on the sketch. Show me progress by adding calendar notes to the work: what came first, last, and so forth. Impress me with your energy and quality. A little humor goes along way, but don't forget that "little bit."

How did you break into this business?

With a really lousy portfolio.

I highly doubt that.

No, it was really awful. In fact, the other day, I showed it to my designers here in the studio and they went, "Oh...that's...nice?" I went to Art Center after I went to University of Wisconsin for a couple of years. In fact, if I could just put little parentheses I would really suggest to any young person who is studying to also not neglect their studies beyond design school. It turns out the courses I took in English literature and critical writing were really, really important downstream, when I needed to involve myself in design management and understand the design process. Don't underestimate that part of your education.

In any case, when I was going into my last year at Art Center, it seemed like the car industry was really bad off, in a very difficult way. There weren't going to be any jobs. I decided to switch my entire portfolio towards Hollywood and try and get a job doing the science fiction types of work for movies. My portfolio was full of cars, as by that time, I had six semesters of car-based portfolio work, but in that last semester I really dialed up that other stuff. I worked on a sketchbook full of spaceships, renderings of the same, etc. I even had an interview set up on a Wednesday after I graduated with Disney's WED studio (now called Disney Imagineering). It was a big, big deal. On the Monday before, however, GM came up and said, "We're not hiring, but we want to see your work anyway," which is typical. I should have probably told them to piss off. But I dutifully showed my portfolio to Chuck Jordan and the head of personnel that came out with him. Jordan didn't hold back telling me it sucked. "This is awful, this is terrible. My God, it's awful. Terrible!" But he kind of hung on the spaceship paintings and drawings and, in particular, the sketchbooks. I had cartoons in them—he liked that.

After that auspicious interview, amazingly enough, the next day the personnel guy called me up and said, "Well, we are going to offer two of you guys a job—you and one other guy." Fantastic. This was probably their tactic back then, to make you feel awful so when they give you a job offer you take whatever it is. So I took this job at GM and never went to the Disney interview, which I regret. An interesting aside is that the other guy who was hired was John Bell, who went to GM with me. I wound up in Germany and he wound up in Detroit, and John—who was a real car guy, a fantastic designer, I mean absolutely fantastic—when he got fed up with GM after a couple of years, he went back to California and went into the Hollywood scene. He joined ILM and eventually was the co-art director on Jurassic Park.

You went from GM to Fiat then to BMW, and after a long and fruitful career you've decided to open your own design studio. What was the motivation behind that?

I had this idea with my wife, Catherine, that I would leave BMW at age 50. I started with BMW at age 35, which is pretty young for that position and 15 years is a nice block. It's two cycles of cars so it's kind of elegantly clean. I thought, although in the end I would end up doing three generations of 3 Series with the team. So we thought, "Where will we retire?" Catherine is Swiss and I'm an American and neither of us really spent that much time in our home countries and Germany wasn't home either. But Italy was where we had spent the first seven years of our marriage, which are kind of important years. We decided we were going to return to Italy, and while we were planning this, the idea of retirement seemed less and less of an issue.

If you were starting off now, what advice would you give yourself?

I would've paid more attention in school maybe. I don't think I was such a good student. What advice would I have given? Maybe I would've relaxed a bit more, not worried so much. On the other hand, I think I started taking up my sketchbooks way too late. I really didn't start sketching seriously until about 1996, and that's something I should've done from day one in a more organized manner. Not overly organized, just a little bit more. I carry sketchbooks now; they come in standard dimensions and that way I can create a bookshelf of them, which is quite nice. In the beginning I

sketched on anything and lost or threw half of it away. In retrospect I probably would've told myself to be a bit more experimental in some things earlier on, but jeez, I was having a lot of fun. I guess I didn't need anybody to tell me to have fun. I hope you're having fun.

I'm trying.

Cool. I mean, this book is kind of a cool idea, so it sounds like you're doing something fun.

Thanks. You mentioned sketchbooks a few times now. I'm curious if you can talk more about that, the importance of them, and any suggestions you may have for up-and-coming designers about how to approach them, what should be in them, and so on?

This is me talking, so I'm sure everyone has their own opinions. I see lots of beautiful sketchbooks that are these little Moleskine guys and people manage to have them filled with these beautiful little drawings. I like sketchbooks, which are about 9 x 10 inches; it's an unusual size, but they fit in the back of your pants nicely so you can carry them around without having something in your hand. I like the kind that are spiral bound so you can wrap the cover back around itself, with slightly heavier paper, not overly toothy, a little bit slick so it takes pen really nicely.

What to fill it with? I fill it up with everything. Literally everything I see or think of. I've never said to myself, "I want to design cars, I'm only going to draw cars." That's, in fact, the last type of thing to concentrate on if you want to understand true car design. Of course it makes sense to draw them when you're working on a project and you're constantly doing these little thumbnails of car ideas. But in terms of how a sketchbook will help you, I think it's less a spot for your fantasy about that one particular issue that fascinates you, and more about disciplining yourself to be observant. Disciplining yourself to record your thoughts and challenge your thoughts by creating logical arguments and dialogues, learning how to storyboard, capturing a moment that otherwise you would've forgotten or was special and that no camera could've recorded. Even just practicing your art skills. That's why I like to carry mine around. When my wife takes me with her shopping, while she's trying on dresses or something, I'll just pop down in a chair and draw the store dummies. They don't move. They're cheaper than hiring a model.

I use my sketchbook as a resource now. I literally go back in and mine them for my contemplations, my dreams, my moments of awareness, ideas and thoughts, and reflect on them. You should do this too because you may be in a position where you have to deal with similar issues once again. A sketchbook is a good place to develop metaphors for life. "You can't understand things if you can't find a metaphor for it," said Immanuel Kant. He's absolutely right. If you can find those metaphors and sketch them and record them for yourself, it will be very helpful when you need to grasp the same concept or communicate the same thought later.

"ANOTHER FEATURE I LOOK FOR IN A PORTFOLIO IS THE JOY OF "INTELLIGENT ABANDONMENT"... WHERE THE PERSON TAKES THEIR IDEA AND GOES BEYOND THE PALE. THEY GO BEYOND THE FIRST OR SECOND BARRIERS, WHICH MIGHT INHIBIT SOMEBODY ELSE, TO TRY SOMETHING NEW...THAT'S WHEN A PORTFOLIO GETS TO BE IMPRESSIVE."

If you are going to use a sketchbook to practice car drawing, then use it wisely. I remember one time this one kid heard that Ferrari was hiring, and he asked me, "How do I get into Ferrari?" I replied,

"Well, have you drawn every Ferrari that ever existed? If not, why not? If you're really passionate about something, why don't you do that?" If he filled a sketchbook with all of those Ferraris, it would be one hell of a portfolio piece. Can you imagine if that showed up on the desk of some guy trying to pick a new designer? Of course, it wouldn't impress the Porsche guys too much.

The history of a car company is really important, and this interview is a little bit about how to get a job and how to get in, so you should be aware of the fact that, with a lot of car companies, if they don't think you're a fanatic about their product, they begin asking themselves, "Why should we hire you?" There's nothing wrong in showing your dedication in a format like that. Plus, it's a fantastic exercise to improve your knowledge of a particular brand. The people inside the company, they know all of those things, they talk about those old products as if they're living today. You can speak with them instantly on their level of historical knowledge after you have attempted that assignment and they really love that.

You are obviously very articulate, and you speak of design in a very inspiring way. Do you have any advice for students on how to add this level of communication that's necessary to turn their ideas into actual products?

When I was in high school I took speech and debate and made my son take it too. If your book reaches far upstream in the food chain of the process and hits the young people still in high school or junior high, I would advise them to do that. I don't know if it is available in all countries or under those names, but that's what they called it in America when I was young. It's rhetorical speaking—a lot of it was spontaneous improvisational speaking. Theater helps. If you can participate in plays, in acting where you have to memorize lines and show some poise in front of people, in front of an audience, you have begun to experience something that's extremely important. Anything that requires you to do speaking in front of a room full of strangers is very, very helpful.

Where do you see the future of industrial design going?

Designers, in general, promote the idea that creativity is a extremely narrow, one-way pipeline. This standard view doesn't leave room for the participation of anybody else in the process. After "the creative person" is done everybody else is just an executor. I think that maybe humankind has to get over the idea that things have to be put into that single state by a creative source. We need to look at the design of a problem as being an unfolding story that may begin at a creative source point, such as a designer, but really won't take shape until it's well in the hands of the consumer. By that I don't mean co-design, where we rely on the consumer or the end user to be a major component in the definition. I just mean more co-creative through the entire process chain, as it once was, where the act of producing something meant you worked with artisans and with people who brought their own touch to the idea and the design along the way. That I think would be a wonderful thing, to put the light of creativity in a much larger arena of humankind and enfranchise people in the productive process. We should strive to give them a sense of participation, instead of saying, "Either you're part of a very, very narrow pipeline of execution or you're one of these creative elites." Instead, we should be saying that there's room for professionals far upstream in the process, but there's also room to incorporate the average person into it. To allow them even a fraction of the expression that we designers enjoy and hope they come away from the experience inspired.

If you want to cross swords then know that I'm specifically talking about a rather arrogant approach we designers have to what we have created. We believe, "This thing is ours, it's our baby, we did it. After that, if it deviates then it's wrong." I am asking us to do more than just say we're open to opinion. I am asking, "Why not try literally opening ourselves to change along with what we have created?" It's like raising kids: they are literally your creation as a parent, but you are only partially responsible for how they come out. The education system, their friends, everything around them shapes them. Why don't we see what we design like that? Wouldn't that be nice?

Is there anything else we haven't talked about that you'd like to add? Any final words of wisdom?

Live long and prosper. No, wait, someone else already took that one. [BI]

To see Chris Bangle's work, please visit http://breaking.in

BILL BARRANCO
FOUNDER
AUTOVISION DESIGN
NETWORK, INC.
PALO ALTO, CALIFORNIA

What kinds of portfolios get your attention these days? What brings in an industrial designer for an interview?

First of all, let me just say first and foremost if there's a lack of illustration skills, if there's a lack of communication skills—meaning the designer can't draw really well but there's some good ideas here somewhere—well, I don't have much time for that and neither do the hiring managers. It's still really basic in that department. If you don't have illustration skills then you might as well go get an engineering degree. That's the key component, the communication of your great ideas, and if you can't communicate those great ideas, it doesn't matter how good they are. That's what illustration does, and whether that's digital illustration or CAD or animation or Flash or whatever you got going, put it together, use the best tools you've got. When you grab the viewer's attention, you're going to communicate. That's the whole point. Beyond that it's the depth: what is the substance of this design? Is it useful? Is it value added? Does it improve quality of life? Is it desirable or clean industrial design? There's the first read, which is illustration, but the second read is content.

Have you seen a portfolio recently that resonated with you, and what about it stood out?

Yeah, several. There was an industrial design candidate for one of my clients who had mechanical-organic forms; he could design anything from a lifestyle product to active footwear. It was fresh, it was new, it wasn't an imitation of somebody else's style, and you could see that he needed to work quickly because his ideas were coming out very spontaneously. Spontaneous, authentic, and fresh. His work just stood out. I submitted his work to the hiring manager and they turned him down because they thought he's so good he probably wouldn't be challenged enough in this role, he needs bigger things than we can offer. It's hard to describe these portfolios in words. It's all about the experience. That's what Apple did—they created an experience and then from there comes the useful function of the product and the interface.

If a student came up to you and asked, "What should my portfolio be like? What do I need to show you in order to work with you?", what would you tell them?

I need to see at least one very strong, exceptional attribute, which might be: exceptional automotive interior design skills, design/illustration skills, deep-thinking problem-solving skills, or creative exterior surface treatments. Then I would say, as my industrial design teacher at Art Center, Ted Youngkin, instructed us, "Industrial designers need to be good not just at one thing, but many things." I would be looking for an overall cohesive and well-prepared presentation—not too graphics intensive—that's concise and visually stimulating.

What characteristics or qualities are necessary to be a successful industrial designer?

If you don't have a passion for this then go get an engineering degree, or go into marketing, or go into something else. Design is a holistic collaboration of many different skills. It's art and illustration, it's engineering and function, there's an understanding of how to work with marketing and product planning. To be a good industrial designer you need to be good at everything. It's no less so today. You need to be good at CAD and animation, but also be comfortable getting up and talking in front of a group about what your idea is. A lot of people want to do this job, and there are very, very few of these jobs available. It's the same thing as professional sports. How many top athletes actually get on a team? Like one in 500; the rest are on the bench. That's how competitive it is. There are more colleges graduating these students than ever, but there just aren't that many jobs. They just don't exist. Having said that, I've never seen so many studios that are looking to hire, but they all want superstars. Nobody is looking for an average, pretty good designer. Nobody wants one. They want the same thing: superstars.

So the number one, the first and foremost fact is that the drawing and sketching skills are still very important. Sit down and draw. That has not changed. No machine, no software, can teach you how to draw. Only you can sit yourself down and learn how to sketch.

How did you break into this business?

It's the path that life takes you down. I had an offer from Porsche that never materialized and so much of it is just chance or luck. I was bound and determined to get into one of these companies. The thing is you just gotta follow your passion, do your best, and just do a great job. Look at you, you're writing a book. Did you grow up thinking that someday you'd be writing a book?

No.

No? And here you are.

Yes, I can completely relate to being lucky.

I didn't know I was going to end up as a recruiter of car designers, but it's just where it takes you. You do what you have to do, whatever that is. I'm so glad you called because anything I can do to help inspire people to take action and go ahead with their lives and do what they love to do, anything I can do to help that I really enjoy.

If you were just starting out now, what advice would you give yourself?

Follow your heart before your mind.

Where do you see the future of industrial design going as it evolves further in the 21st century?

The world has not seen what will happen in automotive interior design—it will truly be this interactive world. Inside your car you'll be inside this womb—the car speaks to you and you speak to it, you interact with it. So there's this huge demand now for high quality, interactive product industrial automotive design, especially for interiors. We are on the verge of a fundamental change in what the automobile is. I mean permanent automotive change. So the designer of tomorrow needs to be a master of many, many, many skills. Only now it's even more so. Now a truly successful automotive designer really needs to be aware of the world of interactive technologies, experiential design, not to mention the same sensitivity to form language and what is automotive and what's not. You still need to have that automotive element, meaning no matter how much it changes people still have to relate to it as a car. Despite all of our advancements, cars are still our most emotional and expensive personal statements.

"SO THE NUMBER ONE, THE FIRST AND FOREMOST FACT IS THAT THE DRAWING AND SKETCHING SKILLS ARE STILL VERY IMPORTANT. SIT DOWN AND DRAW."

That's what I see going on. You're going to have one side that's more like an appliance, and on the other side you'll have the ride-share, community-transport module. Here's an analogy: a hundred years ago a lot of people had a horse. Today if you have a horse, you have a barn, a horse trailer, a truck to haul a horse trailer, a field for the horse to run around, and probably a mansion to go along with the rest of it. Horses are no less coveted or desired than before. In fact, they're more coveted and desired, they're more precious than ever. It's the same way with super-cars and classic autos: luxury statements of excess. This is the fork in the road. We're going to have appliances that get us to work and I-love-my-car-more-than-my-house cars. Both at the same time.

Anything we didn't cover that you would like to add? Any final words of wisdom?

Draw. D. R. A. W. Draw, draw, draw. BI

To see Bill Barranco's work, please visit http://breaking.in

ADAM BAZYDLO MANAGER, INTERIOR DESIGN STRATEGY FORD MOTOR COMPANY DEARBORN, MICHIGAN

Interviewed while Mr. Bazydlo was the Senior Designer at Peugeot Design in Paris.

What kinds of portfolios get your attention these days? What brings in an industrial designer for an interview?

I would definitely say, and we definitely get thousands of them, that the portfolio that gets our attention is the one that corresponds to the job. If the candidate is applying for an interior job and he only has exteriors, or bicycles, or windmills, then obviously it won't work. For people just starting out, they need to give their portfolios more thought for a job they're applying to. The other thing that would really get them in for an interview is the character they have, and we can see this through the work that they do. Whether they're very constructed and logical, or very expressive, or just crazy, it's apparent through their work. We like to see something that tells us that this person is original and has something different to say in his work.

I think those are the two definite things. Admittedly, it's a bit of a numbers game. When you see thousands and thousands of portfolios, you see the repetition of the same elements very often and students will do similar, stereotypical work. For example: the Ferrari—you always see that. There's always a Ferrari, or a Jeep or SUVs, or an eco car. When someone can do something that's beyond that, and it's different and original, I think that comes out of their character. That will definitely get them in for an interview.

Have you seen a portfolio recently that had that level of originality?

Yes, it's actually one of our recent hires. We had a designer who decided to create a luxury car and usually the luxury interiors are made out of leather. So he studied the way the leather folds and the way leather can be cut and put together. He did it all with these little tiny pieces of leather, to show how it could fold and do this. Then he designed a car all around it that had these two states: one that was being passive, which was very slick, and another one where, in a few movements, it would transform itself into a sports car. It was fantastic. It was really impressive.

"WHEN SOMEONE CAN DO SOMETHING THAT'S… DIFFERENT AND ORIGINAL, I THINK THAT COMES OUT OF THEIR CHARACTER. THAT WILL DEFINITELY GET THEM IN FOR AN INTERVIEW "

Or, for example, I remember there was a girl…a very famous portfolio. I think she was from Pforzheim. She decided to create one part that would be repeated thousands of times and that would sort of create a layering of one element over another, creating a whole different look of the exterior. These pieces could move and would react to wind resistance; it was really original.

When you bring a designer in for an interview, what do you expect to learn from them at that meeting?

We want to see their creative process. We definitely want to see what they think. Often at schools you're taught to have good communication skills, whether they are drawing or rendering or talking. At the end of the day, it's also what you can bring to the table in terms of your creativity. So we're looking for the creative process and how they've managed to solve the problem originally and differently from anybody else.

It all comes down to if this person can dream. If they can dream, and if they are dreaming about

doing these products in new, interesting ways, then we can dream with them. It becomes much more exciting.

What are the characteristics or qualities that are necessary for a designer to be successful?

They need to have curiosity and problem-solving skills. They need to have expressive skills. Curiosity, for me, means that, no matter what problem comes along, they're able to find an interesting way to look at it and solve it. Obviously, they should express or design the solution in such a way that makes it interesting. That's what I mean by curiosity and emotional expression. Also, for a successful designer, they have to be able to work with a team and they have to have motivational skills for others.

How did you break into the business?

It was very, very tricky. I graduated right after September 11th, so it was a very, very hard period. Still, I had a goal and I wanted to make it. I came to Europe with my portfolio and got a job at Visteon. I was working for this supplier for two and a half years. But I guess every creative person will do one thing for a while and, once they've mastered that, they want to do something else. I started looking at other places and I came across Peugeot, where I interned before so I had a good contact with them.

If you were just starting out now, what advice would you give yourself?

Well, I made it, but how could I have made it easier? That's really the question, no? It took me a long time to understand that creativity and beauty come from yourself. When you're designing something, it's you yourself who needs to be happy with it. You shouldn't try to do something to make somebody else happy. If you make a project and say, "Wow, this is really good," 90% of the time other people will see it the same way. So don't design for others, design for yourself.

That ties into the sentiment of originality that you mentioned earlier.

Oh yes, absolutely. I think that's important. We live in a world where we have thousands and thousands and thousands of products and choices and one is almost the same as the other. What will make your product different from somebody else's? Sometimes it's just a different color, but you need that originality, that new way of thinking.

Where do you see the future of industrial design going as it evolves further in the 21st century?

Definitely transportation design is a field which fills out a big need that people have, which is moving from point A to point B. Whether we do it fast or electrically or with gas or whatever way, it's definitely going to be the path of least resistance: the easiest, most fun, most enjoyable, and cheapest.

Industrial design is getting more and more creative, more innovative. Thinking back, in the '90s we had sort of a very plastic, industrial-oriented design whereas now the stuff I see from the Royal College of Art, it's anything really. It will continue in that way and find its own path.

Anything you'd like to add that we haven't talked about? Any final words of wisdom?

Just dream. If you're dreaming and you're creative, people will follow naturally. I know it sounds a bit like the '50s, build-your-world sort of thing, but it really comes down to that. I don't think enough designers dream today. They don't believe, they just do a product. We need to be excited again, to find a new way. There are so many ways you can do things, and you should explore them all. BI

To see Adam Bazydlo's work, please visit http://breaking.in

JONAH BECKER
ASSOCIATE VICE PRESIDENT
OF INDUSTRIAL DESIGN
HTC
SAN FRANCISCO

Interviewed while Mr. Becker was the President at One & Co in San Francisco.

What kinds of portfolios get your attention these days? What brings in an industrial designer for an interview?

The portfolios that grab my attention are graphically clean, well edited, and show a range of good skills throughout the design process. They are clearly organized in terms of how projects are presented from brief to research to concept to execution, and most importantly they communicate a fresh perspective and great energy.

Have you seen a portfolio recently that resonated with you, and what about it stood out?

There have been a couple recent portfolios that really stood out. The main difference is that these young designers presented themselves as mature beyond their years. The communication of their ideas—both written and visual—was excellent, the initial vision on projects was maintained in the final execution, and the perspective was fresh. Essentially they presented themselves as designers who could come in and really contribute while at the same time showing a youthful spirit and desire to continue learning. I always like to make hires that are a "two-way street": the designer, even if young, should be able to contribute as much as we will be able to teach them.

What are some common mistakes you've seen students or junior designers make in their portfolios?

There are two mistakes that are most common. The first is poor editing of projects. If a project doesn't portray you in the best light, then leave it out, or redo the project on your own time and show both the original and the new-and-improved version—that shows ambition. Obviously, only show the revised project if the new version is actually improved. Second most common mistake is not communicating the project and idea well. If you show me a design for a bike helmet, I want to know—in a very succinct way—what the challenge was and how you got to your solution. Were you asked to design a bike helmet? Were you asked to design something that protects a human? Or were you asked to identify a new opportunity in any industry of your choice and design a better solution? The original challenge frames my understanding of your solution. I also want to see your thought process—again, clearly and succinctly—from research to concept to execution.

What do you expect to learn from the designer during an interview?

The interview is where I get the chance to connect a person to the portfolio (in almost all cases I will review a portfolio prior to arranging an interview). I want to see how the candidate communicates verbally, reacts to difficult questions or thinks through tough problems, shows passion, and explains their perspective and process. I'm also interested to get a sense of the person's personality, background, and what their interests are beyond design. I'm not the only one who should have questions and be evaluating the fit between employer and candidate. I like to hear what types of questions the candidate has for me—it tells a lot about how someone thinks about their career and what is important to them.

What characteristics or qualities are necessary to be a successful industrial designer?

A great designer is passionate about creating, always looks at the world with open eyes and a fresh perspective. A designer thinks about people and isn't limited by tools or lack of experience, isn't afraid to fail. He or she knows history but isn't bound by it and plays nicely with others.

What are some reasons you have rejected a candidate?

Sadly there are more reasons to reject a candidate than to hire one. The first impression is important

and can be an area where candidates slip up: spelling my name incorrectly, sending a form letter and forgetting to change the names from the other companies to which you also are applying, poor spelling/grammar, unprofessional communication, or even choosing the wrong typeface for a cover letter can be a big turnoff—and generally a good indicator of design sensibility in other areas.

Once reviewing a portfolio the first reason for dismissal is poor design skills. Sketching, form development, CAD, and graphics are a designer's language, and you need to show the ability to communicate your ideas. I'm not necessarily looking for high-end transportation sketches but rather sketches that show thinking, energy, and the ability to solve problems and establish a perspective.

"IF A PROJECT DOESN'T PORTRAY YOU IN THE BEST LIGHT, THEN LEAVE IT OUT, OR REDO THE PROJECT ON YOUR OWN TIME AND SHOW BOTH THE ORIGINAL AND THE NEW-AND-IMPROVED VERSION—THAT SHOWS AMBITION."

Poor editing is another killer. I'd rather have a candidate show me three really good projects than three really good ones and four mediocre ones. Not only do the weaker projects bring down the overall quality of the portfolio, but it makes me question whether the candidate has the ability to distinguish good design from bad design. It's natural to have bad ideas and bad design concepts, as long as you have the awareness to edit them out. Candidates often feel the need to show a certain quantity, but I wouldn't show a project unless you truly feel it puts you in a positive light.

The last area where we might reject a candidate is following an in-person interview. If the person doesn't communicate their ideas and process well, doesn't show energy and passion for their work, doesn't show interest in our studio, or doesn't feel like a good personality fit for our studio, I will move on. Ultimately I want to hire people with whom I'd like to work and spend time.

How did you break into this business?

I'm one of the rare people who knew about industrial design from a very early age. My mom is a graphic designer who is also on the faculty at a design school in San Francisco, so I grew up surrounded by other designers, spending time in my mom's studio, and wondering why our furniture had names ("Keep your filthy hands off the Aalto chair!"). I loved graphics and drawing but was even more attracted to making models using all the materials around me. After getting a degree in philosophy at UC Berkeley I decided to go to the same school were my mom was teaching to study industrial design (then called CCAC, not just CCA). The faculty in the school is comprised almost entirely of working professionals, so as I approached graduation I already had a number of contacts and opportunities in the professional world. So many job opportunities come from personal connections, so it's a great idea to be involved with your local design community.

I was the first employee of One & Co's original founders and eventually became a partner. Over the years they have moved on to other successful design ventures, so I've been the most senior partner since their departures and have brought in other partners along the way.

How do you manage the non-design aspects of running a studio?

Though design is the part that I'm truly passionate about, there are the realities of running a business. As best as I can, I try to separate design work from the other operational requirements of managing the business. I've also gained an interest and respect for what it takes to run a business and not just run design projects. It can be very rewarding to work on the business, as well as in the business.

If you were just starting out now, what advice would you give yourself?

Focus as much energy as possible on the types of projects you want to work on, as anything that is not core to your vision is a distraction. Act like the designer, or the business, you want to be several years down the road—that's the only way to get the opportunities to realize your goals. Make sure every project adds value to the world. Always challenge clients to be better, whether in terms of their design, their attention to environmental or social issues, or any other factor. Never get comfortable. If things get easy you've stopped learning.

Where do you see the future of industrial design going as it evolves further in the 21st century?

I see the future of industrial design continuing to grow along its current path. Design disciplines are merging, and we will be less and less limited to the design of just objects: UX/UI design, environments, branding, etc. A designer should be prepared to tackle all sorts of challenges. Another big area for further growth in design is in the responsibility category: responsibility to business, social responsibility, and environmental responsibility. I look forward to seeing the impact of the next generation of designers who are growing up with this broader understanding of the profession.

Anything we didn't cover that you would like to add? Any final words of wisdom?

Every new experience is just a step in life, so don't be afraid to take a step. [BI]

To see Jonah Becker's work, please visit http://breaking.in

What kinds of portfolios get your attention these days? What brings in a product designer for an interview?

For me, it's always been somebody who's working on the near future. How students can abstract what we have today—how we're living, how we're working, the state of our lifestyle today—and project it into the near future with some new ideas, that's what's interesting. That always creates a stimulating discussion versus just reviewing skills or aesthetic and mechanical or technical abilities.

"HOW STUDENTS CAN ABSTRACT WHAT WE HAVE TODAY—HOW WE'RE LIVING, HOW WE'RE WORKING, THE STATE OF OUR LIFESTYLE TODAY—AND PROJECT IT INTO THE NEAR FUTURE WITH SOME NEW IDEAS, THAT'S WHAT'S INTERESTING."

The 3D skills and drawing skills are expected, but we look for someone who can add something to the type of work that we do. What we do is never about the now or iterative design projects, it's about being focused on what's next. Seeing this in students' portfolios and how in the future they project themselves is what makes them unique.

What do you expect to learn from the designers during an interview?

Cultural fit is really important. We want people who are going to have an initiative. We want people who have a personality. We essentially look for two things: one is a high level of design skills and abilities and the second one is the ability of someone to be complementary to the rest of the team. What is their other passion? What is their other drive? Their other inspiration? Are they an expert snowboarder? Are they passionate about environmental sustainability? For me, it's very important that they'll fit with what's expected within the team and also bring something that's new, different, and fresh.

What characteristics or qualities do you think are necessary to be a successful designer?

I think the ability to think big, to go beyond what's expected, to think in a multimedia type of fashion. How does the design affect the user? How does the user affect the packaging? How does the packaging affect the brand? Design, for me, is more of a ricochet. How we can get to the next idea and how ideas are not isolated from one another? How they all connect into each other is what's interesting to me.

So product design as an entire ecosystem of solutions and experiences, as opposed to just one singular object.

Exactly.

How did you break into this business, and what inspired you to start fuseproject?

Initially, out of school, I didn't have the confidence or experience to start my own studio. I was very eager to learn from others, from working at other places. I spent several years working for three different firms and learning a lot. In the end, I had a vision of something I wanted to do that combined a lot of the different practices of design, hence the name fuseproject. I started in a very old fashioned way: just me at a computer. Then I slowly and organically built a team.

If you were just starting out now, what advice would you give yourself?

The earlier I was able to get a business partner on board, the better. I think being able to focus on the creative part, and finding someone complementary to your skill set to deal with the other things, is key. I think that's what I did, but if I could've done it earlier it would've been even better.

Where do you see the future of industrial design going as it evolves further in the 21st century?

We're going to see making things different for sustainability reasons. I think there is no doubt in my mind that sustainability is going to drive design in the future. On the other hand, I think the future of design is multidisciplinary and requires a holistic approach. That means that industrial design is very much at the center of what makes a business today. It's very much how you look at all of the different aspects, the contextual aspects, the societal changes that are happening, and how they're dictating how you're viewing things.

There's been talk that the field is changing dramatically, that it's dying. How do you feel about that?

That's a ridiculous notion. I think we are probably experiencing a golden age of design because in the last few years design has become a lot more influential than it has ever been. That influence goes beyond restrictions that have been imposed on us by marketing and other people. We're at a stage where we're truly doing product making. I think if you look at the great design periods of the last century, the modernist in the '50s and the mid-century guys, that was when designers had a very deep and profound effect on the core parts of the business. I think the same thing is happening today. It's not hard to see comparisons to this in the way Apple works, or other companies—designers are at the center of their entire operations.

Is there anything you'd like to add that we haven't talked about? Any final words of wisdom?

I would say always look at what's next. Practice design in a way that it is a way of looking at the future, not just a way of answering the needs of the present. [BI]

To see the work of Yves Béhar and fuseproject, please visit http://breaking.in

CHRISTOPHER BENJAMIN
CHIEF DESIGNER, CHRYSLER
INTERIORS
CHRYSLER
AUBURN HILLS, MICHIGAN

Interviewed while Mr. Benjamin was Design Director at Volvo Monitoring and Concept Center in Camarillo, California.

What kinds of portfolios get your attention these days? What brings in an industrial designer for an interview?

The most important thing that I look for in a portfolio is the student's ability to communicate with impact. For example, when you start looking through a project and you get to the end of it, you want to know what it was all about, visually, without having to read too much. It's a lot about visual communication skills. It's about them showing their range, because a designer has to be an artist first, and then a problem solver. He needs to be able to take something from the beginning to an end, from ideation to a finished digital or physical model.

A lot of students these days tend to rely too much on the digital tools without the proper foundation. Even if someone's not the best artist, they can sometimes start to substitute skill with a glossy finish. I started in the age where everything was still manual. I can always tell when someone's good at visual tools but not as strong as an artist. Although you can fool many people with it, if you look closely, you can see the difference between someone who just used the tool and someone who's really an artist.

And then the problem-solving side of it: did they create a solution in a new, different way? Not only the actual sketches but also how they approached the project. Is it the usual target customer or did the student approach it from a more creative point of view? What type of lifestyle does the customer have that makes them need this product? How do those factors affect the way the product looks?

You mentioned you can tell the difference between someone who just knows the tools and someone who is an artist. What gives them away?

Little things. For example, you can draw a car and it's maybe not in the perfect perspective but you can render it really nicely—some people can be fooled by that. A lot of times students will put basic sketches into a portfolio as ideation and then add more finished stuff later on. Especially in the more basic stuff, you see it even clearer: the difference between having a lot of mileage in their pencil versus just putting something on paper and fixing it in Photoshop.

Has there been a portfolio recently that you've seen that resonated with you? If so, what about it stood out?

It was the portfolio of the last designer that I hired over two years ago. When I saw his portfolio—I am not kidding you—I knew I wanted to hire him 30 seconds in. It was the way his projects were laid out, his unique approach to describing how the vehicle fit a certain clientele, his creativity and how the problem was approached and graphically laid out. It was all very concise, the artwork was beautiful, and it was very organized. There was a strong consistency, which means that, as a designer, he was very disciplined and had a method to the way he approached problems.

What do you expect to learn from a designer during an interview?

Two things: the first thing is what inspires them and what makes them want to be a designer. Why is that better for them than doing anything else? Design is really about passion. It's not about just having a job to earn money. It should be something you live, breathe, and something you enjoy. If everything else in life were free, you'd do it anyway. The second thing is, I really want to know what they can bring to us—what new ideas, new thinking. If you look at the whole range of our cars, I would ask what they think is missing and why? What do they think would be a good fit with the brand? What do they think we need to break into? What demographic? It shows that they're not a mindless sketching drone, but that they also think on a higher level about the company that they would ultimately represent and how their

ideas can best fit that company—how they can best create that future.

What are the characteristics or qualities necessary to be a successful designer?

Hard work, determination, and patience—especially as a car designer. When I went to College for Creative Studies [CCS], there were between 80 and 100 freshmen that wanted to be car designers. Twenty were accepted into the automotive program. Not everyone's going to make it, and that's only at the first stage. Then it's getting through school, getting internships, graduating, and getting a job. It's always about being the best of the best. In terms of breaking in, it's really about sacrifice. You have to be willing to sacrifice many things in your personal life. Going to a design school and trying to break into the industry, you have to put the rest of your life on hold, more or less. It's serious. Sometimes I tell young students this and they think I'm kidding, but I'm not. It is really that way.

You have to be relentless in your focus. You have to be better than others, be better than those who inspire you because they're also competing against you. It's really about super-tight focus, drive, and determination. Without that, you get distracted and allow other things to occupy your time. As a result, you will not be getting the practice you need. You're not getting the right mindset.

That's something I went through in school, personally. I lost focus, and wasn't giving the program my full attention. It created a difficult situation to say the least. In the end, I regained my focus, but it's hard to get it back.

One last thing is that being competitive can become a hindrance for some. What I mean is, to continue to be successful as a professional designer, you have to have a great attitude and know how to work in a team and how to collaborate with others. A car is never designed by just one person.

How did you break into this business?

I've heard car designers say that they knew they wanted to be a car designer since they were five or ten years old. To be honest I didn't know car design was a profession until I got to CCS. What I did always know is that I always wanted to do something in the art field. Since fourth grade I was always in magnet schools for the arts. I went to a normal elementary school but one day a week I went to another school and learned art the entire day. Though elementary and middle school it was all fine arts. I learned everything from photography to jewelry making, lithography, and even the classical Renaissance painting methods. We learned all the manual techniques, and because of that I think it made breaking into the industry easier for me. I went to CCS to study industrial design, and when I saw the car design stuff, I immediately knew that's what I wanted to do. During my entire childhood I collected Matchbox and Hot Wheels cars and I've always loved art. That is exactly what car design is: a combination of the love of cars and art. It was perfect for me.

"YOU HAVE TO BE RELENTLESS IN YOUR FOCUS. YOU HAVE TO BE BETTER THAN OTHERS, BE BETTER THAN THOSE WHO INSPIRE YOU BECAUSE THEY'RE ALSO COMPETING AGAINST YOU. IT'S REALLY ABOUT SUPER-TIGHT FOCUS, DRIVE, AND DETERMINATION."

The first year felt easy because I had so many years of the foundation of art and design before attending college. After I got into the automotive program, I quickly realized the sophomore and junior years were definitely not as easy as freshman year. There were some difficult times there, but to be honest, it was my own complacency that hindered my progress. I was not pushing myself hard enough, not wanting it bad enough, and being okay with being in the middle. Getting put on probation after junior year and not

getting an internship sort of woke me up. Senior year I came back and pushed hard. It was the most difficult year. I also worked three jobs at the same time as being a full-time student, but when I graduated I had several offers. This was at a time when Alias was just breaking ground and I had quite a bit of that in my portfolio. I was quite fond of it as a tool. It was a good combination with all the manual stuff I'd learned over the years and I think that really gave me the edge.

If you were just starting out now, what advice would you give yourself?

Be relentless. Be focused. Don't get a girlfriend or a boyfriend. Seriously, when you're in a design school, normal life is a distraction. To be honest, you're going to have friends from high school that you'll meet over the summer that go to a normal college and go to all the parties—and there's nothing wrong with that—but you just won't have time for it. Whenever you're off doing something else, there's another guy or a girl who is focused and practicing and who is finishing their design to a higher level than you are. One thing I learned is that it's not just the end result of what you do, it's the journey. These are the things you may not realize as a student. In the end, it's not only the final result but how you got there. It's your attitude, it's your general outlook. Attitude and personality come into play. Nobody wants to have a problem designer who's super talented but doesn't know how to work with other people or take direction. Those are the things you have to work on as well, in addition to polishing your design skills.

Where do you see the future of transportation design going?

It's all over the place at the moment. Every company that you look at, everyone is doing their own thing. But we've reached a stage in society where there have been so many influential design periods throughout history that people take inspiration from anywhere and that creates a huge variety of styles and form language. In terms of what the companies are looking for, in terms of who to hire, it is sort of a renaissance man or woman—a person who can do it all. We have had the times where we had interior designers, exterior designers, clay modelers, and digital modelers all as separate jobs but I think, more and more, companies are looking for a jack-of-all-trades. Someone who can do exterior and interior and who can take something from sketch into 3D. At least to a stage where you can represent an idea in a good way so a professional modeler can take it into a more developed set of surfaces. As the global economy shifts and budgets grow tighter, companies are growing smarter. I feel that companies will be looking for not just a sketcher anymore, but someone who can take the design from the beginning to the end—possibly take the place of what was two or three people, doing two or three different jobs.

That's a mark of a truly great designer: being able to translate something from an initial idea into something that's tangible. As industrial designers, we're not doing imaginary stuff. We do things that eventually have to be produced. At the same time, it has to be done with creativity and ingenuity. If you're not able to do that, no matter how good of an artist you are, no matter how passionate, you won't be much good as a professional designer.

It sounds like the field is getting even more competitive these days.

Definitely, and I just speak of car design. I read an article back in 2006 in one of the American car magazines where they compared car designers to NFL players. In that year, there were fewer designers graduating from design schools than NFL players entering the draft. That tells you how few there are. But the reality is that there are fewer jobs, and more and more young designers graduating each year. Art Center graduates 12 to 15 students three times a year, CCS graduates 18 to 22 a year, then there's Coventry, Pforzheim, RCA, Cleveland. More and more schools are graduating more and more students. In some of the schools you don't even have to qualify to go into car design. Still other schools don't even ask for a portfolio to get into the program, you just have to pay tuition.

As education becomes more of a business, there are students that slip through the cracks and graduate but without the proper skills to get a job. You can see the other end of the spectrum too. Some young designers are way better than we were at graduation, thanks to access to tools, to ideas, demos, all of the other valuable information you can get online. We

didn't have much of that in 1999 when I graduated. It was actually pretty funny, we would all run down to the bookstore when the latest copy of Auto & Design or Car Styling came out to see what was new. All of the resources are online now and are a great source of information.

Is there anything else you'd like to add that we haven't talked about? Any final words of wisdom?

If you're thinking of becoming a car designer specifically, get all the sleep you can before you start the program. BI

To see Christopher Benjamin's work, please visit http://breaking.in

BLAISE BERTRAND
PARTNER
& INDUSTRIAL DESIGN
DIRECTOR
IDEO
SAN FRANCISCO

What kinds of portfolios get your attention these days, and what brings in a product designer for an interview?

Generally speaking, I am looking at a number of criteria in a designer's portfolio. First, I want to know whether or not a candidate has the "basic" industrial design tools for success: inspiration, research skills, expression tools, and, obviously, technical skills. If one does not have these fundamentals, he or she will ultimately struggle in a fast-paced, high-demand environment like IDEO.

On top of these skills, I see another important dimension, which is the "magic" factor. This is the unique, unexpected quality that we can't see anywhere else. It could be just a way of thinking, a way of expressing an idea, or even a new domain.

When we are looking for designers, we are looking for people who not only know how to answer particular design challenges in the best possible ways, but who also bring individual points of view that will help our clients move forward on their innovation journey. More and more, our clients are asking for IDEO's perspective. Even though we formulate it during the course of a project, we also need to have people who bring a critical and personal perspective.

Furthermore, when looking at a portfolio, I seek the "freshness factor." As you probably know, the field of design is growing rapidly with amazing talents. The ones we're looking for are the designers who are willing to break new frontiers, push the boundaries of the expected, and take risks to invent new paradigms.

We are also seeing a new form of design emerging, which we call "ID plus." Ten years ago, industrial designers were essentially designing physical products based on user, technology, and market needs. ID was a very focused discipline, and we did not believe at the time that designers could be excellent at multiple design disciplines. Over the past few years, however, we have been seeing the emergence of designers who are crossing multiple design disciplines with the same level of talent and excellence. Today, designers think from "kilometers" to "millimeters." Fundamentally, one of the essential strengths of designers is their ability to distill a tremendous amount of complexity and create beautiful and tangible user and brand experiences.

This notion of "ID plus" is actually very important because today, at IDEO, we help brands innovate on multiple levels: service, communication, products, space, etc. So having designers who naturally embrace multiple skill sets enriches the dialogue and increases the impact we have with our clients.

But even with the expansion of personalities and competencies, a designer needs to have a profound sense of aesthetics, which is a very subjective notion that we constantly try to define and redefine at IDEO.

I'm curious then, how do you see this change impacting what's being shown in portfolios? How would one prepare to get a job in this changing marketplace?

Students or young professionals want to have a breadth of work reflected in their portfolio. For example, their experience could go from social impact projects to consumer products. For all of them to connect, there must be a common flow, a narrative that defines the way this designer expresses himself or herself.

Furthermore, I personally love conciseness. Designers should possess the ability to synthesize complexity and to express it in an engaging way. The best candidate is someone who is able to elegantly tell a very complicated story in one sentence, one picture, one scene, or one mock-up.

"THE BEST CANDIDATE IS SOMEONE WHO IS ABLE TO ELEGANTLY TELL A VERY COMPLICATED STORY IN ONE SENTENCE, ONE PICTURE, ONE SCENE, OR ONE MOCK-UP."

Finally, I strongly believe that designers should be able to make others smile, cry, and feel a profound sense of empathy. Humor, for example. Humor connects people. Using it as a way to connect with an audience is very powerful. So, to my mind, the ability to communicate an emotion is fundamental for designers.

What do you expect to learn from a designer during an interview?

Designers generally talk a lot about design process during an interview. It's a legitimate conversation, but to my mind, process does not define talent. Process is a tool that students acquire in school. It teaches how to exercise a rigorous mindset to design. Once they've learned it, I want to see how students apply it, but also internalize it, to make it their own. The application of a process, at times, leads to expected solutions. Sticking to a particular process sometimes is the easy way, but fundamentally, it is important for students to seek the unexpected, the novelty, and to craft new paths. For example, during user research activities, it is easy to cut corners and to extract design opportunities directly based on what people say. Designers should be able to extract patterns to seek opportunities beyond the visible realm of things.

We've been talking about portfolios but there is another part of the equation, which is the way students present their work. If they are able to tell an engaging story, to connect with us very quickly, the interview becomes a conversation where all the parties learn and inspire each other. When it happens it is magical. It means the candidate went beyond presenting his or her work in a high-pressure environment.

During an interview we are gauging someone's talent but also their collaboration skills. Both are important. In the field of design it is easy for designers to have a strong ego. At IDEO we look for people who have a personal point of view, but also who know how to inspire and work in a team environment.

What characteristics or qualities are necessary for the designer to have in order to succeed?

Talent comes first. It is a very subjective notion, but when we see a portfolio we can immediately gauge whether this person has a raw or refined talent. Usually, I never interview people alone. I interview with a diverse group of IDEO designers, varying from junior to senior. There is a sort of collective intuition and trust that guides us during an interview, which allows us to make decisions.

Curiosity is another quality. Being candid and not taking yourself too seriously—that's also important. A sense of humor and great storytelling make a big difference.

Then there is the ability to experiment. Being fearless is important when we need to guide our clients to unexplored areas. So often I meet companies that are willing to take more risks than designers. It always

surprises me. Designers need to be appropriate in their answers to challenges, but they also need to be visionaries. If I ask a designer to solve a challenge that everybody can solve the same way, what's the point? To my mind, it is about understanding the context, identifying challenges, and finding opportunities that no one would have come up with before.

Finally, I personally like the notion of being a "provocateur." It means: "Don't ask for permission, ask for forgiveness."

How did you break into this business?

One of the core motivations for being a designer is to inject humanity, poetry, and emotion into a very functional world driven by efficiency and rationality. I never questioned my choice to become a designer. What really got me into this was a sense of purpose— the desire to improve the human condition in a meaningful way. The second aspect was creating a more sustainable world. The third reason was people. The fourth was aesthetics. It's really hard for me to pull those notions apart; they're part of the same thing. Furthermore, what I love about design is the ability to solve a complex organizational challenge and a minute later, to look at a particular surface quality.

If you were just starting out now, what advice would you give yourself?

I would say: "Go for it. Try. Fail. Try again. Explore. And be more irreverent. Just follow your heart and passion while keeping a personal sense of integrity." I think this advice works for a lifetime, but the earlier you start practicing the better.

A lot of people in design circles wonder whether IDEO even does product design anymore. What are your thoughts on that, and where do you see the future of industrial design going as it evolves further in the 21st century? How is IDEO planning on affecting the future?

First of all, IDEO still does a lot of product design. The reason why it might be less visible today than when we started is simple: the design we are doing today touches so many other areas beyond just product. We have been extending the realm of product design to brand experiences because creating value for our clients means integrating all the facets of brands or systems. We still do a lot of industrial design for startups and Fortune 500 companies, but what we're doing much better than before is inscribing products in larger ecosystems to ultimately create more impact.

Today, we have the best group of designers we've ever had at IDEO. It is refreshing to work with people who are so humble and so far removed from the design "diva" stereotype. Not only are we still designing products, but we are also really pushing our craft in new ways. We are explorers. A few years ago I initiated a global creative white space initiative called Designs_On, which is essentially a platform for creative experimentation and expression. Designs_On is about asking designers to generate unique concepts based on a very simple brief and around important topics such as food and birth. Through this channel, designers have been able to push the limits of design in a safe and very personal way.

Now more than ever, we are thinking about the future of design. Designing life, for example. The field of genetics and biology will become important for designers in the coming years. There are obviously a lot of ethical questions surrounding this topic, but I think designers need to look at it very carefully.

Anything you'd like to add that we haven't talked about? Any final words of wisdom?

Exercise design with a sense of purpose, generosity, humility, passion, and humor. BI

To see Blaise Bertrand's work, please visit http://breaking.in

ROLAND BOAL
HEAD OF DESIGN
PRIESTMANGOODE DESIGN
CHINA
LONDON AND QINGDAO

Interviewed while Mr. Boal was the Lead Designer & Studio Manager at Tangerine, London.

What kinds of portfolios get your attention these days, and what brings in an industrial designer for an interview?

The best things are, in a way, the most mundane. Those portfolios that are just nice and neatly laid out, in many respects, are the ones that leap out at us—where there's not too much stuff on the page and there are not too many pages. Where there is just a sensitivity to how the folio is presented even before you look at the work. Beyond that, we look for people who sketch their designs sensitively. That's really important. A lot of the portfolios we get sent seem to suffer from the owner's belief that they have to—right from the start of their career—demonstrate that they are the greatest designer ever, and that gets in the way of demonstrating their core skills.

The reality is that straight out of the university, whatever one's potential, there hasn't been the time to hone one's skills yet. It is much better when people demonstrate a range of skills—technical skills, as well as their design sense, even if it is inevitably immature. Those CVs that grab our attention are not those with masses of content or those that are really bombastic. If we get sent something, it doesn't have to come beautifully packaged, but there needs to be a maturity about how it's being presented.

Have you seen a portfolio recently that resonated with you, and what about it stood out?

We did have a portfolio fairly recently that was nice and neatly laid out, which I appreciate isn't the most exciting answer to your question. But what was interesting was that it also talked about a design process, and that really struck a chord with us because process and strategy are at the heart of what we do. We have a process at Tangerine that we have refined over the years. Although the person's process wasn't exactly the same as ours, the fact that they saw design as an intellectual process as much as a creative, aesthetic one was something that immediately made us sit up and take note. That really took the form of a diagram at the beginning of their presentation, showing what their process was from the intellectual beginnings, setting up a context for the project, all the way to delivering final design. That was something that was really quite powerful.

What do you expect to learn from the designer during an interview?

The thing we look for most of all is how they talk about the work that they've done—the language that they use. Obviously we want the person to be enthusiastic about their work and about the work that we've done too, but without being sycophantic. We want them to feel like they'll participate well as part of a team, as much as one can tell from a chat with somebody. But most of all it's the terms in which they talk about their work: why they made certain design decisions, and again, the process they went through. If they are able to be articulate about their work than that is a definite plus.

What characteristics or qualities are necessary to be a successful industrial designer?

A balance between the confidence in one's own ability—you're not afraid to suggest something that may seem a little bit left field, a bit off the wall—and being able to work as part of a team, especially if you're a junior designer. If somebody makes a suggestion, or the person running the project says, after all the discussion is over, that something has to be done a particular way, and you're able to take constructive criticism and learn from it, run with it, and do better stuff in the future. I don't mean to suggest that someone's being told off; I mean that whilst it can be good to be really passionate about a design that you're responsible for, if it's not appropriate for the project, there comes a time when hanging on to the idea is no longer appropriate. It's great to have the confidence, but that needs to be married to the ability to step back. And that applies to all of us.

How did you break into this business?

Like most people, when I was at school I did a "work experience" at a few different places. I always wanted to be a designer, but wasn't sure exactly what sort of direction I wanted my career to take. I did a couple weeks at a design consultancy, which got me very excited by the idea of industrial design. I think the most valuable thing that I did at the beginning of my career was choosing a university course that allowed for doing a placement year in industry between the second and third years. That was most valuable because it meant that when I left the university I already had that magical year of experience. Whenever there were adverts for jobs, they would always say: "Junior designer wanted, must have at least one year of experience." Having just left university you're immediately presented with a Catch-22 situation. So whenever I've spoken to people thinking about what sort of design course to take, I've always advised them to take a placement course, not only to give them experience but also because it teaches you a lot more than you could ever learn in a lecture theatre. So, that's what I did.

"A LOT OF THE PORTFOLIOS WE GET SENT SEEM TO SUFFER FROM THE OWNER'S BELIEF THAT THEY HAVE TO—RIGHT FROM THE START OF THEIR CAREER—DEMONSTRATE THAT THEY ARE THE GREATEST DESIGNER EVER, AND THAT GETS IN THE WAY OF DEMONSTRATING THEIR CORE SKILLS."

I worked at a boutique design consultancy, working on high-profile furniture design projects for Italian furniture manufacturers, some interiors and products. Whilst I felt myself more interested in consumer electronics design, as opposed to pure furniture design, it was extremely interesting to get a different perspective on what is really just a different part of the same industry. Including my placement year I was there for a little over four years, and I left six years ago to come to work for Tangerine.

Some advice I would give is that one should always ask for responsibility. It's great when people get really into the stuff they've been assigned, but it's much more pleasing to have people do that and then say give me more, I'd like to do more. That's a real asset. Being proactive in that respect is extremely helpful and appealing.

You mention the importance of having real work experience before graduating from school. What advice would you have for students as to how to go about landing an internship while still at school?

To us it doesn't matter if someone has zero experience or 10 years of experience. If we like the stuff that they're showing in their portfolio, the way they talk about it and so on, that's what really matters. With that said, it does matter to some employers and I think that's reasonable. When people want to do a placement, the key thing is to be very flexible about how long that's going to be and when it's going to be. The other thing is just to call up consultancies and just ask. I know a lot of people shy away from using the telephone to contact people, preferring to send emails or letters. But because we get so many emails and post—of all different types throughout the day—it's very easy for those things to be forgotten or go accidentally unopened.

To get a telephone call of somebody asking if we do student placement instantly elevates that person in our minds, so if they do send an email, it's an extra thing that helps make the connection. It also shows a certain amount of proactive-ness. One shouldn't be scared of speaking to people on the phone. Obviously, you wouldn't want to pester, but being a little bit persistent is reasonable. No one is ever going to get shouted at just for calling, so no one should be frightened of picking up the phone.

If you were just starting out now, what advice would you give yourself?

It sounds a bit trivial, but I think the one thing I've regretted is not always carrying a notebook and a pen. In terms of forming my own design opinions, my own design vocabulary—you see things all the time that are interesting in some way. Having a scrapbook where you've accumulated all this knowledge, be it a sketch or ticket stub or whatever, it's a physical record of where you've gone and what you've seen. It's like a jazz musician having a repertoire of recent riffs that they can drop into their music; their notebook is a mental one but it's the same principle. You want a record of things that you can just flip through. There's never a wasted moment when you're sitting in the tube on the way to work. You can flip through your book and have an idea about something. You record it and it's always there. It sounds trivial but I feel if I had done that for the first few years, it would've been hugely useful. It's something that I try to do now all the time.

What makes this kind of visual note taking important to a designer?

There are a lot of things that I forget when we are concept generating. There have been times where one feels creatively stumped, especially on a Monday morning, staring at a blank sketch pad and thinking, "Where am I going to start?" Being able to flick through some notebooks and finding something to explore is a very useful aide—more to get you going if you're having sort of a barren moment. It's also useful when you look back over it. It's a bit like keeping a diary I suppose, to see where you started a couple of years ago and where you are now. Being able to chart your progress could give you a lot of confidence.

Where do you see the future of industrial design going as it evolves further in the 21st century?

I think particularly with consumer electronic products the future is very much in delivering complete and increasingly engaging user experiences. It's not just delivering a product: here's a phone or a TV, end of story. There are products that offer lifestyle experiences in a way that is interconnected, whether that's to the cloud or web TV or social networking. They are products synced with an overarching, if slightly nebulous, consumer experience.

The most obvious contemporary example of this is smart phones, where you're not just buying a phone but you're buying into an experience that might include iTunes, your phone, your computer, and hi-fi as well. It's a mobile experience as much as it's a static one. It's the whole consumer experience in one product. It's getting broader and broader as we are getting more comfortable with the idea of constant connectivity, and with data existing in the cloud rather than something you'd keep physically. We will have products that fit more into that kind of framework, whereas at the moment we still think of individual products as being completely self-contained. It's about the overall experience of the consumer. For example, traditionally in the airline industry First Class would have just meant bigger seats, more space, better service, whereas now it's about offering people their own space to do with what they want, so there are seat suites rather than just individual seats. And extending the experience into not just bars but lounges and even showers. That principle of extending the user experience beyond the core product also strays down from Business Class to Economy where people are being offered a chance to make their own experience rather than just doing something functional.

Anything we didn't cover that you would like to add? Any final words of wisdom?

In terms of people starting out or sending in folios or CVs, they shouldn't be too long. I can understand people wanting to show the breadth of what they've done, or a case study that shows an entire project, but a 40-page PDF—and we get plenty of those—just isn't going to get looked at in detail. If we can't tell in the first four or five pages what the person's ability is, than 40 isn't going to help. It's just a waste of their time to produce.

A pet hate of mine is when people include a photograph of themselves in a portfolio. It's something that, for some reason, people do all the time. It may just be a personal thing but it just seems like a very odd and slightly unprofessional

thing to do. The design industry is a really exciting one in which to work; it can be quite informal but it is also challenging: marrying business understanding as well as an intellectual side and depth that's exciting, but it is still a professional industry. For some reason including a mug shot just doesn't convey professionalism. So I would counsel people not to do that. Ha, sorry, I got quite a bit worked up around that.

It's interesting you mention that, considering recruiting sites like LinkedIn kind of forced it on people to include their photos.

Yes, having just said that the future of industrial design is a more holistic, connected, and personal experience, and then I go and say that people shouldn't be quite that personal. It's a personal thing, but you wouldn't include a photo if you were applying for a job in, say, a legal firm, so why do it for a design consultancy? [BI]

To see Roland Boal's work, please visit http://breaking.in

ANNE MARIE BOUTIN PRESIDENT AGENCE POUR LA PROMOTION DE LA CREATION INDUSTRIELLE PARIS

What motivated you to create APCI?

In the 1980s the government decided to create a new school that would train designers at the same education level as engineers or general managers, under the premises of the ministries in charge of culture and industry, l'Ensci/les Ateliers. This gave a great impulsion to the whole French education system—at present, France offers more than ten top-level design schools.

At this time, many companies were continuing to place heavy emphasis on engineering and technology when elaborating their strategy and did not see the importance of design as a strategic differentiating factor. To help new graduated designers find jobs, we needed to explain to companies and public organizations what design is and promote the vision of design as a vital tool for user-centered innovation. This is the reason why, in 1983, we decided to create APCI.

APCI is a non-profit organization that is part of a larger international movement that views design as a key factor of company competitiveness and economic, social, and cultural innovation. APCI aims to make companies more aware of the role of design in the innovation process, to educate people towards a demand for well-designed products, and to promote French design in France and abroad.

What would you say are the key ingredients of an exceptional industrial design portfolio?

For a designer an exceptional portfolio must include a great diversity of projects realized in different contexts: for companies of different size, from different sectors, with different kinds of briefs, using different materials and processes, in different marketing environments. But also personal projects without clients. This portfolio will show different methodologies that take into account the needs and desires of consumers, and if possible, that involve them in the innovation process. It must also show the capacity to work at different levels of the innovation process. In general, exceptional portfolios present awarded projects.

For a company a good portfolio is the result of a good design management policy. In many cases this means that design is considered at a strategic level (existence of a vice president of design) and more, as a core competence of the company. These companies communicate about their design as a part of their identity. In general, they received awards that they also publicize.

What characteristics or qualities are necessary to be a successful industrial designer?

Beyond creativity and capacity of shaping concepts, ideas, projects, and scenarios, the main qualities of a designer are curiosity, capacity to listen to people, to understand them, to observe them. The capacity to work in teams with other disciplines is vital. A good designer is not the person who brings ideas to other people; he/she is the person who makes the whole team or company more creative.

How can aspiring designers promote themselves and their work more effectively?

Many ways can do it. Being involved in group projects with a focus on a specific theme in order to bring his or her own fresh ideas and to explore, share it with people. Showing his or her own way of seeing things through the work. This can be done by taking part in competitions, design awards, etc. Also, targeting their connections and networking at specialized exhibitions and conferences. For instance, 13 French representatives were part of a French delegation during the IDA Congress in Taipei last month. They had their own space to show their work in a 300-square-meter pavilion for which we did the scenography. Most of them had business meetings with small and large companies (Asus, etc....). They also went to IDA conferences and roundtables to gain international points of view. That's a way of promoting themselves as well as feeding their creativity.

What would be the one piece of advice you would give to an aspiring industrial designer or somebody who has just graduated and is trying to break into the industry?

I would suggest for him or her to be modest. To listen to people and ask them questions before showing the quality of their portfolio. To show the diversity of their approach and their capacity to work on very different projects.

Where do you see the future of industrial design going as it evolves further in the 21st century?

Our societies are facing deep and heavy challenges. In order to provide a sustainable and desirable world to the next generations, we have to develop a proactive attitude and initiate a process of redefinition of our world. The products and the processes must be reinvented, as well as services and environments. Further, we have to reinvent whole scenarios of life.

"BEYOND CREATIVITY AND CAPACITY OF SHAPING CONCEPTS, IDEAS, PROJECTS, AND SCENARIOS, THE MAIN QUALITIES OF A DESIGNER ARE CURIOSITY, CAPACITY TO LISTEN TO PEOPLE, TO UNDERSTAND THEM, TO OBSERVE THEM."

Design can play a vital role in this process for four reasons. First, it develops a holistic approach, including intuitions and visions, facts and values, which allow [us] to handle complex and changing situations. In multidisciplinary teams, it develops tools to communicate and build solutions easily without specialized languages. Beyond products and services, it can shape concepts and ideas, tell stories, and propose scenarios of life. Finally, its human-centered approach lets people be actors of their own environments and decisions.

This leads decision makers towards completely new attitudes, and allows designers to endorse new responsibilities.

Design has a great future. BI

To see the work of Anne Marie Boutin and APCI, please visit http:// breaking.in

LAURENE LEON BOYM PROPRIETRESS & PRODUCT DESIGN LEAD BOYM PARTNERS INC NEW YORK CITY

What kinds of portfolios get your attention these days? What brings in an industrial designer for an interview?

The right portfolio and candidate for us is probably not a typical T-shaped design school graduate, but rather someone who possesses a broad foundation: a technical expertise in a very broad range of skills that we don't currently have in-house on our team. I call it the A-shaped designer because we are looking for someone who can clearly see conceptual opportunities skyward, then follow the design process to completion because of what they bring to the table when they walk in the door.

I want to knock down the idea that the designs in the portfolio are the only criteria anyone bases their hiring decisions on. We are looking for complementary partners on our team, based on what our clients are requesting. Of equal importance, the individual's thinking should be fresh and unique to that individual, and not some retread from design magazines, blogs, and trade fairs.

Has there been a portfolio that you've seen recently that resonated with you? What about it stood out?

There was one guy from Eindhoven [Netherlands] who had incredible skills in graphic design, new media, and filmmaking. It was a hunch he would excel in product design too...and we were correct. We tried the same formula with a fashion major. She was over her head with an experience design project that didn't have to be out of her league. Ultimately, her personality was sparkling but her process was flawed, and we didn't see that coming. Sometimes that kind of adventurous multidisciplinary thinking is risky for your business because you hire on speculation.

What are some common mistakes you've seen junior designers make in their portfolio?

First, nobody cares about life drawings you did in Foundation, not even your mother. Second, if you email me an unsolicited PDF portfolio, I will automatically delete it and you from the candidates' pool. Thanks for overloading my IMAP account, by the way. Next, don't blast every geographically desirable employer with the same intro letter. You'd be surprised that many people are guilty of doing this type of job hunting. You're not looking for any job, you're planning a career strategy.

Finally, before you consider any design studio as a potential workplace, know what their design philosophy is. It's also helpful to know what work is done in the studio, and what type of projects you will be getting into. It actually helps you consider the best match for your talents and where you can succeed.

What do you expect to learn from a designer during an interview?

I'm looking to exclude any people who would not work well on a team or are unable to take direction. Tell me you want to move to NYC desperately and where my studio is located...well, that's not always a great sign, and it can give me a window into your motives. I sincerely hope you're not a European blogger who will come into work every day hungover and I'm stuck with your sour face until your visa expires because I feel responsible for that fiasco. I've done worse, and probably every employer has misjudged a candidate's enthusiasm for the work, but sometimes the portfolio and résumé were misrepresentations of the skill level of the applicant. This is really a mom's advice: just be honest and you will find the right employer.

What characteristics or qualities would you say make a successful industrial designer?

Encyclopedic knowledge of the decorative arts and other forms of culture need to be constantly updated if you want to create relevant work in the design field. Personal curiosity, intelligence, weirdness, visual talent, a modest but confident attitude toward co-workers. Willingness to go beyond a comfort zone and personal taste to find the best solution for any design problem.

What motivated you to open your own design studio? What challenges have you faced, and how have you overcome them?

Okay, this may surprise people who know the work, but I never wanted to start my own studio. What I really wanted to do when I graduated with an MID [Masters in Industrial Design] from Pratt was to work in a commercial design office for the rest of my life and design tampons, baby shampoo containers, and potato peelers. So I got that job even before I graduated, and this was in the middle of a recession. I loved what I did there, and I excelled at it––so well that I still see products I designed over 20 years ago in the supermarket in the Midwest.

However, I was working for a very unimaginative and unsupportive boss and he was totally freaked out by me as a young, pretty, out-of-the-box thinker. This guy had the biggest share in the company, so he bullied the other partners––after I trained all the other junior designers––to vote me out in the middle of a recession. I really had to fend for myself as a professional without mentors early on, and it wasn't easy. It was good to finally realize that Constantin Boym and I needed to team up professionally because we had each other's backs and our complementary talents were stellar. In a way, I lucked out in the long run that I didn't stay in that huge consultancy where my boss's attitude would have held me back.

Industrial design still seems to be a predominantly male-dominated field. I'm curious what advice you may have for women who are just now starting out?

The gender playing field, luckily, has leveled a bit since I was in design school in the late '80s, early '90s. Today, women are entering the profession, alright, but you have women designers delaying starting a family until their practice stabilizes, or not having a family at all. My advice is to be generous when you support talent and seek support from a network of people out there who you respect as a designer, manufacturer, retailer, journalist, collector, influencer. Have them as part of your professional posse.

If you were just starting out now, what advice would you give yourself?

It's a really different time and place now in design. When I started out in 1988, my artist's background was a very unusual component for a person trying to make a go of it as an industrial designer. That brought up challenges that I was able to turn into a competitive edge, professionally.

PAUL BRADLEY
EXECUTIVE CREATIVE
DIRECTOR
FROG
SAN FRANCISCO

"I WANT TO KNOCK DOWN THE IDEA THAT THE DESIGNS IN THE PORTFOLIO ARE THE ONLY CRITERIA ANYONE BASES THEIR HIRING DECISIONS ON. WE ARE LOOKING FOR COMPLEMENTARY PARTNERS ON OUR TEAM..."

Now, the field is much more diverse in terms of who it attracts. In part, that's because technology has leveled the playing field in tools and dissemination of creative ideas. Therefore, there must be another way to find an edge, but I'll trust the current generation of designers to figure that one out.

Where do you see the future of industrial design going as it evolves further in the 21st century?

The international design vanguard has been through a creative renaissance between 1998 and 2008. The subsequent financial crash has traded the production of innovative ideas for more socially reflective projects. Hopefully, we will see the pendulum swinging back to something in between that adopts both strategies for the future.

Anything you'd like to add that we haven't talked about? Any words of wisdom?

Be kind to everyone. Make your colleagues delight in your presence. Inspire your clients to put out better products. BI

To see Laurene Leon Boym's work, please visit http://breaking.in

What kinds of portfolios get your attention these days? What brings in an industrial designer for an interview?

It used to be that portfolios themselves were kind of design projects and students would hand-build some type of a portfolio. It was very typical in the past that you would get a portfolio class towards your last semester of school and you would learn how to create a portfolio. Now, there's a lot of similarity in how most of the portfolios look and feel because they're on a digital page and share a lot of formatting and almost standardized appearances, particularly the ones that come through websites like Coroflot. You're often looking for an exception, someone who's thinking a bit differently than everybody else. We used to call that "the green haired people." I think the term is still appropriate. It came from the new age or punk scene where people ran around with colorful hair. They were a little bit off-center and interesting.

For an intern, however, you look for something different. They're looking to come in and join you for a period of time, versus someone that you are looking for to join you for a permanent job. There's a lot more commitment there. I always say getting an intern is an opportunity to experiment and try different things. People that think differently can come in and influence the studio.

Has there been a portfolio that you've seen recently that resonated with you? What about it stood out?

It still comes down to design for me. It's less about how well put-together the portfolio is, or the imagery in the portfolio, or the renderings. There's a certain bar to the skill set that you expect the students to have learned in school. You're looking for people to at least meet that bar, but that only gets you through the first level. The second level is really "Are they showing their own design approach? Have they begun to understand who they are as a designer?" It might be a high expectation from someone just graduating school. But if you can find that, then you've got a real opportunity.

If you're looking through hundreds of portfolios, which we often do, you might see one or two of those. Maybe 1% of portfolios coming in really show a student who's looking more inside themselves than they are looking around. Most students look around and see what's out there, rather than try to understand themselves through the influences or inspiration, design, architecture, fashion, or whatever. Of course, sometimes you get that one person who you don't understand where their design inspiration is coming from. Those are the exceptions and often, those are the ones that are the most interesting.

Once you find that "green haired" portfolio and you bring the designer in for an interview, what do you expect to learn from them?

Again, I'll separate between interns and normal hires because you're looking for something different with both. I stopped interviewing interns a long time ago because I wasn't so worried about the risk. I was happy to pick them based on the capabilities demonstrated in their work. I wasn't too worried if they fit in because they weren't going to need to stay there for more than three or six months. For a permanent hire you're obviously looking for a fit within your group, finding what role they will play, and how they will get along with the other designers and engineers and co-workers that are in the studio. You're trying to, in an hour, get a sense of what their personality is. How they deliver themselves, if they can convey their thoughts under pressure, how they react to difficult questions. It's as much about their personality [as their portfolio]. Their portfolio has gotten them in the door and the interview is about assessing the fit and the personality of the individual against the context of the rest of the studio.

What characteristics or qualities would you say make a successful designer?

I really appreciate someone who can be honest about their work and not defensive. As designers we all have some projects that are better than others. Someone who doesn't fight tooth and nail over everything they've designed, who is honestly willing to discuss some of the shortcomings and reflects on their own work is really valuable. Someone who understands their design and when it's good and when it's not as good. Someone who's going to work effectively with others, who has the ability to distance themselves a little bit from the things they've created. Someone who's not too wrapped up personally in each of their creations.

The extreme examples, the prima donnas, where somebody comes in and just thinks that everything they've designed—whether as a student or professionally—is good because they designed it, will get defensive very quickly if you ask them questions about their work. Those typically aren't long-term hires or people who are going to fit in. Not to say you wouldn't consider hiring those folks; some of them may be really good designers and I've hired them in the past because there was a need within that particular studio environment. Again, it's always looking at the fit and the composition of the group and not just at individuals. Even from year to year that will change within a design studio. You're putting together a puzzle and you're looking for a piece that's a right fit considering the rest of the pieces that you've already put together. You've always got in the back of your head that ideal person who would fit with the other pieces.

How did you break into this industry?

It's a story of perhaps luck more than anything. I moved from Ohio State, where I graduated from what I called the "German Design Program," as all of the professors were from Germany. Really to this day I have no idea why that was, but they were. We learned pretty much German design, product semantics. I knew I had to get out from Ohio, as many people from Ohio realize about the time they graduate from college, and it was really a choice of coming to the West Coast. At the time there was a design emergence based on the tech industry in the early '80s. You had Silicon Valley sprouting up and Apple in its early days. I came here in '85 and it was not a good time in the economy. I spent a year doing contract work for a variety of different small design offices. I also painted the house of my landlord and did yard work and side jobs just to put a roof over my head.

"I THINK PROFESSIONAL EXPERIENCE IS VERY DIFFERENT THAN ACADEMIC EXPERIENCE. IF YOU CAN GET THAT WHILE YOU'RE STILL IN SCHOOL THEN IT'S VALUABLE. IF YOU CAN'T, TRY TO GET SOME BEFORE YOU COMMIT TO A MORE PERMANENT JOB."

I got my first real gig, a contractor gig at Lunar, which had just started and broken off from GVO. There were three partners and I came in and helped them out. I worked with Bob Brunner there, and as the web of designers here in the Bay became really connected, the owner of a company called Matrix, Mike Nuttall, called Bob and asked if he knew of any good people around. He recommended me, and Mike then hired me. That actually became my first gig at Matrix, my first full-time job. After five years that turned into IDEO with the merger of DKD (David Kelley Design) and Matrix and ID Two. I went through a lot of interviews not getting jobs, and then only one real job interview to get that job at Matrix that launched it all.

If you were just starting out now, what advice would you give yourself?

I think it depends a lot on where you're at. If you're somewhere where there's an active design community, lots of design offices, consultancies, or even corporate environments, then doing contract work is not such a bad thing because you get to learn

about the different companies and organizations and how they work. Obviously, if you immediately jump into your first job, particularly if you haven't had a co-op program in your school, then you have very little to compare that job to. I remember many years ago the average time a designer stayed at an office was really short, something like 1.4 years and I think that had a lot to do with designers looking for context. They always want to know what it's like somewhere else. They want to know what the next project is. They want to know if someone has a better project.

If you can have that opportunity to experiment and get a better feel for the landscape before you commit to something, then that's a nice luxury to have. If you've had two or three co-op experiences then hopefully one of those will work out. I'm a big believer in that kind of a system. I've hired quite a few people from educational institutions that either support doing co-ops or require doing co-ops as part of the graduation criteria.

So you definitely encourage someone who is just starting out to get as many internships (or co-ops) as possible before finishing up school?

Yeah, I think professional experience is very different than academic experience. If you can get that while you're still in school then it's valuable. If you can't, try to get some before you commit to a more permanent job. The big fork in the road is: do you go into a corporate environment or do you go into a consulting environment? They are dramatically different from each other. I remember when I graduated, I would've taken a job in either one. Now it's been 25-plus years into my career and I've never worked in a corporate design environment, so I have no idea what that would really be like other than from an outsider perspective.

Where do you see the future of industrial design going as it evolves further in the 21st century?

That's a difficult question. I think the academic institutions and the educational systems are largely following professional organizations now. The way students are being trained is not that different than what we use in the professional world. The reason for that is because the process has not been evolving very much in the professional world.

Somehow a shift in how the products are created or manufactured or delivered to people is probably what is going to drive changes in industrial design in the future, rather than industrial design driving those changes. Just as industrial design came into being with the industrial revolution and mass production of products, I think its next evolution will probably again be driven by that type of change. It will be driven by how the world economy works and how the products are manufactured, delivered, and consumed, rather than the profession inwardly looking at itself and changing itself to drive that change.

What do you think would be one of the biggest drivers that would mold industrial design in a different way?

I don't know which one will be the biggest or most likely. I find myself a bit jaded about how industrial design has moved from creating good solutions for a local population, or specific population, to trying to design products that appeal to everybody. Not just somebody in your environment or your country, but everybody around the globe. It's been watered down in that sense, and it does have a tendency to make things more generic. I think a trend around more localization rather than globalization would have an impact on the way we design things and who we are designing for, as well as all of the prototyping processes that are moving into the world of manufacturing process. If Apple can CNC laptops, you can begin to grow products and you don't have to create tools to do those. It opens the door for a lot more bespoke products for things that are really personal, not just marketing personal or marketing customized.

Anything you'd like to add that we didn't talk about? Any final words of wisdom?

I guess the other thing I would say about the interviewing process in particular and the portfolio is that we spend a lot of time talking about a point of view. Again, I think it is a critical part of growing and evolving as a designer. In school you're beginning to develop that, and you're being influenced by others about what that will be. I still see my current point of view being heavily influenced by my lead professor at school, even though, while it was happening, I had no idea it was happening. If I could go back in

time to understand those influences and how they would impact me in the future, that would've been interesting—to have done it differently.

I think the biggest challenge, with developing that point of view, is being able to step back and look at the big picture. To look at what you're doing more globally and then in a very focused way. If you can grasp the holistic nature of something before you jump into the detailed level of what it should look like, or feel like, or work like, then that's going to be a huge advantage in the future. So much of what design is being drawn upon has become system problems, connectivity, and communications. We spend very little time thinking about the individual products and components and much more time thinking about their role within a much larger complex system. Not a lot of that is being taught at the undergraduate level, but that will probably be something we'll begin to see more of within industrial design.

A cohesive story of how a product fits within a whole system of things?

Yeah, to understand its role and then design it. Rather than design the product and then try to force the system that it's going to live in. BI

To see the work of Paul Bradley and frog, please visit http://breaking.in

DR. MARK BREITENBERG SPECIAL ASSISTANT TO THE PRESIDENT ART CENTER COLLEGE OF DESIGN PASADENA, CALIFORNIA

Interviewed while Dr. Breitenberg was the Provost of California College of the Arts in San Francisco.

You've had quite an extensive career and been involved in different design organizations. I'm curious to hear your perspective on how industrial design has evolved over the time you've been part of it?

That's a good starting point. I often talk about the expanded field of industrial design. In the last 10 to 15 years, the opportunities for industrial designers have widened in all kinds of ways; that alone could be the subject of a book. I think certainly this has to do with design of systems and services, not just objects, as many people have said. But I also think it has to do with the ability of industrial designers to problem solve. In other words, to use the design process or design thinking to address all kinds of complex, multifaceted problems. As president of ICSID [International Council of Society of Industrial Design], I was very involved in planning the International Design Alliance (IDA) conference in Taipei last fall. The conference was organized around keynote speakers who talked about international problems in their fields of expertise. They weren't designers. They were experts in fields such as biochemistry, migration and population growth, technology, and the Internet. In response to these keynote addresses, designers discussed how they would address the problem from a design standpoint, often sharing a perspective the experts had not considered. It was really productive. So you've got a host of problems—urban living, urban development, economic development—now within the domain that industrial designers can address. To me that's the expanded field.

A very important aspect of this expanded field of industrial design is that designers have to be broader

in their education than ever before. You can't simply have traditional industrial design skills. Because the problems designers can address are broader and in many cases more systemic, with many integrated parts, you need to have a stronger liberal arts, sciences, and humanities background. This I hear time and time again. It's exciting, but the field is much more comprehensive. Steve Jobs often talked about his work as being at the intersection of technology and the humanities. His success was understanding the human elements in design.

Actually, that was going to be my follow-up question. The education of an industrial designer has focused a lot on craft, technical skills, and ability to create an aesthetically pleasing form. Where do you see it standing today?

I think that the fundamental skills of the industrial designer are still important—the ability to visualize an idea and to communicate it, to prototype and develop through an iterative process. But, because of this expanded field of industrial design, it's necessary to have a broader knowledge base. I think you got to have communication skills, writing skills, the ability to do ethnographic and user-based research—anything and everything that allows you to have your hand on the pulse of our global culture. Industrial design has always been a studio practice, but it's become a humanities or a social science as well. The blend of work that you do outside of the studio with the studio work has become really critical. Business education is another element that's been added. The problem for educators and for students is that you're still getting your degree in the same length of time, and now you've got to understand sustainability and business while still learning the fundamental skills. There's so much more to teach.

What would be your advice to somebody who is considering pursuing industrial design or who is just breaking into the industry fresh from college?

What I hear from employers around the world who are hiring industrial designers is a shift toward the importance of critical thinking and communication skills, as well as having a broad knowledge. They'll say, "We will teach them the new software, we will teach them the new technical skill, what I really want is someone who is a great thinker and a great communicator in language and in visual media." Again, that reflects the more diverse, expanded field of areas in which industrial designers can now work. So my advice is to study the liberal arts and sciences as an integrated part of your design education, which is exactly what a good design curriculum should promote.

How do you see this impacting portfolios and their content?

The best portfolios are more concept-driven. They should reflect a broader array of projects than ever before. I think if you just go out there with household objects you're going to be seen as a fairly narrow designer. You might get hired, but your career advancement will be slower. I have heard from a lot of companies and design firms that they'll bring in someone who is strong on the craft side and has some cool looking prototypes, but they'll really promote someone who has a breadth of different kinds of projects and who shows strong research and thinking in each of them. I also think everyone should have some kind of humanitarian, social justice-based projects in their portfolio because not only are a lot of companies doing this kind of work, they're looking for the character and commitment of the people they hire as well.

How would you advise somebody to get that kind of an experience?

Most schools now have some initiative that promotes this kind of work. Designmatters at Art Center College of Design is one of the most successful. But you should also incorporate your sense of social responsibility in every project you do—it's not an added value, it's a fundamental value.

It's an interesting topic that you bring up, but still, when you talk to industrial design students a lot of their heroes are people like Karim Rashid and Philippe Starck, designers who are not necessarily touching too much on social responsibility.

They should go back to Dieter Rams, who was talking about sustainable design in the 1970s. His work is still iconic and we all know that Jonathan Ive was very influenced by him in his designs for Apple. The social responsibility projects will also add to your "hireability." More and more companies are taking

on this kind of work, so you're just getting ready for the marketplace that you're about to enter. And most importantly, you will find your work more enriching. I think that more and more students think that way, rather than just simply wanting to do flashy aesthetics. This generation of students in college today has a really deep sense of social responsibility.

I know that your own academic background is diverse. I'm curious what sparked your own interest in industrial design?

I do have a background in philosophy and critical theory and I started out after graduate school as a professor at a liberal arts college. But I began to lose my interest in ideas in a purely academic context—ideas that live in academic journals, at conferences, and in books that only specialists read. I was more interested in figuring out a way for ideas to have a bigger impact in the world. I left academia to work in Hollywood for a few years as a screenwriter, but at the same time, I was invited to teach at Art Center College of Design in Pasadena, California, and a couple years later to redesign their liberal arts and sciences curriculum, working with and integrated into the studio disciplines. That was the chance to take the ideas that I've been trained in and define a more practical application for them within design education. My education in design was at Art Center, from their remarkably talented department chairs, faculty, and students.

If you were just starting out now, what advice would you give yourself?

I would've studied design, no doubt. I don't regret my training in the humanities, and ideally, as I've said, you study both. But I would love to have had visual ideation and communication skills I admire in designers. It's not just for the sake of their professional lives. My designer friends and colleagues really see and experience the world differently. I've learned a lot from them, but it's not the same without the deep training they received. Maybe I'll do a design degree at some point. Ideally, it's great to do two years or a full degree in a social science or humanities before you do your design education. I know that means a lot of school, but it really is the ideal combination. If you could study deeply in environmental science, medicine, critical thinking, or psychology, all of these things will make you a better designer.

A designer who is grounded in reality?

That's it. Obviously there are a lot of industrial designers coming out of schools around the world right now. I don't know the numbers in China, but they're staggering. I heard that China has created 1,000 new design programs in the last 15 years alone. Latin America is also drawing more students to the design fields. Design has taken off in Turkey recently. So there are a lot of students coming out with degrees in industrial design and, like any crowded marketplace, the key is going to be what distinguishes you from the other 50,000 who just got their degree in industrial design. It becomes very important to have a specialty within your design discipline, an area of expertise outside of design. Again, it could be any one of many different fields, but you should have your industrial design education plus something else that you bring that's unique.

Where do you see the future of industrial design going as it evolves further in the 21st century?

I think what's happened in the last 10 years and what will continue to happen is that products will be more human-centered in the way that they're designed and used, especially in technology-based products. The iPhone is a great example. Its innovation is not engineering but in the intuitive way you interact with it. Interaction design is going to be increasingly important, if not ubiquitous. We are going to be designing more and more objects that have digital elements or digital interfaces. In general, a fundamental understanding of what it means to be human—our needs, aspirations, emotions, daily rituals—will continue to shape product design in the future.

And it's pretty obvious that understanding the materials in the terms of sustainability and environment has already become a given, an assumption in design. This will be driven by our sense of responsibility to the environment, but also by the marketplace as people become increasingly willing to spend more money on green products.

Anything we didn't cover that you would like to add? Any final words of wisdom?

I have one final thought. I have spent a lot of time in Asia, in industrial design schools and with different organizations, and I want to encourage women to enter industrial design. I've given talks in Korea, China, and Taiwan fairly recently, and I've seen a lot of young women designers who are really good, but who live in countries in which they have almost no opportunity to practice industrial design. It's too bad for them personally, but it's also bad for the national economy because you're eliminating half your creative workforce. It also restricts the success of design companies, who typically have men designing products women buy. I don't want to generalize about or stereotype women, but there are skill sets that women often bring to industrial design that men don't often have. Empathy, for example: we know from studies that girls develop this ability at an earlier age than boys. And this is the basis of being able to understand and design for others' needs. Again, I don't think that men can't be empathic, but I think you find it more easily in women just because of the way they're brought up. Emotional intelligence is also generally more developed among women. I think these qualities are becoming increasingly important in the practices of industrial design.

"...YOU SHOULD ALSO INCORPORATE YOUR SENSE OF SOCIAL RESPONSIBILITY IN EVERY PROJECT YOU DO—IT'S NOT AN ADDED VALUE, IT'S A FUNDAMENTAL VALUE."

The other important trend of course is that industrial design is less and less "industrial." It's all about systems, the ways people interact and communicate with objects and with each other. The old version of industrial design was not appealing to women for all kinds of reasons, but in the expanded field of industrial design there should be a lot of appeal to women, to their interests and their fundamental skill sets. I would like to promote that idea.

Yeah, me too. BI

To see Dr. Breitenberg's work, please visit http://breaking.in

NEIL BROOKER GLOBAL DIRECTOR BMW GROUP DESIGNWORKSUSA NEWBURY PARK, CALIFORNIA

Interviewed while Mr. Brooker was General Manager at frog in Austin, Texas.

What kinds of portfolios get your attention these days? What brings in an industrial designer for an interview?

If I'm looking primarily at automotive designers, then I'm looking for someone with flare in styling capabilities as opposed to product design capabilities. Someone who understands form language, someone who understands how highlights travel across the vehicle, someone who understands interiors and how that whole thing comes together. There is a little bit of different thinking that you're looking for in someone coming in-house, as opposed to someone coming into the consultancy where you're looking for a little bit of the flash in the presentation capabilities to win over a client. There are subtle differences, depending on the side of the fence you're sitting on.

Then, I'm looking beyond just the form factor itself. In a product designer, I'm looking for the understanding of how the product is put together. I would expect the designer to understand how to, for example, put together a cell phone—how do you put the whole thing together. Whereas with automotive, I would be expecting the candidate to understand the basics of the vehicle, proportions, and the package.

Has there been a portfolio that you've seen recently that resonated with you? What about it stood out?

There was a designer—and this goes way back—who had a fantastic portfolio and a great way of showing his designs and presenting his design ideas.

It goes beyond just the portfolio; it's the ability to talk about the story behind the vehicle, for example, or behind a product. That's critical. Some of the better product design portfolios I've seen are where someone understands how to translate a rendered idea into a 3D model.

"WHILE I APPRECIATE PEOPLE THINKING FAR OUT, LIKE THE SUPER FORWARD-LOOKING KINDS OF CONCEPTS, I ALSO WANT TO SEE THE BALANCE OF THAT WITH REALITY. I WANT TO SEE THAT THE PORTFOLIO IS ALSO CARRYING EXAMPLES OF REAL PRODUCTS THAT HAVE BEEN DESIGNED, THAT ARE EXECUTABLE TODAY."

In automotive applicants we would look for someone who knows how to put together a model, but we're not necessarily looking for them to spend a lot of their time building the surfaces of the model, as there are modelers who will do that. But in product design applicants we do expect that. We look for someone who knows how to put together 3D files to construct the product. Some of the better product design portfolios I've seen have been where someone's been actually able to show exploded views of a product coming together and understand the 3D form. Where they are presenting Alias files as opposed to two-dimensional Photoshop or Illustrator files.

It sounds like, for automotive, the portfolios should be based more on the visceral and the aesthetics, and in the product realm, it's the technical aspects that should be emphasized?

Yes, but let me qualify that a little bit. In addition to seeing a portfolio in automotive that just has the flash, I also want to see a couple of situations where someone's been able to take those ideas and translate them into 3D models, like clay models. They need to understand how to take something that's two-dimensional and translate that into three-dimensional properties. Whereas I think in product design you can do that automatically through the 3D file. While I appreciate people thinking far out, like the super forward-looking kinds of concepts, I also want to see the balance of that with reality. I want to see that the portfolio is also carrying examples of real products that have been designed, that are executable today. A typical example from the automotive side is an understanding of drop glass—that it can actually happen on the vehicle, that the curvature on the glass can drop into the body side.

So if an industrial design student came to you and asked, "What should my portfolio be like? What do I need to show you in order to work with you?", what would you tell them?

I would like to see the ability to be creative both with advanced ideas and thinking, as well as ideas that take into account packaging and manufacturing constraints for production in the next generation of products.

What do you expect to learn from a designer during an interview?

I'm looking for someone who can articulate their thoughts, someone who knows how to speak about their design, rather than waiting for an interpretation of their designs. When you're able to put a story behind an idea, that makes it that much more compelling. It's not just compelling from the point of view of the interviewer, but to the boss or the customer. It's going to resonate a lot better when they can remember a story behind an idea.

What characteristics or qualities would you say make a successful designer?

I think it's the ability to collaborate, of course. The ability to speak openly about a problem. There's a competitive edge where the individual has strong opinions about their own ideas and is able to push those ideas through as well. It's a difficult challenge:

being prepared to collaborate with your fellow designers or peers, but by the same token, having a competitive edge to win a design competition. The ability to talk and present an idea is key. Many great ideas get lost because they weren't presented well.

So how would one present their work in that persuasive manner?

First and foremost is engaging the audience. Make sure that you have their attention and bring it to the idea. Then it's again the storytelling behind an idea. It's about being able to concisely, but in a very emotional or engaging way, throw the audience into an idea that you have so they understand it. If you have a strong opinion, make sure that the opinion gets heard by the client. Maybe you have five ideas of which you have two that are strongest, but you put all five up. That dilutes your message. You're better off just presenting the two ideas, if you feel that strongly about them.

A process of self-editing.

Yes. I think a big mistake is taking a shotgun approach where we put too much on a wall for an audience to understand. You lose your message. You have to decide the right level of presentation and the right level of materials you want to put in front of the client to show your message so what you feel strongly about comes through. I've been in presentations myself where we just covered the walls with loads of ideas to show how much work we've done. But that really wasn't an effective way to present the ideas. It got really diluted and you don't keep the attention of the audience. They're looking at the walls, trying to absorb all of this information.

How did you break into this business?

Mine's a strange story. I came in more through an apprenticeship scheme into design, working at the design group and doing the clay models, building properties, doing engineering layouts, and ultimately sketching vehicles. That was the early part of my career, then I got into a managerial role and ended up doing an MBA. It wasn't a typical path into it. I think we are seeing a little bit more of that now because design is more about being creative and innovative, and organizations are recognizing creative thinking is not limited to individuals with design degrees only. It can come out of other key people. We're seeing that at frog right now.

You mention you ended up going back to get your MBA. How have the skills you gained there helped you as a designer? Would you say it added to your success?

Yeah, absolutely. There's a need to understand the tradeoff in an organization because certainly, it's a balancing act. It's understanding the influence that design can have throughout the organization, not necessarily from the creative innovation standpoint, but the business aspects. It's understanding the big picture of the company.

So if you were just starting out now, what advice would you give yourself?

The one thing that everyone benefits from by entering a design school is working with a bunch of other people who are going through the same thing and learning from each other. I would say that experience is critical. I worry a little bit that we are teaching our skills too much on the computer and not making things enough with our hands. Actually, seeing people making things again is a good thing. Understanding the form in 3D through the process of making it is invaluable. We are churning out a lot of people who have a lot of computer skills, who can do whiz-bang on the computer without understanding the form factor.

Where do you see the future of industrial design going as it evolves further in the 21st century?

I see the continuation of what is happening right now. If you look out in the Western world of design, we're moving up in the food chain. Design, creativity, and innovation are being used interchangeably with each other. As the creativity becomes the key differentiator in innovation, I see industrial design being critical to organizations and their ability to innovate.

By the same token, what we're seeing is some migration of key designers to China and India. Some of the work that we would traditionally do here in the west is going to be picked up by the designers coming out of those economies, as they learn to be more creative and develop brand identities. Let's take a look at China right now. If you look at it from the car industry perspective, to date it's been fairly easy for them to just copy what's been done. But they're getting to a point where they're starting to think about exporting. As they do that, they've got to start thinking of their own identity, their own design identity. That needs innovation, a deeper understanding of what a Chinese brand is and how a Chinese brand looks in the North American market or European market.

There's an industry chain here that will shift, where the developed economies will have to move up towards innovation and the developing economies will do the more traditional design we've done in the past.

Is there anything we didn't cover that you'd like to add? Any final words of wisdom?

I think it's making things. Many people can come up with fantastic ideas but if you can't make the ideas, at the end of the day, it's not going to help. Make sure you understand the product itself in its actual form and how to put that together. It is critical to being a good designer. Design, sketch, render, make, present. [BI]

To see Neil Brooker's work, please visit http://breaking.in

ROBERT BRUNNER
FOUNDER & PARTNER
AMMUNITION
SAN FRANCISCO

What kinds of portfolios get your attention these days? What brings in an industrial designer for an interview?

That's a good question because we do see a lot of portfolios and after you interview a lot of people you can pretty quickly decide if it's someone you want to see or not. I really just glance through and I know if this person has a possibility of working within our group. There always is a certain base level of skill and ability [we need to see]. The ability to present a piece of work comes through in a portfolio and, for us, there's also a certain range of aesthetic that we look for that fits within our philosophy. Then it really has to do with a combination of innovative thinking and sophistication. You see a fair number of people developing innovative ideas—something that's new or different. The ones that are more rare have a sophistication about them that comes through. It's more than just a crazy idea. It's progressive and they're thinking about the context of its use and so forth. We look at the baseline of skills and if there is an aesthetic that makes sense for us and the quality of the innovation. You can see, if you're going through four projects that someone has done, those threads. Typically then we'll invite them to talk to us.

Have you seen a portfolio recently that resonated with you, and what about it was different and signified to you that this designer could do all of these things you just mentioned?

When I see someone new I ask if they have "the funk" or not. What that means is that there's just some energy there that's really compelling and you see that they get it. It's really hard to nail down. The majority of the people we have in our studio we've taken on as interns. We really view the intern process as a very extended interview that allows us to spend three to six months, sometimes a year, with someone working really closely and get an idea whether they're going to fit.

We've seen some really great portfolios and a lot of them are, interestingly enough, coming out of France, which has been in development in the last few years from a design talent perspective. We used to see a few schools in the US and a few schools in England and Germany and lately we've seen a lot coming from France and we have three French-speaking designers in our studio right now.

Personally, I like to see models because, when I came up, I always felt that making models was extremely important. It's very easy to cheat in 3D

CAD and you just don't learn about something until you make it. You don't understand scale and proportion and detail until you've actually done it. I really love to see models; it's surprising how the models you see in portfolios are predominantly renderings. For me to see a portfolio that has physical artifacts is exciting because I can get a sense of the designer's ability to actually make something. It's a long way from a model to a real product, but it's a long way from a rendering to a model. To see that is really important to me. Again, we see most students have the 3D skills to develop and visualize things pretty effectively, so that's pretty consistent. The one thing that makes a difference in portfolios now is how well people present. If someone can do it beautifully and articulate a story in their portfolio or a PDF that they send out, it's really important. It tends to allow them to rise to a higher level in the stack when they have done that really well.

What do you expect to learn from a designer during an interview?

That's the opportunity to see the person. We're very careful about who we bring into the team. It's very important because of the way we work. We are a fairly flat company. I have two partners and we have some individuals who are in charge of disciplinary areas, but after that it's sort of everybody else. It is part of the strategy of the way we work; we form and reform teams very quickly. People work on multiple projects with different people and that effectively allows our 40 people to behave like 60. So within that model, it's really important that people fit in from a cultural point of view.

The interview is an opportunity to meet people and see what they're like, listen to them present their work, get a sense about what they're passionate about, what the sparks were that led them to a solution. We really want to understand how they go at something and begin to view them as an individual. We've already seen the work and this allows them to describe it personally. It gives us an opportunity to really get a sense of whether this person would work here or not.

How do you know if they would fit into the culture of Ammunition?

Part of it comes from experience. We are a very close group, and there are no huge professional agendas. That comes from the fact that we don't have a hierarchical group. We look for someone who's easygoing and passionate, who is excited about their work, who has a good sense of humor. We like having diversity. We have designers from US, from Asia, from Europe, and having a mixture of personalities and backgrounds is important as well. It's looking at how this person thinks, how they behave, what they value and asking, "Is that going to fit with this sort of hard-working yet easygoing, fun-loving group of people?"

What characteristics or qualities are necessary to be a successful designer?

Part of it is just loving objects and making things, and that's not always there. Some people like the process and some people like the research aspects of it. What we do and what we look for is someone who has a love and passion for making objects functional, beautiful, and culturally special. That's one of the things we look for and one of the things that's necessary to be a product designer. You really just have to love products, making them, realizing them.

Another one is a natural inquisitiveness in people and having the interest to question things. "Why does it have to be that way? Why can't it be another way? What are people really doing?" Many people just sit down and say, "Okay, here's a problem and here's how I'm going to go solve it." That's great, but what separates a really good designer is asking those questions and wanting to answer them. That's a very important quality.

The last thing would be an interest in things that are technical. An interest in how things are made and how things work and how tools work. All of those aspects make a good product designer. You're interested in techniques, how things are done, and how things work.

How did you break into this business, and what motivated you to start Ammunition?

It's an interesting path for me. I started off in engineering school. My father was a very

successful engineer. My mother was a fine artist, fashion model, and an entrepreneur. I started out in engineering and, while I was doing alright, I didn't like it. I literally wandered over to the art department, thinking of moving into fine arts and discovered industrial design. I didn't even know it existed. I started, and I don't remember why—probably because I needed a job—but I started working very early, during my second year of school in some internships. Eventually, I worked part time at a design-consulting firm in the Bay area, and the great thing about that company was that if you were good, if you had skills, they kind of left you alone. Now that I'm running a business that sounds like a scary idea, but they did that. I've always been an independent person so it actually helped me learn a lot. I started working with two guys very closely and we eventually left and formed what became Lunar design.

I literally went to school, worked as an intern, learned about the business and how design happens. Really, the important thing for me early on was finding those really great projects that allowed me to demonstrate my skills and [growth]. When there was something that came into the studio that I thought was a really great project, I figured out a way to work on it somehow. Not only to learn but to build my portfolio. You can't be too aggressive, but at the same time you can't just sit down and be too passive and hope things will just happen. One of the things I give as advice to people is to understand where you want to go and seek out those opportunities to get there.

So, Ammunition wasn't my first business. After school we started Lunar, and then I went to Apple and then to Pentagram, which was kind of like starting a business within a business. When I decided to split off to start Ammunition, it was really a couple things that were driving it. One was, while I felt I had learned a lot running design at Apple and being a partner at Pentagram, I didn't feel like it was the best platform to do what I wanted to do, which was to create brands around products. I wanted to develop things and really drive an idea, not just a product, into a market. I wanted to build a team to do that. Secondarily, as a designer, you're usually just happy to get a good project, and so if you can get that good project, and work on it, and pay yourself and your people, you're happy. But what you end up doing is giving away really valuable intellectual property very cheaply. I wanted to start building models where we were partnering to participate in the value that we create. That's part of what we've been doing with Beats and a few other entities, and we get a return on our success.

If you were starting out now, what advice would you give yourself?

The one thing that was never taught really well at school, and it's extremely important, is the ability to communicate and communicate about your work. You really don't get a heck of a lot of training on how to write about it, how to tell a story, how to convince people, and how to make arguments. If you're at a certain talent level and you want to be a great designer, your abilities to motivate people to develop your designs are as important as your abilities to develop, implement, and manufacture.

As a young designer, you think, "If it's a really cool idea everyone will want to do it," right? Turns out, that's not true. You actually have to do a lot of work to move something from an idea to reality. People are involved and you have to learn how to convince people, how to motivate people, and play politics. All of those things are necessary to make good things happen. None of that is taught at school, so I guess if I were starting over, in addition to the things I was learning in design, I'd spend more time on how to communicate, how to write, and how to present.

Where do you see the future of industrial design going as it evolves further in the 21st century?

I don't consider myself as traditionalist as some who think product design is a craft and it should remain a craft, and it's always about the art, the inspiration, and the designer. Then there are other people who say that it's about process and design thinking—and that's the future of design—to really be more focused on broader ideas as opposed to this object you are trying to make. I think the future of industrial design really is continuing and broadening the idea of craft. The notion of making something really great extends beyond the forms

and the details to how things work and how they behave and communicate. How they're seen by the world. It still needs to be something that's incredibly well crafted, well thought-out, beautiful, emotional, exciting. Those are all the things that have to be there.

"WHAT WE DO AND WHAT WE LOOK FOR IS SOMEONE WHO HAS A LOVE AND PASSION FOR MAKING OBJECTS FUNCTIONAL, BEAUTIFUL, AND CULTURALLY SPECIAL...YOU REALLY JUST HAVE TO LOVE PRODUCTS, MAKING THEM, REALIZING THEM."

It's not saying that the designer is a craftsman who sits and makes this perfect object. It's taking that passion for perfection but broadening it into many, many things around the experience people have with things, and using the way we're trained as designers to be effective at it. I think that's the future. It's becoming more and more recognized, whether it's interaction design or product design or communication design. The people who are very successful aren't just technically adept; they have a vision and a passion to bring excellence and a great experience to their work. When people can feel that passion come through something, whether it's software or an object, it's always there.

Is there anything we haven't talked about that you'd like to add? Any final words of wisdom?

Ideas are very important, but what's probably more important is that you see that idea through. Design is one of those things that is 10% inspiration and 90% perspiration. We put a lot of focus on that creative idea and it's very important, but those ideas never go anywhere unless you see them through and it's a long, hard battle to do so.

You have to stay committed to it. Being dedicated is extremely important, especially if someone wants to be entrepreneurial and do things on their own. ▣

To see the work of Robert Brunner and Ammunition, please visit http://breaking.in

MAX BURTON
FOUNDER & PRINCIPAL
MATTER
SAN FRANCISCO

Interviewed while Mr. Burton was Executive Creative Director at frog in San Francisco.

What kinds of portfolios get your attention these days? What brings in an industrial designer for an interview?

For me it's a very instant read. I know pretty much immediately if it's in or out. I can do a fairly quick sort of 20 portfolios, narrowing down to the three I like in just a few minutes. I'm looking for work that's original and beautifully presented. Since I am an industrial designer, the physical form has to be amazing. For what I call the "first read" or the "instant read," the design must be iconic and memorable. Then there's the second read, which is where I really get down into who I might choose, and that's when I dig into their process—making sure they've done research and identified a user and a need. Ideally, I like to see an insight discovered during the research phase turned into a solution. This shows a good process and the candidate's inclination towards empathy. For the third read, I like to see that they've demonstrated all the necessary skills and knowledge to be an invaluable industrial designer. This is where I look at prototyping, drawing, rendering, and 3D CAD skills, as well as choices they made on materials and manufacturing techniques.

Has there been a portfolio recently that resonated with you? What about it stood out?

Interestingly enough, I don't see as many great portfolios as I used to. I think partly because people who are choosing to study design aren't choosing industrial design as their first choice anymore. Even the volume of portfolios is less than what it used to be. I actually liked the portfolios of the two interns we have coming into frog; both of their portfolios were really excellent. They had a lot of original thinking and a thorough process. They tackled some unusual spaces, which is appealing, rather than seeing yet another sketch of a shoe or a car. You could tell immediately by looking at their final forms, which were quite fresh. An original solution demonstrated that they looked at a problem from a different angle, or a new perspective.

What do you expect to learn from a designer during an interview?

The tough part about hiring a designer for their first job is that they have to be firing on all cylinders. They have to be creative and skilled in all key areas, and that's asking a lot. I expect not only a great idea, but also a great articulation of that idea through form, colors, materials, and finishes. I expect a great ability to present their work with exceptional rendering skills, 3D CAD, as well as good process. I like to see a good process book. I want to see that not only is their sketching good, but more importantly, that they think through sketching.

They also need to have the ability to present well. Can they stand up in front of a group of people and potentially a client and communicate their ideas confidently? We are not just hiring them for this year or next; it's an investment for years to come and we have to look for their ability to one day become an associate creative director or creative director. Those positions require great interpersonal skills.

What are the characteristics or qualities necessary to be a successful designer?

The biggest shift I've seen is that once upon a time product designers were trained very much in technical skills. While this is important and I support technical competency, the design world is expanding and we have to take on more of the upstream thinking on a project. That means defining what the opportunity is as opposed to simply refining a pre-existing idea. This means working as a team, alongside strategists, researchers, and business people to look for these opportunities. The way old-school industrial design was set up was that the industrial designer was the first step in the assembly line of the production process. The marketing or engineering department handed the design to you and the industrial designer simply styled a product based on current market trends. The exciting opportunity for industrial designers now is that they can get involved in the definition of a product much, much sooner and that's a really exciting place for designers. Today, successful designers are using their brains as well as their skills.

How did you break into the industry?

I know it's tough for every student graduating because, in a way, design school is really just a beginning. Designers really advance their education when they start working, so the first job or two is really important. In the beginning I focused on learning rather than making a good salary. I was very fortunate that I won a scholarship that was sponsored by Royal Society of Arts (RSA) in England. The scholarship paid for half of my salary for a year to be employed in a company. The RSA connected young graduates with a company that never had a designer before.

I was matched up with a company in Nottingham, England, that manufactured robots. I was fortunate to start there, as it was a factory that actually made things––which was not only really cool, but a great learning experience. Upstairs was the design and engineering department and downstairs was manufacturing and assembly. I started out as the only designer in a huge factory in an industrial part of town. I started designing robots, making them much easier to use, more ergonomic, and of course, more beautiful. One day I had a prototype on my desk and the general manager of the factory walked by and noticed it. At the time he didn't even know who I was; I recall he looked at me and said, "Who are you, what are you doing here, and what is that on your desk?" I said that I was an industrial

designer and that I had just designed the prototype in front of him. He was completely blown away. He thought it was amazing and immediately saw the value of good design. He became my biggest fan and supported me during my time there. The same day he asked me how much I was getting paid. I recall I was earning 7,500 pounds, and the next day my salary was doubled. The design team later expanded to three more people.

"I LIKE TO SEE A GOOD PROCESS BOOK. I WANT TO SEE THAT NOT ONLY IS THEIR SKETCHING GOOD, BUT MORE IMPORTANTLY, THAT THEY THINK THROUGH SKETCHING."

After the first year, I knew I had to move to London because that's where all the design activity was. But as soon as I got there, there was a huge recession in England. I sent about 150 letters to many different design consultancies and I only got two responses back. I was interviewed at Tangerine by Jonathan Ive and at PDD by Brian Smith. PDD offered me a position as a junior designer. It was during my year at PDD that I really honed my skills. After a year at PDD, I knew I needed to go to the Royal College of Art to propel my career.

If you were just starting out now, what advice would you give yourself?

Being a designer today requires both depth and breadth. If I were to start afresh, I would demonstrate that I have core competency in my area of expertise—industrial design—but then I would show breadth in my ability to think beyond the physical to solve a problem, or originate an idea. In design today we tend to be discipline agnostic when we create. I don't think I would have to prove to everyone that I am an expert at interaction design or strategy but that I know enough to collaborate and communicate with other experts and occasionally contribute an original idea. It's very rare for an industrial designer to work in isolation these days, so I would show how I worked on a group project. I would show how I was effective at collaboration, and show what I contributed, as well as how my thinking helped influence the results in a positive way.

In the early days I would also advise graduates to interview as much as possible. The interview process itself is an invaluable method to practice telling your story, communicate your designs, and gain confidence.

Where do you see the future of industrial design going as it evolves further in the 21st century?

As the world becomes more digital and more virtual, one would think that industrial design is becoming less relevant. I think the opposite is true. We are humans and we inhabit a physical world. It's a fundamental human need to connect with each other and the world around us in a physical way. I can't imagine a world where this no longer exists. At some point, even if a product is mostly about software or digital content, we as humans need to access this data and content. This is where industrial design plays a crucial role.

Physical design has become a tangible expression of a company's brand and ethos. The physical product is the moment where a person literally touches the brand. Physical objects are powerful symbols where abstraction of software and brand become real. Industrial design is less and less about functionality and more about meaning. Industrial designers who understand this shift will be hugely relevant in the future. They not only need to personally understand this shift, but they also need to be able to express it to the companies they are working for, as very few companies are grasping this shifting territory.

Anything you'd like to add that we haven't talked about? Any final words of wisdom?

Follow your heart. Do what you are good at and what you enjoy. Like me, you probably chose to become a designer because you love to be creative and make things for people. You probably enjoy seeing people use your products and the delight they experience when they use your design. Creativity, empathy, and compassion for people are the virtues of a great designer. If you possess these qualities and aspirations, your career as a designer will be long and rewarding. If your motivations are about money and climbing the corporate ladder, you will be disappointed and frustrated. For the long haul, you have to love what you do. Take this approach and everything will just simply fall into place. [BI]

To see Max Burton's work, please visit http://breaking.in

MORAY CALLUM GROUP VICE PRESIDENT & CHIEF CREATIVE OFFICER FORD MOTOR COMPANY DEARBORN, MICHIGAN

Interviewed while Mr. Callum was Executive Director of Design at Ford Motor Company in Dearborn, Michigan.

What kinds of portfolios get your attention these days? What brings in an industrial designer for an interview?

I think what's changed a lot is people's abilities in terms of skill levels and different techniques. Obviously, it's not just looking at sketches but has a lot to do with their ability to create those in 3D and ability to use additional programs. There is a technical level we look for and flexibility within that level. We don't want a person who can just do one thing, we need a range of abilities.

We are looking for creativity and new ideas. I like to see a chronology through the portfolio. If they've been in college for three or four years, I'd like to see where they've started and how they've developed throughout these years. You can tell a lot about a designer through the range of improvement, and it's also kind of interesting to look at. The appropriateness of design is also important. A lot of designers tend to design for themselves and they need to realize you're not designing a car for yourself. You're designing not just for a specific brand, but for specific clientele and the tastes that they have. It's an ability to put themselves in their customer's shoes and those of the employer they may be working for—the ability to design appropriate to the customer and appropriate to the brand.

I think becoming a transportation designer is pretty straightforward. You go through a specific course and decide that's going to be your career quite early on. Obviously, they look at brands that they want to work for and where the work is going. There's nothing complicated about why they would come to us. They hear we are hiring and they are looking for jobs. We like to think we're a design-led company, so what we do will attract designers to come interview to work with us, not just because they're wanting a job.

Has there been a portfolio recently that you've seen that resonated with you, and can you talk about it?

There was a student from Art Center recently who had a range of work. His ability to design for different brands was very indicative of how he matured as a designer. He designed a car for one brand and then another, and there was very little surface language connection with the two but it still came from the same designer. It showed his flexibility in being able to design appropriately for the brand he was working for. I think that shows a level of maturity. It's not something design students always think about. They try to put their best foot forward and pick a design they want to do, as opposed to what's good for the brand.

We still look for people who can sketch and draw and who can understand a form through drawings. I think that tells you a lot about the designer. If they can sketch and draw, then we can understand the forms.

What do you expect to learn from a designer during an interview?

We employ designers not just for their design ability but for their opinion as well. I like designers to be quite strong in terms of describing why they did things.

They need to have strong opinions of design and be able to explain why they're designing something specifically as opposed to just letting the portfolio do the talking. Their ability to present shows maturity and potential as a designer, to put forward their opinion and explain why they're doing things, as opposed to just being automatic. I think that's really important.

What are the characteristics or qualities necessary to be a successful designer?

Be very patient.

I think it depends. I think a lot of us who have reached senior management in design probably never aspired to that. To be frank, the higher up you go, the less you get to design. I think it's a necessary evil, just being able to control what the right thing to do is. I think in terms of characteristics, it's the ability to articulate what you're doing and why you're doing it. A lot of our job is communication and collaboration and negotiation. For a successful designer, you need to be able to do all these things. It's not just about doing a great design. If you can't convince a company to spend the money to build that design, it will stay in the sketch form. It takes a bit of salesmanship and also the ability to articulate, communicate, and negotiate a design to move forward.

How did you break into this business?

A little bit by default, I suppose. I don't know if you know my brother Ian; he's the director of Jaguar design. He's four years older than me and he was the one who knew from age zero he wanted to be a car designer. I kind of grew up with the same enthusiasm for cars that he had but went off in a couple of different tangents. I actually started studying architecture and then moved to product design and then realized I was just trying to avoid the inevitable. It's a little bit different from other people. Ian, being a few years ahead of me, sort of paved the way as to knowing what schools to go to and giving me contacts as well. So I was really lucky because he was the one that struggled to find some of these things. Scotland is really not the car design capital of the world. I owe a lot to him to be able to get into this business.

If you were just starting off now, what advice would you give yourself?

While you're actually designing, it's going to be the happiest part of your career and as you move up the ladder you'll do less of what you love and more of what is necessary. So I'd tell myself enjoy the good times while you've got them.

Where do you see the future of transportation design going as it evolves further in the 21st century?

You get a couple of different reactions to that. Some people say cars aren't changing at all relative to other technologies and I think they have actually changed quite a lot. In the '50s we thought we'd have flying cars by now, so I think we're getting a bit more realistic as to where the future is going to go and the pace of change. That pace will actually accelerate due to new technologies. I obviously think that different fuel sources and different technologies have the potential to change how the vehicles look.

> "A LOT OF OUR JOB IS COMMUNICATION AND COLLABORATION AND NEGOTIATION. FOR A SUCCESSFUL DESIGNER, YOU NEED TO BE ABLE TO DO ALL THESE THINGS. IT'S NOT JUST ABOUT DOING A GREAT DESIGN."

I think the interesting thing will be if the people are going to be open to that change or not. If we get fully autonomous electric vehicles, for example, if the engine doesn't need to be where the current engine is, and you can change the package around, I think time will tell if that's acceptable to the public or not. People are reluctant to major changes,

especially in car design. I think the potential is there as we move forward to dramatically change vehicles. The public will tell us whether they want that or not.

Is there anything you'd like to add that we haven't talked about? Any final words of wisdom?

I hope I'm not sounding like a real cynic. I think people need to understand that design, and especially automotive design, is a business. Be prepared to really be in a business atmosphere, where decisions are made not as emotionally as most designers would like them to be made. They're made quite rationally and based on a lot of data, which is quite difficult for designers to accept sometimes. I think designers inevitably know what's right from a design viewpoint, but that's not always as easy to communicate to the non-designers as you may think it is. You have to perform a really rational case, which is not something designers are used to doing.

So I think you need to be very aware of the fact that you're going into a major industry to design, and that the business decisions will be the ultimate decisions that people make, even around design. Don't expect the emotional part of the design business to be overpowering and be prepared to collaborate and negotiate to really get what you want. BI

To see Moray Callum's work, please visit http://breaking.in

LUCA CASINI
DIRECTOR
LUCA CASINI DESIGN STUDIO
MILAN

What kinds of portfolios get your attention these days? What brings in an industrial designer for an interview?

Certainly the objects in the portfolio, the style, and its presentation. It should emphasize the fundamental design skills like personal taste, proportions, sensibility, CAD, and the layout know-how. Every day we receive many CVs, and it's very important for the applicants to give an immediate good impression, so allow me to share with you some practical advice.

Should they use a PDF or .doc file for their CVs? If they're using a PDF file the recruiter will know that the CV probably will contain not just text, and that probably it will be visually more interesting. I personally prefer receiving PDF files. When naming the file remember to include your name, for example: "John-Smith-CV." We receive so many files named just "CV." Normally we download the document in a general CV folder and if it doesn't have a name we need to add it manually, or we forget to change it and risk losing the file. So the name association between the e-mail and attachment is very important.

Next, do not send heavy attachments. Design studios don't like receiving heavy files. Keep the attachments to 3 MB maximum. We often receive portfolios from 10 to 15 MB. Designers should know that receiving 10 to 20 files a day of this kind could create problems.

It is common to receive CVs and portfolios together; this is good considering that design studios can have a complete idea of the designer's skills, but often it is not necessary. It is enough to send just some nice images, just the best three to four images in order to leave a right impression, then on request more material can be added. Most of the studios hire junior designers first to assist in 3D or 2D CAD or graphic design of the presentations—then it will be a natural process to get involved in more creative phases after a certain time—so "concepts" aside, it is very important to show images that can emphasize these technical skills together with indication of the personal style.

Avoid sending the complete history of your work and definitely do not send all of your personal new concepts and ideas. Sending just a couple of representative images: a rendering, a 3D wireframe, a sketch, a graphic or illustration layout, included with the CV is a good choice. It is also important to know that some studios or companies don't open the e-mail or don't reply to an e-mail that includes portfolios due to legal issues. The sender could

claim copyright on a concept that may be similar to the one a design studio or company may already be working on. It's something difficult to explain, but it's something similar to what happens between a design studio and a client. A design studio will rarely receive feedback from a company, nor will it send them a new concept proposal without signing an agreement firsthand. That's why in some website disclaimers you will find something like this: "Any unsolicited suggestions, informations, ideas, will be deemed not to be confidential and nonproprietary. By sending to us any information or material, you grant to us an unrestricted irrevocable license to use, display, perform, modify, distribute, transmit those informations or material, and you agree that we are free to use any idea, concept, know-how that you send to us." So if the designer would like to avoid problems of this kind, he should include in the e-mail text a declaration considering this aspect in favor of the design studio. In general, the student or the designer should avoid sending images or information about original projects with which the student or designer intends to develop a possible business with, and especially not if these concepts are not yet patented or in some way already protected.

"AVOID SENDING THE COMPLETE HISTORY OF YOUR WORK AND DEFINITELY DO NOT SEND ALL OF YOUR PERSONAL NEW CONCEPTS AND IDEAS. SENDING JUST A COUPLE OF REPRESENTATIVE IMAGES… INCLUDED WITH THE CV IS A GOOD CHOICE."

In regards to the CV graphic design and the layout…a designer is not a financial consultant or a lawyer, so he has the opportunity to show his graphics and communication skills when composing his CV. This way a recruiter, a design studio, or a company will receive important visual information about the designer's capabilities starting from the analysis of the CV graphics and visual organization. This doesn't mean to exceed with over-designed graphical elements; this just means to organize the CV in a clear way using the right fonts and a nice composition, adding some personal touch in the layout.

What do we look at when we first look at a submitted CV? First, we look at the computer skills, then the kind of studies one has done and general skills, eventual previous experiences, and then we look at the images of the works. Sometimes CVs include the designer's portrait, and this image is supposed to reflect the person. The quality of image chosen speaks volumes, so in general pay attention if you decide to include a portrait. It's a delicate matter that could tilt the final decision in a positive or negative way.

Naturally, students understand that some studios receive thousands of CVs each year, that the available places are normally few, and that sometimes it is not easy for the studios to reply back to everybody. So, some students decide to send letters by post or to make phone calls, and some others ring the doorbell directly to schedule an interview. Some of these initiatives could certainly create a more personal contact, but normally when a design studio is really looking for assistance or to hire, it starts to look at the internal CV database trying to find the person with the right skills for the specific need. So in the end, contacting via e-mail is the right way, and it is always a plus to send it in the right place, at the right time.

What do you think of showing work that's not industrial design in a portfolio? Things like art, photography, hobbies, etc.?

Initially, I think it would be better to send a short portfolio with few beautiful images, I mean a really great selection of industrial design products. Then, it would be good to indicate in the correspondence the possibility of sending a "complete portfolio" on request in which more subjects, such as the non-industrial design works, could be included.

What characteristics or qualities are necessary to be a successful industrial designer?

An industrial designer should understand and be able to consider a multitude of aspects: from trends and needs in various target markets, marketing basics, production technologies and processes, material knowledge, to logistics and transportation issues. Then, of course, all this knowledge should be used and translated in a winning design proposal where ideas and style are represented with a good graphic layout and with reliable 3D models supporting a perfect presentation to the client, and with the right tools, to let him easily proceed to the engineering and production phases. The other aspect, once the portfolio of products has the right quality, is the personal promotion of the work done, to communicate in the best way possible your work to the companies and media.

How did you break into this business?

After some training and various timely experiences, I opened my own studio immediately after the university studies and started knocking at potential clients' doors, asking to support them with my skills. Before doing this I felt the need to get the right tools to visualize and build my concepts and ideas. That's why I dedicated time to learn the proper software in order to materialize my thoughts in images and 3D models, simplifying the process. We were one of the first studios in Italy working with advanced CAD surfaces in 1997.

What motivated you to open your own design studio?

It was a passion I had since I was a kid. I then pursued artistic studies, marketing studies, and architecture and design studies, to follow my desire to create objects of any kind.

How do you manage the non-design aspects of running a studio?

I don't know yet, I have to improve! Because my time is dedicated to design aspects of the business, this part is certainly less than 50% of my activity.

If you were just starting out now, what advice would you give yourself?

Move to the right place, where you think it would be easier to develop and grow with your job, and the same advice that I gave myself in the past: think different and don't do the same job that everybody else is doing.

Where do you see the future of industrial design going as it evolves further in the 21st century?

Good and well-designed products around us will always be accepted, as well as the right people that guide this process: good designers will always play an important role for the various industries. I see an impressive evolution in many different fields of knowledge and the question is how will these resources be merged. Networks and web communication are simplifying the matter, but the interaction between the participants is a good thing to focus on. The amount of information a designer could play with is becoming relevant. Designers could have a key role in mixing and playing with this new knowledge and contributing new, exciting products. So designers should spend part of their time researching new technologies and solutions that can be merged with new ideas, even when they are not involved directly by companies in this process.

On the other hand, in the short term I see a huge number of product designers trying to enter the workforce, I see many designers looking for a job and companies that are looking for product development experts and CAD operators, all of which do not exist in high numbers. So, another thought is that maybe it would be better to start off a career with a more "technical" approach: to find a place, to evolve there, and then in a second step, move to a more creative, but technologically conscious sphere, but this suggestion is not for everybody. BI

To see Luca Casini's work, please visit http://breaking.in

**ERIC CHAN
CEO & FOUNDER
ECCO DESIGN
NEW YORK CITY**

What kinds of portfolios get your attention these days? What brings in an industrial designer for an interview?

You need to have a good portfolio with skill and sensitivity about form, about design, and more importantly now, the humanity. Design is for human beings and we need to make sure that people can use the object we design. I think design used to be only about the aesthetics, but nowadays there are a lot of challenges in the world. There are all sorts of issues like the energy impact, ecology, material choice, recyclability. Everything needs to be beautiful, useful, affordable and needs to perform, but that alone is not good enough. We need to produce a more sensitive product and thus design is given a new challenge on how we make decisions: how can we help this consuming world be a little bit more sensible?

How would you say that affects the content of portfolios? What should students be focusing on, or how should they be presenting their work to reflect these changes?

I think a designer needs to know the background, research and understand how the product will be used, and what the content should be. Research skills are a very important piece and the student needs to show a logical understanding of their problem. At the end of the day, it's down to the designer's sensitivity, or the magic touch, that pulls all of those forms together to make a desirable object that is long-lasting and that people can use. That design skill is not only aesthetic or technical, but also psychological, cultural, and intellectual.

Have you seen a portfolio recently that embodied that, and can you share what about it stood out?

You can see from the project how the student has expressed themselves. Design is still in a commercial environment and we really need to meet the objectives of a market success. Many of the portfolios we see are more focused on that area, which is not necessarily bad. But if you think long term, and see how the designers understand and describe their mission and their goals, you can see beyond the portfolio. When they interview, you can see and hear from the person as to how they think, how their design relates to the culture.

What else do you expect to learn from them during the interview?

We would like to know the person's integrity, and their values. Can they work with a team? How do they communicate their own ideas and express themselves? When we look for young people, we are looking for long-term prospects. We look for those who can work as a team over a long time.

What characteristics or qualities would you say are necessary to be a successful designer these days?

You need to be confident in expressing yourself, honest, and genuine about your own values. Be open-minded about other people's opinions. Be hard working and understand where you place your energy. Continue improving yourself, learn, and expose yourself [to new things]. Design is not just a learned skill. Be open to new situations and challenges. Read a lot, travel a lot, talk a lot, do a lot.

How did you break into the industry? What motivated you to open your own design practice?

I was born in China, in Hong Kong, and was educated there and then I came over to the States to get my master's degree from Cranbrook. It was a very comprehensive program that pushed my intellectual and cultural boundaries. I worked for a company called Henry Dreyfuss Associates. He was the founding father of industrial design so the ergonomic theory was applied to commercial products: how human beings can interact with a product in a more comfortable way, in a more psychologically sensible way. There were a lot of people around me, and a lot of people who inspired me.

Having your own firm has a lot of challenges, but it gives you a voice to communicate how you see

design, and you can help impact it. So far I've been fortunate; we have a good team of people working here. We are not a big team but we do interesting, game-changing projects. It is very rewarding, not only financially, but emotionally and culturally. Design is an industry, but it is also a profession and a rewarding one at that. You enjoy what you're doing every day.

If you were just starting now, what advice would you give yourself?

I would definitely tell the younger me to take more risks. Do more things that seem risky. Read more and learn more outside of the design field. It's a very different world now, the young people have a lot more opportunities and are not as confined as how we used to be. That's also a new challenge—noise is everywhere. Information and noise and insight are different. How can we get to actionable insights that we can use to make better societies or better ourselves?

Where do you see the future of industrial design going?

We are not able to make more products, or more waste. Product design, by nature, already creates objects to consume. This is the double-edge sword that we need to figure out how to balance. How can we design a product that is consumed less but creates more value and performance through energy and material? How do we discard the objects? How do we recycle them? How do we reclaim the energy? There's a lot we can learn from nature. Look at the tree: it consumes less and it recycles itself, returning back into the ground and regenerating. We are not, as a society, able to do that, but design can help us define ourselves. I think the next generation of design will be how we are using the new technology— biochemical, sensors, and wireless—and combining it to make less product, less stuff, but smarter, more sensible things that can contribute to a better world.

You see industrial design shifting towards more sustainable design, a cradle-to-cradle emphasis, that focuses on system solutions?

I think by nature we have to understand that, but not many do. We have a lot of room to improve. In the everyday practice we still design products as usual. The process bar needs to be raised. Every day we can challenge ourselves to be selective about every decision we make. A demand for a higher order of things will happen. People will feel satisfied—not just by the luxury, superficial enjoyment—but also on a deeper level.

"EVERYTHING NEEDS TO BE BEAUTIFUL, USEFUL, AFFORDABLE AND NEEDS TO PERFORM, BUT THAT ALONE IS NOT GOOD ENOUGH. WE NEED TO PRODUCE A MORE SENSITIVE PRODUCT... HOW CAN WE HELP THIS CONSUMING WORLD BE A LITTLE BIT MORE SENSIBLE?"

It's a huge challenge and I hope that the younger generations will have more potential to improve upon it than our generation. We're hoping for the best.

Anything we didn't cover that you'd like to add? Any final words of wisdom?

Design is not like being a lawyer or an engineer—those are very pragmatic, measurable, and very tangible professions. Design has different measurements. They are very intangible, the rewards are very intangible—the intellectual profit, the ecological profit, the cultural profit, in addition to financial profit. You can have immense rewards if you know how to cultivate your career. [BI]

To see the work of Eric Chan and ECCO Design, please visit http://breaking.in

CHRISTOPHER CHAPMAN
CHIEF DESIGNER
HYUNDAI DESIGN CENTER
IRVINE, CALIFORNIA

Interviewed while Mr. Chapman was Director of Automotive Design at BMW Group DesignworksUSA in Newbury Park, California

What kinds of portfolios get your attention these days? What brings in an industrial designer for an interview?

After 20+ years of looking at portfolios, the truth is I flip through them rather quickly. I can usually tell in a matter of seconds who has original ideas and who is a copyist. I also can tell who has put the time into sketching. It's all about mileage. The ones that catch my eye contain the least amount of flash. Usually, this means they are "DWP." No, it doesn't mean Department of Water and Power, it means "Deadly With Pencil." If you take away the computer, they can still capture and command attention with a simple, monochromatic sketch. It's really apparent when someone hasn't used a pencil enough. They try and compensate by "bedazzling" their audience with flash and color and digital filters. It's a smokescreen for laziness. Beyond that, I look for someone with graphic sensitivity and overall craftsmanship and layout skills. The true professional has the ability to tell a visual story in a concise manner. It is, without a doubt, the true differentiator.

What do you think of showing work that's not industrial design in a portfolio? Things like art, photography, hobbies, etc.?

Nothing wrong with that...why not? Inspiration usually comes from places outside the main subject matter anyway.

What do you expect to learn from the designer during an interview?

We are a satellite studio, so beyond shear design talent, we need to know if an individual would be a good personality fit. It's a nightmare if even one person doesn't "get it" in such a small environment. We can't "hide" them away somewhere.

What characteristics or qualities are necessary to be a successful industrial designer?

Most of the successful, and happy, designers I know are humble people. They have a quiet confidence. They are aware of what they have achieved and even more aware that they have not done it alone. Fill in the antonyms in my sentence and you have the basis for the unsuccessful.

What are some reasons you have rejected a candidate?

Lack of "sketching mileage" tops my list. I can always tell when someone has made excuses not to draw. Another is mistaking arrogance for confidence.

What do you think is a good way for people to improve, to get better?

I am a big believer in homework. There is no substitution for practice and repetition. Unless you're da Vinci, you need to be sharpening your pencils all the time. In addition, we need to be in support of a culture that rewards risk-taking and mistakes. Sometimes I think we're being too careful not to break eggs.

How did you break into this business?

Like most, I thought cars were designed by engineers, so I was late to the industrial design party. After reading an article in Smithsonian magazine, I realized Art Center was in my own backyard. So I switched majors from engineering and began studying design. My "ah-ha!" moment was when I reflected on my science fair projects in high school. They lacked serious content, but looked really great.

What would be the one piece of advice you would give to an aspiring industrial designer or somebody who has just graduated and is trying to break into the industry?

Find a way to dream and seek optimism because the future is your business.

Speaking of the future, where do you see the future of transportation design going?

Process-wise, I see that we should not aspire to use one toolset to design. While the pressure is on to do things faster and cheaper, this should not mean sacrificing the best ways to get the job done. Secondly, transportation design has always depended on great visionaries and futurists who have the capacity to convince others of that vision in order to move the standard upward.

> "IT'S REALLY APPARENT WHEN SOMEONE HASN'T USED A PENCIL ENOUGH. THEY TRY AND COMPENSATE BY 'BEDAZZLING' THEIR AUDIENCE WITH FLASH AND COLOR AND DIGITAL FILTERS."

Vision becomes blurry in times of uncertainty. The best of the best understand that by taking risks during those times; the results are great products, which coincide exactly as things get better.

Anything we didn't cover that you would like to add? Any final words of wisdom?

It surprised me how deeply affected I was when Steve Jobs passed. Somehow I think we all took his existence for granted, as I think we can take our own lives for granted. I can't speak to the type of person he was, but it seems he inspired others to demand more of themselves than they think they could endure—pushing to new limits they did not previously know they possessed. Design is a young-minded person's game. If you want to stay relevant, it's important to hit the reset button from time to time, and re-invent yourself on a consistent basis. [BI]

To see Christopher Chapman's work, please visit http://breaking.in

ALLAN CHOCHINOV
EDITOR-IN-CHIEF
CORE77. COM &
CHAIR OF MFA IN PRODUCTS
OF DESIGN PROGRAM
SCHOOL OF VISUAL ARTS
NEW YORK CITY

What kinds of industrial design portfolios would you say are getting the most attention these days?

Portfolios with strong visuals and evident skills. Employers also like to see process so it's important to show what decisions you made during a project, research, prototypes, iterations—the stuff that led to the final product.

How would you advise an industrial design student to prepare their portfolio in order to land their first job?

I would think in terms of "projects" instead of products. Very often, the artifact is the result of deep research, analysis, experimentation, synthesis—a whole lot of steps before the idea is actualized in form. You want to tell a comprehensive story by including all of those elements.

What characteristics or qualities are necessary to be a successful industrial designer?

Point of view would be my first answer. I've written in the past that a skilled designer with nothing to say is a very dangerous thing. The impacts of design— the consequences of production and consumption— are significant, and because design deals in scale, those impacts multiply out. You want people participating in this practice who are extremely thoughtful, and who consider things from many different perspectives.

In addition, multiple fluencies and an understanding of motivations and stakeholders are critical in a designer's toolkit. Empathy is key, of course, but rigor and finesse are close behind.

Part of the mission of the new MFA program at SVA is to prepare exceptional practitioners for leadership in the shifting terrain of design. Can you talk more about what that means?

Sure. At some point I have written that we are not in the business of training great designers as much as we are in the business of equipping people to do great things in the world of design. The shifting terrain of design really has to do with several different factors. There has been great and positive change in the processes of design— from concentrations in research, ethnography, anthropology, and social innovation, as well as a keen eye toward business design, strategy, and work around policy. The participants of design are changing, welcoming professionals and sub-specialists in all the areas above. But there are also people using the tools, processes, and language of design who may not be trained as designers at all: makers, hackers, and entrepreneurs of all flavors are embracing the practices of design thinking— user-centeredness, iteration, and systems. Then on the flip side, you have designers using the language and the tools of people in the making and artistic communities (open hardware like Arduino, platforms like Kickstarter), the crafting communities, as well as the social and policy sectors.

Perhaps the most significant change in design is that the consequences of our actions are becoming very, very apparent. What designers are engaged in is fundamentally systemic, and we are plainly seeing our natural and social systems pushing back, providing sobering feedback to what we have been engaged in during the past century. If you consider the collapse of so many of our natural systems, social inequality, lack of access to clean water, disease, human trafficking...there are just so many systems that are broken. Designers have this tool kit—a way of studying and assessing and imagining possible futures—that leverages a unique set of skills. Through prototyping, designers make the invisible visible and present us with options that we can assess, debate, and make decisions around. We now see more designers turning their efforts from artifacts of convenience to contexts and experiences of real need and value. These areas require more skills and different fluencies, but it's a privileged time for design to contribute more positively.

"THROUGH PROTOTYPING, DESIGNERS MAKE THE INVISIBLE VISIBLE AND PRESENT US WITH OPTIONS THAT WE CAN ASSESS, DEBATE, AND MAKE DECISIONS AROUND."

Designers have long been referred to as "problem solvers," but I should add that we may need to move away from the word "solution" and more towards an idea of "negotiation." I think one of the reasons people feel so helpless—and often hopeless—right now is because we're looking for solutions to problems that seem absolutely impossible and unsolvable. Most problems are dynamic, systemic, moving targets, they're made of people and policy and politics and prejudice, and they are living things. So instead of setting ourselves up for solving problems, perhaps we need to be looking to negotiate problem spaces. This may require a change in how we describe what we are engaged with in design, and how we actually engage will likely change as well.

Where do you see the future of industrial design going as it evolves further in the 21st century?

Product design can be seen as a kind of hub for design practice, where all sorts of different things come together—from brand, brand experience, and interaction to usability, physicality, manufacturability, and desirability. But at the end of most design processes, you are often, literally, holding something in your hands. This something can be very smart with embedded technologies, or can be very ephemeral and fleeting. It can be a set of instructions or something hand-made just for you. But it's an artifact, and artifacts speak to a very primal, human thing. They're hugely powerful as touchstones, and I think people recognize that making stuff—whether it's cooking or it's MakerBot-ing—is a fundamental human gratification. Humans have this need for making things with their hands as a way to sort through problems and

make sense of the built environment and of the world. I think solving through making is fundamental.

A designer's unique ability is to imagine something that isn't there: to prototype, to create renderings of fictional products, to create ad campaigns for services that don't yet exist—to try things on for size, so to speak. "Are these the products and services that we actually want in our world?" That is what design can help us find out.

Would you say that we're witnessing an important pivot in the evolution of industrial design? What would be your suggestions, then, to somebody who's just started studying industrial design in order to be prepared for this change once they're out?

Design in general, and industrial design in particular, is moving from a noun to a verb. Most people have considered design as a noun—something that is aesthetic, and which comes at the end. Now we are seeing design as a verb, as a process—something that is strategic, and coming at the beginning. The products of design can be a social intervention, a piece of design art, a hack or a craft or myriad embodiments in between, but it's long been true that the discipline of industrial design has been defined much too narrowly, caught in the domains of engineering and styling rather than responsive to the realms of behavior and experience.

In terms of preparation for leaving school, certainly there have been lots of amazing, destabilizing developments in the past few years that are going to impact the kinds of work people do. Crowd-funding platforms and their impact on product development, for example, or ubiquitous, geographically aware computing and the explosion of interaction and product-service pairings are changing the field.

I see a lot of designers being entrepreneurial, and instead of getting a job, actually creating jobs right out of the gate, launching design projects on Kickstarter and other platforms, and utilizing powerful social and connectivity tools to find collaborators and customers. The ubiquity of social, prototyping, and engineering technologies is lowering the barrier of entry to practically zero, and we are seeing a design landscape with less and less friction. You can launch something, get press on it in a day, find partners and funding in a month...or a week. So just a few years ago, where the overriding goal would be to get a job—I think that's not going to be true for a lot of design people moving forward.

If you were just starting out now, what advice would you give yourself?

I would concentrate on people as much as skills. I would be engaged with communities of creative people who are doing stuff, who are making stuff and just be around them, work for them, volunteer for them. There's just no substitute for that kind of firsthand, visceral experience. It's more collaborative, and more fun. The way that you learn when you are working on a project is just very, very different than the way you learn when you're studying something in abstraction; it's an essential kind of learning.

Finally, many designers will tell you that what they most regret—or wish that they learned in school—is business fundamentals. So get your business knowledge up. Especially in this time of entrepreneurship and quick turnaround, knowledge of how markets operate, how supply chains are managed, how brands think and how intellectual property is handled—all of these and so much more are critically important.

Anything we didn't cover that you would like to add? Any final words of wisdom?

We are living in dizzyingly dichotomous times: How can it be that we have the most powerful tools in human history—in terms of science, engineering, visualization, manufacturing—and yet at the same time be facing the most daunting problems in human history? I find that an extraordinary condition. And on top of that, we have what I think is the central design challenge of our age: How can a group of people be charged with birthing "new goods and services" into the world, and at the same time be held accountable for stewarding their environmental and social impact? That's where our work is next. [BI]

To see Allan Chochinov's work, please visit http://breaking.in

MATT CORRALL
LEAD UX DESIGNER
DNV GL
BRISTOL, UNITED KINGDOM

Interviewed while Mr. Corrall was Senior Designer at Kinneir Dufort in Bristol, United Kingdom.

What kinds of portfolios get your attention these days? What brings in an industrial designer for an interview?

It will depend on what kind of role we're looking to fill. Some designers at KD [Kinneir Dufort] work mostly at the conceptual, innovation-focused end of the design process, some work mainly on mechanical design and development for manufacture, then there are some that work right across the board. At KD my work is most often at the front-end, so that's the kind of role I'm more likely to be interviewing for. If I'm interviewing a candidate, I would want to see evidence of certain skills and working process captured in their portfolio. Evidence of innovative thinking and problem solving, the ability to interpret research, empathize with users, and work harmoniously with other disciplines such as engineering. Then in terms of core design skills: sketching, model-making, CAD, and understanding of manufacturing processes.

I also try to get an idea of how this person thinks, what their personal working process is like. Several times in the past I've received portfolios which have beautiful finished renderings of design work, but don't tell me the story behind the design. What I'm more interested in seeing is how the designer arrived at that rendering—I want to see sketches, prototypes, and the design development to really get an idea of how this person works and how they think—not just the end result. I'm really interested in the story.

Can you give me an example of a good way to tell a story about the product development process?

One important skill for designers is the ability to communicate quickly and clearly to a variety of project stakeholders, so I expect a candidate's portfolio to explain their work simply, over just one or two pages, in an image-based format. I'll be flicking through and won't stop to read a lot of text. What is this project? What exactly were you trying to achieve in this project and for whom? In a nutshell, how did you get from start to finish?

For example the finish might be a manufactured product, a conceptual rendering, or a physical model. I'd want to see some photos of the research that was done, some sketch work and prototypes that show concepts and let me understand why one was chosen over the others. I'd like to flip through those pages and see a snapshot that tells me the story of your project in just a few images and captions. I pay attention to the skills of the designer and I'd like to see that communicated in a sincere way. Sounds like a lot, doesn't it?

"I WANT TO SEE SKETCHES, PROTOTYPES, AND THE DESIGN DEVELOPMENT TO REALLY GET AN IDEA OF HOW THIS PERSON WORKS AND HOW THEY THINK—NOT JUST THE END RESULT. I'M REALLY INTERESTED IN THE STORY."

No, it makes complete sense for what's required of an industrial designer.

Also, if I'm looking at student work then I don't expect this person to have all the skills and to have mastered the entire design process just yet. Of course, I'll view the portfolio with perspective on the level this person is at, where they are in their education or their career. We bear that in mind. For someone junior, if I can see that the basic skills are covered and there's evidence of passion and

intelligent design thinking, that tells me this person has potential. As with any interview the skills we look for will depend on the role we need to fill.

If you had an opportunity to guide an industrial student on how to create a portfolio that would resonate for you, what would you tell them?

The person viewing your portfolio will likely have many to look through and be pushed for time, so avoid a lot of text and use good quality images and captions. Your portfolio will need to get their attention with some impactful work on page one, and communicate your greatest strengths over the next few pages, simply and efficiently. Start and end on a high note with your very best work, as this will be most likely to stick in their mind. Take good quality photos of your work—including rough prototypes—which are equally as important as the finished design.

Also bear in mind your audience and if necessary tailor your portfolio to suit them. You should already know a fair amount about the company and if possible the person who'll interview you, so show them work that's relevant to their business if you can. Finally, if you're sending a sample portfolio by email, make a good first impression—a single, good quality PDF or a link to a well-maintained online portfolio will go down well. Send a hard copy in the post too; those are becoming rarer these days and will certainly get looked at.

What do you expect to learn from the designer during an interview?

When a candidate comes in with their portfolio, usually I will look through it with them and ask them to talk about their projects as we go. I may have already been sent their sample portfolio and seen some work in there that interested me, so I may stop on those projects and ask more about the process or thinking behind the design. One thing I find quite nice about interviewing designers is that it doesn't have to be too formal. There's the portfolio, tell me a bit of the story and I can drop in with questions, such as "Why did you do it this way?" or, "Tell me a bit more about why you chose this concept instead of that concept?" Through that discussion the details of how this person thinks and works will come out. As most projects in the industrial design world are team efforts, I will probably also want to learn what the candidate's contribution to each project was, and what they were responsible for. This will help me understand how they might fit into a project team at KD.

What characteristics or qualities are necessary to be a successful industrial designer?

Generally speaking, good designers have curiosity, drive, and an obsession with detail. I'm looking for someone who's passionate about what they're doing; you tend to need that sort of tenacity. In a project team comprised of many different disciplines, the designer should be the person who can get along with everyone from marketing to engineering to the CEO. The designer should be able to speak their languages, help them all towards a shared vision and be tenacious enough to overcome the inevitable obstacles along the way. I guess designers are affectionate in a way, there's a real love for the product they're creating, there's a drive to get to a better design, to find a better way of doing a product, to explore new avenues, new materials.

Core skills such as sketching or CAD are important, but clear thinking and the determination to make that product the very best it can be are more important, in my opinion. In an interview I'll try to find out who this person is, ask if they could fit into the team at KD, and if they're flexible and fast enough to join in. Being a consultancy, we can find ourselves working on just about anything. We could be working on medical equipment one week, a chocolate bar the next, and a mobile phone the next. One of the things I like very much about consultancy work is that you have to very quickly become familiar with a different industry and project stakeholders. You have to understand their business, listen to input from research, marketing, and engineering, and after digesting all that information, produce designs that will make them glad they came to you. What a challenge!

How did you break into this business?

I studied a BA (Hons) Design for Industry degree at Northumbria University, which is in Newcastle upon Tyne in the north of England. I started out studying mechanical engineering but switched to industrial design after a year. I'd never been introduced to industrial design at school but had an interest in creativity and building new products, which the

engineering degree wasn't satisfying. I remember walking into the university product design studio for the first time and thinking immediately: "This is definitely for me." My degree was a four-year course, which included a couple of work placements over summer breaks, one at a consultancy and one at a small manufacturer. After graduating, we exhibited our work as a group in London, hoping to attract some potential employers. I ended up with an interview at LEGO, the Danish toy company, and that was my first job. Whilst I didn't set out to become a toy designer, there was a playful streak in my work and a cartoon-like sketching style that probably got me noticed. I moved out to Billund, where the head office is in Denmark, and lived there for three years working as a toy designer.

I think all product designers grew up with a severe LEGO fetish.

Yeah, a lot of us still have it. It's a wonderful toy that really gets kids, and adults, using their imagination and creativity, so it makes sense that it appeals to designers. At least having worked there I have a good excuse for the LEGO sets lying around at home.

So, after three years of Danish living, I decided to get back to the UK and moved to Cambridge, working at a couple of the many product design agencies in the area, but it was really the toy design that got me started.

It doesn't necessarily mean that the industry you start off in defines your entire career?

No, not at all. When I left LEGO my portfolio was full of toys, which showed my design skills and my professional working process. I was applying for work at a product design consultancy where, as with KD, the projects can be really varied. I decided to complete a couple of quick projects in my spare time to show I could be flexible and adapt my skills, to show that it's not just toys I can design, that I could do consumer goods too. It worked.

Industrial designers are lucky in being able to work anywhere in the world for a huge range of industries, but you will need to demonstrate to prospective employers that you can be effective in their business. A mini project or two done in your spare time can make all the difference and can be done over a weekend. If you want to nudge your career in a new direction, as a designer it can be reasonably easy to show you can adapt.

If you were just starting out now, what advice would you give yourself?

The perfectionist streak that a lot of designers tend to have, which is a very good thing when working on design details, did mean that as a student and a young designer I tended to keep working in pursuit of perfection and sometimes messed up with time management. One skill I could've improved on in the early days was working efficiently and managing my time. As a graduate I spent a long time making my portfolio as perfect as I could and I realized in retrospect that I could've done it in half the time. Set yourself deadlines and stick to them; the portfolio should look great but it doesn't have to be a work of art.

Where do you see the future of industrial design going as it evolves further in the 21st century?

That's a big question. I'm certainly finding one major trend in our work at the moment is the increase in integrated industrial and user interface design, which isn't something I studied, but is becoming more and more prevalent. Since I graduated, touchscreens and other new technologies are becoming more and more affordable and interesting for companies, so I'm working on more and more products that have some software element to the design. To achieve a great product, we need to consider the user experience as a whole and so both hardware and onscreen interaction should be designed together. There's certainly more of that coming. At KD we have industrial designers who understand and design GUIs (graphic user interfaces) as well as the hardware they're displayed on. In the future I think some understanding of interaction design would be beneficial.

The other trend is a broader scope for the work of the designer and more collaborations. At KD we can be involved in a project right from the first research and innovation work, right through to manufacturing or anywhere in between. We may also find ourselves collaborating with other partner organizations or working with clients outside of the UK. Traditionally an industrial designer might have just worked on the product itself, but I think this is already broadening

to encompass service design, brand and packaging, and of course user interface. Designers here need to be flexible and able to communicate clearly with people from all walks of life. That's where the ability to visualize and sketch becomes really valuable; it's a great way to communicate quickly and it cuts across language barriers. With the collaborative nature of work in a consultancy I'd say both of these trends are going to continue.

So even with the growth in digital interfaces and digital objects, the ability to sketch with your hand is still important?

Yes, I think very much so, because it's very fast and everyone can understand it. When you're meeting with a client, you can discuss a concept and sketch an idea right there in front of them, which they can immediately understand. It adds a lot of value to the service you offer. These days I sometimes sketch digitally with a tablet, sometimes on paper depending on the situation but the core skill is the same. In any design project, sketching is an important tool—it's fast, flexible, and all you need is a pen and the back of a pizza box. I don't think that will ever go away.

Anything we didn't cover that you would like to add? Any final words of wisdom?

The pressure is on now. Good question. When you're starting out, some projects will be failures. You'll be learning and not everything will work out the way you hoped. Don't be afraid to talk about the projects that failed as well as the successes—they show you're not afraid to take risks and that you're learning and developing as a designer. Even for the professionals, projects don't always go smoothly, but that's the nature of innovation and trying to create something truly new. ⃞

To see Matt Corrall's work, please visit http://breaking.in

JONAS DAMON
EXECUTIVE CREATIVE
DIRECTOR
FROG
NEW YORK CITY

What kinds of portfolios get your attention these days? What brings in an industrial designer for an interview?

It's a combination of things, but most importantly: the ability to be an author and tell a story. By this I mean having your own point of view and being able to articulate it. It sounds a little clichéd, but it is ultimately what we as designers do. Isolated images of isolated products without context are meaningless. A designer needs to understand the greater world in which their work lives, and needs to be able to communicate that. And then fantastic execution skills as well, of course. There are certain schools that are difficult to hire from because, while they educate a designer to think well, they don't exactly train them to shape or visualize their ideas well. That's fine for somebody later in his or her career who may have already mastered these skills through previous experience, but fresh out of school you really need to be able to execute. The combination of storytelling and craft is what ultimately makes you hire-able.

Have you seen a portfolio recently that really resonated with you?

I keep thinking about this designer that interned at our San Francisco office a couple of years ago. He sent me his portfolio originally, must be three years ago now, and I thought his work was fantastic. He had a great ability to tell stories about his work, to give insight as to where some of his thinking came from. The work had real depth to it. It was rich enough that you could look at something and see multiple layers of things going on. Unfortunately, we couldn't offer him an internship here in New York, but our San Francisco studio snagged him and I think he worked out quite well. He ended up working for Apple's Human Interface Group after he graduated in 2012, so he's doing quite well now.

It sounds like it's a given that they need to have technical skills, but if they can't tell the story...

Yeah. Authoring or storytelling is the more important of the two because we need designers who can create compelling products first. We don't need any more meaningless products in the world. If you're able to design something with relevance and give it cultural weight, then you'll be well off. Ultimately, technical skills can be learned on the job or in-between school and job. While it is hard to get a design job out of school, if you don't know SolidWorks or if you can't create a rendering to sell an idea, you can always learn those specific skills on the side while job hunting. In the meantime you can be a barista or sell clothes to make a living.

When I came out of school, I couldn't get a design job. I didn't have great technical skills. For the first three or four years out of school I did many non-design related things. I was a nanny in Paris. I sold clothes and was an office manager for a photographer in New York. I was not working in a design firm. Eventually, on my own, I did build up the skills to get hired as a designer.

What do you expect to learn from a designer in an interview?

I try to get a sense of their passion for the work. I want somebody who's really dedicated to what they do, somebody who's really curious. I want a personality that's open, someone who is willing to learn, who is in it for the right reasons. I feel like design has gotten to be very trendy in the past 10 or 15 years through exposure from all the design blogs and now, most recently, with Kickstarter. Industrial design has become fetishized by the public in the way fashion is. It's become very easy to reach a lot of people with easily good-looking but ultimately meaningless work. That kind of design attracts a certain person, and that's not the kind of person I'm too interested in having on my team. I want somebody who is crazy curious about how things work and how to make things, as opposed to being after the glory of design.

What are the characteristics or qualities that are necessary to be a successful designer?

That passion I just spoke of, as well as perseverance and luck.

You touched on this a little bit earlier, but how did you break into this business?

I took a hammer and I hit it until I broke in. When I graduated in the early '90s, things were similar [to how] they are now. We were in a recession, there was not a lot of work to go around, and America had not really woken up to design. There were not a lot of jobs that were interesting to designers. Companies were not too eager to work with young designers, and I also felt ill prepared. I knew how to think about design but not how to execute. So for the first four years I did other things. I had a workshop where, on nights and weekends, I'd build stuff. I moved to London in 1997, as there were a lot of exciting things happening in Europe at the time and London had an incredibly vibrant scene for young designers. Tom Dixon, Jasper Morrison, and Ross Lovegrove were really getting going, and coincidentally that year Wallpaper magazine launched, a magazine that opened up the excitement of what design could offer.

"ISOLATED IMAGES OF ISOLATED PRODUCTS WITHOUT CONTEXT ARE MEANINGLESS. A DESIGNER NEEDS TO UNDERSTAND THE GREATER WORLD IN WHICH THEIR WORK LIVES, AND NEEDS TO BE ABLE TO COMMUNICATE THAT."

In London I got a job with Tom Dixon, and worked at his studio for about a year. After that year, Habitat, a large European homewares retailer, hired him as a design director. He asked me to join him. We had the task of building their in-house design department up from two designers to 15. During my three years there I had the opportunity to travel a lot around Asia and Europe as part of our design and manufacturing process. I visited a lot of factories in China, Thailand, Vietnam, India, Bangladesh, Poland, Czech Republic, and Portugal—all over the place. We went to small villages where everybody's house is a part of the assembly line and also to very modern factories that manufacture IKEA lighting. I got a real handle on what design means in terms of actually building things, and the ability to communicate with people across different cultures about making objects.

When I came back to New York in 2000, I opened up my own design consultancy and kind of left the whole furniture design scene. I focused more on consumer goods for companies like Tupperware, Vitra, and Target—a good variety of companies. I did that for about six years. Towards the end, some friends of mine started a company called Areaware, which I became involved with, and still am. I started to get tired of working alone in my office. I felt like maybe I was going looney working by myself and I wanted to dive into reality again and be around a larger group of people, and do work that would reach a larger audience. So I closed shop and became a director of industrial design at Arnell, after which I came to frog.

If you were just now starting out, what advice would you give yourself?

Don't give up. It feels hard and you can't see the future, so you don't know if you're making the right decisions or if you're moving in the right way. I feel like creative people don't have a choice in terms of doing or not doing what they want. I felt driven to do design work; it's a passion that I can't live without. When I'm at home, I keep thinking about making stuff. When I'm on vacation, I think about making stuff. So stick with it and things will happen. I think other people appreciate this passion.

Where do you see the future of industrial design going as it evolves further in the 21st century?

This is a big topic. It's going where it's always been going in its short history. It's continuing to evolve the tangible experiences. The digital-physical divide is not that important. What's important is being in a world that we can interact with. Industrial designers will continue to define the world around us.

Anything you'd like to add that we haven't talked about? Any final words of wisdom?

Believe in yourself. Just keep banging away. Throughout my career I've been wrongly frustrated at times, not believing that what I do matters or that people notice. Sometimes I've given up and now, in hindsight, I can see everything that's ever happened was because I persevered. Forge ahead and things will happen. [BI]

To see Jonas Damon's work, please visit http://breaking.in

THOMAS DEGN
PROGRAM DIRECTOR FOR
THE MFA IN ADVANCED
PRODUCT DESIGN PROGRAM
UMEÅ INSTITUTE OF DESIGN
UMEÅ, SWEDEN

Industrial design is such a broad field with many options. How would you suggest students best prepare their portfolios for the jobs they want? How should a portfolio for someone applying to a design consultancy such as frog be different from a portfolio for someone applying for an in-house design position??

Even though most of the designers' skill sets are necessary both in-house and at a consultancy, I do believe that in-house designers should be able to display a higher level of consistency in understanding of brand values and the importance of research, continued development, and refinement of both a brand and its products. On the other side, many design consultancies rely on fast-paced teamwork qualities and designers who can think on their feet and quickly understand their different clients' needs and generate concepts where the value proposition is clearly

defined and understandable, both in text and initial concept visualizations.

If an industrial design student came to you looking for advice on how to prepare their portfolio to get an internship or a job, what would you tell them to do? What should be in their portfolio?

I would advise them to display, as truthfully as possible, their present tools, skills, and mindset. Ideally each designer should master being a thinker, a decider, and doer, as well as being the unique individual person they are. All of that doesn't matter if they are not able to portray it in an understandable way.

When you say "to portray it in an understandable way," what do you mean?

They should try to display their tool-, skill-, and mindset by visualizing their work, thought, and decision process with sketches, graphics, short texts, timelines, and photos. The portfolio should been seen as a help to the potential employer to assure that the candidate applying is a reflective, efficient, and professional industrial designer. I personally appreciate if an applicant has the ability to answer and include the following in the portfolio: What was the starting point/ problem or design opportunity of the project? And who were/are the stakeholders? How was this addressed? (Methods, conclusions, and decisions.) The result of the different phases and the final designed solution, and final reflective conclusions. How did (or might) the designed solution solve the initial problem?

What kinds of student portfolios are getting attention from employers these days? What's the emphasis placed on?

Different employers put emphasis on different skills depending on their present needs and the focus of their company. As an absolute minimum one has to be able to display and communicate the basic creative skills of producing quick, understandable, and inspiring ideation sketches, the ability and wish to work in a team, and the professional and social skills required for this. We want our students to prepare and be able to display their work for employers who truly understand and appreciate the industrial designer as one who, through a structured and thereby quality ensured process, can design the best possible solution to a given self-identified problem or design opportunity textually, digitally, and three-dimensionally. The pedagogical strategy and studies at the Advanced Product Design program have been designed for this specifically.

"THE PORTFOLIO SHOULD BEEN SEEN AS A HELP TO THE POTENTIAL EMPLOYER TO ASSURE THAT THE CANDIDATE APPLYING IS A REFLECTIVE, EFFICIENT, AND PROFESSIONAL INDUSTRIAL DESIGNER."

We teach and enable our students to communicate and show that they can enter an organization and contribute from day one as productive designers and team players.

As the school year just wrapped, was there a particular graduating student who dominated the job offers this year? What about his or her work stood out? How did they showcase their work to the employers?

The soon-to-be professional designers who really stand out at the end of their studies are the ones who not only master the complete process of design—from problem identification, analysis, conclusions and ideation, and after that, selection of the most suitable direction for finalization— but who are also able to communicate all of this through both traditional (physical presentation models) and dynamic media (videos).

What kind of feedback do you hear from employers about the content of students' portfolios? What are they doing well, and what are they lacking?

It is my impression that some design managers are experiencing that the digital tools of design have made their way too far and too early into education, in such a way that the basic understanding of the form and even construction can get lost. In a 3D digital environment everything is possible; there are hardly any limits, including the things you would realize are impossible or at least not logical if it was tried out with quick mock-ups or physical proof-of-concept models. It is so important that we do not loose the tangible and analog understanding and tradition of design. After all we are creators and makers of physical solutions, functions, and aesthetics.

What characteristics or qualities are necessary to be a successful industrial designer?

There are three overall qualities I believe should characterize a successful industrial designer. These are empathy, understanding, and communication. A designer should be able to feel empathy for the client and in particular the present and future users for which the best possible solution should be made. A designer has to understand what the problem or challenge really is, how it could be solved and the various consequences of the same in terms of usability, costs, production, environmental impact, etc. Finally, a designer has to be able to communicate this and the proposal for the final design in a verbal, textual, visual, and even physical form.

If you were just starting out now, what advice would you give yourself?

Embrace and combine analog and digital sketching into one and keep developing and refining these basic skills until these have developed into a strong, efficient, and personal technique. Communicative ideation sketching is by far the most time and resource-effective media for engaging oneself and others in creative dialogues and visual brainstorms. This applies no matter what design discipline one decides to specialize in at a later stage. "We sketch therefore we are." I have included tips for some inspiring sketching books with student works from UID and Advanced Product Design such as Design Sketching by Olofsson and Sjölén and Learning Curves by Sjölén and Macdonald.

Where do you see the future of industrial design going as it evolves further in the 21st century?

Right now everything is design. I see a future where there will be an even greater need for creating, designing, and producing the right things the right way. To quote the late Danish engineer and former director of the Danish Design Centre Jens Bernsen: "Design is about turning a purpose into a tool." We must never, ever, lose our creative and analytical ability to identify, analyze, understand, and solve problems. This is, in my opinion, our greatest asset and responsibility as industrial designers. I see true industrial design as a craftsmanship, and I imagine that we will see a future where the importance for structured and disciplined designers who understand and master this increases.

Anything we didn't cover that you would like to add? Any final words of wisdom?

I don't know if I am experienced enough to share words of wisdom, but it seems obvious to me that the field of design in terms of tools, skills, and possibilities is constantly developing and growing. At the same time, the basic tasks of the professional industrial designer have stayed the same: to be able to—from a specific challenge, a planned schedule, and defined deliverables— use and control both brain halves. Reason and rationality on one side and feeling and passion on the other in order to fulfill and complete an undertaken assignment. BI

To see Thomas Degn's work, please visit http://breaking.in

ANDREW DEMING & RACHEL GANT FOUNDERS YIELD DESIGN ST. AUGUSTINE, FLORIDA

You have had a successful Kickstarter campaign not too long since graduating. Can you talk a bit about that experience and how you see it affecting your long-term goals?

AD: Kickstarter was a natural way for us to put our story out front and convey the personal inspiration that led to the creation of our company and our initial product offering. As a platform, Kickstarter is excellent at tying products to their makers and giving backers a sense that they are investing not just in a product, but in people and in a belief.

Although our first product was a bag, after Kickstarter we began working to offer a much wider range of product categories. In that sense, Kickstarter served as an initial spark, a means of introduction. It also provided some real momentum that helped us break through numerous manufacturing and logistical barriers to get the product into the hands of our first customers.

When you start looking to grow your team, what kinds of industrial design portfolios will get your attention? What would bring an industrial designer in for an interview?

AD: We've recently started looking to bring on an additional team member and have been discussing this very question. As a small team working closely together, it is something we're intent on getting right.

Our most important requirement is that a candidate be hungry to learn. We are in the stage where so much of what we do is new for us. We are constantly learning and always evolving and expect that those we work with will be interested in learning new skills and problem-solving their way through unforeseen challenges. While good design appears clean and effortless from the outside, the process is a messy one and we need people who are willing to get their hands dirty.

We believe that there's a balance to be had between asking the right questions and digging in and executing. It's really about being emotionally aware and sensitive to the occasion. No one wants to work with the contrarian who's always eager to spout out every reason why this or that cannot be done. On the other hand, rigorous questioning and open discussion on the front-end of a project can obviously help keep things on track.

Have you seen a portfolio recently that really stood out? What about it caught your eye?

AD: Versatility and perspective revealing a wide range of ability and interest. We're not against being specialized, so long as there's an ability to zoom out and see the bigger picture. We respond well to those who can observe, translate, and react to a variety of problem sets, audiences, and mediums. Those are the portfolios that stand apart.

As far as the design of the portfolio itself, the best portfolios we've seen fluidly express a consistency and care for not only the 3D design projects, but the 2D elements on the page. Typography and layout must be well considered in order to achieve a level of simplicity and elegance that elevates the work rather than detracts from it. If graphic design layout is not your thing, lean on a friend. It'll go a long way.

What are some common mistakes you've seen junior designers make in their portfolio?

AD: A focus on polish over depth. When reviewing portfolios, aside from good execution, we are looking for work with meaning and character. If there are elements that lack a bit of refinement, that doesn't scare us. We can work with that. What we can't work with is bad ideas presented as a final solution. We all have bad ideas, and they are important to get out during early stages of development, but if someone isn't willing or motivated enough to move past a bad idea, it is a red flag that they are likely not opening up to constructive criticism.

What do you expect to learn from a designer during an interview?

AD: What drives them. What they want out of an experience. Where they see themselves going. It takes care to convey future goals without making a potential employer feel like a stepping stone, but communicated correctly, honest ambition is admirable and apparent. If ambitions don't align, then it's good to understand that up front.

What kinds of characteristics or qualities are necessary to be a successful designer these days?

AD: In many ways it's the same as it ever was: a designer must be interested in and engaged with the world around them. More than an interest in itself, "design" should serve as a lens through which we view the world and see areas ripe for improvement.

Adaptability. Any student of foresight will tell you that one of the greatest changes we face today is the very rapid increase in the rate of change, meaning that individuals and organizations must be ever more adaptable. As designers, I think this means that we must be driven by values and principles, not defined merely by skills or knowledge of programs. Those things, while important, are a means to an end and will turn over countless times throughout the course of a career.

Confidence in communication. Whether in internal design reviews or external presentations, the ability to clearly articulate concept and intent is absolutely crucial. I think good designers always really want to understand the "why" behind the design decisions made...why this subject matter? Why this material choice, etc.? When we are thoughtful and consistently ask ourselves those questions throughout the process, it's easy to clearly convey to others what led to a particular outcome.

How'd you break into the industry?

AD: While we are both fairly young and relatively early in our careers, we share a gratitude for the winding paths that have led us to where we are today.

RG: My original studies as an architecture student were a product of discovering that my diverging interests had a place to meet. In my early education, I loved everything; it was quite confusing. One day I wanted to be an engineer, the next an artist, and then a psychologist. Architecture was boasted as that intersection balancing logic and creativity, so it seemed like a natural fit. Even though it wasn't my final focus, I spent three years studying architecture, which proved invaluable when making the switch into industrial design. The skills I learned from one design perspective shifted into a new, yet parallel, world of design.

"IF THERE ARE ELEMENTS THAT LACK A BIT OF REFINEMENT [IN A PORTFOLIO], THAT DOESN'T SCARE US. WE CAN WORK WITH THAT. WHAT WE CAN'T WORK WITH IS BAD IDEAS PRESENTED AS A FINAL SOLUTION."

The places I've lived and studied also made a huge impact on my approach: from the deep south, to the midwest, to Scandinavia, and of course here in San Francisco. All places and cultures were very different, but again, I naturally tend to focus on a contrast and comparison type of perspective, contemplating how and why people live and approach their lives day-to-day and found my place in design to be tying those threads of daily life together. These immersions in different worlds, whether it's a new city or a new discipline, play an incredibly important part in how I see and develop my role as a designer.

AD: Early on, my very first successes were in the music realm. I was a bit late to discovering design, shifting into it partway through my undergraduate years. But I felt that the process I'd grown to understand in writing music—that chaos leads to potential solutions which lead to refined outcomes—prepared me well for the shift.

My first degree was in graphic design and the jobs I had right out of school fit squarely within that role.

It was a great starting point, but I realized I was not going to be wholly satisfied on that trajectory. Wanting a better understanding of how design fits into the context of business, I went back to school for an MBA at CCA [California College of the Arts]. That's where my path crossed with Rachel's. Not long after we met, she convinced me to leave my graphic design job to take a position at fuseproject. The original title felt like a step down from the position I was in, but in hindsight it was absolutely the right move. It was there I felt for the first time that the full range of my ability was being put to use. I had the privilege of working with and learning from some incredibly talented people on some remarkable projects.

Both the job shift and grad school were scary moves at the time, but they were pivotal moments that really shaped me and prepared me to venture out on my own.

Can you talk a bit about your decision to start your own studio? What challenges have you faced, and how have you overcome them?

AD: It's an idea we tossed around since we first started dating—realizing that we shared a similar design sensibility while each bringing to the table very different and complementary skills. We've done everything together, from the design of our first product to the design and development of our website, to the design and physical renovation of our office space—the list goes on. It's been an incredible experience, but not without significant challenges. Manufacturing and supply chain operations have proved to be the most complex and consuming investments both financially and psychologically.

Where do you see industrial design going as it evolves further in the 21st century?

AD: We've already begun to see, and will continue to see, a greater demand for a more integrated approach to design. Everything is getting tighter: the distance between design disciplines as well as the distance between design and production. It's evidenced in a continuing trend towards flattened hierarchical structures in organizations.

Look at the example of GE moving much of their manufacturing operations back to the US to be nearer to design and marketing. It's happening with companies big and small. As the world strives to become more efficient both environmentally and economically, design is being acknowledged more and more as a critical partner in achieving this goal. Designed efficiency can cut costs from a systems perspective, but also a materials perspective. With an increased emphasis on the importance of close relationships between disciplines, it's an exciting time to be practicing. BI

To see the work of Yield Design, please visit http://breaking.in

MICHAEL DITULLO CHIEF DESIGN OFFICER SOUND UNITED, ENCINITAS, CALIFORNIA

Interviewed while Mr.DiTullo was a Creative Director at frog in San Francisco, California.

What kinds of portfolios get your attention these days? What brings in an industrial designer for an interview?

I'm seeing so many portfolios that are merely adequate. They are filled with projects that seem designed to show skills. When I close a portfolio like that I think to myself that this person has everything on the checklist and yet there's nothing I can remember in the portfolio, nothing that stands out. What I look for right away on a quick flip-through of a portfolio is a project that is memorable and stands out as being exemplary of that individual's personality, ethic, and philosophy. Is there something that makes me say, "Oh that was the girl who did this..." or something that doesn't feel like an academic school exercise that was given by a professor? It's not any one particular thing that I'm looking for, rather something that feels like it came from the root of who the person is.

When we work on production projects it's like we are climbing Mount Everest together. We are going to run out of food, there's going to be a snowstorm, and there's going to be perils along the way that will

make us question ourselves and our journey. It can feel like that when you are on the path to making something truly unique and industry leading. There will be obstacles on our way to that grand summit that we didn't predict. I need to know that anyone we are going to bring onto the team is going to have the kind of passion, the gumption, and the stick-to-it-iveness along with the ever important skills to make it through so we can get to the top of the mountain. So I'm looking for any hints of that. Usually it comes through on one portfolio piece where somebody found the right opportunity to really be themselves and give it something extra.

I will also share a tip that a mentor shared with me when I first started reviewing portfolios. I always look for the worst sketch in the portfolio and assume that is the candidate's average operating level. People are going to put their best work in, and obviously they're not going to put their worst work in—they will omit that—but to get a little bit of that extra volume, they're going to put some of their average work in. That worst sketch in the portfolio is an indicator of what their day-to-day working style is like. If that worst sketch in that portfolio is still very good, I find that that person is able to operate at an above-average level. I haven't been wrong about this yet.

The other major attribute I look for is an understanding of the bigger picture, an understanding of cultural "connectedness." Now that you're creating a service or an object, or whatever it is you're designing, it's crucial to understand there are other things in this person's life. Perhaps the thing you're designing for them is actually—while very important to you—not very important to them. I look for people who can acknowledge that. A truly successful and timeless design has a sensitivity to culture, brand, and emotion. It has a resonance that goes beyond being a clever functional solution, which it also must posses. I think designers that understand that move beyond the plateau of average design.

Have you seen a portfolio recently that resonated with you, and what about it stood out?

One of our past interns is a great example of a portfolio that stood out so much that I knew I wanted that individual on the team from the first glance. I first came across his work when he was 16 years old on Core77 forums. I'm always looking at portfolios, at work through my connection with Core77. I immediately pegged him when he first popped on that radar as someone who's going to be really very good. What I saw in him was that he was very passionate and very dedicated, but never married to a solution. He would do a project and then six months later redo the same project, and then redo the same project again. It was as if he acknowledged that he had learned more so it was logical for him to redesign the entire project to see how he could tackle the problem with his improved skills and outlook. That impressed me.

I've had students tell me, "Oh I have a portfolio but it's not ready yet," and I think that outlook does not acknowledge that a portfolio is a living document. It should always be changing, never static. This is very different from when I was in the school in the '90s. At that time you had no choice but to submit a finished book. Now we can see somebody's portfolio evolve over a period of years: their life, their growth, their education becomes the focus of the portfolio. I think it's really important for students to understand and embrace that. The portfolio is not something you ever finish, it's an organic thing that grows and expands. If you want proof that I believe this, take a look at my portfolio online. It's just a mess—a collection of things, ideas, notions that are on display so someone can get a sense of the breadth of work I think about. I get calls all the time so obviously it's okay. It organically grows and you can see the years that projects were added and understand the context of the projects to one another. This is not to say that I am necessarily looking for tremendous amount of volume, but I'm looking for someone who is just intensely curious.

What about the portfolios that don't make it through. What relegates those portfolios to the "no pile"?

I think there are three variations on the no pile. The first one is the adequate but unmemorable pile. We interviewed a young man the other day who fit into that category and I thought, "I really want to like you, but all of your work looks so standard, so stock." When you get a job, you're going to grow as a designer obviously, but I need to know that you're going to add some sort of unique spice into the dish. The second category is someone who so narrowly defines themselves. I looked at a portfolio recently

that was very good. I really liked the work but the aesthetic displayed across projects was very singular and niche. Because the candidate had defined a set style for himself to work in, he limited himself to what kinds of solutions he would explore.

The third group is comprised of portfolios that are simply sub par. Honestly, that's the bulk of them. We were at the Swissnex SFMOMA Dieter Rams event last week with Yves Béhar, Catherine Bailey, Joseph Becker, Markus Diebel, and myself on the panel discussion. A student asked us what the designer of the future will be, considering there is so much for young designers to learn, so many forces pulling them in different directions that they cannot go deep on any one thing. It made me think of the portfolios I'm seeing that are not very good and I see that they're affected by what that young man was talking about. They are trying so hard to be everything to the point of failure. There's so much more that design students have to learn today. If you try to be decent at all of those different things, you're going to end up not being very good at any one of them. The task for young designers now—and this is very difficult to do when you're 19 or 20—is to start deciding what kind of designer you want to be, at least what designer you want to be right now. Then you can hone the three or four different things that you'll need in order to excel in that particular area. From there you can use that base to expand out into the industry and evolve over time.

We have so many different kinds of designers here. We're able to have someone who is really good at these three things, and someone who's good at three other things, a third teammate that has yet another skill set and center of passion. We put strands of individuals together and twist ourselves around a singular problem and make a cable so unbelievably strong that we are able to do things we never could as individual contributors. Diversity of ideas, abilities, skills, and passions is the secret to a really strong team.

You touched on this a little bit, but what do you expect to learn from the designer during an interview?

When they come in for an interview, it's really their job to lose at that point. We've determined that their work is good. I'm not looking to learn more about their skills per se, as long as the work is truthfully their own. I always ask some questions to make sure that it is, especially for team projects. Barring that, it's all about the personality fit at that point. It's important for people to understand that every question I ask is a part of the interview. As a candidate comes into the room I may casually ask, "How is your hotel, how are you liking San Francisco?" and if the candidate responds with something to the effect of, "Oh, it's so rainy here, I don't like San Francisco," the interview is over. Everything said after that point won't surmount that fact that the candidate is not happy in the city we work in so it won't be a good fit for them in the long run.

If I ask what interests a candidate about our company, they should be able to respond with one interesting story about us, our projects, something that shows me that they've been to our website and have a point of view on our work. This will help me to understand how the individual may relate to us. I'm looking for all of those little telltale signs that help us to know if this is a person who wants to be here for a while.

I ask questions about specific design decisions on the projects, not to know why something is the radius it is or why they went after a specific solution, but just to see how passionate someone is about their design, how they think on their feet and how open they are to criticism, input, and direction.

What characteristics or qualities are necessary to be a successful industrial designer?

I asked this very question of someone when I was a young designer. I believe the answer I got still holds true. A successful designer must be savvy. The image of a designer in a studio for 20 out of 24 hours in a day, pounding his head against the wall until inspiration strikes is outmoded. The ability to be savvy and navigate an organization to understand what the success criteria are—the spoken as well as unspoken—is paramount. As is the ability to mix with people who have different skill sets than yourself: researchers, marketers, executives, operations guys, accountants, project managers, and engineers. I've probably hung out more with those guys than designers because I was trying to understand them. I understood my own kind. I could navigate the pecking order of our own, but in order for my projects to be successful I had to understand the pain points and priorities of these other people in the process that

spoke very different languages than me. I wanted not only to learn their language, but also to teach them ours. Then they would understand that my priorities might seem more non-linear, and much harder to measure, but they were important to our shared success. This way they would care about them even if they didn't understand them. In essence I was trying to make them understand that there were things they didn't understand.

It's one of the interesting tasks of designers, the ability to frame a solution. We have to make a solution that makes it desirable to us as designers, and have a legitimacy within our own community. But then we also have to be able to reframe that solution and present it to engineers who have a totally different set of success criteria, as well as the business people who again have the third set. I can't stress enough that in the process of doing this that we do not lose our own language, goals, and priorities. I feel that in the early 2000s, through the whole design-thinking thing, we started to lose our own identity. As our identity started to dissolve around the edges, so did our value. We became just another person in the chain concerned about money and manufacturing instead of the human side—the sticky irrational parts that are not as comfortable to talk about because they cannot be measured. In this place expertise and ability combine to form a kind of intuition that can be scary to linear thinkers who like clear and measured progress and decisions. Every amazing game-changing product was thought to be stupid and useless the day before it came out. The day after it comes out people say how genius it is and how they alone knew how it would change the world. It's that irrationality, that disconnect from the linear progression of things that makes design special.

You've had an online presence for a while, and you're very curated and obviously very passionate about design. What are your suggestions to young designers on how to promote themselves?

When I was going to school it was hard to know what was going on in the next design school over. You only knew the 20 people or so in your school and what they were doing. You could've been the best person in your school, but there could have been a girl or a guy in the next school over who was bananas way better than you and you'd have absolutely no idea. Now there's no reason to ever see a bad portfolio because everyone should know the level of everybody else. We are interviewing people from all over the world because of that. I'm looking at portfolios from Tokyo to Paris; there is really no limit or boundary to the kind of person we can bring in. We are seeing this even with the US students who are going to school abroad more. It's happening in both directions.

When I first saw Core77 back in 1995, it just went live. Somebody showed it to me in a computer lab [because] no one had their own laptops or Internet connection back then. They said, "Look at this thing, it's a design website." It was a page, literally one page. I realized there is actually going to be content on there that we won't see anywhere else, or we will see it much faster than we would in traditional media. It was an immediate realization that design books and design magazines were not going to be the future source of the latest in design. The world moves so fast now that by the time something gets into a book, it's past tense. A book is a fantastic medium to archive and preserve something. The book As Little Design as Possible on the work of Dieter Rams is great because that's not changing; it is a moment in time with a start date and an end date. By contrast a blog focuses on this hour's best design, this minute's best design. The ability to get your work out there is immense because those blogs need food in the form of new content to sustain themselves. You have to have a thick skin—that academic bubble where it's safe to explore doesn't exist on the Internet. As soon as something goes live it's subject to both praise and ridicule, and that's okay. It's a good thing. What I see in the designers that expose their work online, whether it's Core77 or somewhere else, is their work gets better, faster. They get feedback on things that are working, and they get criticism on things that aren't. No matter how hard it hurts, you can't help but learn.

I notice this particularly in the Core77 discussion forums. There have been so many designers that started as sophomores and posted work and we have seen them evolve over time right in front of our eyes. If someone hits a 1,000-post mark, I start to pay much more attention to them. I give them more feedback because I know this is someone who's part of a community, who wants to contribute, improve, and give back to something bigger. At some point that person may get my phone number and we'll start talking. There are designers I've never worked directly with but who I've given career advice to, or helped them get their first job because I see they're a good designer and a good person, and if I don't have a place for them I'll help them find somebody that does. It's a small world in many ways, and the creative directors at the big firms and companies all know each other. If I find somebody good and I don't have a spot I'll want to make sure they work for a friend who will mentor them and grow them. I think having an online presence has exposed me to that sense of a global community that has been personally beneficial to me. I have no doubt that I would not have been able to go from a consultancy to Nike, to frog and now to DEI had I not had that online presence to develop my voice and commitment to design beyond my personal needs.

How did you break into this business?

I wanted to be a designer since I knew what that was. I came from a pretty normal family, whatever that means. I think everybody's parents want them to be something. My father wanted me to be a professional baseball player of all things. That just seemed so ridiculous to me, but I got really good at something I didn't like through discipline and hard work. At one point I finally rebelled, told my father I didn't want to do this, I didn't like it. He asked me what I wanted to do with my life, and I said: "I want to draw the stuff from the future." It was a very innocent statement from my 13-year-old brain, but I thought that must be somebody's job. A few weeks later, he brought me this article in the Wall Street Journal about Giorgio Giugiaro and he said, "Is this what you want to do? It's called industrial design." I said, "That's it," and I asked for a drafting table and markers for Christmas. It was probably the weirdest Christmas wish list of any 13-year-old.

I always knew what I wanted to do. I don't know if designers are born but I certainly know there are people who have an absolute aptitude, that I do believe. I believe that designer is not a title. You can have the word designer on your business card, but it doesn't mean you're a designer in my book. However, you could be a trash collector and you could be a designer at heart. It's a person, not a job.

I had a really hard time at school. I almost failed out my sophomore year. I'm not able to learn in a very linear, academic way, it always feels artificial to me. I tend to learn organically by doing in a more real-world scenario where there is real risk. It was a problem as a student. I had prepared so hard to be a design student, applying all that discipline and rigor I had learned early in life trying to be a designer. I read everything I could read, and spent all of my money I made working at McDonald's on design books. I had taught myself to sketch, render, draft. I got into school and freshman year, I loved it. It was hard core, it was boot camp, the professors were trying to destroy you, and I loved that. By contrast my sophomore year felt soft, overly academic, didactic even. There were four professors in industrial design, two had just graduated the grad program so they never worked professionally, one was an architect and one was a graphic designer and I just felt between all four of them put together, I knew more than them. I stopped coming to class and worked at home on my own self-directed projects. On critique days I would come in with these totally different projects than everybody else and the professor would ask me, "What is this?" and I'd say, "This is the project you should've assigned if you knew what you were doing." The academic system rejected me as much as I rejected it. I wasn't dealing with it well, but I dealt with it the only way a 19-year-old can: by rebelling.

"THE PORTFOLIO IS NOT SOMETHING YOU EVER FINISH, IT'S AN ORGANIC THING THAT GROWS AND EXPANDS."

I found allies in a couple of professors who luckily somehow saw something in me despite of all my posturing and difficulties. They helped me to work out of that hole, and they helped me set a path for myself in which I ended up doing a lot of industry-sponsored projects, studying in Milan, as well as doing an exchange semester with another school. Ironically, I ended up graduating with a faculty award.

With all that effort school didn't really prepare me for the real world. RISD has a wonderful tradition of teaching you these fine crafts techniques. You have

to learn how to hand cut a dovetail joint in wood with a Japanese saw perfectly, and that's a wonderful technique exercise. They did a wonderful job teaching us very conceptual thinking skills, but at the time there was no bridge in between those skills at the time. There was no sense of the professional world. Keep in mind this was more than 15 years ago, things have changed there, but that is how it was at the time.

I didn't do any internships because, frankly, I was an idiot. I graduated and thought, "Great, when does my phone start ringing?" I had no idea how to get a job. There were no online portfolio hosting sites, Coroflot was essentially a couple of classified ads at the time. Eventually, I had to move back home with my parents, which was traumatic. Nike had offered me a job two months prior to graduating while I was doing a sponsored project for them, but I was very cocky and didn't want to lock it in because I thought something better might come along. It sounds unbelievably stupid to me now. I asked if I could wait until I graduated to decide, and they said sure, no problem. When I graduated, they didn't have the job anymore. They had just gone through a tough year and had a hiring freeze at that time. I remember thinking, "I am an idiot. I should've just accepted that job two months ago." So I had nothing other than a couple of little freelance leads. I remember my parents had this giant ping pong table in the basement. I made that into a makeshift home office. I'd work down there for 14–15 hours a day, into the night, redoing my portfolio over and over again, and would send it out. I got rejection after rejection from every big design firm.

Finally, I got good enough where I got a month-long contract from a design firm out in New York. It was a horrible firm that will remain nameless. It was literally the worst place that I've ever worked in my life, and yet it was wonderful because it was the first professional design setting that I was ever in. The creative director there was a tyrant who would just chew you out at length given any opportunity. He was very conservative and he never wanted to push the clients, but I learned what it meant to do professional-level work. I would go to work, do the work as the director wanted it because otherwise you'd get sworn at for three hours. Then I would come home and redo the project as if I was doing it on my own so I could get a sense of where I would take it if I had the freedom to explore. The one-month contract turned into two months and through that time I was able to build a portfolio where I was finally getting responses from design firms.

A new boutique firm pinged me from Connecticut, called Evo. There were only five or six people there at the time. It was in a loft of this old New England barn. On my first visit something about it just felt right. They wanted to take a chance on me and I thought this would be an amazing opportunity to grow with a firm that was also growing. They gave me a job offer on the spot, and on January 5th—six months after graduation—I finally got a job. Those six months were the hardest six months of my life.

If you were just starting out now, what advice would you give yourself?

Get an internship. I think that's why schools with co-op programs tend to have stronger graduates, because they have experience. Design is not an academic activity. There are certain baseline knowledge sets that are best learned in the academic setting, for example basic skills, design theory, and design history. Once you get out of that environment, you think you're a designer, but really you're just formed enough to begin your real education as a novice professional designer. Those first few years at Evo, every month I thought to myself: why didn't I learn this at school?

At first I was really angry at school, but now I realize that it's just not possible to learn some of those things at school. It doesn't work that way. The reality is it is only possible to learn at that level in real situations. When you leave school you're still this lump of clay that can be further shaped. My biggest piece of advice is to get an internship, or four, because you will learn things that you will not have learned otherwise. You will bring that learning back into the academic environment where it will be safe for you to really figure out what you just learned, and bring it into your working process, share it with other students, and expand on it. You'll also develop a sense of the type of design you want to do. As I said earlier, younger designers have to decide earlier than ever the kind of designer they want to be. Internships will facilitate that. They will help you auto select, because you'll learn if you want to work in a corporation, or if you want to be more of

a generalist or be more of a go-to-market designer.

The other one would be to put your work out there, into the world, to set up some kind of a digital presence. To seek input on the things you're not good at from complete strangers. I see so many young designers continually build on their strong parts and it would be like if your right arm is stronger than your left, and you just kept working out your right arm, now you have a huge right bicep and a wimpy left bicep. So I think you should be running towards those weaknesses, not away from them.

Where do you see the future of industrial design going as it evolves further in the 21st century?

I think ever since I graduated school in the '90s I've been told that industrial design is dying. I remember clearly my first day in the industrial design program at school the head of the department gave a speech in which he clearly stated without a shadow of a doubt that all the jobs in industrial design are gone. This was 1995. Back then it was because of outsourcing, it was because the factories were giving away design for free and supposedly nobody cared about it anymore. That ended up being false, a poor excuse for people who weren't good enough to be professional product designers. That was their sour grapes, a reason why they were never able to get the job they wanted. The factories were and still are giving design away for free, it is just not very good, not culturally relevant nor emotionally resonant.

Now the excuse is that it's all about digital, that people only care about digital experiences. The truth is we're physical beings, we experience everything through sight, through touch, through smell, taste, and sound. Until that changes, there will always be an unquenchable need for better physical design solutions, both functional and emotive. In a way perhaps even more so because the digital world is becoming more enmeshed with the physical, screens are becoming more ubiquitous, so the pretty little box that we design over and over again will be less important and the physical things that surround and input into those digital augmentations will become ever more important. Why would anyone ever buy a Montblanc pen when a Bic does the job just fine? The answer is because they want to. Right, wrong, or indifferent, it is important as a designer to understand and account for the irrational side of our decision-making process. It is another lever to pull when crafting the right solution to a problem.

There will always be room for great designers because physical experiences will always need to be reevaluated. I do think that there is a commoditization trend, there will always be work for subpar designers who work cheaply. In a way I think the middle has fallen out. There's not really much room for mediocre designers anymore. My biggest piece of advice is, if you don't love this, if you don't get out of bed in the morning ready to do this—that's not to say you won't have bad days where you won't feel like doing this—if you're not just ready to live this and let it shoot out of every pore of your body like you were lit from the inside, you won't do it for very long. The industry won't tolerate that anymore. If this is something that you love to do then it will sustain you emotionally and physically. If you find design just ekes out of you even when you wish it wouldn't then you will find you are among others like you. If you're willing to push and always improve yourself, then there will always be room for you in this global community we call design. In fact, you will find it will welcome you with open arms because real recognizes real.

Anything we didn't cover that you would like to add? Any final words of wisdom?

The last thing I would add would be that I would be nowhere today if it wasn't for other people who saw something in me and reached down and helped me. I had to find them, but when I looked, it turned out they were there the whole time. Find a mentor or 10 and really soak everything up from them. There are people who I've found throughout the years without whom, without question, I wouldn't be where I am. The only way you can repay those people who have helped you is to help other people. I've been trying to do that my whole career. I find the more that I repay that debt, the more I get out of it. By helping people, I learn things about myself. Don't just do your job, be a part of design. BI

To see Michael DiTullo's work, please visit http://breaking.in

TODD ELLIS
HEAD OF STRATEGY &
OPERATIONS: INNOVATION &
SUSTAINABILITY
PUMA SE
BOSTON

What kinds of portfolios get your attention these days? What brings in an industrial designer for an interview?

Regardless of experience, the first thing we look for is project diversity, meaning a range of different projects that highlight various design skills, design thinking, and the ability to visually tell those stories. Looking at a portfolio with limited subject matter, such as automotive design work only, it is difficult to gauge the individual's ability to transfer those experiences into footwear design. But if the individual has a range of projects or product designs in varying physical scales while utilizing different materials, colors, and finish solutions, it allows us to better judge their initial design capabilities and interests.

Has there been a portfolio that you've seen recently that resonated with you? What about it stood out?

There was one that stood out. The individual had a couple of years of professional design experience. Their experience only encompassed consumer electronics, but they were interested in obtaining a position in athletic footwear design. To facilitate this interest, they created a number of simulated footwear designs, focused on design thinking and biomechanical problem solving for the activity, in this case the sport of basketball. They clearly illustrated the project process and design solutions by telling the story of the user. This included developing a good consumer profile by researching and identifying the user's personal abilities, interests, and consumer brand affinities. From a qualitative perspective, this was some first-rate storytelling and legitimate design research that helped me believe that the design proposals presented were the correct and appropriate product solutions.

If you had an opportunity to guide a student on how to create an industrial design portfolio that would resonate for you, what would you tell them?

The first thing I tell any student who is seeking a position within a particular business sector—consumer electronics, footwear and apparel, medical, transportation, software or social media, design consultancies and services, et cetera—is to do research on the companies that make up the sector of interest. Be familiar with the companies, product ranges, user benefits, consumer targets, brand messages, and company histories. Form opinions and questions on what you like and don't like. From there, develop your own mock project—projects that offer solutions, alternatives, new market opportunities for the targeted business sector. In other words, when soliciting for work or employment, know your audience and their core interests, and speak to them on their level.

So once you bring in a designer for an interview, what do you expect to learn from them at that one-on-one meeting?

First impressions are critical. Generally, if they are coming in for a face-to-face interview with us, they would have already been screened on the phone a couple of times, to make sure they can communicate well verbally. When they come in for an interview, we like to look, not only at the work, but also how they conduct themselves and explain their projects and work experiences. How people handle themselves professionally is a highly underrated capability. In my view, it is one of the most critical assets any individual can have. In some cases, we have looked at incredibly talented designers who don't carry themselves well from a verbal communication standpoint. They have difficulty explaining their ideas verbally. As a manager, I may consider hiring the person because of their strong visual storytelling skills. But then I must assist them in developing their verbal presentation capabilities. Don't expect every hiring manager to think this way. Therefore, there is a legitimate need to have a balance of both visual and verbal storytelling abilities.

With that said, what characteristics or qualities are necessary to be a successful designer?

There are many characteristics necessary to be successful in life, and that starts with being well rounded in business and social skills. Coming up with a wonderful idea is one thing, but executing the idea to make it real is just as important. Making stuff real requires hard work, perseverance, and being inclusive of various stakeholders who embody more than one idea or solution. Team players make great product champions.

How did you break into this industry?

The footwear industry is certainly the last place I thought I would ever be. I started out designing in the bicycle industry. That led me to work for an ID consulting office in southern Connecticut, where we worked on everything from medical to consumer products. One of our clients was a large athletic footwear company. For them, we worked on industrial design, mechanical engineering, and material solutions for footwear and user solutions involving footwear cushioning and stability technologies. The projects had a heavy dose of functional requirements, fashion, and product styling. My boss at the time was a former automotive designer. Rhetorically he said to me, "Wow isn't this footwear design stuff great! It reminds me of automotive design studio work. Wouldn't you love to do this every day?" I looked at him and thought, "This is fun for a single project or two, but I am not blown away working in footwear. There are other things to design. Where's our next client? Let me at them!"

But, as time passed, the footwear projects grew on me. I found I had a natural affinity for footwear design and development. I left the consulting world and took a full-time position in athletic footwear design, starting at the factory level in Korea. There, I received the "school of hard knocks" training in the footwear business where, in addition to design, I was exposed to product development, commercialization, quality control, and the financials of running a business. This led to other opportunities in the industry, where I grew from designing footwear to leading teams of design, product development, engineering, biomechanical, and marketing professionals.

If you were just starting out now, what advice would you give yourself?

I don't want to date myself here, but things in ID or product design are certainly a lot different than when I started. On a general level, it is clearly more competitive now, and the quality of the work is much higher. As a result, for young designers to enter the business, the playing field has leveled. Therefore, it is harder "to be seen." To stand out for an employment opportunity, you need to show more focus, interest, passion, and conviction. Raw design talent is not enough. As I previously mentioned, if there's an industry you're interested in, learn about it as much as possible. When you approach a potential employer, show your extreme interest and what you know. Ask key questions because everyone likes to talk. You asked me some questions and I'm talking right now.

Where do you see the future of industrial design going as it evolves further in the 21st century?

From a Western perspective, the locations where we make things have changed dramatically over the last 30 years. For various business, political, and economic reasons many American and European manufacturing bases have shifted to Asia. As the business of industrial design involves the manufacture of goods, it's only logical that some portion of design will follow where the manufacturing is. I think that a lot of Western-trained designers need to look at some of those new job locations as opportunities. This is a great chance for individuals to experience new things and carve out new opportunities for themselves.

A designer as business manager is another area where I see the profession evolving, or at least where I would like it to go. I'd like to see more classically trained designers take a lead role in business. That's easier said than done, as first you have to have an interest. The best way to do this is to expose yourself to non-design business elements. You can take continuing education courses, but on-the-job exposure is really where you will learn the day-in-day-out important issues.

You mentioned the connection between design and business. Can you elaborate further on the importance of designers entering that business side? What's the advantage there? What's the benefit?

I think having more designers enter into critical business decision-making can result in better product solutions for the user. Ultimately, better solutions can mean increased revenues.

"TO STAND OUT FOR AN EMPLOYMENT OPPORTUNITY, YOU NEED TO SHOW MORE FOCUS, INTEREST, PASSION, AND CONVICTION. RAW DESIGN TALENT IS NOT ENOUGH."

When the designer has a better understanding of the totality in business—sourcing, marketing, distribution, finance—there is greater opportunity for the designer to see things in a different way and deliver something better and new to the market. But the designer has to have the interest to make this happen. If you only take the approach as a single cog in the machine, you only know the couple of cogs around you. You need to pull yourself out of the gears and take a broader look at the whole machine.

So it's a combination of both long-term and systems thinking.

Exactly. You want to be able to take a bigger view. I know not everyone is interested in that or has the affinity to go there. There are capable design people out there who, if they spent more time on the business side, could become top management-level professionals and help drive better opportunities for companies. I think it's up to the designer to make that choice.

Anything you'd like to add that we didn't talk about? Any final words of wisdom?

I've always considered design as a business function and I've always approached it that way. Design equals business. This could maybe explain why my career has gone towards the business management side of things. If you only think of design it's just going to be design, and nothing more. If you think of design as a business tool and as a business itself, then you think about it a bit more broadly. That opens up the ability to communicate what design can do for the total organization. BI

To see Todd Ellis's work, please visit http://breaking.in

DAVID FELLAH
CEO & CO-FOUNDING
PARTNER
DESIGNIT
COPENHAGEN

What kinds of portfolios get your attention these days? What brings in an industrial designer for an interview?

If they are right out of school, then we are only looking for talent. It doesn't matter if they have experience or not, talent matters the most. We have a philosophy in hiring people at Designit that transcends everything, and that is our employment mantra: chemistry, chemistry, competence. To us collaboration is everything, especially because we are so globally dispersed—just in Denmark we have two offices. We need to be able to work across cultures, across time zones, across language barriers—so the chemistry has to be right. We need to have a perfect chemical balance between the people. That's more important than anything, than talent, than experience.

How do you define someone who has talent?

You're a product designer yourself, so you know what I mean. When you look at portfolios you know by the "handshake"—by the first pages of the portfolio. You just get that feeling. It's so intuitive for us. You sense the level of craftsmanship and the conceptual strength in a split second and whether this particular talent's style fits into the Designit way of designing.

You mention chemistry and cultural fit. What kind of a person would work well for Designit?

It's all about how you fit within our cooperative culture. The way you look, the way you talk, what your handshake is like—it's a delicate, but actually rather simple assessment to make. Within our frame of reference there are few clear giveaways if you'll be able to contribute in our group process. Some of those are visual, like your personal style. Is your appearance dominating and are you trying to stand out instead of trying to be a part of the group? It's hard to explain, but we are all able to interpret these signals. We then know if this person, with this kind of appearance and attitude, will fit into our "it's-not-about-me-it's-all-about-the-project" process successfully.

What characteristics or qualities would you say make a successful designer?

We moved away from the "classic product design." Everything we do has a technological component, not necessarily inside the product but maybe it is tied into some kind of service. As soon as you talk about a technological component, you're talking about connectivity, or something that's a part of a different set of opportunities. So you need to know that a product designer has to understand more than just ergonomics, or standard beautification tools. A product designer today needs to understand everything else in the complete horizon of design disciplines surrounding a product. Everything from understanding that this product at some point has to become part of a brand, has to be able to fit into a packaging concept, and so forth. Product designers nowadays are much more multi-skilled, or multi-understanding than we would think was important 10 years ago.

I remember 20 years ago, if you were interested in packaging design and you were a product designer, you were an idiot. It had nothing to do with your "art," and of course this is different today. We're a multidisciplinary design agency and it's important that you as a designer can design, say, an intelligent electric toothbrush, some new service experiences to enhance the use of it, and also understand where and how it is supposed to be positioned in the store among competing products. You need to know how to interpret that complexity and use it in a product design process that embraces not only the product, but also packaging, instructions, brand, product portfolio, etc.

It's shifting from an individual product to an ecosystem of solutions.

Exactly.

How did you break into this business?

We just started. We were three guys who started Designit about 20 years ago and we were all fresh out of school. We didn't really break into...well, of course we did, but we were never really employed anywhere before Designit, if that's what you're asking. We didn't have any other options at that time. There were no jobs for us in the city we lived in. They were hard times, and we just went for it.

What were some of the challenges you faced as you started Designit?

Actually, the major challenge we faced was that we wanted to approach establishing a design company in a new way, where business was above design. We were focusing on the business goals of our clients rather than designing for ourselves. This sounds so basic nowadays that it's embarrassing, but it wasn't basic 20 years ago. We had a mantra outlining a very important value: think before you draw. Twenty years ago you weren't thinking before you drew, you were an artist if you were a product designer. We set out in a world where product designers were artists, and where technology was something only engineers cared about. We set out to change that and do something different. We were almost l'enfant terrible. We were looked at as "What are they thinking? They are bringing business into our wonderful world of design." Things of course changed since. Damn it, this makes me sound old—I'm not old.

But that was our challenge, to make the local market understand they need to approach any product they were working on with the entire ecosystem in mind from the get-go, including branding, positioning, the product portfolio strategy, and so forth. I guess we succeeded in that.

If you were just starting out now, what advice would you give yourself?

We have learned a lot along the way, but we haven't done anything specifically wrong. I would say, stick to the design business because we tried other business adventures alongside, and none of them succeeded. So, spend your energy on design. Other than that, I can't say, "If only we had known this or done that." Maybe I would say that I wish we all had more experience from somewhere else so that we knew about product management before we started, but in the long run those are details. I mean, the reason why we've got Designit is because we're the kind of guys who aren't employable anywhere else.

Where do you see the future of industrial design going as it evolves further in the 21st century?

That's a really, really interesting question. There's no doubt that the world has become more and more focused on user experience, and user experience is more about interactions between products and services, between products and other products. I have a feeling the world will end up with fewer products and more services, more opportunities for products to work together rather than just more products, products, products. So the future of "classic product design" is about understanding multidisciplinary synergies and understanding that the product in the future is probably more a product platform wrapped in services than it is a product by itself.

How can a student in school right now prepare for that kind of an environment?

I have no experience with how it is in the States, but my feeling from Europe is that most industrial design students are nerds. You've got to be a nerd to be a certain kind of product designer. You have to be able to dive into complex design tools and the detailed values that make up a world-class product. It is a nerd profession.

So in two words: look up. It's so easy to just look into your computer display and see the world from there, but if you look up you'll see that the world of products and brands is changing rapidly around us. You can easily understand then the demands expected from you. You should work hard to possess more skills than just the ability to make something look and feel beautiful. It also has to tap beautifully into the entire ecosystem and you need to understand so many other things than just materials. I sincerely think that amazing things happen when it is the designers who are thinking that way, and not the business owners, because we bring a different kind of creative thinking into the strategic mix.

"YOU SHOULD WORK HARD TO POSSESS MORE SKILLS THAN JUST THE ABILITY TO MAKE SOMETHING LOOK AND FEEL BEAUTIFUL. IT ALSO HAS TO TAP BEAUTIFULLY INTO THE ENTIRE ECOSYSTEM AND YOU NEED TO UNDERSTAND SO MANY OTHER THINGS THAN JUST MATERIALS."

If I were only interested in aesthetics, I could find five Chinese product designers that would be way better at the price than one Danish designer. They would not understand how to make that thing tap into the rest of the world, but the basic skill set is easily found. We get hundreds of applications from India to Germany from designers who are very technically skilled. But the technical skills are a given these days. What sets you apart?

Is there anything you'd like to add that we haven't talked about? Any final words of wisdom?

It's difficult to have any final words of wisdom right now, as we're in the middle of a disruption, both in business and technology. I just realized that Nokia, who was always shelling out tons of different designs, is now basing their entire business on just a few devices. If those few devices fail, they will fail. Nokia is doing it. Apple has done it: narrowing their portfolios of many, many devices to a few, and finding different ways of making money through

services around those few devices. The Chinese brands will follow suit soon too. So we're in a time where some of the old paradigms of how our clients make money are changing. Therefore our business is changing as well. It sounds like something you'd say in the 2000s but it's true now.

I have no way of saying what product design will look like 10 years from now. I know it looks dramatically different today than it did 10 years ago because product experience is going towards service experience. And service experience has to do with technological opportunities, and those develop so rapidly these days. We can only expect everything to be dramatically different in both the near and far future. ⊞

To see the work of David Fellah and Designit, please visit http://breaking.in

**FELICIA FERRONE
FOUNDER
FFERRONE DESIGN
CHICAGO**

What ingredients are necessary these days to make a strong industrial design portfolio, one that stands out?

Portfolios need to reflect a broad spectrum of types of work and show a range of scales. Often portfolios look very similar and it's the ones that have a strong graphic sense that really stand out. The work also is presented in very much the same way. It's the ones who approach presentation of the ideas in a completely different way that really stand out.

So if an industrial design student came up to you and asked, "What should my portfolio be like? What do I need to show you in order to work with you?", what would you tell them?

I would say the portfolio must be considered as a whole: a strong graphic design sense and layout, font selection down to the paper selection, if it is presented physically. The designer should immediately indicate their level of attention to detail and sensitivity. The projects, of course, must also be strong and easily understandable.

What was the motivation for you to open your own design studio?

I've always known I wanted to work for myself, and I always knew I wanted to be in some kind of design director role. It really wasn't until the Revolution Collection of glassware that it finally happened. It allowed me the opportunity to figure out all the "moving parts" from finding manufacturing to designing the packaging to figuring out distribution.

"OFTEN PORTFOLIOS LOOK VERY SIMILAR AND IT'S THE ONES THAT HAVE A STRONG GRAPHIC SENSE THAT REALLY STAND OUT."

These were things that I felt required my full attention and couldn't be done well while working for someone else. I knew I also wanted to be free to pursue design with established brands along with more self-directed work and having my own studio allows me that freedom of choice.

How do you manage the non-design aspects of running a studio, of doing this whole self-funded thing?

I do everything from accounting to boxing and shipping, which all takes time, so it is finding a balance between the creative time and the production time. I take great pride in figuring all of that out, as well as having my hand in it. I think it is crucial to have an understanding of all aspects of your business, as ultimately it's your responsibility. With self-funded work there is freedom and that is the ultimate luxury.

What advice would you give to somebody who is just starting out in the industry and has a desire to open their own studio?

When you come up against resistance, do not give up. Just find another way to accomplish your vision. Much of life comes down to tenacity and perseverance.

Industrial design seems to be a predominantly male-dominated field. Still, I'm curious what advice you may have for women.

This goes for anyone: I think you need to be absolutely 110% prepared and be able to achieve your vision against any resistance you may encounter. As a woman, you probably have to be more prepared, so as not to be dismissed when running into problems while trying to innovate and push your ideas through.

If you were starting out just now, what advice would you give yourself?

Set clear goals and be more strategic about how to achieve them. This covers everything from design ideas to business aspects. I have so many ideas going on in my head at once and of completely different subject matter. It's a question of how to organize all of this so that you can use it to move yourself forward towards your goal more efficiently.

So what would you say it takes to break into today's very competitive marketplace?

It's about people and perseverance. It's about meeting the people you want to work with and finding a way to bring your ideas to fruition.

The network is important.

Yes. Absolutely. Whenever I hear that word it makes me cringe, but ultimately it's just getting to know people and having people get to know you.

Where do you see the future of industrial design going as it evolves further in the 21st century?

I see it as an enormous economic engine that will have ever greater importance within the world economy, especially in the US. It has tremendous power to impact our economy through the increase of smart manufacturing, sales tax revenue generation, job creation, and providing a new framework for seeing our world. I see it also adding to the category of really large-scale problem solving; people really are looking at design as a solution to larger problems.

As designers, we are constantly connecting seemingly unrelated dots and looking at human factors involved in all of these complex issues. It's so much more comprehensive than the traditional linear approach to problem solving in business. Design and design thinking are critical and will become more and more critical to our future.

Anything you'd like to add that we didn't cover? Any final words of wisdom?

I really can't emphasize enough this sense of perseverance. I think that's something that's innate in most entrepreneurs, but I think it is a skill that can be acquired and honed over time. Not taking no for an answer, staying true to your vision, and finding a way to see it realized. [BI]

To see Felicia Ferrone's work, please visit http://breaking.in

BRYON FITZPATRICK PROFESSOR EMERITUS TRANSPORTATION DEPT. COLLEGE FOR CREATIVE STUDIES DETROIT

You have had quite a long and illustrious career as a product designer—probably the longest of any of my interviewees. So I'm curious: what is the hallmark of a stellar or successful industrial design portfolio? What is the common thread?

Portfolios are a visual indicator of how an applicant is looking for a position in the design business—how they present themselves and their skills.

A great cover design can help set up a positive feeling about the work inside, assuming there is the quality material to back it up. Good graphic design and layout, first-class sketches, explanatory notes, and so on are all helpful. Errors of project sequence, insufficient—or too much—coverage on projects, and lack of a good story are all factors contributing to an overall bad portfolio.

Have you seen an industrial design portfolio recently that resonated with you? What about it stood out?

Of the portfolios I have seen recently, one fulfilled the good design criteria perfectly. A great cover graphic, carried over to each page on a smaller scale, an intro index, sections devoted to various product designs and all divided by a titled acetate sheet. Everything was illustrated by a full range of skills––sketches, digital work, explanatory text–– with superb depiction of the design process.

If an industrial design student came to you looking for advice on how to prepare their portfolio to get an internship or a job, what would you tell them to do? What should be in their portfolio?

The basis of any good or great portfolio would be the control of the content. That means illustrating a good range of expertise without overdoing it in any one area––which is often a temptation––to attain a good balance. Some applicants may have a preference for specific areas of industrial design, and even though the portfolio content may be wide ranging, it may be useful to show more emphasis on their preference, be it product, furniture, etc. to show their area of focus.

What has been the most common mistake students (or junior designers) make in how they present their work or their portfolios?

Two things come to mind regarding mistakes students seem to make. One of those is trying to show too much, sometimes including lesser works to pad out a portfolio. Too often viewers have to wade through too many pages of stuff to get to the real substance of a project. The second is the lack of a "good story." That will always put a bit of a dampener on a presentation.

What advice would you give to someone preparing for an interview at a design studio?

Lots of things have to be considered before any interview. Apart from the obvious: being neat and tidy—basic as that is—or talking too much and not listening. It's okay to state a preference for a particular area of design if asked, especially if one has the appropriate portfolio content. I can't stress enough the importance of having a good sketch book—or two—as they can sometimes contain more evidence of a good thought process in the development of a design, or observations not even connected to products, cars, and so on.

What characteristics or qualities are necessary to be a successful industrial designer in the long term?

A big plus is flexibility: being willing and able to approach any design area and see it as a challenge. Being basically a product designer—but sketching around cars—I once volunteered to work on a new motorcycle project, a complete departure from my "normal" area. With that move, I generated a shift to another country and further experiences in new fields.

"THE BASIS OF ANY GOOD OR GREAT PORTFOLIO WOULD BE THE CONTROL OF THE CONTENT."

I made it a point to work on both interior and exterior automotive design, giving me more flexibility—plus, it was more interesting.

How did you break into this business?

I had initially studied architecture for three years, built furniture, worked freelance, and then switched to product design. When a position was advertised in a car studio, I applied for and got it. Five years later, I went back into product design again full time. It was a more interesting and varied experience, and then into teaching.

If you were just starting out now, what advice would you give yourself?

I would suggest taking any job just to get into the business instead of waiting for the perfect spot. Build a great portfolio, keep updating it, and establish a network of contacts. It's easier now with LinkedIn and other Internet social networks. Back in the day, you had to have a card file and would have to keep track of people.

Where do you see the future of industrial design going as it evolves further in the 21st century?

Obviously the emphasis has shifted to the digital and materials technology side of things. It's so much easier to source information, materials, contacts, and get prototypes made almost instantly for lower prices, and so on. Another important trend via the prototyping phenomenon is the prevalence of the designer/entrepreneur—people like Dyson, Veronika Scott, and from the past, Craig Vetter. People who are able to put their own designs into production. You can see even more of that now via Kickstarter.

Anything we didn't cover that you would like to add? Any final words of wisdom?

If you've applied for a dream job, and did not got it, drop them an email every couple of months as a check-in, anyway. Things change, and something even better may become available, so keeping in touch is not a bad idea. ◰

To see Bryon Fitzpatrick's work, please visit http://breaking.in

FRITZ FRENKLER
FOUNDER
F/P DESIGN GMBH
MUNICH

What kinds of portfolios get your attention these days? What brings in an industrial designer for an interview?

We are an international studio, looking for talented people who are able to work in a team. We look to find young people who are able to work in multidisciplinary teams, to work hard and not just sketch, because bringing the product into the market is a difficult task. Still a lot of young designers think they can be a star designer immediately, but from my point of view, all star designers are not designers—they are artists. As far as I know, there are few schools and universities where you can get an experience learning about multidisciplinary teamwork. Nevertheless, there are still some young designers who can work in a team, who are intelligent and do not only believe in what they already know. It is important that they are able to learn something during the process. Those designers are hard to find.

Would you say that there is plenty of talent out there, but not enough industrial designers who can work in a team environment?

I think first of all, there is a wrong understanding about design outside the industry. In different societies and different countries there are different ideas of design. Design is very hard and detailed work. Design is not fine arts. Design is engineering, research, understanding and setting up developing processes—not just sitting in a beautiful environment and making nice colored sketches or renderings. I don't believe it is important to operate a computer for design, because the computer is mainly needed for presentation. You don't need a computer for developing products. Since we started to use computers in the fields of industrial design and architecture, the design quality has decreased. Therefore, I need employees who understand

proportion, usability, and ergonomics, but first of all who understand people and their culture and society.

What are some common mistakes you've seen students or junior designers make in their portfolios?

The lack of consistency in quality of work throughout the portfolio is usually the most common mistake. I hold a view that good design and good design projects primarily result from a strong idea and the consequent pursuit of this idea. Most portfolios don't show this consistency neither within single projects nor throughout the whole portfolio.

What would you say it takes to be a successful industrial designer?

I think you have to be able to moderate processes. Of course the problem is that designers have enemies in companies—we don't have many friends. The marketing likes to do our job, engineers believe they are the better designers—but to break the ice, designers have to moderate the process of product strategy and product development. Designers have to do this because nobody else can do it—engineering is naturally related to technology, marketing is related to markets, but design is the only one related to people. Lots of designers feel the same way, they see themselves as lawyers of the users of the products. If you can explain this to companies, if they take this path of developing, then designers can moderate the process and things would be much more smoother, with less problems than now.

If you were just starting out now, what advice would you give yourself?

First, patience. Always trust yourself, study the history of design, study the process of developing products, and learn from it. Don't believe that today's new media and new technology can help us to create better products—this is nonsense. We have to understand the change of societies and the new needs of the people. This is the way to make companies successful. From my point of view there is only one company in the world which understood that people need and like to have easy-to-use products and like to have products that are linked together with systems. It is Apple. Today's product development has no idea how the people are using products and what the systems behind them are all about. I tell young designers: think about processes and systems and not just about the product. You have to create systems and services for systems—this will be the new challenge for design.

Where do you see the future of industrial design going as it evolves further in the 21st century?

Design has to be the supervisor of processes. As I mentioned before, too many people are trying to do design at the moment. Today, decisions about products are made by engineering and marketing. The design fulfills ideas of the marketing and tries to envelop technology—this a wrong approach. We have to create products which fit in systems and societies. Designers have to be the inventors of products. We have to invent products, think products, create products—this will be the chance, the evolution of design.

"I HOLD A VIEW THAT GOOD DESIGN AND GOOD DESIGN PROJECTS PRIMARILY RESULT FROM A STRONG IDEA AND THE CONSEQUENT PURSUIT OF THIS IDEA."

To achieve this aim, we have to leave fine arts behind and move towards science. If we try to make nice drawings and sketches to impress people, we will never create good products. Nobody asks why this has happened during the last 30 years, why we had nice drawings, but 70% of the products on the market are rubbish and nobody is able to use them. Thus, we need new kinds of products—products that are serving people, society, and environment. We need new kinds of designers and a new kind of education in line with science.

How would you change the process? What would you recommend students do?

As I said, it is a question of education. This is the reason why I got involved in the university to teach the students. We have to understand and to explain why this is the right form, why it is the right product. It is not only a question of aesthetics, it is also a question of engineering and—once again—science. But you need time. You cannot say: "I like it, so it's okay." We have to make it clear to the client, the market, we have to give answers: "This is the right product for you because..."

Therefore we have to change education programs at universities and we have to get closer to engineering and science and get away from fine arts. Of course, we have to be able to make sketches to explain what we thought, but even one of the most important and best architects, Walter Gropius, could not draw, yet he was able to change the whole field of architecture. I think it's not the question of drawing or doing renderings with a computer, but it's a question of thinking about processes aside from just the aesthetic point of view.

If you had the opportunity to give advice to a graduating class of a design school, what would you tell them?

We have to get back to the real world. We have to leave the artificial world where design is located at the moment. The real world is full of different people and environments, and we have to understand this and study it. If you think in terms of ecology, we have to be able to say: "No, we cannot realize this product. This product makes no sense." Maybe the task of designers of the future is not making products. For example, Apple, once again, is the leading company in this way of thinking: Apple introduced the new iPhone 4S, without changing the design. They only included some new technology and improved some existing technology. This is the future of design—not making a new form but understanding the process and understanding what people need.

It sounds like you are almost saying that industrial design needs to grow up and become mature.

Yes, exactly. Design had a strong position in history. The philosophy of Bauhaus for example was very strong in process and development. At the moment we are killing brands, together with marketing. I'm really concerned about this kind of marketing strategy. There is no understanding about the market and the people. We are designing against competitors, not for people. This is the problem. Again, look at Apple, they never care about competitors. Just think about mobile phones. Apple appeared on the market, when it was already "closed." Nokia, Sony-Ericsson, LG, and so on had 150 different kinds of mobile phones on the market—each company.

Apple came out with its one phone, and said: "We don't care, we invented a product for the people."

Anything we didn't cover that you would like to add? Any final words of wisdom?

I believe that design is one of the most important professions, but the profession has to take people's needs seriously. If we don't do it, the profession will disappear. It's the moment of truth. We have to think about how to teach young designers. If we just entertain with software or renderings, the profession will disappear, but if we educate the right way, this profession can change the world. [BI]

To see Fritz Frenkler's work, please visit http://breaking.in

TYLOR GARLAND
CO-FOUNDER AND CEO
BOOMBANG INC.
LOS ANGELES

What kinds of portfolios get your attention these days? What brings in an industrial designer for an interview?

The first thing that catches my eye is usually the craft. Traditionally, in industrial design there is some type of form giving, so the ability to create a visually compelling and well-crafted presentation certainly catches my eye. Then, I move pretty quickly to understand their motivations, strategic process, and rationalization frameworks. If, upon first glance, I see poor sketching, renderings, or form development it's a turnoff. However, if they are applying for a research or strategy position, then I would reverse the order of importance.

Have you seen a portfolio recently that really stood out, and what about it caught your eye?

It depends on the position we're looking for. Whether we are looking for someone with product design and engineering skills or someone that's more strategically focused on consumer and marketing insights, or someone who is more brand focused. Each portfolio resonates differently depending on the position we're hiring for. But the portfolios that have caught my eye recently are the ones that demonstrate prolific divergent thinking. By that I mean a broad range of interests and tools that they're using: everything from conducting meaningful consumer and market research to materials and technology aptitudes to the creation of novel business models. I tend to be drawn to designers that are wide in experience and interest, with deep super skill in a few particular areas.

A combination of really good technical skills and critical thinking skills are important in their portfolio?

Absolutely, two sides of the same coin. If you're sending in a portfolio without the benefit of being able to present it, you need to be aware of both your audience and your craftsmanship. People are very busy these days and are bombarded with content, emails, and portfolios. It's a different kind of portfolio than the one you would use for an in-person pitch deck. There is a reason magazine ads look the way they do: no one spends time to read them, it's all headline and picture. I'd suggest you think about your portfolio in terms of progressive disclosure. Catch their eye with high-concept headlines and visuals that show off technical skills and allow them to read on if they would like to delve into the critical thinking—or skip to the next project. My guess is that, in your absence, most folks will decide if they like your work in about five seconds and a few page flips, assuming your portfolio doesn't get accidentally buried in their email.

When you bring in a designer for an interview, what do you expect to learn from them at that one-on-one meeting?

For junior designers I look for maturity, passion, openness, and verbal skills. I've met several very talented designers who had egos the size of the Hindenburg and, well, you know how that story ends. When you join a studio, you join a culture and that culture is made up of people who all have unique temperaments and skill sets. In all cases, being a team player that can lead but also follow is important, so I try to get a sense of how they will fit into our culture. They've already made the cut in terms of their design skills by that point.

What would you say are the characteristics or qualities needed to be a successful designer?

A deeply integrated perspective on innovation is the short answer. People who strive to uncover meaningful consumer insights and market gaps and translate those insights into the unmet rational, emotional, and symbolic needs of people. Then, how to create a solution in the form of a product or a service experience. They need to understand the marketing aspects. How to get the word out around what they're creating and ultimately have it connect to a business model. An integrated understanding with the complete ecosystem of design will put them in a position of influence with a wide range of audiences.

So understanding the entire scope in which the product lives, not just the product itself?

Yes, thinking beyond the object is critical at Boombang. We are moving away from designing just objects to designing systems, from business systems to software and experience systems, service systems. Product is usually just one part of a bigger equation. For a designer to be able to have that awareness is, in my opinion, the primary hallmark of a design leader.

How did you break into this industry?

I graduated from Art Center in '93 and, prior to that, I made the decision that I wanted to be on the consulting side. I wanted to be able to work on many brands and categories, with different types of management teams. I wanted to go broad— maybe it's my attention deficit disorder. I did my research and chose frog design as my target. They were the only company that I interviewed with and I was pretty relentless about getting the job. I think

I just wore them into submission until they brought me on as an intern. It was either that or they would have had to issue a restraining order. I guess the internship was easier for them.

"...THE PORTFOLIOS THAT HAVE CAUGHT MY EYE RECENTLY ARE THE ONES THAT DEMONSTRATE PROLIFIC DIVERGENT THINKING."

After the internship, I went back and finished up my degree at Art Center. Post-graduation and a few gigs later in LA, I found myself back in the Bay Area right when the whole dot com thing was exploding. I spent about six years collectively at both Fitch and frog in San Francisco during the dot com heyday. I was very lucky and was overpaid and under-qualified for most of the positions I held.

A few years later, I started Boombang because I fundamentally sensed a breakdown in the traditional consulting model where companies would hire design teams comprised of people that had never run a business, but were very quick to give business advice. So there was a disjoint there for me. The whole fee-for-service structure was a bit challenging as well. These companies would hire a firm and pay them their fee whether they did a great job or a crummy job, measured by how well that product did in the marketplace. Fundamentally, there was a breakdown in getting creative interests aligned with business interests so that was one of the things I tried to solve for at Boombang.

We spent a lot of time developing new client engagement models, most of which were underscored with a spirit of entrepreneurship, meaning we were willing to take on some level of risk with the client. We also launched a venture group that incubated new technologies, products, and brands in addition to working with early stage companies in which we would waive a portion of our fees in exchange for product or business equity.

We put our money where our mouth was, so to speak. This wasn't something I could do at other firms at the time. Their appetite for risk was too low and their overhead was too great, so that was one of the main reasons why I started Boombang.

If you were starting out now, what advice would you give yourself?

Probably to plan less. We spent a lot of time modeling our multiyear plans. What I've experienced is that, although you have a target and an idea of what you are managing towards, there are so many variables that are unknown. Our ability to trade up to higher value opportunities along the way is part of the key. Where we entered into the business plan is certainly not where we exited. It's a series of pivots and shifts along the way, and those are just impossible to predict. We spent a lot of time planning and it really never turned out the way we thought and I think that's okay, because sometimes it turned out better.

So I would definitely tell myself not to be so strident, not to be so rigid about designing the business, to be more organic about it. The power of intention and law of attraction can take you where you want to go if you are clear in your heart about what it is you want. The details seem to sort themselves out if you're focused on your cause and are open to evolving your vision. Embrace the unknown, that's where true potential hides.

Where do you see the future of industrial design going as it evolves further in the 21st century?

I think that "industrial design" is an antiquated term. When I look at what's happening in our world and specifically the companies we work with, the need is much more broadly around innovation and combining technology, business strategies, and design in new ways to solve problems. It really transcends the idea of industrial design per se, which seems to be an artifact of the industrial age, where the focus was on manufacturing and mass-production products. The term bothers me because it focuses on the object and I think where the profession is going is much more expansive. In order to transcend, we must include, and I'm in favor of that. I would like for someone to rebrand

the ID profession. I think it marginalizes the real innovation that ID thinkers can bring to community, business, and humanity at large.

Anything you'd like to add that we didn't talk about? Any final words of wisdom?

If this book is for young designers looking to build their careers and find their way, I would have them read The Hero's Journey by Joseph Campbell, which talks about many things, one of which is the paramount importance of following your bliss. There are so many different ways of expressing your personal passion that will naturally seek out like-minded audiences. This is where your power and happiness live. The more you can be conscious about selecting partners and projects that inspire a deep, intrinsic sense of purpose, the more successful you're going to be. It's a combination of looking outside of yourself and seeing where your fellow man is heading, to find what your personal journey is. Only you can answer that—not a school, a teacher, a colleague, your parents, your mate, and certainly not me. BI

To see the work of Tylor Garland and Boombang, please visit http://breaking.in

RALPH GILLES
SENIOR VICE PRESIDENT OF PRODUCT DESIGN & PRESIDENT & CEO OF SRT BRAND & MOTORSPORTS CHRYSLER
AUBURN HILLS, MICHIGAN

I'm sure when it comes to portfolios, you've seen it all. What gets your attention these days? What brings in an industrial designer for an interview?

A nice range of very, very forward-thinking ideas. I'm excited when people take risks with design. At the same time, I like a few bookends. I like to see that the person can do more immediate stuff because sometimes we have immediate projects. We can see if the person can latch onto those. I'd like to see a couple of different themes. What I mean by that is when someone does a very loose sketch and they're able to translate that into a design, without losing the essence of the sketch, you can see the theme survives the process of maturity and evolution. I also like designers that include their inspiration. What's their philosophy? Some kind of a philosophical base in their work is very important to me.

Is there an example of a recent portfolio that you've seen that blew you away? Have you seen a portfolio recently and thought, "Wow this is awesome"?

Generally, I think the quality of portfolios has come up dramatically. I think a lot of it has to do with the computing power available to students nowadays. Some of them have personal computers that are more powerful than our professional stuff was five years ago. It has definitely opened up the quality of work, the rendering quality, even the presentation, so I'm a little bit distracted by the vis com [visual communications]. Some of these kids are publishing books or quarter-of-an-inch thick magazines of their work. How did you afford that? The tools that they have make the work appear of higher quality, so it's actually harder for me now because I have to look through all of that and see the pure designer. It's very easy to be drunk on all the "Hollywood," so to speak. With that said, I think the modern designers are handling the tools really well. They design the vehicles through and through. We are seeing exteriors and interiors—a package design—so they're really doing a nice job making industrial designers into not just theme people.

What do you expect to learn from a designer during an interview?

In all cases, and this is personally my point of view not a general design-head point of view, my first impression is always the ego. Does this person come in with some kind of outside ego or not? That's the thing we hate the most at Chrysler. We're very much about sharing. We all share. We are willing to adapt and learn from each other, so the ego is the first thing I deal with. If they say "I" a lot in their interview, or talk all about them becoming the world's best designer in

five years, and not about contributing to the company, they're out. The humility is very important to me and the willingness to be a team player.

What characteristics or qualities would you say make a successful designer?

I think the ability to spin a design in your head. The ability to draw a singular theme in all views—the command of form. You can tell if someone sketches the same idea, but it's really different in every view, it means they're not quite able to design it in their minds. That's something I notice right away. That technical skill where you're almost able to create a mental 3D property, where you're basically illustrating it in various views...that's a very powerful skill.

Then, believe it or not, the written word. There are still a lot of illiterate designers out there. Designers need to be pretty intelligent in terms of what they write and how they write descriptions or describe their vehicle orally, or the technical content in their portfolios. I'm looking to see how good that is, and sometimes I'm actually shocked to see spelling mistakes and grammar issues. It just shows me that maybe they're not as well rounded as they could be.

There's more to being a successful designer than what I just mentioned. A lot of it is the emotional intelligence. I think artists in general can be so one-dimensional sometimes. It's nice to see a designer who's also potentially a good leader. It's one thing to be a great designer, but can you campaign your concept? You have to be very socially functional to be able to sell your idea, so I'm always looking for that. Are they comfortable in their skin? Could they be a good speaker someday? Do they look me right in the eyes? Do they have those kinds of leadership qualities? It's more than just being a great artist, it's also: "Are you a good candidate as a leader?"

How did you break into this business?

That was long before the Internet, so I actually literally had to write letters to car companies. I wrote one to Chrysler and that's how I knew there was such a thing as a designer. It really was about the magazines, reading about Giugiaro, and former design leaders. I tried to reverse engineer their careers. I am, like most people in this industry, a car lover, and while I don't think it's necessary to be a car lover to succeed, that's where I came from. I grew up in the '80s when cars were ugly, so I always thought I could do something about that—try to help. It's grown so much since then. I used to think of the Big Three, now it's the Big Seven. There are studios all over the planet. In every nook and cranny there's a design studio, and then, outside of automotive, there are a lot of places to be an industrial designer. It has been a very exciting field for many years.

You're one of the rare industrial designers with an MBA. I'm wondering if you can share some insights from that experience. How have the skills from that helped you as a designer? Did it add to your success, and would you recommend it?

Absolutely. I don't think it's necessary in the first stage, for sure. It's not going to make a difference whether you get hired or not—especially at the beginning. But once you're inside a company I highly recommend it. The automotive business is a very complicated business. I think the MBA really helped me to integrate myself with the rest of the community because finance people, most of the engineering people, and all of the marketing people have an MBA. You're swimming in a pretty elite field, so it's really important and nowadays it's almost a requirement in business if you want to go further. So I highly, highly recommend it. It is tricky because it will kill a little bit of your innocence. You can talk yourself out of good ideas too early, so that's something I'm always fighting. I have to be a little ignorant or force a little ignorance in my mind so I don't shut things down too soon. I think overall, the benefits outweigh the risks. Especially if you see yourself as a leader someday, or want to manage a studio, because a lot of design is also managing the cost, the materials, the staffing. It's more than just making cool cars.

Knowing what you know now, what advice would you give to your younger self?

Get mentorship. I think it's important to really seek out information. We tend to work a little bit too quick, too fast, and regurgitate things. You have to reset yourself every couple of years and see outside of your profession for inspiration, or encourage your people to do that. Be as fresh as possible. Be hyper-aware of the design world, not just automotive,

but anything going on in design. There's inspiration in every corner of life. That's helped me. Seek out senior managers, if not in your company, then outside. They can help you understand that there's always a big picture, there's always tomorrow. Some designers will fall on their swords for something today, but think what long-term impression you're making and what kind of immediate life you're leading for yourself. Think of your career in a 10-year space, not just in the moment.

As you mentioned, the industry can be pretty tough, and it often requires a thick skin. What advice would you give to a design student on how to navigate these very "sharky" waters?

Yeah, it's very tough. I think you do need a thick skin, you really do. Oftentimes, especially the more progressive you are as a designer, your ideas may be seen as outlandish and people tend to cast you off as being not as forward-thinking. A big part of the challenge is to bring them along and help them. I used to call it "intoxicate them with the vision." It's extra work to get non-right-brained people to come along with you, but you have to be able to put yourself in their skin and think about it through their eyes. Think, "Well, how can I divert my message here to be digestible to them?" Introduce them to what you're trying to do. It takes more effort.

"IT'S ONE THING TO BE A GREAT DESIGNER, BUT CAN YOU CAMPAIGN YOUR CONCEPT? YOU HAVE TO BE VERY SOCIALLY FUNCTIONAL TO BE ABLE TO SELL YOUR IDEA...IT'S MORE THAN JUST BEING A GREAT ARTIST, IT'S ALSO: 'ARE YOU A GOOD CANDIDATE AS A LEADER?'"

Typically, what I've found is that they don't see what you see. Designers think that everyone sees the world the way you do. It's amazing to me when an executive pulls me aside and says, "Ralph, I have no idea what you're talking about. I don't see it." They can't see the design, especially if it's in a sketch or rough model, they're almost terrified of it. Designers need to invest more time in the campaigning of the idea, and also the explanation of the basic foundation. Don't take the position of "Oh, he just doesn't get it"—that just alienates the designer. It's more work but, eventually, they'll respect you more over time and you become known for reliable solutions, and earn that respect. I'm sure the first time Frank Gehry sold a building, people thought he was insane. It's just the way this works, there's always an uncomfortable pioneering phase, but if the designers like it, they'll just have to push through. Don't give up.

You've seen the industry at its highs and its lows, and you've been at Chrysler since the start of your career. Where do you see the field of industrial design going?

It's been quite an interesting trip. I joke that I've worked for about 80 different CEOs. The last four CEOs had very different views—different interests in design. You need a thick skin, but you have to be careful that it doesn't become too thick and you lose yourself. What keeps me going is that there's always a future. We're one product-cycle away from being on top of it. We're one car away from winning the awards. That's always kept me positive. At the same time, cars take four years to come to fruition, sometimes even five to 10 years. So you have to invest in your people; try to make them comfortable at work. Find creative ways to make them at ease, to work out the culture side of business.

I think the culture is overlooked sometimes. If you work hard, you tend to forget that culture-building is as important as the products you make. When times are rough, it's what keeps people together and creates bonds. Without forcing it, having social parties and social events really makes a fertile environment for friendships and bonds. So if they get another offer they have to weigh the new job for a couple more bucks against this value that they have. I take this very seriously. Personally, it's kept me at Chrysler. I mean I could leave tomorrow, but I'd be leaving 300 of my friends behind. So I've been trying to create that type of an environment. It's not easy, but it's something I'm striving to do.

Anything that we didn't cover that you'd like to add? Any final words of wisdom?

I think there are two things. One thing is that you're going to come across, as I have of late, some pretty tough personalities. It's challenging because not every style works with every other style. There are times where you have to look at whether you need to reinvent yourself, or you wait and betray yourself. There's always that difficult moment in a designer's career and a designer's life where they have to reassess themselves and never forget what they're made of. Just be aware and just know that the world is always a changing place. Be ready for change, accept it, and realize that, at the end of the day, sometimes you're talking to yourself. You really have to take a deep breath and make sure you're a balanced person, and there are a lot of other things that make life worth living, so to speak. Find outlets beyond your design career. Find other things to give yourself a mental break. If you overwork the muscle, you'll fatigue it. Keeping your mind as fertile as possible, and as positive as humanly possible, is where great ideas come from. [BI]

To see the work of Ralph Gilles and Chrysler, please visit http://breaking.in

MARIANNE GRISDALE VICE PRESIDENT & CREATIVE DIRECTOR TEAMS DESIGN CHICAGO

What kinds of portfolios get your attention these days? What brings in an industrial designer for an interview?

During the height of the worst recession, about a year ago, we had placed an ad on Coroflot and we got over a thousand responses. Part of it was because the ad was for a junior designer. Unfortunately, in our field people like to hire someone with a little bit more experience, so a position available for a junior designer was very rare, and they all jumped at the opportunity. That meant I had to figure out some way to wade through all the applicants because we don't have a human resources department.

The first thing that I do is to actually read the cover letters. I'm looking to see if the person has enough writing skills to be able to correspond with our clients and kind of understand the intent. You'd be amazed at how poorly written some of these things are. I'd get things that were more like text messages where they don't capitalize their I's, they write things like "LOL." I also look at their résumé. I got some résumés where they put everything they've ever done into a résumé that is literally 10 pages, even though they've never held an actual design job. I reject that sort of craziness right out of hand. Basically, even before I get to their portfolio, I've weeded some people out.

"AS FAR AS I'M CONCERNED: WRITING, SKETCHING, SPEAKING—THAT ALL FALLS UNDER COMMUNICATION SKILLS. GOOD IDEAS DON'T MATTER IF YOU CAN'T COMMUNICATE THEM."

When I get to the portfolio, I'm looking for mechanical ability. There should be some sort of project that shows parts moving through space and an understanding of what a product must do. Lots of junior designers have a hard time understanding the support that is needed because we often have to submit our products to FDA, UL, or CE, the European certifications. We are not expecting

someone with a portfolio to know everything, but we're expecting them to have a certain level of understanding. In addition, we are looking for aesthetic ability. It's not just about understanding what looks good, it's also about understanding what happens when two forms meet. If I see a portfolio that's all iPhone shapes, I'm not really interested because I can't tell if that person understands more sculptural forms, things that are more organic and what happens when those organic forms meet. Obviously, we look at the writing and the sketching. As far as I'm concerned: writing, sketching, speaking—that all falls under communication skills. Good ideas don't matter if you can't communicate them. A certain level of sketching skills is important. They don't have to be a sketch virtuoso, although that's always nice, but they need to be able to sketch well enough and comfortably enough to communicate their ideas.

That leads to one of the most important things that needs to be in their portfolios, which is showing us their thinking. To me, a portfolio should be telling a story, and the story should be about them. I want to know what was happening in their head during the course of that project, what decisions they made and why they made them. Obviously, it's hard to understand but if I don't see that progression in a project, then I can't really tell if that person is just a one-hit wonder, or if they actually have multiple good ideas and if they chose an idea for a logical reason. When we do a project, we will write a proposal and we might have to show six to eight good ideas to the client. Each one of those ideas has to be viable, and they should all be good ideas. It never fails that the idea you like the least will be the one the client will pick, so you really don't want to show any bad ideas. So if you're hiring an employee that can only come up with one idea, that places a lot of burden on the rest of the team. We really need people who can come up with multiple good ideas to any given solution.

We get a lot of applicants for whom English is not their first language. Their language skills may not be as good as somebody who was born here. Nonetheless I look for craftsmanship in the portfolio and some of that comes down to spelling. Obviously, if somebody is from another country I can sort of overlook some things, but I'm looking for how careful they are and if they are smart enough to get somebody else to help them. I've seen some amazing, well-crafted portfolios from people from other countries whose English skills aren't that great; that craftsmanship and attention to detail is as important as an amazing idea. You need to have both of those abilities.

Out of those thousands of portfolios you went through, I'm curious to hear about the one or two that caught your eye.

We had two people who really impressed us. One was a woman who had sensitivity to certain projects. The other was a man from a local school and he had creative projects and had a confidence about him that we could use. We tried them out for three months and then we hired them all.

If you had an opportunity to guide a student on how to create a product design portfolio that would resonate for you, what would you tell them?

Students should focus on telling a great story from start to finish about what was going on in their head during the project. They should show that they came up with other good ideas and that they made logical decisions. The craftsmanship in the portfolio, cover letter, and résumé should be their very best.

So once you bring in a designer for an interview, what do you expect to learn from them?

My boss has done several speeches at conferences about the personality of teams and how to put together a good team and how we look at teams. One of the things that we noticed is that we had too many introverts on our team at the time. Some of our introverts are some of our best designers—they are absolutely amazing—but the problem is you can't work with them in front of clients. We were really looking for somebody who was more outgoing.

We interviewed somebody who was really talented, with a great portfolio, but he just didn't interview well. He said things like, "Getting back to the grind..."; he just didn't sound excited or enthusiastic about working. We don't want to hire somebody like that. We want to hire somebody who's enthusiastic and likes their job. Let's face it, some days it's easier to get up and go to work than others. It's natural; that's life. But we really want people who really enjoy design

and enjoy the kind of design we do. We're not doing beautiful, sculptural objects that go into MoMA every day. Sometimes, if we get lucky, we'll get items that get placed in their gift shop, and that's great. A lot of what we do is similar to the Bosch power tools, where the person who is appreciating it is some contractor who's dirty, and storing it in the back of his truck. That should be equally rewarding to a person and equally as glamorous. If it's not, they're not going to be happy here.

What characteristics or qualities are necessary to be a successful industrial designer?

I think it depends what you're applying to. One of my complaints with these applicants was that, because of the job situation in the last few years, people have been applying to jobs that maybe weren't their first choice. They don't bother to hide that in their application or their portfolio. Look to personalize and show your passion for the job you're applying for. I would say passion for your job, for design, has to be there in order to be successful. You have to enjoy it. I think there's room for a lot of different personality types. We have some designers who are very much introverted—they don't like to talk in meetings. Sometimes I feel like my job is to purely be a translator because they don't feel confident about talking in front of clients. They're shy and not terribly verbal to begin with, so I'm left to talk for them. That's okay because they have great talents. On the other hand, somebody who's very verbal and great at presenting things—able to see the big picture and organize things—there's a lot of room for people like that, too.

I worked for a place where they tried to make us all cookie cutters, and you had to be good at everything. Nobody is good at everything. Nobody. The best you can do is to try to balance your team with a combination of personalities and make sure that all the different skills that are needed are covered by various aspects of the team.

How did you break into the industry?

There aren't too many women in design. When I was in high school, because I was good at math and science, they tried to push me towards engineering. They thought they needed more female engineers in the field. That was never my interest. I was much more interested in art. I took a lot of art classes and really enjoyed that aspect of things. I was lucky because my mom worked for a university, and I was applying to architecture schools and they had a program that I was interested in. It was a more art-based rather than civil engineering-based program, so I was applying to things like that. In the meantime, I had been taking classes in architecture that the college recommended, and one class that I took was a portfolio class for high school students at the College for Creative Studies in Detroit. While I was there, I really liked the school and I met a lot of people and had a great time that summer. I took a bunch of classes in the fall of my senior year in high school, and one of them that I took was "Intro to ID" and I fell in love. I applied to CCS and got accepted.

It really fit me well; the instructors encouraged me a lot. I graduated at the time when the market was really bad. I basically called every design firm I could find. This was before the Internet, so I went to the library and used the yellow pages. I applied to anybody I could find that looked like they might do industrial design. I called all of them and made appointments and then drove out on my own dime, stayed with friends and interviewed with anybody who would let me in the door. I got a bunch of job offers and then I picked one in Chicago.

Out of about 50 interviews I've completed so far with global industrial design leaders, you're only about the fifth or sixth woman that I've interviewed. This field is undoubtedly still dominated by men. What would you say to women who are considering pursuing industrial design? Do you have any words of advice for them?

I think it's a lot easier now than it used to be. I still ran into some issues when I was interviewing—when I was first looking for a job out of school. Things that I had hoped were more issues of my mother's generation unfortunately were not. I think a lot of that, with each decade, is going away. I've been working for more than 20 years now and I see that there's a lot less of that than there used to be. I'd say just stick with it. It is a little intimidating. You have to be a strong personality to go into a room full of men and hold your own. I think with every generation women are being taught that they can do that. I think they have the skills.

I'm not quite sure why there aren't more women in the field. Perhaps there still isn't a lot of awareness in high schools about what kind of career path this is. They don't know much about industrial design and how it fits women as well as men. I also think that there are a lot of projects that are suited really well to a woman's point of view. I've worked on projects that were products designed for women, that had men as well as women on the team, and some of the men came up with the best ideas, and vice versa. What I'd say is that teamwork is really important on any given project, and having the gender roles and points of view represented on a team is very important. I know it sounds cheesy because our name is TEAMS, but we really do look at it that way.

If you were just starting out now, what advice would you give yourself?

I thought I got a good education. I had a good portfolio. It got me job offers and it gave me the foundation for the skills that I needed to get started. Obviously, I've learned a lot since then, but what I wish is that I had gone to a school that had more internships. I think that understanding what the real world requires of you helps. It also helps if you understand what you need to learn and that motivates you even more. It gives you a better idea of what you do and don't like, so when you go out into the world looking for a job you can pinpoint what fits you the best. That's beneficial for both the employer and the employee.

I feel that internships are good because they show you why you need to learn things; they also open your mind up to new topics. For instance, if you told me in school that I'd be interested in anthropology, I would've told you that you are nuts, because I had no interest in it at the time. Now that I understand how anthropology relates to design and how it could help me in doing a better job for the end-users, I would welcome the chance to study it. I would embrace those courses in a whole different way than I would've back then.

Another thing I would've done is that I would've gotten a master's [degree] earlier. I never got it and I regret that. Whether it be in anthropology, or business, or product development. I think that gaining that extra knowledge would've helped me do a better job and it would've helped me in my career to get to a certain level faster. Personally, my interests are in the research aspect of design because I've seen how initial discovery research can really give you great insights into how you can make a product better, or completely different. There are a lot of unmet needs in many different kinds of products, and the only way to discover those is to go out there and follow somebody and really understand how they're using their product.

To me that's more of my passion, but on the other hand, if you're better at the selling, the strategy, and the numbers and business end of it, I can certainly see where an MBA could help. Quite honestly, an MBA would help me too, because I ended up going a little bit down that route. We do research at TEAMS but it's not our primary focus and because we are small, the three of us that run the office wear a lot of different hats. One of those hats has to be running the business end—the numbers. I think again one of the great things about being a designer is that we are sort of jacks-of-all-trades, masters of nothing. That ability to put yourself in someone else's shoes or design something for them also allows us to put ourselves into a lot of roles within a company.

Where do you see the future of industrial design going as it evolves further in the 21st century?

I think that understanding how different disciplines understand each other is really important and that seems to be the future. Not so much being everything to everyone but being really good at what you do and how you support the other disciplines that must go into developing a product. What that means is, for instance, one of the things that we do a lot of is visual brand languages. What we're looking at is how can we make product experience—from the moment you take it out of the box, to the moment it has to eventually get recycled in some fashion—more positive? How can it reinforce the brand attributes? The design of the packaging, the design of the product, of the support materials, how something is displayed, all of those experiences add up to a successful brand. That's more and more how the future is going to go. I hear more and more companies trying to repeat what we're doing.

The other thing that I see is that, while the US is still strong in terms of design, I'm seeing a lot of other countries starting to produce some really amazing

designers. So the future of design is going more global. We are going to get a lot more competition. Right now we have an intern who's from India, doing his master's in Sweden with an internship in Chicago. That's pretty cool. BI

To see the work of Marianne Grisdale and TEAMS Design, please visit http://breaking.in

DAN HARDEN
PRESIDENT, CEO &
PRINCIPAL DESIGNER
WHIPSAW
SAN JOSE

What kinds of industrial design portfolios get your attention? What brings a potential candidate in for an interview?

Portfolios that grab my attention are visually captivating, communicative, different, and holistic in skill representation. I look for a vision, attitude, or approach that reveals the designer's personality. Good problem-solving abilities must always be demonstrated—the fluffy portfolios without it are rejected. A good portfolio is clear and concise with a natural flow to it like a good essay. We look for good skills too such as sketching, CAD, model making and storyboards because candidates will be producing these kinds of deliverables for our clients if they are hired. It helps if some of the work in the portfolio was produced while at an internship in a consultancy so they're not completely green. We look for evidence of passion in a portfolio. Passion is a powerful internal force that spawns creativity, feeds ambition, and makes one naturally curious about learning.

What is this passion that you're looking for? How can you tell this person is as passionate as your team?

Well you really need to meet them to gauge their passion, but what we produce as designers should represent what we believe in and that's what we look for. Your design solution says a lot about you. We look for emotionality and rationality at the same time. We also look for fearlessness, cleverness, and curiosity because those are telltale signs of a passionate mind at work. Surprise me—make me think, "What the heck is that?" or "Wow, that's brilliant!" Don't be afraid to stick your neck out, and always express your passion in your own unique way.

Could you talk about the latest industrial design portfolio you saw that really captured your attention?

A young woman from Korea sent her portfolio and it was very minimal, clever, and even poetic. Nothing fancy, just very real and very simple. Her cover letter even had the same stream of [consciousness]. She connected on every level.

It sounds like what gets your attention is something that's aesthetically pleasing with functional resolution?

Yes, because that's a lot of what good design is. Aesthetics are personal, and therefore reveal the most about a designer. The aesthetics of a portfolio are important because it's the first impression and if you blow that, it's over. You might be a good problem solver but if your aesthetics are bad you'll struggle selling the idea. Beyond aesthetics we look for functional resolution in all forms: Does it work? How do users benefit from it? Is it feasible? Is it relevant?

What characteristics or qualities do you look for in an industrial designer? What do you expect to learn about them during the interview?

Designers are complex and emotional right-brain types and sometimes difficult to interview because they aren't verbal. We just try to uncover their virtues, talent, and passion by having them share their work and philosophy. We look for energy and enthusiasm but, at the same time, we're looking for sincerity and authenticity—people who are trying to do good things with their creative abilities. We have wonderful employees who, on the surface, are not openly passionate, but they are intense, quiet, and brilliant. Others are loud, artsy, and completely nuts. We look for all types. It makes the environment dynamic plus

it serves our clients well. For example, a serious medical client may not be comfortable with a wacko emotional designer but a gaming client would be. In a consultancy, people are everything so recognizing good qualities in designers is critical.

How did you break into the industry?

I've never really thought of myself as ever breaking into the industry because I have thought about design practically my whole life. As a kid I was always drawing, painting, and taking things apart to figure out how they worked. I built a lot of dangerous things like go-carts, mini-bikes, and bombs. Let's just say my parents were very patient as I expressed my unfettered creativity. It wasn't until design school that I realized there was a profession for someone like me called industrial design. I went to the University of Cincinnati, which has a co-op program where you alternate work and school quarters.

I suppose my first break into the design industry was that series of three co-op jobs. My first co-op was at Richardson Smith, a very notable ID firm in the seventies and eighties. I was asked to sketch, render, and build models alongside professionals at the top of their game, solving real-world design problems. This is where I had an epiphany about design and my future. I was 19 years old and enlightened from then on. My second co-op job was with the great design master George Nelson in New York City. George was an inspiration because he encouraged "design thinking" way before we called it that. My third co-op was at Hewlett-Packard where I got a taste of what it was like to be a designer in a large corporation. At HP a design competition took place to create the new design language for all HP products, and my design direction was chosen. By the time I graduated, I had products on the market not only for HP but also Chemical Bank, Galion, and NCR. I was on a roll without really knowing it.

Throughout school I was always crazy about European design, especially work from Mario Bellini, Ettore Sottsass, and Dieter Rams. I decided to move there after school to learn more about it. I found a good job in Germany at Dolphin Design where I did automotive and housewares work. During that year in Germany I was curious about a radical design firm down in the Black Forest called Esslinger Design (later renamed frog design). I got on a bus and went to meet their leader, Hartmut Esslinger, and we hit it off right away. He and frog design would later play an important role in my design career.

After a year in Germany I missed the creative energy of the US and went back to New York to work at Henry Dreyfuss Associates, a renowned old design agency. There I was able to break into the "big" design industry, designing major products for AT&T, Bell Labs, Polaroid, and Johnson & Johnson. This is where I built a portfolio and learned the business of design like how to write a proposal, sell design, run a project, and achieve financial results. These business skills are essential, especially if you want to be a successful consultant.

At this point in my career, at age 29, I had built a solid base and I wanted to work for the best firm in the world, which at that time was the one and only frog design. No other firm had reached that level of respect and admiration, highly acclaimed for their Apple and Sony work. I went to see Hartmut in California this time and he said, "What took you so long, can you start next week?" Other than founding my own firm later, that was the move of my career. It was my big "break" as most designers who went to frog design back then would admit. I tore into that job with vigor, designing as much and as fast as I could, loving every minute of it. I had the good fortune to work with great clients such as Steve Jobs at NeXT, Larry Ellison of Oracle, Rupert Murdoch of News Corp, and Stan Shih of Acer. We hired talents like Yves Béhar, Brett Lovelady, and Gadi Amit and we built a world-class team. The company quadrupled in size. I was there for 10 years starting as a senior designer and eventually became president by 1998. After being there for 10 good years and about to turn 40 I decided it was time to start my own firm. Whipsaw was the culmination of almost 20 years of hard work and a dream that is still unfolding.

Looking back at my early and mid-career I suppose I had many breaking in moments. My ultimate goal was to have my own company and I drove toward that goal step by step. I looked for experiences and jobs that would teach me the most, that fit my design values, and that didn't compromise my beliefs. I looked for firms whose work just spoke to me. Choose your experiences well because the path behind you brings you to the path in front of you. Fate takes care of the rest.

If you were starting out now, and knowing what you know now, what advice would you give yourself?

First, that design as a profession is not only immensely gratifying to do but it's one of the best ways to make positive change in our world today. Now more than ever, designers are sought after, listened to, respected, and even revered for their creativity. You must jump on this opportunity. Drop all fear. Try new things, stretch yourself, experiment, and have fun. As an imaginative person it's important to keep your mind open so that inspiration comes to you naturally, without overthinking it. Most of all just go for it. Don't care what anyone thinks, especially your design peers who are all trying to out-cool one another. Also, don't rely on formulas. Much of the world is driven by them—just look at education, medicine, and law. Of course, repeatable formulas have advanced civilization. If you want to go to the moon you need them but if you want to imagine going to the moon, the algorithms don't do a darn thing for you.

"WE LOOK FOR EVIDENCE OF PASSION IN A PORTFOLIO. PASSION IS A POWERFUL INTERNAL FORCE THAT SPAWNS CREATIVITY, FEEDS AMBITION, AND MAKES ONE NATURALLY CURIOUS ABOUT LEARNING."

It's kind of cliché, but the best advice, especially for a young designer, is to never stop learning and be terminally curious about everything. Knowledge and insight gleaned from observing and candid living are the best source of creativity. This profession is directly affected by advancements in technology, behavioral science, material science, process methodologies, business models, and many more. Every time I think that the ultimate new way for doing something has been found, boom it's reinvented. Instead of being daunted by this flood of changeful information, revel in it.

As a consultant you become an "amateur expert" in many fields. It's an absolute joy to learn about so many fields, especially when you know how each would benefit from what you have to bring to the table. I have designed many products for the computing and communication fields, but what is really interesting are the obscure vertical markets that require ground-up learning on the part of the designer and often where more innovation can be had. For example I have done baby-feeding products, slot machines, surveyor's GPS, vascular surgery equipment, agricultural guidance systems, ion chromatography equipment, and sleep apnea machines. In every case I knew little to begin with but after swimming in the problem and becoming the user, answers came. After a while one sees the common elements between all fields, realizing they are all united by end-user pains, desires, and a quest for simplicity. I am convinced that raw learning and curiosity fuel most innovation.

Where do you see the future of industrial design going?

ID is becoming more complex and has a much wider definition than it did in the past. On one end of the spectrum, design is returning to its roots where craft, materials, and product quality are the primary focus. At Apple, designers start with a block of aluminum and experiment with what to do with it, the same way Charles Eames did when he experimented with laminated plywood 70 years ago. I will often go into the shop and experiment with foam or clay when trying to solve a design problem. This intimacy with the problem is still one of the most gratifying and effective ways to discover a solution. For a while it seemed like an outdated process considering all the CAD and rapid prototyping available today but I'm happy to see more designers embracing craft again.

On the other end of the spectrum, design is being transformed by technology where ID will continue to be tasked with creating our digital experience, which is decidedly not like the above description. Industrial designers are great at digital UX because we relate to a material world where reflected light paints a surface, tactility is tangible, and buttons actually go "click." In the future, this rich dynamic someone has with an analog experience will be better replicated in the digital experience, making them more integrated and therefore more intuitive.

The scope and reach of design will grow in the future too. I've seen design go from styling a product, to styling an experience, to styling a business, to styling infrastructures. I am very interested to see where this goes, especially where design is applied to social problems. This will force industrial designers to work with a wider variety of disciplines including architects, government officials, policy makers, etc., and this will surely expand the definition of ID.

Industrial designers (and the world) must soon figure out what it really means to be sustainable and this must become a mantra of the profession in the future. People will always need things, and industrial designers will always be asked to create them in as great a quantity as possible in order to "feed the machine." That's the paradox for ID. We help to create millions of good things that take energy to produce and that fill space.

We're likely not going to change the construct of our consumption-focused capitalist society. However, in the future designers can influence how people feel about their products by building in sustainability values. I think there are two parts to this. The first are the more obvious external things we can do to make products more responsible, for example, using less material, reducing manufacturing energy consumption, and making products recyclable. You should be doing this already. Thanks to technology, we will be able to come closer to achieving these goals on a much larger scale. Things are getting smaller and more efficient all the time. Designers need to keep the pressure on the technologists and engineers to continue this reductionist trend. We do this by making sure that less being more is a most desirable trait to consumers. We make sure that sleek, slim, minimal stuff remains cool. We beautify simplicity. This presents an economic stimulus too, which is often the only way to get clients to do the right thing.

The second part of the sustainability solution is harder. It's internal to what users and their societies believe about material wealth and conservation. The biggest sustainability problem by far is the sheer quantity of things humans make, consume, and desire, and it's only getting worse. Developing a global positive attitude about conservation is the key. To make and consume less is opposed to capitalism but that's what we have to do in the long run. We have to accept that no economic growth or even negative growth is okay. We all seek peace of mind and fulfillment on some level, but that does not have to mean more stuff. Is it possible for designers to help change attitudes about conservation? Absolutely. Design is a communication tool that needs to express quality of experience, not quantity of experience, and although marketers may disagree, timeless high quality/high value design is the most sustainable in the long run.

Finally, in the future I think design and business will eventually eliminate cultural diversity. At the beginning of my career I noticed way more cultural diversity. It was easy to see the difference between Japanese design, German design, French design, Italian design and American design. Now, if you didn't see a logo on a product you'd be hard-pressed to tell me where it comes from. I once mimicked the tri-bar K'un elements from the Korean flag into the ventilation pattern of a Korean computer called Trigem, and it took over the number one market position because their customers said it looked "distinctly Korean and that makes me proud." I miss that differentiation and pride of place that comes from designing products with cultural expression. However if better design is being produced all around, and if a global style built on common values is more effective at bringing us together, should cultural diversity even matter?

You asked George Nelson once what is was like being a designer, so now I'm going to ask you the same question: What's it like being a designer?

Being a designer is fun. I get to be creative all day long and I get paid for what I love to do the most. Design is such an integral part of my life that I don't see it as work or my profession but rather as my purpose. I do it because it feels right. If you don't feel design in your bones, don't pursue it as a profession.

Being a designer entails wearing lots of hats, especially as a design consultant. Every day I assign about 50% of my time to solving design problems; I sometimes work individually, sometimes with our team, and sometimes with our clients. The other 50% of my day is spent running a design firm, which involves strategic planning, business development, accounting reviews, recruiting, public relations, and more.

Working effectively with clients is an art form. You have to be pragmatic when working with their engineers, ebullient when working with their marketing [people], and visionary when working with their CEO. To be a successful consultant, one needs to be able to turn these traits on instantly. I find it helps to be really honest about the issues, tell a client your sincerest opinion, and also express enthusiasm and passion, of course. People follow when they witness your honesty and see competence in action. ⊡

To see the work of Dan Harden and Whipsaw, please visit http://breaking.in

PAUL HATCH
FOUNDER & PRESIDENT
TEAMS DESIGN
CHICAGO

What kinds of portfolios get your attention these days? What brings in an industrial designer for an interview?

There's the obvious: looking for a well-rounded set of skills. For the junior designer, we need to see the skills demonstrated, but the most important thing is to see the "right" thinking. The type of thinking that has the ability to explore and find multiple solutions, and chose the right path—the demonstration of using both the left and right half of your brain. The ability to explore and feel your way around a problem, using a certain amount of empathy and a general sense of optimism that show multiple solutions to a problem. Finding those solutions, whether they are for styling or practical solutions, is a very creative process. Then you've got to use the other half of the brain to show rational judgment on how they can be combined and how you can make something better. When it comes down to the portfolio, we are looking for the sort of person who can already show that ability to look at multiple paths simultaneously and be able to use rational judgment to find the best one.

Have you seen a portfolio recently that embodied those qualities, and can you talk about it? What about it stood out?

The work that a good portfolio shows catches your attention—it attracts your initial interest. The second line of judgment isn't just on how good the sketches are or how good the products look; it's to understand how they came to these good designs. The recent ones that I've got in mind showed a lot of loose sketches—not doctored sketches—they were the real thing. You could see this person is thinking on paper and having a conversation with the paper back and forth. They can draw the ideas rapidly, reading them through their eyes back into their brain, and then they react again with another idea and the cycle continues. You can witness if that happened on the paper. Having that ability shows that they can get in that creative mindset while also judging and weighing up what they see. So sketches obviously demonstrate thinking on paper.

When you bring in a designer for an interview, what do you expect to learn from them then?

The interview conversation gives you some clues as to the knowledge they have behind their ideas. Did they explore? Did they get passionate about their idea or their work? Are they self-critical about it? If they did it again would they do it better? We are looking for signs of an inquisitive, passionate, and critical designer. Those three elements show creative and critical thinking working in combination. We also study what we call "designer's DNA" to help us think of how the skills of individuals balance out. The "DNA" is not attained by looking at their set of skills but their mental attributes, their inherent personality traits. If you're interviewing someone and the job entails a fair amount of research, and if the person has never done research, how do you know they can do it?

You can't just judge a person by a set of skills or the list on their résumé; you need to understand who they truly are. Does this person have empathy? Do they have a good "gut feel"? Is that demonstrated when they are sketching a product? When I'm talking to this person do I get a sense that they're listening and taking in the information? Those are the attributes that, for instance, could make a

good ethnographic researcher. They would need to connect with people, observe, and mentally record a lot of information in a very rational way. So we try to bring the interview away from skills and towards these "DNA" attributes.

It sounds like an industrial designer has to wear multiple hats.

Absolutely. Here at TEAMS we stretch all of our industrial designers' depth as far as we can. We don't pigeonhole anyone. Projects are run by multiple people who bring different things to the table. While everyone might be very well rounded and have a good set of skills and attributes, each person has certain things that they can do better than anyone else. A junior designer coming straight from school may not have all the experience, but they do have those traits inside them such as empathy, gut feel, a good eye—with those we can move mountains.

What qualities or characteristics are necessary to be a successful designer in the long term?

Experience and skill. You gradually build skills that utilize your strongest traits. Your skills evolve drastically as you develop from a junior into a senior designer and head towards management. However, your personal traits stay with you. For instance, you use empathy differently as a senior designer—you're not just putting yourself in the shoes of the user as a junior designer does, but you're also connecting with the client in a personal way and motivating your team. Design has the ability to utilize all kinds of traits really. Long-term success for a designer is about finding the right path for you moving forward and not squeezing into predefined boxes. You will only excel in the areas that truly suit your traits.

How did you break into this industry?

A lot of graduating designers expect that you go through three to five jobs and that in five, 10, 15, 20 years you'll have your own firm, your own place. It seems to be a kind of standard expectation. There's nothing wrong with that per se, but it's not necessarily the right path for everyone. I guess I had the same expectations coming out of school, but what happened was quite different. I was working at TEAMS Design in Germany and was at the right place at the right time. I was given the opportunity to open up an office in Chicago for TEAMS Design, their very first branch. It was a great opportunity and a huge challenge. There was a lot to learn about setting up a company and managing people—it was a big transition. The company has had very steady growth since the very beginning. We've been very lucky. The advantage I had, compared to someone setting up their own company, is that we already had a portfolio—not an individual's portfolio but a wider TEAMS Design portfolio. In 1998 when we incorporated in Chicago we were unknown in the States, so arriving here was like starting from scratch— except with a large portfolio of successful products.

If you were just starting out now, what advice would you give yourself?

In this current economy there are a lot of people who are motivated to do their own thing, to set up their own shop almost straight from school. Very few will end up successful. It's very hard with those few years of experience and lack of produced products to do it. Their design abilities may be top-notch and they may be very talented, but there is a lot to be learned from a good few years working within a business.

> *"YOU'VE GOT TO LOOK INSIDE OF YOURSELF AND SEE WHAT MOTIVATES YOU. WHY DO YOU DESIGN?...THAT WILL GIVE YOU SOME CLUES AS TO WHAT KIND OF A DESIGNER YOU ARE AND WHAT YOU CAN BRING TO THE TABLE..."*

It's hard to say how long that is, maybe five or 10 years, but bringing true experience to the table can make up for the lack of market successes a startup company typically would have. It sounds cliché to talk about personal experience being so important, but the company gets built very much upon the individuals. The DNA of the company is the DNA of individuals. The difference defines whether you run just another design company, or run a successful design company. To be successful at something, it's not just motivation and knowledge; you also have to have the personal traits, a broad skill set, and real-world experience. It makes a big, big difference.

So what advice would I give? Gain all the experience you can get before starting your own company. Another thing is to understand your core strength; do not try to be everything to everyone. As soon as you realize who you truly are and what you can do, things get a lot easier and you become more successful. The answer is inside of us. You've got to look inside of yourself and see what motivates you. Why do you design? What do you get your kicks from? That will give you some clues as to what kind of a designer you are and what you can bring to the table—to the world—that may be different from other people.

Where do you see the future of industrial design going as it evolves further in the 21st century?

Industrial design has gained a lot of credibility over the last decade, but it's still in its teenage years. It's getting its first recognition from the world around it. In the near future we will see a phase of maturity. Understanding how industrial design and user experience are merged together and how they can become much stronger together. There are now many industrial designers moving into design management and strategy, defining design thinking as a recognized tool. Many designers are going deeper into research and getting to the source of inspiration before any design sketch is made. It's expanded into lots of different areas beyond what it traditionally did. Industrial design originally had artisan and craft roots, but I think we've now expanded it into many tangential areas. That's all exciting, but where does it all take us? That has yet to be understood. This is the maturity stage I'm talking about. At some point we will realize what it means to be us. It's an interesting path, and the next 10 years are going to be the most interesting years in industrial design yet.

What makes you say that?

There's now recognition, experimentation, and a holistic expansion of the field. This post-teenage stage will bring the understanding of who we are and we'll have the ability to deepen that. There's a lot of what we do that's less than perfect. There are a lot of products in the world that are far from being truly solved and meaningful. But we're soon going to have a lot more truly meaningful products that tie in experience with user interaction, with emotions, with the brand, and the entire product line. Designers will look at products as part of a family and not just as a singular icon. The profession needs to do that a lot more than it is doing right now. We very often get caught up in a singular product and a singular idea and the singular visualization of that idea, but it could be so much more. BI

To see the work of Paul Hatch and TEAMS Design, please visit http://breaking.in

JULIE HEARD
OWNER
MIXER DESIGN GROUP
AUSTIN

What kinds of portfolios get your attention these days? What brings in an industrial designer for an interview?

I like to see a balance of thinking and skills, substance behind the pretty pictures. I love to see sketches; that's kind of a lost art as people focus more on 3D CAD and making beautiful renderings. You can make a beautiful rendering of an unattractive or poorly designed product. Sketching by hand shows raw talent, though 3D CAD and visualization have become essential skills.

Have you seen a portfolio recently that resonated with you, and what about it stood out?

I've seen a few that resonated with us and the work we do. We are primarily a technology-focused firm, so if I see a lot of furniture or consumer goods, they don't interest me as much as something that's more relevant to the work we do. And, of course, the portfolios that really have beautiful sketching, those are the ones that catch my eye.

If an industrial student came up to you and asked, "What should my portfolio be like? What do I need to show you in order to work with you?", what would you tell them?

Show the whole process, but in an efficient way: research, concepts, refinement, final design. Carefully consider the graphic design/layout of each of your projects and only show work you are proud of and can talk confidently about.

What do you expect to learn from the designer during an interview?

We are a small office so personality is very important. We wouldn't hire someone—as talented as they might be—if they don't appear to be a fit for our organization. We want to learn a bit more about them, how they got interested in product design in the first place. We also make sure that people understand what our company is about, what we do.

"I LOVE TO SEE SKETCHES; THAT'S KIND OF A LOST ART AS PEOPLE FOCUS MORE ON 3D CAD AND MAKING BEAUTIFUL RENDERINGS."

If they show work from team projects, I like to understand what contribution they've made to the process. When we interview students from the same school, we usually see the same project more than once, and it's interesting how they talk about it. From initial research and concept development to the implementation and documentation—the right brain, left brain stuff—can they communicate all of these things effectively and confidently?

What characteristics or qualities are necessary to be a successful industrial designer?

Talent! Communication, both visual and verbal, being able to quickly communicate your ideas, and think on your feet. Open-mindedness. What I mean is, you can't love your ideas so much that you're not willing to let other people influence them. You have to let your ideas evolve to best solve the problem and meet the needs of your client.

How did you break into this business?

I thought I was going to go into graphic design, as it was among the few creative careers that I was aware of at the time. When I started looking at colleges, I quickly focused on the College for Creative Studies in Detroit. They encouraged me to apply to the industrial design department, which turned out to be a very good decision. My first job out of college was at a small consulting firm and I learned a lot in the 10 years I was there: design skills, customer service, and what makes a good business. I became a member of IDSA [Industrial Designers Society of America] in college and was able to meet mentors and fellow designers because of that common connection.

What motivated you to open up Mixer with your partners?

I had worked with my business partners for about five years and we were all ready to do something different. There is a good balance between the three of us—we all have different strengths we bring to the business. We have been very considerate about the people we choose to work with and the way we position our company. It's all about relationships, and a little bit of luck.

If you were just starting out now, what advice would you give yourself?

Be confident in yourself. Authentically confident.

You're one of the few women that I'm interviewing, as there aren't that many in the industrial design field at the leadership level. I'd love to hear what advice you have for women who are trying to pursue and break into this field.

I feel really fortunate. I know to some extent that some people treated me differently. If anything, they had lower expectations of me, and that was motivating. It drove me to work harder because I didn't want people to think I needed an unfair advantage. I felt like I was rarely treated unfairly, certainly once I got into the workplace. I've heard from other women who have unfortunately had the opposite experience. At the last IDSA district conference a designer from Korea shared her story and though it was totally different culturally, I think she had a similar attitude to it as me—it just made her work harder. You don't need to work for or with people who don't appreciate your contribution. You're probably not going to change them, but you can find a school or career situation that's better for you.

Where do you see the future of industrial design going as it evolves further in the 21st century?

There's a lot of outsourcing that's being done for economic reasons and we need to figure out what unique value we provide. I think we are always going to be more in-tune with the needs of our own market: the Western consumer. We will continue to do the things that we are best at and create intellectual property in the process. Industrial design has traditionally been about the object itself, but now it is more and more about the entire experience.

Anything we didn't cover that you would like to add? Any final words of wisdom?

Send your résumé and portfolio by email—anything sent by regular mail will probably get filed away and forgotten. Know who your audience is. Don't address the cover letter to the wrong person. Do a little bit of research on the company you're targeting. In an interview we may ask you, "What do you think we do?" and we've interviewed people who really didn't know. When you send out an email, don't just ask if we have job openings and expect a personal response. Always include a résumé, a bit of a portfolio, and follow up. [BI]

To see Julie Heard's work, please visit http://breaking.in

TODD HERLITZ
DESIGN DIRECTOR
RADIO FLYER
CHICAGO

What kinds of portfolios get your attention these days? What brings in an industrial designer for an interview?

Before digging into a portfolio, I always give it a quick flip-through to get an overall sense of the designer's work. The things that usually grab me initially are exceptional sketching skills and a good feel for refined form development. These two things tend to jump out immediately because they are relatively rare.

Sketching is always a key indicator. I think of it as a language that we speak and the more competent you are at it, the greater your ability to communicate with others around you. If you struggle with visual communication, it can impede your ideation and adversely affect the thought process. Fluency is ideal.

Beyond the sketching skills, there has to be evidence of great creative thinking and problem-solving skills. This is the most important thing that we do from day-to-day in product development. While I love a beautiful sketch or rendering as much as anyone else, without some deeper thinking informing them, they are illustrations, not concepts.

The form development skills are an important indicator of the ability of the designer to cover the entire development process. There are some designers that have great ideation skills without form development abilities. There are some great form-givers with weaker problem-solving skills. Ideally a candidate will have great ideas, can communicate them well, and is able to resolve the design in a beautiful and elegant way. Form resolution and refinement is that magical bridge from the concept to the physical product.

Has there been a student or junior-level industrial design portfolio that you've seen recently that really stood out? What made this particular portfolio successful in your eyes?

Something that always stands out as exceptional is a consistency of quality work throughout the whole portfolio. It's common to see varying degrees of maturity in a young designer's portfolio from project to project. They, after all, are learning, growing, and trying to find their "voice." When I come across a young designer's portfolio that's exceptional from cover to cover, it stands out immediately.

When you dig a little deeper, more often than not, you find that the designer has been focused on art and creativity since they were a kid. They generally will have a very supportive family and community that provide encouragement, education, and resources for them. I don't want to generalize too much, but this is definitely a pattern that I've witnessed in talking to a lot of younger creative people.

What do you think of showing work that's not industrial design in a portfolio? Things like art, photography, hobbies, etc.?

I love seeing designers have other interests like art, music, photography, etc. That said, I think that those interests belong on the résumé, and not necessarily in an introductory design portfolio. If I receive a PDF portfolio as an initial contact about a design position, I like the portfolio to be design-focused. If the candidate has a website where you can then find out more about them and their work, I think this is a good forum for sharing other work, interests, or hobbies.

Also, if they come to the office for an in-person interview, this is a good time to have examples of other interests to flesh out the conversation and give a broader picture of themselves. Having well-rounded individuals is extremely important and having activities outside of their profession indicates that they practice a healthy degree of work/life balance.

What are some common mistakes you've seen students or junior designers make in their portfolios?

Over-designing the portfolio itself. If there is visual

clutter in the layout and design of the portfolio, it detracts from their work. A piece of advice that I always give students is to think about your portfolio like an art gallery. Gallery spaces are usually designed to recede and let the artwork within it stand out. Portfolios should be treated this way as well—a clean, simple backdrop against which the strength of the designer's work can be presented. The work itself can then communicate everything the viewer needs to know about the designer's strengths, personality, and values.

What do you expect to learn from the designer during an interview?

One of the first things I like to look at is where the person went to school. Every design college has its own teaching philosophy and approach that gives you a clue into how the designer was trained.

"...THINK ABOUT YOUR PORTFOLIO LIKE AN ART GALLERY. GALLERY SPACES ARE USUALLY DESIGNED TO RECEDE AND LET THE ARTWORK WITHIN IT STAND OUT. PORTFOLIOS SHOULD BE TREATED THIS WAY AS WELL..."

I like to see examples of great work, but also want the candidate to be able to provide examples of other professional experiences. Times they've led a design direction or process, challenged an internally accepted idea, taken initiative to follow ideas they believed in, how they work in a team, even examples of past failures and what they learned from them.

I also like to get a read on work ethic. That's usually very evident in the amount of work in their portfolio. It's also interesting to find out about their earliest

work experiences: lawn mowing, paper routes, etc. I personally had a number of restaurant jobs growing up—bussing tables, washing dishes—and I know how much that makes me appreciate what I do every day. That's a perspective that I like to look for in potential candidates as well.

What is the interview process like?

I always start off with a phone interview before bringing anyone in, even if they are local. You can learn a lot about someone from a half-hour conversation. It always helps to have them walk through their portfolio and explain some things you may have missed just by reading through it. It also gives me a chance to give the candidate background on the company, the Product Development Department, and the position they would be interviewing for. You can also get a good read on personality and gauge interest in the position to see if there is potential. Then you can make an informed decision on whether or not to have them come in.

Sometimes the conversations are engaging and energizing, and those are always the people that I'd like to talk to further. When their passion for design is evident even over the phone, that's a very good sign.

What are some reasons you have rejected a candidate?

Lack of interest or passion. I have had interviews where the candidate is clearly not interested in the position and just wants to find out how much it pays. In these cases, I get off of the phone with them as quickly as possible.

What characteristics or qualities are necessary to be a successful industrial designer?

Being able to find just the right balance between creative and analytical thought.

In design, you need to be able to think as unconventionally as any artist, yet be able to pull back and frame new ideas within the context of a "real world" business. This balanced mind is the ideal, but also the most difficult to find.

How did you break into this business?

My father, John Herlitz, was a car designer, so I was always encouraged to draw and follow my creative interest from a very young age. I had originally planned on going into graphic design/illustration. When I went to college at the Cleveland Institute of Art, I fell in love with 3D design in the foundation program and changed my focus to industrial design. I was fortunate enough to have a few different job offers upon graduating college in 1996 and my first full-time job was on the Playskool team at Hasbro in Rhode Island. I then went on to work for some design-consulting firms including Altitude, Insight Product Development, and HLB.

If you were just starting out now, what advice would you give yourself?

I would give myself two pieces of advice that I now give to every student that I talk to. Be nice: it's a small community and a healthy network can lead to a strong career. Design hard: what you get out of it is a direct result of what you put into it.

Where do you see the future of industrial design going as it evolves further in the 21st century?

More and more, the value of design as a driver of intellectual property, brand integrity, and business strategy is being understood and appreciated. As a result, the role of the designer is becoming increasingly complex and we are being asked to help find solutions to more than just aesthetic problems.

There are always going to be terms of the moment like "design thinking" or "disruptive innovation." When it comes down to it, though, the designer's role is to be a functional creative entity within the business organization and use their skills to better and beautify the lives of their customers. From a junior-level designer to a senior VP of product development, this is something that we all have in common. [BI]

To see Todd Herlitz's work, please visit http://breaking.in

JASON HILL
FOUNDER
ELEVEN, LLC
LONG BEACH, CALIFORNIA

What kinds of portfolios get your attention these days? What brings in an industrial designer for an interview?

When I look at portfolios I want to see not just a shiny oh-look-I-made-a-model or I-did-this-great-Alias-rendering, but I want to see the process of how you got there. The process is the biggest thing for me. What's the inspiration? What problem are you trying to solve? Are you using some sort of philosophy? Is it driven by manufacturing process or limitations? Is it driven by purely an aesthetic nature? Or are you reinventing something that exists? Are you combining things? How did you get there? Again, the process. Is it inspired by biomimicry and nature, or is it just "I wanted to design a new bike and I wanted it to look cool and it's made out of plastic"? There are simple things and complicated things. I look for the spectrum of not what you did, but how you did it.

Have you seen a portfolio recently that really caught your eye, and what about it resonated with you?

It was a transportation design portfolio and it was the manner in which it was presented. The format was such that it was just like an existing hardcover book. The designer took examples from the book and redefined each one in his own style, as well as recreated the original designs from the book. He juxtaposed the two together and put forth his own kind of presentation. You're almost looking at a future book. It was so well prepared, and so deep, it just worked well all around. It had a great narrative alongside really good work. It had a process—you could see all the sketches that were part of the presentation, instead of just final shiny photos of the result.

It used to be you would put together a portfolio in a book, meaning a folder. Then we went along in the '90s with DVDs and eventually it was "go to my website" or "I've emailed you a PDF" or "here's a thumb-drive." It became all electronic. Now we've kind of come back to the actual, "Here's my book," and it's literally a hardcover book. That seems to be a dominant thing these days. Instead of just a website or bunch of files on an industrial design website, there's a personal touch. It's an actual hardcover book, not just bound at Kinko's, but a professional looking artifact of either their school experience or their design career.

Once you bring in a designer for an interview, what do you expect to learn from them?

I am looking for enthusiasm of the process and also whether they are able to quickly and with clear, simple language, describe what the process and the result is. I am also looking for confidence.

What qualities or characteristics are necessary to be a successful designer these days?

They need to have their finger on the pulse of things, but also be grounded in reality. And a good understanding of applications of processes to get to their result.

How did you break into this industry, and later what motivated you to open your own studio?

I was pretty focused from high school to go to Art Center and get a degree in automotive design. I was able to do that in four years with a couple of internships. At the time I graduated it was a pretty good time in the business and I was able to have a choice in which studio I wanted to work for. It was based purely on the right time and the right place. I also had the right stuff to get an offer. Once I was in the business of working for a car company, it was easy to switch to other companies. I did that for over 14 years and during the last five years I noticed the way the business model was working. There were a lot of opportunities with outside clients that were in transportation but not necessarily car design. I thought if I were a consultant doing what I do and doing it for these companies that are in need of design services, that there was a business opportunity there. To be honest, I reached a point where I didn't want to build a career anymore, I wanted to build a business.

I thought of it as a challenge; I wanted to take a look at it from a business side. Why are these companies coming in? What are they paying for and what are they getting? The importance of design in the marketplace now is, every year, gaining more traction. It's always been important, but now it is recognized as a strategic business advantage, which is even better. I saw an opportunity to create that business for myself. It also gave me control over all aspects of the process and the results. I knew I had the personality to deal with multiple clients instead of just one boss and one company.

"WHEN I LOOK AT PORTFOLIOS I WANT TO SEE NOT JUST A SHINY OH-LOOK-I-MADE-A-MODEL OR I-DID-THIS-GREAT-ALIAS-RENDERING, BUT I WANT TO SEE THE PROCESS OF HOW YOU GOT THERE."

With your first job or your internship, you should really be paying attention to what happens and why on the business side. Even in the automotive industry you have to know what's going on in the bigger picture. One should strive to be successful in the business of design, not just the process of design.

If you were starting out now, what advice would you give yourself?

Be open to every and any job. You think your specialty is one area, but if you examine it it's really your job to figure out what is the benefit of design, no matter what the client or what the product or what the industry wants. What is your value?

Your job is to communicate why design is important and to be paid properly for it. Do not underestimate or undersell the importance of design. The bottom line is, don't be afraid to charge for what you're doing.

Where do you see the future of industrial design going as it evolves further in the 21st century?

There are always opportunities, whether the economy is good or bad, if you've got the right attitude and the right product to offer. There's never been a better time, whether it's design for user experience, the application of new processes, manufacturing, anything. There's never been a better time. The future will get better as long as designers show their level of importance and don't fall short.

Anything that you would like to add that we didn't cover? Any final words of wisdom?

The beauty of young talent is that there's no fear, there's a high level of inspiration and talent, and economically that's advantageous for companies. They're relatively cheap. BI

To see Jason Hill's work, please visit http://breaking.in

HARM-WILLEM HOGENBIRK & MARC NAGEL CO-FOUNDERS PILOTFISH AMSTERDAM & MUNICH

How did you break into this business? What motivated you to start your own design practice?

HWH: I studied industrial design in Amsterdam, at Rietveld Academy, which is more of an art academy with emphasis on personal creative development and conceptual thinking. They had a very small department which was industrial design, which I felt most attracted to. During my studies, I started to work for one of the bigger industrial design agencies in Holland, where I learned the technical aspects of product design and I stayed there after my studies. This is also where I met Marc, and maybe before we continue the story, Marc can introduce himself.

MN: I am from Hamburg, Germany, where I studied industrial design, and then I went to postgraduate studies to a school in France called École Nationale Supérieure de Création Industrielle. The master's course didn't exist at the time there; it was sort of postgraduate studies. This was a very specialized industrial design school, compared to Hamburg Art Academy, and similar probably to Harm's school. Then, I did quite a bit of work in the field of interior architecture in this small office, and then I went to the agency where I met Harm. We did some projects together, and the story continues from there. We decided one day to open our own company and the main reason for that was that we wanted to have more influence on the creation of the product experience.

HWH: In the late '90s we both had the opportunity to work for a while in Taiwan. At that time the Taiwan OEM/ODM industry focused on consumer electronics. Technical developments and innovations gave enormous momentum to new product developments. Marc and I decided to specialize ourselves in the fast-paced 3C [computer, communications, and consumer electronics] business field; it just seemed to be so much more dynamic and more fun. Having an office in Taiwan gave us the opportunity of selling Western design to the local ODM industry, while selling Asian competences, like engineering, tooling, and production in Europe via our Munich office. This proposition paid off.

What were some of the main benefits of having studios at these two different locations?

MN: Taiwan was for the speed. You could get easy assignments. It was impossible in Europe at the time, because it was incredibly slow. In Europe we were looking for more strategic projects, let's say bigger projects, but it just took a lot of time to get these projects in. So as Harm said, we got a flying start with projects in Taiwan, and something [like] that was for a designer from the Western world almost unbelievable. We could realize many, many projects. When you work at a typical European agency, the number of products that end up on the market in three years is probably one project, one product. In Taiwan, in three years you may have 10 products. So the ratio, the speed and the dynamic is much bigger there, and that's something that we wanted—to create a mix of both worlds there: let's take the speed of Taiwan, and let's also get the depth of Europe that's happening, and let's mix it up together.

HWH: Yeah, speed and also the specialization and skill set of the societies there in developing consumer electronics or professional electronics.

MN: Yeah, I don't know if we said that already, but at the time we completely specialized in consumer electronics, mobile phones, notebooks, and all that. The development of that was not happening at all in Europe at that time.

What kinds of portfolios get your attention these days? What brings in an industrial designer for an interview?

MN: Well, we can draw up the ideal person which can cover the entire process, who in reality doesn't exist, but what we want to see is somebody who shows strong analytical and research skills, who is able to translate that strong product vision into a result, and who goes further into strong visualization, and in the end into realization. But this of course, is a little bit of a theoretical thing because nobody in the world can fill the whole role of this. What we like to see is somebody who is intriguing us with their story and can actually show that they dove really deep.

I can give you an example of what we'd like to see from an industrial designer: that he really tried out what he was doing. We see so many renderings and it all looks pretty, it's all nice, but then we want to see that he tried it out. That he built the prototype, that he tested it, that he met some people, that he did a video to see how these people are reacting to it, a little bit out of the ordinary. In the standard ID portfolio, you show some nice pictures, you have maybe a mood board at the beginning and then this is it, and this is something we definitely don't want to see. Everybody has it more or less, some people are better at visualization skills, some have less, but the story is really important. Understanding where you're coming from.

HWH: I'd like to add something. It is of course a very dynamic thing. First, the applicant's email is already the first screening. We get emails where they say: "Dear frog," and they continue the story, or "Dear people of Pilotship." Not careful and disinterested in really what they're doing, that is already the first screening. Then when you're looking at the portfolio, that's the second screening, so that is all fairly normal.

As the applicant you have it all under control. I would say to the applicants do your homework, and be very dedicated to what you're trying to reach from the start. So, do that in a very thorough and good way, and then when the portfolio is interesting and appealing, that means we have a nice mix of exactly the ingredients what Marc just referred to, then we can invite them in for an interview. Then we can see if the person is authentic or not. If you are authentic and you can talk with passion about how you look into the world, in combination with a good portfolio, that's such a powerful combination.

MN: It's the passion.

HWH: Yeah, the passion. It's the key.

MN: And passion can be your whatever, let's say you're a surf freak, and you tested something around that or you did something to realize your passion, there's always something that makes the story behind the product—that shows that somebody has a dedication to what he's doing. Some designers are, and this goes much deeper probably, but some designers are not able to work according to requirements or briefs. It means that they may have a brief for a project, a sort of introduction on what it is supposed to be, but then they simply did what they think is good, regardless of the brief. So there's no link between the analysis and research with the product. This should be very correlated, otherwise it is very visible immediately to somebody who knows about design that this doesn't work. Either the research was made up later, so it shows: "Hey, we also did research," or the designer is simply not capable of translating the research or a brief into a product. So, definitely the biggest issue is somebody who is not able to translate what has come up from personal analysis or briefing he gets from the client, let's say the product vision, into a design, into a product. That's maybe the thing we would look into the most.

You mentioned research. What do you expect to see in a designer's portfolio from that realm? Do you expect them to show that they went out and talked to the potential market?

MN: Yeah, I wouldn't say potential market, but potential user. We are not expecting, and it's not what we provide to our clients, this sort of market analysis—but at least when someone is presenting to us a medical product, then I expect from him that he has actually been on-site, and that he took some videos, did some interviews with the doctors, if it's a product that a doctor would use. If it's a consumer-related product, then I expect from him that he is characterizing or understanding what kind of a user will actually be using it. I'm not talking about the young dynamic user who's 24, which is more or less the dream of the designer himself, but it should be thorough, should be something you can understand—that he really stepped into the shoes of the user.

Then, we would like to see some technical reflection, there's no flying carpet yet—so, they should respect, or either they should position the product in the right time context, or simply have an understanding if what they're doing is also realistic. It doesn't mean it has to be produced tomorrow, but it can be realistic in 20 years, it has to be logical in that sense: "Well, we're using technology that's not out yet, but we positioned the project in that time context."

The last thing is the market. Let's say the more micro understanding of what kind of products make sense and having a reflection on what is out there, maybe the idea already exists and how do I differentiate myself from that, so a little bit of a business case reflection on that.

"IN THE STANDARD ID PORTFOLIO, YOU SHOW SOME NICE PICTURES, YOU HAVE MAYBE A MOOD BOARD AT THE BEGINNING AND THEN THIS IS IT, AND THIS IS SOMETHING WE DEFINITELY DON'T WANT TO SEE."

HWH: And I think it's a combination of your own imagination with the research results which in the end makes a difference. What Marc said at the beginning is so true, there are always people who have emphasis on

a very good research skill, but not so on translating it yet. Or there are people who can use research skills of others to translate that to concepts, right? There are other people who translate the research with a styling direction. That's the benefit we have being an agency of 40+ people, that you have team members with different backgrounds and skills sets to create meaningful products.

So they kind of complete each other?

HWH: We always make decisions based on what our needs are, yes. So that is the HR policy to have a balanced team with different skill sets.

You touched upon this a bit already, but what characteristics or qualities are necessary to be a successful industrial designer?

MN: I think one of the qualities we mentioned already, but I can mention it again, is the ability to translate a vision into a product, or into an experience. It sounds so simple but it's the most difficult thing.

HWH: Maybe we can make it even shorter. I think a good designer is very much able to communicate through his design, what are the values of what he is trying to do, of the service, or the product. It's communication, actually.

MN: Then of course, he has to master certain tools. Sketching is still essential. This is the quickest way to express yourself. Then you have of course, the tools like 2D or 3D renderings, or build up, these are the tools that these days more or less everybody brings in, but at different levels of expertise there. Usually somebody whose sketching is really good, he's less good in 3D, but that's not a problem. If you have a really good sketcher, who isn't as good in 3D that is okay for us—but less good is if one cannot sketch, that's the bigger problem in the end.

Why such emphasis on sketching?

MN: Because it's the quickest way to express yourself. Ideally, you are already able in the meeting with the client or workshop to sketch ideas that already show some direction.

HWH: I think it's also so intuitive, sketching. On a meeting table with a customer, you can directly show and explore your ideas and product vision, which is impossible with 3D programs. And by sketching, you can come to integrated concepts much more efficiently, because your thinking process is supported by the sketches or your sketches are supporting your thinking process.

MN: It's also easier to throw ideas away, because the sketch only takes about 30 seconds. But if you build it up in the computer, it takes you maybe an hour or something. You are very able to throw away something that just cost you 30 seconds. I think that's one of the nice things about the sketch—it's not so concrete, it's still open, it leaves space for interpretation. But of course, when it comes to presenting something to the customer, the sketch is not enough. So you have to either take the sketch into the computer. You're either going to rework it in Photoshop to come out with something that is more thrilling, or you're gonna build it up in 3D to show more detail. Actually, in 3D we need someone who's more quick than accurate, because after that there comes the process of how to implement the 3D anyway.

What are some reasons you have rejected a candidate?

MN: Maybe one thing we have to explain is that we have quite a special hiring process. Junior designers, if possible, are invited to join us for between one to three weeks, to work with us. Once we are convinced that the portfolio is good, or we had a phone interview or we met, then he or she will work with us for let's say two to three weeks, and will get paid on freelance basis. After that trial period we usually know if we will hire them. We will see how this person is interacting with the team, and also for them to see how we work, if there's a fit. This has to do with how much someone has to bring in and how quickly they can adapt to a new environment. If you have an access to a company for only two to three weeks, you have to be present from day one, be completely awake. Of course, we take this into account, but there are big differences in how people are able to create something interesting in this rather quick and rushed time.

If you were just starting out now, what advice would you give yourself?

MN: I think what is important today, and what has

changed in the last 10 years, is that you need a much broader view, meaning that you have to understand other fields as well. You have to have an affinity for the business model of your project.

HWH: What I really am much more aware of now is the position an industrial designer has within the whole product development process. I really did not have a clue back when I started. I had a dreamy, very dreamy idea about that. A designer plays a very small role in the product development process. What I maybe would've loved to have is deep knowledge of the commercial side of design, which I wasn't taught at all.

MN: Actually, the eagerness of the designer should be to take on a bigger role, bigger responsibility in the whole process. Otherwise, it's just a styling job and that's over. I mean, you have these sort of craftsman designers who are just like craftsmen doing the design job, but I think the designer that we are thinking of and who everyone probably wants to be, is a designer who has a bigger influence on the entire process. You can only have that when you take bigger responsibility in the whole process, you go beyond your typical skills of a designer, in order to also be someone who talks at the same level with the marketing guy, the technical guy, or even a CEO. In order to be able to do that you need to have the knowledge.

Where do you see the future of industrial design going as it evolves further in the 21st century?

HWH: We believe that you have to start from the user perspective to create unique user experiences, which is our mission. I see the future of design in design of services—when product development and product design are combined with user interface design and combined with business models, using modern digital infrastructures and technologies.

Anything we didn't cover that you would like to add? Any final words of wisdom?

MN: I wish the designers would actually just send us a small PDF sampler and perhaps a link to a more extensive portfolio which includes the process that we can check out online, or they can send us a second portfolio. Speed, how quick and how accessible this information is, is actually quite important. The CV that shows what you did, including your interests and experiences, this is something that's important to us. To understand who the person behind the designer is, because again—it's all people business—and it's essential that someone fits the team. [BI]

To see Pilotfish's work, please visit http://breaking.in

EDWIN JAMES DESIGN MANAGER OF STYLE INDUSTRIALIZATION, PSA PEUGEOT CITROËN PARIS

What kinds of portfolios get your attention these days? What brings in an industrial designer for an interview?

There isn't one specific type that gets my attention. The standards of creativity and presentation required will obviously be very high, but I personally look for a good technical understanding of how things are constructed as well. I work on car interiors and follow the industrialization phase of projects, which explains this specific need. I like people who can work out the big volumes, but are capable of going into great detail as well.

Design is fun. It's not just a job; it's also a way of life, a state of mind. I love people who show artistic ability based on other things than cars, the non-petrol heads.

Have you seen a portfolio recently that resonated with you, and what about it stood out?

Yes, but I can't name names. By the time you print this, I will have seen a better one.

What made this one stand out was the artistic level and the student looked like he was having fun. The trick is to get to the point as a student where you can draw anything that you can imagine, and not just imagine what you can draw. If you can draw

on automatic pilot, you will be surprised by the pertinence and innovation of what just flows out of you. In this case, I thought that the cars in the portfolio were the worst part, but when he stopped doing what he thought was expected of him and moved on to other forms of transport he revealed much more of his design potential.

One of the challenges with "standing out from the rest" is that design schools often have a way of working which tends to format a student in the direction of uniformity. A kind of "house style" where you advance based on adherence to the norm. The other dilemma is, if you are too strange and out of context you become a risk. This will mean seriously reducing the number of jobs open to you. The best thing is to show that you can play it both ways, make employers believe that you can do everything from show cars to a re-skin.

What do you expect to learn from the designer during an interview?

Their degree of motivation to join us, obviously. But I can't help thinking about how long it will take before this young person could be trusted to start running a small project, negotiate with a supplier, or be sent to the other end of the world to do design in a challenging environment.

"DESIGN IS FUN. IT'S NOT JUST A JOB; IT'S ALSO A WAY OF LIFE, A STATE OF MIND. I LOVE PEOPLE WHO SHOW ARTISTIC ABILITY BASED ON OTHER THINGS THAN CARS, THE NON-PETROL HEADS."

In short, what I expect to learn is what potential they have and how rapidly they—and we—will be able to develop it.

What characteristics or qualities are necessary to be a successful industrial designer?

Artistic ability, technical understanding, personality, and at least one built-in crystal ball.

What are some reasons you have rejected a candidate?

Rejection or acceptance is a joint decision with other managers and the Human Resources department. The most common reason is personality. Here, things become very subjective. Designers have very different profiles from the rest of the population in a company, but at the end of the day it's a team sport with a vast diversity of personalities. Will this person be complementary in the mix?

How did you break into this business?

My father had been to art school. He was a good jazz musician and a good illustrator—he worked for Disney at some point—and he drove Peugeots and Panhards in '60s and '70s England. Peugeots had a high-quality aura; they were quite a rare sight in Britain at the time. Back then, when two Peugeot owners crossed each other on the road, they used to stop, shake hands, and exchange phone numbers. Anyway, my father and his dreams certainly influenced me a lot.

So I went off to Farnham Art School, then Birmingham Polytechnic, to do industrial design, and went on to the Royal College of Art to specialize in automotive design. The trio of tutors there—Ken, Peter, and Nigel—were nice, accessible guys who cared for their students. Meeting them was decisive: they sponsored me and put me on the right tracks by introducing me to Wayne Cherry and Geoff Lawson at Bedford Trucks, then Art Blakeslee at PSA Peugeot Citroën. They basically helped kick-start my career. In the end, the key to all this was just a love of drawing and curiosity about how things are made, but I also got lucky and met the right people at the right time.

If you were just starting out now, what advice would you give yourself?

Assuming that you have mastered Photoshop, learn a 3D modeling tool, like Alias or ICEM, to a basic level...quick. Selling your ideas to management by a slick graphic presentation has always been important, but over the last few years it has become a very sophisticated art. Even if you are not the best modeler in the world, it is a great advantage to build a quick model to show the direction that you wish to take. To be able to check the quality of what others have built for you, it is essential to master a few basic functions of any tool used in the studio.

Where do you see the future of transportation design going?

Intelligent on the streets and very numerical. Efficient and reactive in the studios.

Can you elaborate a bit more? What do you mean by that?

Very hard to give you a straight answer, because this is a strategic direction for us and I can't go into detail. Detecting the changes in market direction and anticipating these trends with products is what we do. The key to this is to look beyond cars and keep an eye on the world at large: economic, social, ecological, and even geopolitical movements. If you like, a designer is somewhere between a forward-looking mirror and an amplifier of weak signals. Designers soak up all that is going on around them and must be capable of projecting their ideas at least four years into the future. For the numerical comment, it is obvious to me that the car has become a "connected" object, part of your personal network. This will give us all a lot to think about in terms of interfaces with other objects and systems. Automation will also probably play a role in the future driving experience.

Anything we didn't cover that you would like to add? Any final words of wisdom?

Yes, if you want a job, remember that there are about 400 parts to be designed on the inside of a car. So there are other things to imagine than the exteriors of red Italian sports cars. On the other extreme, environmentally friendly small-vehicle projects don't need to look like potatoes. In the end, the biggest challenge is to design a normal, mid-range car that looks great. BI

To see Edwin James's work, please visit http://breaking.in

DEREK JENKINS
DIRECTOR OF DESIGN
MAZDA NORTH AMERICAN
OPERATIONS
IRVINE, CALIFORNIA

What kinds of portfolios get your attention these days? What brings in an industrial designer for an interview?

It's hard to really qualify because you just know it when you see it. Certainly I'm looking for someone who's got a natural taste and sense of balance in their work. They look like they're drawing, illustrating, and modeling nice proportions. This is a priority for me personally, and for our brand. Second is real creativity, someone who's pushing form language, some kind of graphic language that we find fresh or appealing or relevant to the direction we are going in. Also, an awareness of technology, brand awareness, industry awareness. Someone who understands the broader picture because those demands are put on us quite regularly. The portfolios that I review on a regular basis run the gamut of really conservative to very professional but somewhat predictable, all the way to really extreme, creative, inspirational type [of portfolios], and pretty much everything in between.

We try to keep our team balanced; it's very important. Oftentimes you can get a relatively normal, predictable team but they can execute an idea really well. You'll get a successful design that way versus if you end up with a radical idea, poorly executed. Then, you're really risking success. So having a solid, experienced team with a fresh insight is really important.

Has there been a portfolio that you've seen recently that resonated with you? What about it stood out?

I feel like for the last several years the automotive design has been really pushed and dominated by the European schools and by the European brands. The last six or seven years have been really dominated by

BMW and Audi, and now it's shifted towards French brands. Most recently some of the portfolios coming out of the Strate [Collège] and some of the other smaller French schools have just been outstanding. They're very creative, very fresh, very vibrant, and very professional. The level of execution of freehand drawing all the way through digital sketching and digital modeling and then clay model execution [is excellent]. It's the whole presentation. I monitor what's going on at American schools, and I'm getting portfolios from all over the world at any given time, and I really think there's a lot of strength in France right now.

What makes their portfolios fresh?

I think a little bit of it is that we've gone through this era of very disciplined, structured, linear design dominated by Audi and I think it has had a very broad influence on Asian brands and American brands. Somehow I feel what the French offer is the next chapter. The discipline of execution is there, but with more risk-taking, breaking more rules. Not having to be so consequent with every single line and shape. Not being afraid to go just slightly over the top. It's very entertaining. The work looks very sophisticated and very artistic at the same time, and very expressive. I think that's a great balance to have, especially to push things to the next level. It's just nice to see—very nice to see.

What do you expect to learn from a designer during an interview?

I need to understand a little bit about their thought process. What motivates them as a designer? I need to know that there's an inherent natural passion and drive to do this kind of work. I think to be a successful car designer you need to be passionate about one or two things. You either really have to love cars and understand cars and be passionate about the automobile. That's where you really dig down and get your emotion, and that drives you. Or you are very passionate about creating and designing. I know designers who have their benefits and their limits. I know designers who don't really get along with people but are really amazing and deliver results. They can almost take anything and make something great out of it. I look for what drives the individuals. It inevitably leads into car discussions and cultural differences and things like that.

A major part of what designers are being asked to do today is very strategic, and I think it's a great role for design because we have a broad view on things and we are trying to look past the daily clutter to the bigger overall movement. Not everybody in the company has that skill and we naturally have to have it. I think being part of that strategy thought process and being able to articulate our view in a professional, business-like manner is extremely important, versus, "Hey, I'm here to do fresh stuff, look out."

"PEOPLE ARE PULLED HERE FROM EUROPE AND ASIA, AND GERMAN COMPANIES ARE PULLING IN THE AMERICANS AND THE JAPANESE. IT'S BECOME INTERNATIONAL SO YOU HAVE TO MEASURE YOURSELF AGAINST THAT, AND BE HONEST ABOUT IT. IT LEADS TO HARD WORK. IT TAKES A LOT TO BE COMPETITIVE."

Basically it's about the personality. If they're not jiving with the team, if they're not respectful to the team, if they have the wrong attitude and are too extroverted or too introverted [it won't work]. The general attitude is extremely important for me.

What characteristics or qualities would you say make a successful designer?

You do have to know where the business is going and generally understand how people live—what people really want. It's important that you're always applying your experience and knowledge of general life in a creative, yet thoughtful way, to what you do. That you're coming up with types of vehicles that you think would be leading in the industry, but

also capture the desire of a broad audience. Finding that balance is not easy to do, so you have to have that strategic touch and be aware of how people live. We've all seen examples of products that have come out that are just too boring and we've also seen products that really pushed boundaries but were just ahead of their time. Finding that balance is a skill within itself.

How did you break into this industry?

My story is probably somewhat of a cliché. I grew up drawing cars and loving cars, but I didn't grow up loving drawing. It was more about loving cars. I grew up here in Orange County and my dad was into air-cooled VW Beetles, Baja Bugs, dune buggies, and that kind of thing. There was always a lot of tinkering going on in the garage and a lot of remote-controlled planes and cars, and later shaping of surfboards. That all led to creative things and wanting to tinker more. I found out about Art Center through one of my coaches in high school, and at the time I didn't even comprehend what car design was. I thought it was just engineers. There was no Internet. There were no design celebrities per se. Once I visited the school I got the picture and just pursued it from there. I did a series of internships while at Art Center, first with Porsche and then later at VW/Audi in California, which ultimately led to working there for several years.

If you were just starting out now, what advice would you give yourself?

My number one advice I give to students is don't measure yourself within a certain niche, or against this student sitting next to you. Don't narrow your ability. You have to look at it on a global scale. You need to be an individual and pursue your style, but you also need to make sure that you're head and shoulders above people around you. The competitiveness is the biggest challenge for the students because the talent pool is really global. Before, it was more segregated into clusters, and now that's all gone and the field is wide open. People are pulled here from Europe and Asia, and German companies are pulling in the Americans and the Japanese. It's become international so you have to measure yourself against that, and be honest about it. It leads to hard work. It takes a lot to be competitive.

Where do you see transportation design going as it evolves further in the 21st century?

The last 10 years have been so exciting and there's been a real design renaissance. We are in the golden age right now. I started school a few years after the first Miata hit the road and that was such a big deal at the time. This fun, little, affordable, emotional car. I see how much more expressive and emotional the car design has become today, and the technology that's going into it. I think the next 10 years will be amazing. More and more vehicles are diversifying; there are subsegments of subsegments now and I think the choice for the consumer is getting broader. There's a technology boom going on right now and that will probably have the most profound effect on the way vehicles look. Whether you're talking about lighting technology or battery and powertrain technology, glass technology. The biggest challenge is just keeping up with it all. It's exciting.

Anything you'd like to add that we didn't talk about? Any final words of wisdom?

At the end of the day, it sounds very complicated but so often I find that the decisions that we're faced with are obvious. Oftentimes, the most difficult thing is to convince people. The hardest thing for me has been to train myself to have those rational arguments. So often as a designer your job is to persuade, in a gentle, professional, and respectful way. If you can persuade decision makers to make a difficult choice and make the process easier for them, that's really such a major part of your challenge and task.

It gets back to character, demeanor, and working well with people while respecting the process. You can't go in guns blazing, because, eventually, the tide will work against you, so you have to find that work-life balance. It's a hard thing to do; it's taken me years and I still come up against that. I still win some and lose some. [BI]

To see Derek Jenkins's work, please visit http://breaking.in

LAMBERT KAMPS
ARTIST & DESIGNER
LAMBERT KAMPS ART & DESIGN
GRONINGEN, NETHERLANDS

Your work blurs the line between art and design. Can you discuss your approach and share an example of the challenges that you face in designing for a very niche market?

The first five years of my own practice, I concentrated on art projects. I made a lot of big objects for exhibitions in galleries, in festivals and moved during that period a bit in the direction of autonomous architecture. After those five years, some interior projects came along and I started to use art concepts in interiors and vice versa. It wasn't a choice, it just happened. I think that it is interesting to make an artistic, political, or critical statement in design. There are enough products, empty products, which are only made because of the shape, color, or technique. I need a reason to design; just making a product is not interesting enough for me. It is not so easy to earn money with this approach, so I didn't become a rich man, but people are interested and I can tell them something through my designs.

What characteristics or qualities are necessary to be a successful industrial designer?

First, you need interesting and inspiring ideas and different ideas work in different fields, techniques, and interests. Next thing is that you have the skills to do it and create something out of those ideas. More importantly, you have to start and just do it, find people who can help you with problems, because it is impossible to know a solution for every problem. Another thing is that you have to take care of your money; you are running a company and you need to earn some money to live from and to pay for your experiments.

What motivated you to open your own design studio?

I started my own studio during the summer of 1999. After finishing art school where I was trained as a visual artist, I had to start my own business or work for another company. The choice was simple—there were not a lot of jobs available and I am a determined person, so Lambert Kamps Art & Design was born.

How do you manage the non-design aspects of running a studio?

Running a studio is at least 50% of your time, working to make it possible to create a design. As I am working on my own, it means 50% of my time is doing things like bookkeeping, making offers, billing, discussing, having meetings, traveling (a very important aspect, if one of your customers is not next door), presenting, et cetera, et cetera.

"I THINK THAT IT IS INTERESTING TO MAKE AN ARTISTIC, POLITICAL, OR CRITICAL STATEMENT IN DESIGN. THERE ARE ENOUGH PRODUCTS, EMPTY PRODUCTS, WHICH ARE ONLY MADE BECAUSE OF THE SHAPE, COLOR, OR TECHNIQUE."

I also have a workspace with a lot of machines and materials that need care, that need to be cleaned and calibrated, so this is also part of the job. Some things are nice to do and others are boring, but still part of the job.

Can you talk more about your approach for how you go about landing projects from clients? What works and what doesn't?

To find clients, I show my own designs at fairs. I show what I stand for through my personal projects. Those objects are often so special that they don't sell, but they are interesting for publishing, getting picked up by press and appearing in newspapers, magazines, blogs, newsletters, etc. That way I can leave an image of my work in people's minds and hopefully they remember me when they need me.

In case of clients for whom I work, I first need to see where we match, so I can understand them and do a good job. Producing good, quality work is very important, as today's happy clients bring the new ones in the future. Clients who are not satisfied can easily kill your business.

What advice would you give to a young designer who wishes to start their own practice?

Just start, and see what happens. If you are young you can always integrate into the ordinary work process, doing it the other way around is much more difficult.

Where do you see the future of industrial design going as it evolves further in the 21st century?

I think that it will be more custom made, probably there will be some digital design kits available so you can design something at home, send it to a producer/printer/CNC or some future machine and after a week, you would have your own product in your home. Or, we will all have our own 3D printers and just buy a document or a design online, and print the product at home. It is also important when people have money to spend and are willing to pay for good, interesting products. The economic crisis of these days will hopefully end the endless consumption of products that we don't need, and bring focus to more quality in our lives.

Anything we didn't cover that you would like to add? Any final words of wisdom?

For me design is about vision. BI

To see Lambert Kamps's work, please visit http://breaking.in

Your fairly young studio focuses a lot on ecology and social enterprise. Can you speak more about this path and why you have chosen this career direction, fresh out of school?

Our work is extremely collaborative. My partner and I started working together right out of school. Danny's background is in architecture and landscape, and I have a degree in product design, so right off the bat we are coming from different perspectives. We are very interested in melding our disciplines together and seeing what happens. We have shared interests in urban ecology, sustainable design, and lately social design, which is trying to understand what design's role is on a local, community level. We feel that the work we're doing is at the intersection of all of these points, trying to experiment with how all of them can fit and work together in an interesting new way.

I think we understand that we can't always start with a clean slate. With limited resources and the way most cities work, it's important to design within an existing system and try to improve it, instead of creating something totally new.

What are some of the challenges you guys are facing as you're launching a new design studio?

All of our projects stem from our mutual interests we talked about earlier. What is really difficult is figuring out what to do once we've completed a project. We've been struggling with various different paths where we can take our work. Should we just share it and talk about it? Turn it into a business or a non-profit? Each one of these has its own issues and responsibilities and non-design problems that we have to contend with. For example with Greenaid, since we're not coming from a business background we had to do some quick on-the-job learning. At the same time it is really exciting and we've had a lot of support from people who have been willing to fill in the gaps for us. It's been stressful, but good.

Can you tell me a bit more about the decision to pursue your own studio as opposed to going the typical route of getting a job at a consultancy or an in-house design studio?

It happened organically. When I graduated it was the year before the recession really started to affect designers. I was working in a more traditional job but personally felt very frustrated. My idealistic bubble burst when I graduated with all of these sustainable projects and couldn't find a creative job in that realm. All I knew is that I didn't want to design corporate showrooms, which is what I was doing. My partner felt similarly and we just started doing the work we wanted to be doing, on the weekends and after work. For the Buckminster Fuller competition, which was our first collaborative project, we had to submit our entry as a studio. So it was kind of a joke, us as a studio, something we had to do. Once Greenaid took off we, maybe naively, made a decision to jump right in and said let's see what it means to get this product into production, to turn it into a social enterprise. That actually ended up launching our studio. It was both unexpected and surprising.

When we look back, we realize we didn't have much choice, not if we wanted to make a living working on projects we felt passionate about. When we talk to other designers, they have similar experiences. Everyone in grad school is super competitive, everyone is vying for the same jobs, no one can move out of LA because it's the same everywhere. We're not alone in starting our own studio, our own business. I think almost one in three of our friends has done something similar. I think it's going to be a common trend. Creatives are going to need to create their own jobs.

How do you manage the non-design aspects of running a studio?

It helps that there's two of us, I'd recommend that to anyone. If you're going to launch a business or a studio, definitely think about collaborating. My partner and I kind of balance each other, personality-wise. He's good at managing the sales and strategy, the day-to-day work and I tend to be better at numbers and overall vision. It's really about dividing tasks and playing to our strengths. Everything we can't do, we outsource. People are incredibly supportive of us and we've always found wonderful people to work with.

Can you talk about how you land projects and clients and what works and what doesn't?

We've always ended up doing the opposite of what we were taught to do. For our studio work, we usually start a project based on some selfish interest or need. Lately it's been shifting a bit as clients have started to approach us for specific projects. These projects are very collaborative, and have been supporting and balancing out our personal work.

We just launched COMMONgood, which is a volunteer collective. Formerly Project H LA, it has recently become its own entity under the umbrella of COMMONstudio. It gives local LA creatives a chance to work on local projects and experiment.

What advice would you give to a young designer who may wish to start their own studio right after school? Do you recommend it?

Yes, certainly. More than anything I would recommend pursuing projects that are personally interesting. Definitely try and find a partner who can round you out a bit. Work is always better when it's with more than one person. Don't be afraid or wait too long. There's a balance between slowly perfecting a strategy and having to just dive right in and throw something out into the world. Being too cautious can really come back to bite you.

Where do you see industrial design going?

This is a really exciting question and everyone is thinking about this right now. There's room for everyone. There will always be a need for more traditional industrial design that tends to be more object-based. I do think there is a trend in designers manufacturing their own goods. Not only starting their own studios but figuring out how to make it locally. That will be interesting to see how it plays out.

I also think social design is trendy now. Consumers have picked up on it and bigger brands have definitely picked up on it. As a result, consumers will get a bit more savvy, and hopefully start to ask harder questions. This will affect how social design actually operates, and how it's packaged and sold. I think the projects will get deeper and more local and I'm hoping there will be more transparency in how things work and how things are affecting everyone.

Can you talk about your experience being a woman in a very male-dominated industrial design field? Do you have any advice for other women who are starting out?

I've been lucky to collaborate with both men and women in a number of different ways, and I'm happy to say that I've never felt any bias or weirdness just because I'm a woman. My advice would be to just continue the work you're interested in. Be yourself. Don't let gender get in the way.

"WE'RE NOT ALONE IN STARTING OUR OWN STUDIO, OUR OWN BUSINESS…I THINK IT'S GOING TO BE A COMMON TREND. CREATIVES ARE GOING TO NEED TO CREATE THEIR OWN JOBS."

We as a studio are coming from a grassroots level— nobody would give us jobs, so we made our own. No one wants to fund us, so we fund ourselves. It's definitely more equalizing, for sure.

If we had not pursued our own studio I think things would have been more difficult. I'm not a classic industrial designer. I can't draw like the wind and I'm certainly not the best 3D modeler. It's a shame because I think there are a lot of creative people out there, who if given an opportunity, can prove themselves. Hopefully this has less to do with me being a woman, and more with having, or not having, a specific skill set.

Anything we didn't cover that you'd like to add? Any final words of wisdom?

Design is really shifting and it's exciting to be a small part of it. Beyond discrete spaces, there's a lot of exciting work to be done in the realm of services, experiences, social enterprise, etc. Who knows where we'll be next year. 〔BI〕

To see the work of Kim Karlsrud and COMMONstudio, please visit http://breaking.in

CATHY KARRY
DIRECTOR OF CAREER
& PROFESSIONAL
DEVELOPMENT
ART CENTER COLLEGE OF
DESIGN
PASADENA, CALIFORNIA

Industrial design is such a broad field with many options. How would you suggest students best prepare their portfolios for the job they want?

Prepare a list of companies they aspire to work for, research what is important to a company, the types of projects showcased on their site, and the skills requested on job postings. Then, revisit their portfolio to determine if there are any gaps in skill sets. Showcase relevant personal projects, the projects that show ambition and passion, while making sure the craftsmanship is just as stellar as school studio assignments.

How should a portfolio be different for someone applying to a design consultancy such as frog from someone who may be applying for an in-house design position?

A consultancy may need someone who is more versatile, where a large corporation may be okay with a designer who is more specialized. If you can design it, model it, and animate it, all the better. Companies

are counting on the fact that students have gained some experience through internships so they can hit the ground running, to have the ability to contribute from day one.

What kind of feedback do you hear from employers about the content of students' portfolios? What are they doing well, and what are they lacking?

I always ask employers this question. The following content is an overview of feedback from multiple employers who receive and review portfolios from design schools around the world.

New graduates from top design schools generally show a high level of sketching and rendering abilities. More often than not, design students show strategy as an integrated part of the design process, but it oftentimes lacks connection with the final outcome. Also the final execution many times lacks the detailed information employers look for. Students can get hung up on what they want to design vs. meeting the design challenge. What they don't realize is that all companies will question their ability to deliver on brief.

Students want to write a mini-novel to describe their process and decision-making points instead of developing a visual narrative whether it is through the use of 2D tools or animations. The latter makes portfolio reviews more enjoyable for employers as they can comprehend the work without a lot of explanation from the candidate. Students need to remember that their portfolio must speak for them when they are not present.

Many times there is more depth to a project than is communicated in the portfolio. This lack of information, or the ability to showcase complex information visually—even though it may exist—can end the possibility of an interview. There may be five other portfolios on a potential employer's desk that do communicate the information thoroughly, and therefore, the employer is not going to take the time to call you for clarification.

Being an intermediary between the students and their prospective employers, what trends have you seen developing over the years in regards to what employers are looking for in industrial designers?

The expectations of employers have been on the rise for at least the last five years. Don't lose the ability to sketch, but add business acumen, digital tools, branding, manufacturing, sustainability, etc. Internship experience has become mandatory. It's like getting a high school diploma. I have even received a request for an intern with internship experience.

A student may say that it's difficult to get an internship or that they don't know how to or whom to contact. What advice do you have for them there?

Some schools do a better job than others when it comes to educating students about the importance of interning and what resources are available. Students should work closely with their mentor(s) to develop a strong portfolio based on the companies they aspire to work for, network through their mentors, faculty, career services, and alumni relations. There are also so many design sites that post internships from around the world and encourage portfolio uploads.

"BE VIBRANT WITH YOUR WORK. THERE ARE A LOT OF 'CAPABLE DESIGNERS,' BUT TO REALLY STAND OUT, A CANDIDATE MUST SHOWCASE ORIGINAL THINKING AND TECHNIQUES."

LinkedIn is a powerful tool. Professional conferences hold portfolio reviews and most schools have on-campus recruiting. These tools give students a longer reach, but applying from a distance makes the development of strong self-promotional materials, including their portfolio, extremely vital. Once interest is established, Skype is one option for the student and the employer to get a better sense of what working together will be like, once again shrinking the playing field.

As the school year just wrapped, was there a particular graduating student who dominated the job offers this year? What about their work stood out? How did they showcase their work to the employers?

There are always a few students that get multiple offers. There is vibrancy to their work, a passion that is apparent, consistent high level of execution. Strong sketching skills still draw attention, but strong ideas and strong solutions keep that attention, pique interest. Strong students showcase personal projects as well, which allows them to differentiate themselves from their classmates. In regards to showcasing work, Art Center hosts industry events on campus, giving students the opportunity to display the outcome of multiple projects in a large format with the addition of models and digital work. We also aggressively promote our online portfolio site. Students must have a strong online presence, as this is the way most companies want to receive portfolios.

With the current economy and the ever-expanding pool of global talent, it seems that it's getting harder and harder to get into the business these days. What does it take to stand out?

Creativity and passion. Be vibrant with your work. There are a lot of "capable designers," but to really stand out, a candidate must showcase original thinking and techniques. Have the ability to identify opportunities in the marketplace vs. "re-skinning" existing products. Showcase proof of interdisciplinary exposure. Understanding of manufacturing and product lifecycle, as well as sustainable practices, speaks volumes.

What has been the most common mistake students make in how they present their work or their portfolios?

I review hundreds of student portfolios every year from multiple design schools, and one common mistake is thinking that one size fits all—not treating portfolio development as another design project. We encourage students to explore personal projects: the projects that really showcase ambitions, personal passions, and differentiate their work from other designers. I often also see students having difficulty extracting vital materials from personal sketchbooks, and struggling to drive a strong story through visuals—putting complex information into easy-to-understand formats. We work with our students to communicate a solid snapshot of the ideation phase—really showcasing the important decision-making points and the existence of additional viable options, a strong balance between blue sky and more production feasible ideas, and sensitivity to brand, as well as the end user. Diversity can be great, but there should be some apparent focus.

What would be the one piece of advice you would give to an aspiring industrial designer who is trying to break into the industry?

Be curious and aware. Request informational interviews with designers and companies of interest. Find mentors. Do what you love. Intern!

How did you land your first job?

I applied to ads in the paper. I know, so old school. My current profession was much more calculated. I am passionate about design education and helping students prepare to enter the creative marketplace, so Art Center is a perfect fit.

Is there anything we haven't covered that you would like to add?

I understand that employers need thoroughly educated designers to help them create competitive products in today's global marketplace. I feel strongly that the collaboration between design education and industry is a win-win situation. When industry invests time in education through internships, projects, and curricular reviews, they help to create a strong talent pool of future designers. ⒷⒾ

To see Cathy Karry's work, please visit http://breaking.in

**STUART KARTEN
PRINCIPAL
KARTEN DESIGN
LOS ANGELES**

What kinds of portfolios get your attention these days? What brings in an industrial designer for an interview?

The very first thing I look for is a state-of-the-art skill level in design—smart and creative use of color, proportion, form, etc. This is the minimum threshold that a candidate must meet. But beyond that, I'm interested in portfolios that demonstrate a breadth of capabilities, from research through concept development. The way a portfolio is formatted should present a narrative thread that lets me know where an idea originated, what research—what consumer or market need—supports the idea, and what thematic visual inspiration drove the design.

What do you think of showing work that's not industrial design in a portfolio? Things like art, photography, hobbies, etc.?

I think this is a good idea. It helps me gauge a candidate's passions and areas of interest that might inspire his or her designs. However, outside interests should only be a small percentage of a portfolio's content.

What advice do you have for preparing the content for web versus a printed portfolio for interviews? Or has everything gone digital these days?

For the most part, I would say that things have gone digital these days. Many people come in for interviews with portfolios that they present on laptops or iPads. That said, it is easier than ever to create a high-quality print portfolio. One candidate came to an interview with an amazing book of his work that he created on Blurb.com. Whether to have a printed portfolio or both printed and digital is up to the candidate.

Would you suggest sending just a teaser or full portfolio from the initial contact, and why so in either case?

I recommend sending a teaser at the point of initial contact and using your full portfolio during an interview to open up a deeper discussion of your work. This is my personal approach when speaking to potential clients. Prior to our discussion, I will send a one-sheet or very short portfolio to capture their attention, but I wait until we speak in person before presenting our larger body of work and capabilities. This allows me to personally guide the audience through my work and frame the exact story I want to tell, rather than leaving things up to interpretation. I think this approach is equally valid for an interview candidate.

Has there been a student or junior-level product design portfolio you've seen recently that really stood out? What made this particular portfolio successful in your eyes?

Yes, what made it stand out was the storytelling component combined with a truly innovative solution. Both aesthetic and functional innovation were addressed.

"GOOD DESIGNERS ASK QUESTIONS LIKE 'WHY?' AND 'WHAT IF...?' THEY QUESTION THE STATUS QUO AND PUSH PARAMETERS."

What are some common mistakes you've seen students or junior designers make in their portfolios?

A few mistakes I've seen is that often they don't make the portfolio function as a standalone. There is no graphical hierarchy or clear story around each project and oftentimes the graphics and layout overpower the work itself.

What do you expect to learn from the designer during an interview?

When I have the opportunity to talk with a candidate in person, one-on-one, I am evaluating their communication skills. How do they talk about their work, their ideas, or their creative process? Can they get me excited about it? To succeed in a career as a designer, you will often need to "sell" your ideas to co-workers and clients. You may think you have a good idea, but unless you can articulate it and get others to buy into the idea, it will never become a reality.

Do you have any suggestions on how one may improve on this essential communication skill?

The first step is to realize that communicating and presenting is important and to take it seriously. Prepare what you're going to say ahead of time. Create talking points and rehearse as much as possible. Take every opportunity to speak in front of groups. This could be as simple as presenting to classmates or coworkers or as involved as joining a professional organization like Toastmasters.

What characteristics or qualities are necessary to be a successful industrial designer?

One of the most important things to me is an inherent, natural curiosity about the world. Good designers ask questions like "Why?" and "What if...?" They question the status quo and push parameters. They are constantly seeking out new information from magazines, blogs, events, other designs, and even television. But they don't just absorb information—they synthesize it into inspiration and actionable concepts.

What are some reasons you have rejected a candidate?

My pet peeve is when people come in for an interview and they haven't done their homework. They don't understand who we are at Karten Design and can't articulate where or why they would fit in with the company. They don't ask any questions about the company or our way of working or the opportunities they'll be able to pursue. All of this represents poor communication skills and a lack of curiosity.

How did you break into this business?

I discovered industrial design by chance. My older sister was studying fashion design at the Rhode Island School of Design and told me I should check out this field called industrial design—she thought I might enjoy it. She was right. I was the kid who loved taking apart the family remote control or vacuum cleaner. I was driven to know how things worked. I fell in love with industrial design because it bridges intellect with the process of making a physical product.

What motivated you to open your own design studio?

I recently discovered that entrepreneurism is a genetic trait that runs in my family. My dad and my grandfather both had their own businesses before me. I worked for several years as an in-house designer in the corporate environment and I wasn't satisfied. I noticed that, to succeed in this type of environment, you couldn't display emotion. People never got mad or excited in meetings. But emotion is such an important part of design. I wanted to create an alternative atmosphere that nurtured creativity and free expression.

How do you manage the non-design aspects of running a studio?

I enjoy all of the aspects of running my own design firm. I get just as excited about leading a creative team as I get by executing a design. Today my focus is on relationship management—ensuring that Karten Design delivers the highest level of service and innovation to all of our clients. I've learned a tremendous amount of business over 27 years. Karten Design has survived three recessions, and maintained a very strong portfolio of work during this latest downturn. I've done this by surrounding myself with smart people who can guide me outside my core competency.

If you were just starting out now, what advice would you give yourself?

There is such a long laundry list of things that designers have to know and do to succeed today. They have to be research-friendly, they need to understand business and marketing strategy, they need to be lateral thinkers as well as visual thinkers, they

need to work quickly in 3D. My advice is to get really good at one thing. Find a niche that you're passionate about and develop a depth of expertise that no one else can replicate.

So there is a benefit to specialization despite the broad, generalist knowledge an industrial designer must possess to succeed these days?

Yes, there's definitely a value in specialization. That's not to say that general skills do not need to be fairly strong across the board. But specialization—either in a discipline like research or user interface, or a customer segment like women or the elderly—will go a long way toward making yourself stand out in a field of generalists. If you are a specialist, you possess a body of knowledge that is hard to duplicate—something that will be highly desirable to the right employer.

Where do you see the future of industrial design going as it evolves further in the 21st century?

Design used to be about the ability to make things look good. This is still important, but it's now just the foundation of what design has to offer. The future of design lies in functional innovation—researching people and developing empathy that allows you to design new ways to solve classic problems, from improving a product's usability to growing a client's market share. Because of design's new strategic place in the business world, designers can't talk about their work in terms of design. They need to understand the value it brings for its clients and end users.

In your opinion, what is the value that design brings to business?

Design is all about connecting to people's emotions. Designers can help businesses connect their brands with their customers.

Anything we didn't cover that you would like to add? Any final words of wisdom?

I'd like to take one last chance to reiterate the importance of presentation and storytelling. People understand their lives as narratives. The best way to capture someone's attention and create desire is to tap into that propensity with a well-crafted story of conflict and resolution. You need to show people the value of your design by demonstrating that you're solving a problem. ⊞

To see Stuart Karten's work, please visit http://breaking.in

MICHIEL KNOPPERT CREATIVE DIRECTOR FOR NEXT GEN PRODUCTS & EUROPEAN STUDIO LEAD DELL AMSTERDAM

What kinds of portfolios get your attention these days? What brings in a product designer for an interview?

Beyond an excellent skill set of sketching, 3D CAD and such, we look for widely and broadly educated system thinkers with an analytic mind. They need to be good observers of life, and have an opinion and voice of their own, original and conceptual.

What specifically in a portfolio showcases to you that an individual has these aforementioned skills?

I don't just want the pretty pictures, I want them to tell a story. I want to see someone truly understand a problem, form an inspired vision and—based on insights—create a unique and relevant solution to that problem. That solution should be in the form of a stunning design that shows that same vision, translated into form, function, materials, and color.

Have you seen a portfolio recently that really stood out? What about it caught your eye?

Over the last few years I have seen a few portfolios that really stood out. Those that did all had two things in common: they conveyed a sense of personal style that was apparent from exploration to final proposal,

and they were like story books. Not all the work that was shown was super polished, but all of it was interesting. I'd hire these individuals so they could apply that creativity and sense of style to our challenges.

What are some common mistakes you've seen students or junior designers make in their portfolios?

I see two common mistakes in the work that students and young professionals show. One common mistake is to focus on the polished result. Styling exercises outside of any context fail to communicate a skill set that solves actual design problems, and they show un-thoughtfulness. The other mistake is quite the opposite: where portfolios focus on creative exploration and process, without a solution. It's nice to see process and wildly creative ideas, as long as they're a means to an end—the end being a great product.

What do you expect to learn from a designer during an interview?

First, I try to see if the person in front of me matches the work they show in their portfolio. What part of the work were they really responsible for? I like to give them a chance to fill in some of the blanks. Then of course, I try to gauge the fit with the group on a personal level, and if they get excited about what we have to offer.

Finally, I try to learn about their aspirations. In our group, we're looking for types who deeply care about content, strategy, and design execution—not so much people who aspire to be a manager, or are interested in just shipping a product for their portfolio. This is easier to assess in an interview, especially since candidates are not always aware of their personal aspirations.

What characteristics or qualities are necessary for the designer to have in order to succeed?

That depends, but for our group at Dell, they need to be analytic observers. Everything we create is for people. Failing to understand what drives our consumers results in a flawed product. I believe designers need to be extremely observant. This applies to pretty much anything: from people's behavior to technology to corporate politics.

Next they should be synthesis visionaries. The design problems we work on are complex, multidimensional problems. As a designer, they will need to take all the pieces of the puzzle and put them together to create a clear and compelling vision. Designers need to be great communicators and integrators—seeing the opportunities and examining the breadth of solutions and problems. They need to excel at visual communication and creative problem solving. These qualities are required to function at the core of complex, multidisciplinary projects.

"ONE COMMON MISTAKE IS TO FOCUS ON THE POLISHED RESULT. STYLING EXERCISES OUTSIDE OF ANY CONTEXT FAIL TO COMMUNICATE A SKILL SET THAT SOLVES ACTUAL DESIGN PROBLEMS."

Finally, they need to be craftsmen with an eye for the big picture, as well as detail. They are responsible to deliver great design work, which means they have to sweat the details. They need to work tirelessly on design problems with engineering, refining the CMF [color, material, finish] specifications, perfecting the 3D models, and so on.

How did you break into this business?

There were two important moments. First, my graduation project with Springtime in Amsterdam got noticed by Tucker Viemeister, who dropped by the studio to say hi. This resulted in him starting a New York office for Springtime and connecting us with some big American clients like Nike and Coca-Cola.

The second moment happened after spending some years with Springtime. My girlfriend and

I decided we needed to broaden our horizons. I interviewed with Philips in Hong Kong and Nike in Portland. Scott Wilson, who I knew from social circles via some Nike connections, had just moved to Chicago and invited me over for an interview at Motorola. Soon enough, we were moving to Chicago where I started to work with a group of super-talented designers.

If you were just starting out now, what advice would you give yourself?

Travel and make yourself uncomfortable. Take part in research, talk to business people, work in the model shop, get an understanding of everything that is involved in creating a product.

Where do you see the future of industrial design going as it evolves further in the 21st century?

Industry is changing. Real problems will be solved by small impromptu groups of highly motivated experts. Designers will play a pivotal role in these new clusters of diversely talented collaborators. They will keep oversight and be catalysts for the innovation process. They will also be the ones to make the ideas tangible and communicate them to the manufacturing parties. These groups can work within organizations, but modern technologies and networks will, more and more, empower designers to do things on their own, adding entrepreneurship to their skill set.

Anything you'd like to add that we haven't talked about? Any final words of wisdom?

Have something to say without being a loudmouth. ⊞

To see Michiel Knoppert's work, please visit http://breaking.in

BRIAN KUTSCH
GLOBAL DESIGN LEAD
LACOSTE
LONDON

What kinds of portfolios get your attention these days? What brings in an industrial designer for an interview?

The portfolios that get my attention these days show thought process and the candidate's ability to sketch or generate ideas quickly. I look for a really good grasp of the fundamentals or the classic thought process that a student would learn in college. Showing the combination of solid research, ideation sketching, then pulling the strongest designs from the ideation stage into a more finalized product that has a cohesive story behind it, is one way to create a strong portfolio. Ultimately a recent graduate portfolio should showcase thought process and skill.

Have you seen a portfolio recently that has blown you away? What about it stood out?

I have seen a number of portfolios that have blown me away and really appreciate the few that basically check all the boxes well. These portfolios I find are really solid. Overall I haven't really seen anything that really came out of left field as a whole new approach to things, but for me it's about finding that special something within a portfolio that will bring someone in for an interview.

Can you share a bit about what made those portfolios "really solid"?

Well, over the past few months I have seen a range of portfolios, but the strongest ones generally seem to come from people that have spent time at the larger brands. The thought process of the way that these bigger brands go about design and creating great product, they're just really good at checking every single box. They know how to go through the process of problem solving all the way through to product launch.

I'm assuming this also means a level of competency and ability to draw, the technical skills, as well?

Right, correct.

When you say they've "checked all the boxes," what do you mean? What are those boxes?

In-depth research, ideation or sketching phase, problem solving, refinement, refinement again, beautiful renderings, details, technical drawings, product sampling, color and material refinement again, then to a launch strategy.

If you had an opportunity to advise a student on creating a portfolio that would resonate with you, what would you tell them?

Currently I appreciate portfolios that are pleasant to interact with. I would suggest putting the portfolio online so it can be accessed from anywhere. If I can view it easily on my smartphone, even better. Additionally, have a PDF version that can be printed and emailed. An eight megabyte or less PDF file size is preferred. Make sure you showcase your skills clearly. Balance in-depth projects that take five or six pages to explain with some punchy one-pagers.

When you actually bring in a designer for an interview, what do you expect to learn from them then?

Well, for me it's a lot about the personality and if they're willing to learn and grow, ask the right questions. I really want to get a sense that they want to be within the company that I'm working for and be a part of the team. At the end of the day you spend more time together with your co-workers than you actually do with your family. That's the reality. Ultimately, bare bones, do I want to spend time with this person? Let's say you go on a business trip for three weeks in Asia, you'll get to know each other pretty well. You need to get along.

So the key question to answer is "Can I spend three weeks in Asia on a business trip with this person?"

It's a balance. Skill set, willingness to learn, and being

open to change. Then, yes, one important question is: "Can I spend three weeks with this person on a business trip?"

What characteristics and qualities are necessary to be a successful designer these days?

Designers are problem solvers. One very important characteristic is the ability to communicate well. I think the scope has gotten so big as to where you can go. There are so many different directions, it's really about trying to figure out what you want to do, and sort of think about three steps ahead. When you do that, you should be able to identify who to ask the right questions to, as well. You may have the right question and ask the wrong person and get the wrong advice and end up in the wrong place. If you're able to ask the right questions to the right people, they'll generally direct you down the correct path.

As far as some other qualities that are necessary to being a successful designer: an ability to sketch and applying that ability to a really great thought process of solving problems. From there, stylizing the product to be market-relevant or commercial is one way people grade designers as successful.

How did you break into the industry?

Well, it was really from a connection I had from college. A good friend of mine had gotten a job at Converse and at that time I was working within the automotive world in Detroit and he said, "Hey man, I think you'd be a really great fit here, there's a lot of potential." He really opened up the opportunity for me to break into footwear. I then worked really hard honing my skills and sketching footwear specifically for Converse. After that I applied for and landed a six-month contract position, which then turned into full-time work.

If you were just starting out now, and knowing what you know, what advice would you give yourself?

I probably wouldn't sweat it as much and focus on having more fun. Right now I'm designing shoes and managing a team that's creating a fun product. I think the stresses of "Get that job, get that job" can kind of make you lose sight of what the reality is

and that is that it should be fun. You're doing what you ultimately love to do, which is solving problems through design and creation. I think if I could go back, I'd have a little bit more fun with it.

"SHOWING THE COMBINATION OF SOLID RESEARCH, IDEATION SKETCHING, THEN PULLING THE STRONGEST DESIGNS FROM THE IDEATION STAGE INTO A MORE FINALIZED PRODUCT THAT HAS A COHESIVE STORY BEHIND IT, IS ONE WAY TO CREATE A STRONG PORTFOLIO."

Also, I just think the most enlightening experience as a designer is to get right into the manufacturing process because that's the whole half of it, the half you don't learn in school. You can read about it, but actually going there and getting into the thick of things, you learn a lot. If at all possible, visit a manufacturing facility within the region where you're going to school. It will help tremendously to understand what actually happens in a mass production environment. One example would be understanding the amount of waste created—it helps you as a designer to learn how to reduce waste. It goes back to the environmentally, socially responsible designing.

How have you managed to make your own designs more environmentally or socially responsible?

The group I work for holds environmentally and socially responsible design as highly important. So, these two subjects are constantly being discussed and implemented within our business model. Beyond that the rules and regulations within the greater industry surrounding chemicals and responsible best practices are continuously being improved. In general, if you stick to the basics, so to say, and stay away from chemicals and waste—it's the little bits over time that can make a really big impact, if you're making a product that's being made a million times over. Even just reducing that one small piece can make a big impact.

Where do you see the future of industrial design going as it evolves further in the 21st century?

It's a really difficult question, actually. To me it seems there are two major factors that will shape the future of the profession: information flow and technology. Overall I think industrial design will become more and more of a global amalgamation because of the Internet and increased communications. There are bigger shifts of trends that I'm finding because of this.

Also, technologies like 3D printing and others surrounding the industry are quickly opening up many new opportunities for anyone to be an industrial designer. The combination of information flow and new technologies will create a need for large-scale mass production while at the same time allow for very small production runs aimed at niche markets. Things seemingly always balance out and the future of industrial design will too.

Anything that we didn't talk about? Any final words of wisdom?

It goes back to "have fun with it." If you have fun doing the design work, it will show through to your portfolio and your sketching. Just have fun with it. [BI]

To see Brian Kutsch's work, please visit http://breaking.in

CHELSIA LAU
CHIEF DESIGNER, STRATEGIC
CONCEPTS GROUP
FORD MOTOR COMPANY
SHANGHAI

What kinds of portfolios get your attention these days? What brings in an industrial designer for an interview?

A product designer needs to have a really good sense of proportion. We also look for creativity and innovation. We often see portfolios with really strong sketching techniques but sometimes the design is not original or innovative enough, so we will not be particularly interested in those. We are looking for people with well-rounded skills, there has to be good problem solving, offering new solutions, really going beyond just a beautiful sketch.

Have you seen a portfolio recently that resonated with you, and what about it stood out?

The auto industry in China is still developing. We see a lot of portfolios, but I feel most of the time the students' work has not yet reached the level of refinement or sophistication we are looking for—but we do see the potential. I'd say that we pay more attention to originality and design thinking.

What do you expect to learn from the designer during an interview?

Designing in the car industry is all about teamwork. As good as a person's artwork may be, we're looking to understand their personality. Is this somebody that can work in a team environment? At the end of the day, we will have to work with different cross-functional teams and those teams will be constantly changing depending on which program they're working on. This person really needs to have a lot of interpersonal skills, be willing to work with the team—that's very important. Then we will, for instance, look at a sketch and will want to know what the thought process behind the sketch was. What triggered all of this creative thought, what exactly are they solving, and is this design for a specific type of target customer? And what kinds of things will be inspiring them?

I'd much rather see a selective portfolio than a portfolio containing lots of repetitive work. For some reason students tend to include a lot of work of different variations on the same theme, but if you go through and categorize them there may be only just a few ideas. Let's say you have one project; you might be able to show multiple perspectives or different aspects. You can have different solutions or ideas versus one idea with many variations of the same theme. Technically, I see it as one design versus four ideas generated from solving a particular problem. We really like to see people pushing the design envelope rather than presenting very limited creative thoughts of maybe one or two ideas, just doing slight changes based off of the same theme. It's very important to see the potential in candidates and that they have the ability to generate lots of good ideas, rather than just one idea over and over.

What characteristics or qualities are necessary to be a successful industrial designer?

You need to have a good sense of design and taste. Certain technical skills can be taught in school, but certain things like aesthetic sense and taste cannot be taught. It has to be within you. That is the difference between a mechanical mind versus a creative, imaginative, visionary [mind].

How did you break into this business?

I grew up in Hong Kong and at a very young age became very interested in drawing and fine arts. My parents recognized the talent in me and encouraged me and my younger brother to take private lessons all the way from primary school through high school. After high school, I studied at a school in Hong Kong, which offered a product design course. At that time I didn't know a whole lot about industrial design, but I knew my career had to be something related to art or design. I even thought about going to Paris to do portraits to earn a living. After completing my studies in Hong Kong, I worked for a year and then had the opportunity to study at the Art Center College of Design in Pasadena, California.

I didn't really know much about car design at the time, and I thought I would just further my education on the product design side. When I first enrolled in the college, I was so inspired by walking into the senior classes. They had walls full of sketches and scaled clay models; it was overwhelming and impressive. I never knew that design could be so expressive, and from then on I was hooked.

"CERTAIN TECHNICAL SKILLS CAN BE TAUGHT IN SCHOOL, BUT CERTAIN THINGS LIKE AESTHETIC SENSE AND TASTE CANNOT BE TAUGHT. IT HAS TO BE WITHIN YOU."

During school, I was selected to do an internship at Ford headquarters in Michigan and those few months totally changed my life. Although it was for only a short time, I got the opportunity to work on a special project and they were very good about allowing the students to visit different studios. We were able to see different stages of many programs. Some of them were heavy on ideation, preliminary sketches that really stretched the design creativity, some were programs with heavy feasibility trade-offs involving aerodynamics and engineering, and some were concept vehicles. We were able to see a lot in a short time and to understand that designing a car is not just simply doing a beautiful sketch. It's a lot deeper than that. I knew that this was the career I wanted to follow. I went back to school and chose automotive design as my major and, after I graduated, I started working for Ford.

I'm sure you hear this question a lot, but as we know industrial design is still very much a male-dominated field. So I'm curious to hear what advice you'd have for women who are trying to pursue and break into this field?

Even back when I was a student, yes, product design was very male dominated—and car design especially. It was really rare to see a woman involved. However, nowadays they are encouraging more women to enter the field, with some success. I have in the past helped out at events, whether it's going to a high school or talking to design students, sharing with them my experiences, my struggles as a car designer and to let them know that there is a car industry and to get them interested in the creative field. Things are changing and I see a lot more female designers in the industry.

I think, first of all, it's a tough industry. It's highly competitive. There are only a very small number of car designers in this circle. On the other hand, to do a car is a huge task. A car will contain easily many thousands of parts, and then as a designer there's a lot we have to consider. As your career progresses, you'll take on a more leadership position to orchestrate and lead a team in shaping a compelling design that resonates with the customers.

It is rather complex. I think if any young females want to enter this field, first of all they must ask the question: do I have the passion for doing car design or industrial design? The passion is what will keep you going. I think to be truly successful in the industry you need to have the push to continue to improve and reinvent yourself. You have to have the desire to see beyond, doing more than you think you can: endurance, perseverance, and determination.

It's tough, it's challenging but you should enjoy the journey. Just be determined and don't look back. Just go all the way. Push as hard as you can.

If you were just starting out now, what advice would you give yourself?

The love, the passion to do the work will keep you going. You'll have ups and downs, and it can be very challenging at times, but you need to keep up the positive optimism. Remember why you came into this industry. It's all because of that dream. Keep this clear in your mind. It will keep you going.

Where do you see the future of industrial design going as it evolves further in the 21st century?

I think the whole world is global now, especially here in Asia and China. The future will depend on the growth and development of the urban mobility infrastructure. As designers nowadays we are also thinking of offering more and more solutions that are sustainable and sensible for the environment.

Anything we didn't cover that you would like to add? Any final words of wisdom?

I feel that the personality of the individual is really important. You need to be strong and open, always optimistic. I feel that sometimes people like to isolate you if you are different, and there will be times where you will naturally feel isolated. I felt that really contributed to me being stronger and more independent. As young ladies get into the field today, they need to open up and try to engage themselves, be involved and be part of the bigger team. There are a lot of talented people in our industry: experienced designers, engineers, clay modelers—all of whom have lots of knowledge and are great artisans in their own way. By expanding your circle, getting help, and talking to people, very soon you'll feel that you're integrated into a bigger family.

It was a struggle for me at the beginning, but after I integrated myself, I overcame—not just the language barriers, but the cultural ones as well. I was taught in traditional value that when you have an idea to not express it too strongly, that was not polite, that you're supposed to keep everything to yourself. What I found in the design world is that if you have a good idea, you need to express yourself and really seek the opportunity and grab it. Over the years, I've changed and I feel that once I moved away from that state of mind, things started to improve. BI

To see Chelsia Lau's work, please visit http://breaking.in

What kinds of portfolios get your attention these days? What brings in an industrial designer for an interview?

The main attributes that I look for in a product design portfolio will heavily depend on the candidate's experience and seniority. But in general I look at four attributes. The first is the layout of the information. How is the information communicated and organized? What points are the candidates trying to highlight? More often than not, many design portfolios are overly cluttered with too much information that is hard to digest, in particular when there is a lack of explanation to go with a project. Portfolios that get my attention are ones that are concise and to the point, laying out the problem statement, what was undertaken, and the solution it provides.

"PORTFOLIOS THAT GET MY ATTENTION ARE ONES THAT ARE CONCISE AND TO THE POINT, LAYING OUT THE PROBLEM STATEMENT, WHAT WAS UNDERTAKEN, AND THE SOLUTION IT PROVIDES."

Secondly, I look at process work and richness of content. What activities were undertaken by the candidate from conception to final solution? Many portfolios only present the final result fully rendered and resolved. What is more of interest is how the candidate worked through the problem to get to the end result. It's not to say that a beautifully rendered and modeled solution is not wonderful to see; it certainly shows technical skills, but it's more about the design thinking process that resulted in the solution that is of interest.

Next, form development and technical skills. This is a core competency that is expected. Candidates should be able to communicate intent, form details, and technical information through sketches and illustrations. CAD creation skills are important in how the candidate tackles surface creation and their understanding of 3D forms and construction principles.

Finally, show relevant work. Category relevance is important. It is great to provide a variety of projects and work type but understanding your target audience is also important. For example, we receive many applications solely comprised of automotive sketches and illustrations—which is great to see—but is it relevant?

Have you seen a portfolio recently that resonated with you, and what about it stood out?

Every year we look for design interns and this year's crop of candidates has been surprisingly strong. Brigham Young University, Virginia Tech, and Cleveland Institute of Arts had some strong students that stood out, in part because of project selection and how problems were identified and resolved through a product or service. In particular this year's candidates were stronger in showing their process thinking.

What do you expect to learn from the designer during an interview?

How they communicate and convey intent on each project. How articulate the candidate is and how well they understand the subject matter.

How do you know if the designer you are interviewing will fit your studio culture?

After identifying a prospective candidate, the first stage is the phone interview where—along with discussing their portfolio—we would get a sense of their personality over the phone. After that we'll have the selected candidates on-site for an in-person interview. We'll have the design group meet the candidate on a one-on-one basis and have the team report back on their thoughts of the candidate.

What characteristics or qualities are necessary to be a successful industrial designer?

Process thinkers. A candidate who is able to step out of their own shoes and position their mindset in the eyes of the user will make for a successful designer. Being open-minded and unbiased to explore a wide range of ideas in different solution spaces.

How did you break into this business?

I broke into this business through an internship in my third year in the UK. In addition to the school project, I developed my own personal projects that supplemented the variety of work and technical skills that I wanted to portray. An important aspect that helped me break into this business was learning from peers and senior students in how they treated programs and the processes with which to tackle a problem.

If you were just starting out now, what advice would you give yourself?

Put yourself in the shoes of the design firm: understand their needs, what they do, what values you can provide, and what they would want from a candidate.

Where do you see the future of industrial design going as it evolves further in the 21st century?

The trend in the industry is moving towards conceptualization through 3D CAD and high quality rendered visualization tools. Illustration and sketch development is a casualty of this trend. It is very easy for candidates to get enamored with the tool and lose sight of the design thinking and development aspect of the work.

What is it about sketching that makes it so powerful and necessary to the process of industrial design? Why not just jump into 3D CAD?

CAD tools have certainly made it a lot easier to jump straight into 3D but there are many situations where quick communication of ideas—such as in brainstorming sessions—is vital to communicate ideas and intent. In addition to storyboarding and framing of concepts, sketching is the only medium that can be effective without heavy time investment in generating 3D CAD. [BI]

To see Philip Leung's work, please visit http://breaking.in

RONALD LEWERISSA CREATIVE DIRECTOR FLEX/THE INNOVATIONLAB DELFT, NETHERLANDS

What kinds of portfolios get your attention these days? What brings in an industrial designer for an interview?

The quality of the work. What triggers me usually is when I see enough skill and craftsmanship in the work. Their imagination is very important—their creativity. Also because strategically, we are looking at designers more and more as design thinkers, I truly hope to find that skill in young designers as well. Those are basically the three most important elements that we are looking at in portfolios.

You mentioned "design thinkers." Can you elaborate?

I see many designers who find solutions for non-existent problems. They are creating products that miss a certain relevance. What I mean with design thinking is that there's a very broad consensus that people trained as industrial designers are capable of tackling all kinds of problems that are not necessarily related to physical objects. They can tackle all sorts of problems because they are trained to think from a problem to a solution. That's a different way of thinking than what people do in physics, mathematics, etc. We feel that the new generation of designers should be very skilled in that way of thinking. Not necessarily to just design physical products but to tackle all kinds of problems that we see in society.

Have you seen a portfolio recently that exemplifies that, or one that really caught your eye? Can you share a bit about what stood out?

I see quite a few portfolios that focus on scenarios that could be solutions for sustainability, for instance. They're not necessarily looking for what's the best material to make this product out of, but to develop products that truly change the way people behave around the products. A very obvious scenario could be that you don't design cars anymore to be owned but you design them for sharing or renting. There's quite a few students that come up with very innovative solutions for problems like that and they catch my attention.

If you had an opportunity to guide a student in how to create an industrial design portfolio that would resonate for you, what would you tell them?

Make the portfolio look stunning and convince me in an intelligent way that the problems you are trying to solve are relevant. Prove that your solutions work and show that your solutions will or can be recognized in the marketplace.

What do you expect to learn from them during an interview?

When you see a portfolio that holds a certain promise, you see beautiful images and very well-outlined problems and solutions. Very often those portfolios were made in the ideal circumstances of having the right tools, the right amount of time, etc. In the real world, those situations are usually never there. You have to perform really, really well in difficult circumstances: not enough time and budget, different stakeholders with different opinions, very high expectations, and so forth. When we interview candidates, we talk about their work, their motivations, but we also give them a little exercise where we ask them to design something under difficult circumstances. So in one and a half hours, they have to develop a simple product but the result really shows their ability as design thinkers. It shows their skills in drawing, visualization, and their creativity under time pressure. Do they come up with really out-of-the-box ideas or scenarios? For us, that little exercise is really

important. It shows that they can do something well under really difficult circumstances.

As a relatively small design agency in the Netherlands, we also have to work under very difficult circumstances all the time. Budgets are always really tight, time is always limited, freedom in the choice of production methods is always limited. You always have to work with low investment production methods. So those are very difficult circumstances and, if under those circumstances you can create something really outstanding, that is, for us, a very important sign.

What characteristics or qualities are necessary to be a successful designer?

Top of the list for me is creativity and it has to be extremely well developed. You have to have a certain openness to cooperate with other designers and other disciplines, and also with other people that you feel are not necessarily helping your process. Within every project we face sometimes political, but also technical issues, that we have to resolve. Communication is, of course, very important. How do you verbalize the choices that you've made? I still think technical skills are very important—the speed in which you work. We are an agency and basically we sell hours. If we don't do enough in one hour, it's going to be an hour we're not going to get paid for, so speed is important.

"MAKE THE PORTFOLIO LOOK STUNNING AND CONVINCE ME IN AN INTELLIGENT WAY THAT THE PROBLEMS YOU ARE TRYING TO SOLVE ARE RELEVANT."

The ability to learn fast. You have to adapt constantly to the needs of your client, the type of product you need to develop. You have to learn with every project and the faster you do that, the better equipped you are to work successfully. Adaptability in a project, where things change all the time, and your ability to adapt to this new situation is very important. More and more of our clients work in a global sense so you have to be able to bridge different cultures, even though you're not from a country where your product is being sold. You still have to understand what the drivers are in that country, how the society works, the role the product plays in that society. Of course, English language is important but an ability to speak Dutch, German, or French will definitely increase effectiveness.

What motivated the opening of FLEX/the INNOVATIONLAB?

I started my career at GE, working in the US. I felt that designers were mainly hired to beautify products—they were stylists. That didn't interest me very much. I learned that many corporations were that way in the US at the time. In Europe, it was almost as if designers were designing something for a museum. In my opinion, design played a totally different role. It was a means to reach a very specific objective. For companies, it was to create meaningful brands, make a profit, guarantee sustainable growth, or reduce cost. For end-users, it was all about increasing the quality of life and, for our society in general, it was a shared objective of a more sustainable society, fair distribution of wealth, and so on. For me, it was not fulfilling to play traditional roles that were very common for designers at the time. I started my own studio together with Jeroen Verbrugge because we felt design was much more important than beautifying products and making museum pieces. We wanted to try and do it differently.

If you were starting out now, what advice would you give yourself?

If I were 23 years old now and had to start my own business I would say "use your ability as a design thinker to come up with a different business model than selling hours," which is what we do today. Be more of an entrepreneur and come up with a truly innovative business model for designers. I think that's something that we as a profession should start to think about. You have to stay very true to yourself and try to define what makes you unique as a designer and make it part of your proposition.

I think there's still great value in smaller groups of designers. I would not want to work on my own. In creative processes you need the input of other people to reflect on work and to utilize all of the different backgrounds, culturally, socially, and in terms of expertise. You have to think about what type of organization really maximizes creativity, openness, and design thinking.

Where do you see industrial design going as it evolves further in the 21st century?

It would be more built on design thinking as a skill, rather than on technical skills. Perhaps it's less product oriented and more service design and brand-driven innovation. It's interesting to see how objects that surround us have a huge influence on how we behave. Twenty years ago, when we didn't have cellular phones, the way we communicated with each other was totally different than it is today. Also the intensity, the types of information that we shared with each other. The products that surround us influence the way we behave as people. I think it is very interesting if designers would use that skill, the skill to change people's behavior, to make our society a little bit more livable and a little bit more sustainable.

Something else that I see is that producing things, making things, is becoming less and less the domain of large corporations. Of course today we still need a big company to make a car, a safe car, but then, in the future, especially when you look at electric cars, the technology is very simple and anyone with a garage could build their own electrical car. The manufacturing is becoming less the domain of large corporations, so that means there could be a lot more smaller scale projects for industrial designers. That's a different way of working. Instead of making huge volumes of the same thing, perhaps we make much smaller volumes of a lot more different things.

Also I see that designers have a tendency to want to do it all themselves. I would think that it would be important for them, in the future, to start to invite other disciplines to join in on a much more regular basis than they do today. Do less yourself. Involve other disciplines and people in the work that you do.

Is there anything you'd like to add that we didn't cover? Any final words of wisdom?

I'm not sure if I'm wise enough to give you any words of wisdom. I hope that the future generations of designers truly love what they do. I hope that they have so much passion in their work that they create opportunities for themselves in which they can do really meaningful and great work, making our society and future a little bit better. BI

To see Ronald Lewerissa's work, please visit http://breaking.in

BRIAN LING
DESIGN DIRECTOR &
FOUNDER
DESIGN SOJOURN
SINGAPORE

What kinds of portfolios get your attention these days? What brings in an industrial designer for an interview?

It depends on the position level of the designer applying for the job. At the junior to mid-level, I would expect to see portfolios that show a lot of the designer's thinking process. You really don't have a lot of time to get to know a candidate as most interviews last an hour, so you can't really tell if they are completely up to par. However I've found that designers who can articulate their thinking process make good hires. I've found that the thinking is the most important characteristic.

Designers looking to interview at a mid- to more senior level will need to show, in addition to the thinking process, evidence of commercialized or realized products. They don't all need to be award-winning designs, but a portfolio with a consistent trend of designs that have been brought to market is a very powerful way of getting my attention.

Have you seen a portfolio recently that resonated with you, and what about it stood out?

Yes. He was a fresh graduate, but exhibited a level of maturity that was impressive. All his projects were presented in a way that showed how he came up with the idea and developed it into a design solution. The interesting thing about it was that he turned it into a story. Instead of the usual A leads to B to C and then to D, he presented the work through scenarios by using simple illustrations that were very clear and easy to understand.

What do you think of showing work that's not industrial design in a portfolio? Things like art, photography, hobbies, etc.?

It would be interesting to see what else a designer is passionate about. However, it does not add to the discussion as my concern when I hire a designer is: can he deliver the goods on time and to the quality required?

What do you expect to learn from the designer during an interview?

The ability to think critically about a problem and how they go about solving it, the sort of technical skills (sketching, 3D CAD, presentation, etc.) they have, and how comfortable they are with them. Will they be a good fit for the team? I have rejected good designers who don't complement the team as, for example, there may be too many people with similar skills. Soft skills and hygiene factors like eye contact, ability to take criticism, and communication skills. I have on occasion asked candidates out for a chat over coffee so that they will be in a less formal environment.

"I'VE FOUND THAT DESIGNERS WHO CAN ARTICULATE THEIR THINKING PROCESS MAKE GOOD HIRES. I'VE FOUND THAT THE THINKING IS THE MOST IMPORTANT CHARACTERISTIC."

Is this designer reliable? Design is a serious business and any designer needs to show they can step up where required. What are the candidate's aspirations? I like to have designers be with the team for at least two years, as I need at least six months to get them up to speed. Only after that time will they be considered productive. A candidate will usually be a no-go if they "smell" like they are in it for the money and a flight risk.

What characteristics or qualities are necessary to be a successful industrial designer?

As mentioned in the previous question, the ability to think critically about a problem. This is much less common than you would expect. Creativity and the ability to create strong design solutions. To a certain extent, being a designer still boils down to being creative. The ability to empathize with consumers they are designing for and being able to relate with people in the team from other disciplines. A good work ethic, no point being super creative, but lazy. A resourceful problem solver.

You've mentioned "the ability to think" as a key skill for a product designer several times now, and with good reason. This may sound like an odd question, but how would an industrial designer demonstrate this skill in their portfolio or during an interview?

I would say that this is a combination of a designer having a habit of questioning everything—in the context of the design problem—showing evidence of deep problem analysis and signs of pushing oneself to the edge and beyond.

What are some reasons you have rejected a candidate?

The most common is not being a good fit with the team or the job one is being hired for. Call me fussy, but I've rejected a candidate for small things such as wearing a cap to an interview (not serious), and presenting a moldy portfolio or a poorly designed one (attention to details). I've also rejected candidates who did not make an effort to learn about the company and brand before they came to the interview.

How did you break into this business?

I was actually going to be an architect, however after my National Service, I lost my connection with architecture. The good thing though, was that I knew

I wanted to do design. It was along the halls in the Faculty of Built Environment at the University of New South Wales that I discovered the department of industrial design, and the rest is history.

What motivated you to open your own design studio?

I wanted to try and do something different, as well as have more control over my career and time. After a certain amount of time being a corporate or employed designer, you tend to be exposed to the same stuff over and over again.

How do you manage the non-design aspects of running a studio?

Very painfully. I consider it a necessary evil and I have many good entrepreneur friends who give good advice. I also learned to outsource things that took up a lot of my time such as: bookkeeping, web design or branding, and communications work, etc.

If you were just starting out now, what advice would you give yourself?

Manage your cash flow well, have a safety net, and most importantly have a good network of friends and industry contacts. I always say that "I stand on the shoulders of giants," as these contacts, colleagues, and friends have been vital in getting my business going through recommendations and collaborations. I'd like to take this opportunity to thank them for all their support.

Where do you see the future of industrial design going as it evolves further in the 21st century?

Industrial design is fast evolving. New technologies are changing the way people buy and subsequently how we design and make or manufacture things. Take a look at Kickstarter. Designers have the opportunity to share great ideas with people with very little financial risk. What is even more exciting is that now anyone can be a designer. So how will professional designers step up? Here's a clue: take a look at how affordable digital cameras turned everyone into a photographer and how professional photographers adapted to this. ID is also becoming a more humble activity as the focus is shifting to solving more important matters like sustainability and improving the quality of life. When you start looking at improving the quality of life, you will see that these ID problem-solving skills can be used in the context of larger things such as systems design and even in government policy making. As a result, the role of the designer will evolve to become more of a facilitator of conversations with and between people who themselves have been empowered to create.

Anything we didn't cover that you would like to add? Any final words of wisdom?

If you see where ID is heading, you can see that design is a very multidisciplinary activity. While designers don't need to learn to wear many hats, they will need to learn to empathize with the different people they work with by having the ability to speak their language. This is so they may apply their skills in an effective manner. [BI]

To see Brian Ling's work, please visit http://breaking.in

ANTON LJUNGGREN DIRECTOR OF INDUSTRIAL DESIGN BIOLITE BROOKLYN

As you're looking to grow your team, what kinds of industrial design portfolios would get your attention? What would bring in an industrial designer for an interview?

As a start-up with a smaller team, we look for multifaceted individuals who can play different roles at different stages of the process. In contrast to a consultant, we define our own projects, plan our own product pipeline, and set up our own timelines. That means there are great opportunities to affect the direction of the business, which in turn means

a lot of responsibility. We look for all the basic skills of the trade such as research, sketching, and most importantly, the ability to identify an opportunity, understand any potential challenges, and solve for them through great design. Passion, curiosity, and self-motivation are other essential qualities as we look to grow our team.

Have you seen a portfolio recently that really stood out? What about it caught your eye?

When I look at portfolios I look at what makes it unique. It can be the projects they choose to work on, the solutions they come up with, or the way it's presented. If there is passion and a strong vision in the work, it will shine through.

What are some common mistakes you've seen junior designers make in their portfolios?

The unfortunate reality is that the review process of design portfolios is often stressed, leaving little room for in-depth understanding of each concept in the first round. It is therefore important to build your portfolio with a clear and purposeful visual hierarchy. In a 30-second first pass, I should get the high-level of each project and walk away impressed and wanting to come back for more. Make the presentation as visual as possible and try to capture the take-away from each page in the headline, so that it can be understood at a glance.

In the second round of the review process it is vital that the work has depth. Explaining all the considerations that went into a design decision can be quite complex. Showing the process and highlighting insights from it is an important tool. It is important to walk your audience through your thought process. There is a fine balance between showing just enough to get the message across, but not too much. Make every photo or illustration count; each one should tell the story of what you learned from it. It's irrelevant that you did hours of research and heaps of models if your design is not informed by them. Make the connection between insights and design solutions crystal clear.

If an industrial design student came up to you and asked, "What should my portfolio be like? What do I need to show you in order to work with you?", what would you tell them?

I want to be surprised by the energy and creativity in your thinking. Industrial design is about problem solving. Show me that you see what is broken around us and that you have ideas for how to fix it. Think about what you can bring to the table that can compensate for your lack of experience.

"IT'S IRRELEVANT THAT YOU DID HOURS OF RESEARCH AND HEAPS OF MODELS IF YOUR DESIGN IS NOT INFORMED BY THEM. MAKE THE CONNECTION BETWEEN INSIGHTS AND DESIGN SOLUTIONS CRYSTAL CLEAR."

I want to see an aptitude in creating forms by showing a variety of styles. I want to see passion and curiosity that shows that you love what you are doing and will take on any challenge with great enthusiasm and pride. I want to see a fluid ability to visualize ideas in sketches and models, both analog and digital. All in all, I want to see a varied toolbox including 2D and 3D software, sketching, functional and aesthetic 3D model making, problem solving, structure, and methodical thinking. But most importantly, again, is the mindset and will to improve anything you work on.

What do you expect to learn from a designer during an interview?

I want to see the reasoning behind the work. Why they made the decisions they made and how they came to their conclusions. One of the best crits I ever attended was at an architecture school. The professor asked one question again and again. He asked: "Why?" There was often some reasoning at the surface, but when he kept pressing the students, many of them came to the realization that they had actually made their decisions based on assumptions or their own likes and dislikes, rather than the needs of the users or other objective constraints.

In my opinion, good design is a mix of this type of rational reasoning and the artistic vision of the designer. The rational reasoning is based on the given constraints such as user needs, cost, competition, and manufacturing. The artistic vision is more subjective but equally important. If you do the first part well you solve the problem, but if you nail the second part you create an emotional bond with the user. That's when it becomes a product of desire.

There is a natural tension between the two methodologies. Designers are creators and some want to create for themselves more than for someone else. Rational thinking alone won't make a great designer. But mixed with creative, critical thinking and a strong artistic vision, it will. Similarly, artistic vision alone won't make great design, but it can make great art. Great art can be aware of and participating in its context or it is driven by the artist's individual need to express him- or herself from a more self-centered standpoint. Either can create great art that others appreciate and see as meaningful for them. But my definition of design is that it solves a problem; perceived or real, it doesn't really matter.

What characteristics or qualities are necessary to be a successful designer these days?

Curiosity, cross-disciplinary thinking, and openness to explore how to use your skills in different disciplines.

How did you break into the industry?

I got my first internship through a friend of a friend. It was before college and it was unpaid. In many ways, it was a favor to take me in since I didn't have any experience. Working at a small design consultancy with only six people allowed me to see and learn the process at a close range. Having the practical experience of real-world projects helped me get the most out of college. I started doing my own projects on the side at a small scale throughout school. After graduating, I did more consulting work, often in small teams. I found the work through my personal network and brought in designers and engineers as needed, partly to be able to take on larger and more interesting projects and partly to learn from others.

As I started applying for jobs I had my aim set for the US. I applied to over 30 design studios by sending out emails from my native Sweden, and then following up with a printed hard copy of my portfolio to the few that answered. After months of hard work and only one real lead, I realized that I could not apply for a job from afar and saved up for a trip to New York and San Francisco. When I arrived, I found that almost every studio was open to meeting informally. The difference in responsiveness when I was there showing that I was committed versus sending emails from Sweden was dramatic. It seems obvious now, but the pleasant thing that I've learned was that people were so open to helping me out when I showed some commitment. The informational and informal interviews led to a real interview and an internship at Smart Design's headquarters in New York. The internship later turned into a job and I found myself on the other side of what had once been such an intimidating wall.

Can you talk a bit about your decision to join a startup and what industrial design can bring to the table in that type of environment?

As a consultant, you get experience in a wide variety of fields working with different industries, clients, and products. You learn to solve all kinds of problems, often on very short timelines. What you don't get to do as often is to follow through and see the product all the way from start to finish. You often enter too late to define the product, or you hand it off too early and don't get to control the details through to production. At a startup, no one is going to tell you what to make. You need to define who you are, what you should make, and how to go about making it. I feel very lucky to work at a product-based startup where I get to help form the brand, the design language, and the vision for where to take the company.

I see my role as helping bring the voice of the user, the market, and the brand into the equation of our business. By being a part of a startup, I'm hoping that my work will have a bigger impact than it would as a consultant or even as part of an in-house design group in a large corporation. We have an interesting business model developing products for the outdoor recreational market in parallel with

emerging markets in developing countries. To me, the social and environmental mission is an important part of why I joined this team. I believe we can make a positive change in the world by helping people live healthier, richer lives, while improving the dire state of our environment in the process.

If you were just starting out now, what advice would you give yourself?

Learn as much as you can. Work with great people and build your network to one day start your own business. Not everyone has the will, or drive, to start something from scratch, but if you do, you should do it early when you have time to fail and come back again.

Maintain a vision for what you want out of your career and your life, and check in with yourself every couple of months. Ask yourself if you are achieving what you set out to. Continuously re-evaluate your goals and never settle.

Where do you see industrial design going as it evolves further in the 21st century?

We are physical beings living in a physical world so there will always be a need for well-designed physical products. The big change that I see coming is the merge of digital affordances with physical products. Computers, phones, or even household appliances are no longer just boxes housing the smarts of a microprocessor. They are starting to become smart objects, aware of their users and their environment, able to interact with it. Some people find the advent of the digital revolution threatening to product design but I think it is the most interesting time to be an industrial designer since the Industrial Revolution.

Up until now, the design of an object has been constrained by the physical and emotional context it lives in. The rules for that context haven't changed much over the last hundred years. It's been primarily based on the laws of physics with some advancements in manufacturing techniques. While the human body is constant, we now have the option to define interactions without mechanical constraints as the primary driver.

Visual and tactile communication have been the predominant qualities for products, but we're now adding an array of sensors allowing objects to see, hear, talk, and more. There is a lot of opportunity, a lot of responsibility to get it right, and a lot of work ahead for the new generation of industrial designers. BI

To see Anton Ljunggren's work, please visit http://breaking.in

THORNTON LOTHROP
ADVANCED INNOVATIONS
DIRECTOR
DESIGN CENTRAL
COLUMBUS, OHIO

What kinds of portfolios get your attention these days? What brings in an industrial designer for an interview?

The first thing I look for is the ability to draw, to think on paper. It's one of the things that separates good designers from the average: how well can they think on paper and work through various design challenges.

Thinking on paper—what does that entail?

It's more than just sketching. It's a different manner of drawing. There are different kinds of drawing in design, aside from the typical skill that's taught: the design sketching, learning how to draw straight lines, circles and stuff like that. Thinking on paper moves away from simply exploring aesthetics and initiates a cognitive process, going to a place where you're having a conversation with yourself, expressing things you don't really understand. Usually when you're sketching, you are drawing things that you do know. But when you're thinking, you're trying to examine categories

of information that you're unsure of. The ability to do that in a fluid fashion, you don't see it very often. It's certainly an essential language that designers use to communicate with each other.

Has there been a portfolio that you've seen recently that really stood out, and what about it resonated with you?

It's been a long time since I've seen that particular skill set. I generally see it with more senior designers or people with a background in drawing who learned design versus those who learn drawing through design. The current generation of students appears to be under considerable pressure to learn digital media as a primary form of communication. I think eventually the discipline will learn that digital visualization, while essential to the industry, is secondary in the design process. Engineering and architecture have already gone through this experience and realized how critical drawing is to the design process and the ability to learn 3D software. Research has shown that people react differently to drawings versus computer-generated images. It's why the movie industry is struggling with the "Uncanny Valley" effect. While digital renderings may be dazzling, they can elicit a negative response.

I think that many senior designers are discouraged by what's coming out of the schools these days. It's not as if there are no good students, it's just that there aren't enough of them. The transportation and entertainment programs still appear to be setting the benchmark for visualization skills.

Sketching ability, or the analog skills, is the foundation for anyone who wants to be a successful industrial designer?

Drawing is still the most difficult single skill to acquire in the design process. Software is becoming intuitive to the point where nice digital renderings require just basic linear thinking. Now you can get your engineer to do computer renderings and there are engineers who can draw better than some designers. The profession has to continually reinvent itself in order to maintain a critical presence, from a business perspective, in the development process. Visualizing while facilitating a development meeting with the business client is one of the skills of a good designer.

When you do find that designer that meets your qualifications and you bring them in for an interview, what do you expect to learn from them then?

It's important to see how intelligent they are. You can't really tell that until you actually speak to them and see how they handle certain questions. Certainly a portfolio that they send in is refined and they had a chance to do that on their own, but when you come in for an interview you have to see how they interact with other people. The nuances of that social interaction are what firms will rely on as an indicator of the responsibility that they'll be able to shoulder. The maturity that comes out during an interview is pretty critical. Once you hire someone there's an expectation they'll perform.

You've mentioned that intellectual curiosity is a characteristic that's necessary to be a successful industrial designer. Can you tell me a bit more about that?

One of the things that I like to see in someone's portfolio is a collection of creative endeavors they've done outside the design curriculum. When you see portfolios coming out of different schools you start to see kind of a sameness because they do similar projects. I think most designers realize sometime during their first job that it marks a beginning of their education and not the end. Intellectual curiosity is not just something that makes people unique or interesting. Many creative ideas come from sources completely unrelated to a project at hand.

How did you break into this business?

When I was in college the first time, I was interested in design but pursued architecture, not knowing about industrial design. I realized quickly that architecture wasn't what I was seeking and devoted my time to fine arts. It took some years to discover industrial design and realize how well it fit my interests. I remember some of my classmates also started in another discipline, like architecture and engineering, and made the switch when they realized that industrial design existed.

If you were just starting out now, what advice would you give yourself?

Trust your intuition. Looking back on what people said to me at the time about design, there were certain impressions I had that were dismissed or simply discounted. In hindsight, a number of those intuitions were pretty accurate for me, but when you don't know anything you have to rely on others and hope for the best.

Where do you see the future of industrial design going as it evolves further in the 21st century?

When I first started designing, and people would ask me what I did, the first comment they would make about industrial design is that they thought it had something to do with designing factories. That's still the case. I think one of the biggest challenges the industry faces is helping business and the public understand what industrial design really is, the difference it can make. Business still treats it like a commodity, a secondary profession. The Asian manufacturers who offer free design and engineering services for tooling and manufacturing contracts aren't helping either.

"THINKING ON PAPER MOVES AWAY FROM SIMPLY EXPLORING AESTHETICS AND INITIATES A COGNITIVE PROCESS, GOING TO A PLACE WHERE YOU'RE HAVING A CONVERSATION WITH YOURSELF, EXPRESSING THINGS YOU DON'T REALLY UNDERSTAND."

I teach an introduction to design general education course and ask the students, most of whom are from other majors, to describe the profession. The diversity of responses points to a certain invisibility in the arena of public perception.

It is interesting that it's still a big question mark of what we do in our field. Our process, it's still a big mystery.

It is. It's really unfortunate, although people are beginning to appreciate it more with high-profile products like those of Apple.

Anything that you'd like to add that we haven't talked about? Any final words of wisdom?

There's a disconnect between education and practice that I've observed and which has been in place since Raymond Loewy's time. I see many senior ID graduates with very little understanding of how the profession operates and how best to prepare for it. The internship experience is still the single best route to getting full-time employment after school. The problem is that many students don't have the skills even to get an internship.

Research has indicated that this "disconnect" is not exclusive to industrial design but a widespread concern across many industries. I don't think there's one specific culprit, but students suffer the consequences of being ill-prepared, while businesses may be challenged to find the skill set they need without extensive on-the-job training. BI

To see Thornton Lothrop's work, please visit http://breaking.in

BRANKO LUKIC
FOUNDER
NONOBJECT
PALO ALTO, CALIFORNIA

What kinds of portfolios get your attention these days? What brings in a product designer for an interview?

Their thinking. There are way too many portfolios out there that are the same. It's very rare to see unique thinking—the ability to not be drawn into the paella of the Internet. The unfortunate side effect of the Internet is that everyone becomes a similar thinker because of the fact that people get insights by what they see. So what gets my attention is unique thinking—big, broad thinking that expands beyond the norm, beyond the status quo, and the usual practice of design.

Have you seen a portfolio recently that had that kind of thinking?

Not yet. I've seen good bits and pieces here and there, but not an entire portfolio.

How would you suggest to students to break out of this same old vortex that you mention?

They should start using more of their inner Google.

What do you expect to learn from a designer during an interview?

It's about being human and how they communicate with other humans. To understand if they have passion and enough empathy to understand the world around them, how design can reduce the noise and enhance life. That's one of the most important things I look for. How do they think about the problem? How do they see themselves contributing in the world?

What characteristics or qualities are necessary for the designer to have in order to succeed?

Hard work and passion. This access to convenience has made the newer generations not so eager to work hard on their own practice—on their own journey to discover the purpose of design. To work hard just like Michelangelo did in his time. It's about practicing your art, practicing the art of innovation, of thinking for practical purposes, for emotional design, for how you live, for questioning things continuously. Keeping your inner child alive, always pushing forward.

Designers who do interesting work are driven from within. They're interested in the evolution of their own work. Like a good musician, they're not creating a song to just win awards but to create amazing melodies. A violinist will practice for years for that one concert.

How did you break into this business?

That story is pretty long, but I come from Serbia where not much industrial design existed at all when I was studying. Nonetheless we had a great school for it. I was always sketching and drawing, you could say even before I started to walk. When I was 14, someone told me that there's a job called "designer," and they explained what it was. I was so fascinated by the fact that I could design products—I couldn't believe this job actually existed. So I went to a design high school, which when I think about it now, was pretty advanced. I spent a lot of time practicing, did a lot of analog design work. There wasn't any computer software for it at the time. We drafted, sketched, and did all of the visualization stuff as well as machining, prototyping, and building real, physical objects in the shop.

"SO WHAT GETS MY ATTENTION IS UNIQUE THINKING—BIG, BROAD THINKING THAT EXPANDS BEYOND THE NORM, BEYOND THE STATUS QUO, AND THE USUAL PRACTICE OF DESIGN."

When I finished high school, I applied to the five-year-long program in industrial design at the University of Arts in Belgrade. They only accepted five students in the whole country—and Yugoslavia at that time had a population of 20 million people. I was extremely excited and happy about getting in. It took me through many years of experimentation and practice.

After University, I started a company with a couple of friends of mine. We worked until about '98. I also manufactured furniture, designed office interiors, branded products, and printed a book of my work. I sent it everywhere—to IDEO, to frog, et cetera—to get feedback. People would tell [me] I was crazy; no one was going to reply to some

guy from Serbia. Coming from Serbia meant a much harder starting position than for some other people around the world. I had to work a lot harder to break through, but I continued to send out my material. Eventually, Hartmut Esslinger from frog design got back to me. He offered me a job and I was very excited to join his team in California. It was always my dream to try California and Silicon Valley because the area was coming out with some major technologies and products that were on cutting edge of what's possible.

Finally, I always knew I was going to start my own studio. I wanted to redesign the way design is conducted as a profession—how it's practiced. I wanted to design for reasons beyond just economic. So I started first working on my book NONOBJECT and finally in 2007 opened the studio with the same name. Since then, we've been working on really exciting stuff and continue to grow as a firm.

If you were just starting out now, what advice would you give yourself?

Follow your intuition—it's very important. And work hard. Ask yourself why are you doing this? Have a very positive outlook and attitude toward the world. Optimism is critical. When you run into an obstacle always know that there's a way around it. That optimism will help you drive forward.

Where do you see the future of industrial design going as it evolves further in the 21st century?

It's a lot more than the future of industrial design; it's the future of design and its positive and meaningful impact on the world. [BI]

To see Branko Lukic's work, please visit http://breaking.in

MYK LUM
PRINCIPAL
LDA LLC
IRVINE, CALIFORNIA

What kinds of portfolios get your attention these days? What brings in an industrial designer for an interview?

We review all portfolios closely, but the first hint of the quality of the portfolio is in the résumé. After viewing thousands and thousands of résumés and portfolios, we find that if the résumé is poorly designed, the contents are sure to match. Once we start looking through the portfolio, one of the first things we pick up on is the candidate's sensitivity to form and aesthetics—not only in the products themselves, but in the layout of the portfolio and the sense of graphics. If the products are aesthetically appropriate, we'll start to pay attention to how they derived the design, the research and strategy, and the level of innovation. Is it beautiful, but boring? Or did they first solve a problem or rethink how the product works, then made it beautiful?

We look closely at their sketches, because we like to see the progression of ideas and where they came from, and to see what else they came up with. If we see glimpses of this in an emailed portfolio, we'll usually ask them to come in. We also value internships in recent graduates, especially if it was with a design consultancy, and if you're more experienced, we want to see that you worked in a very design-driven environment.

What do you think of showing work that's not industrial design in a portfolio? Things like art, photography, hobbies, etc.?

Depends on what it is and how good it is. We've seen some candidates with incredible sketchbooks of non-product-related works that showed us an amazing attention to detail and sensitivity to form. Other candidates, who appeared very serious, showed their whimsical side by showing some very amusing sketches that showed a great sense of humor. But

we've also had some candidates show us poor quality sketches and art that brought the level of their portfolio down a few notches. In general, we recommend sticking to ID-related work unless your other work is of exceptional quality.

What do you expect to learn from the designer during an interview?

We are hoping to find a little information that is not obvious from looking at a portfolio. What kind of a work ethic does the candidate have, can he get along with other designers, is he defensive about his work, how passionate is he about his work and being in the design field? We want to see what his working process is, and what kind of thought went into his design solutions. We are also trying to determine if he is interested in the types of projects that we frequently work on, and if there is "chemistry" between the candidate and our team.

What characteristics or qualities are necessary to be a successful industrial designer?

We believe someone who is passionate about design, and can't imagine themselves doing anything but design, is an essential quality. They are determined to be a great designer. They eat, sleep, and breathe design. They are constantly trying to improve their design skills, whether it's learning the newest program, analyzing products when shopping, reading books, magazines, and understanding that everything is connected. They are naturally curious about everything, and are not afraid to take a risk. We think a creative thinker who can look at a mundane product, and imagine what it could be, would make a great designer. We also think "teachability" is a great quality— someone who is willing and eager to learn, and hopefully someone who can teach us a thing or two.

What are some reasons you have rejected a candidate?

In most cases, we reject candidates because their skill set is not aligned with what we are looking for at the time. Sometimes we reject candidates because they have a reputation for being difficult to work with—the design community is small, so if you're a difficult personality, word will eventually get around. Sometimes geography is an obstacle—we can't fly everyone in to meet with them, so if we're not confident in your ability to do the job, we won't call you in.

What motivated you to open your own design studio?

After graduation, I worked for a small design consultancy for a number of years. Tough times came, and the office eventually shut down. Since I was unemployed, I decided to work part time at another consultancy, and part time as a freelancer. As the freelance projects started to get bigger and bigger, I eventually went off on my own full time, and started hiring employees.

How do you manage the non-design aspects of running a studio?

We're a relatively small firm, so I manage most of the business aspects myself, which keeps me quite busy. In general, I spend most mid-mornings answering emails, afternoons doing design direction, and evenings are spent on general business-related work.

If you were just starting out now, what advice would you give yourself?

Not long ago, I gave a lecture at California State University Long Beach, and part of that lecture was advice to students. Here are some of the talking points of that lecture:

If you are starting as a junior in the ID program, be strategic in your decisions in school—they affect the rest of your life. Pick design projects in the area that you want to get into (broad, such as product design or research/strategy). Pick design projects that allow you to show off your design skills. Develop a strong work ethic—don't miss deadlines, don't accept mediocrity because of time. In fact, don't accept mediocrity, period. Strive to be the best. Design is a competitive field. Okay and fairly good are not acceptable— exceptional and awesome are what you should be shooting for. If you want to design products when you get out of school, pick projects that end up with real products, not conceptual "cloud" projects. Don't ignore the mundane—it shows a design firm your ability to take something you use every day and make something unique and innovative out of it, which is what we are frequently called to do. Get an internship,

a good one, as soon as you can. Your senior thesis project should point the direction in which you want to go. Network.

"DESIGN IS A COMPETITIVE FIELD. OKAY AND FAIRLY GOOD ARE NOT ACCEPTABLE—EXCEPTIONAL AND AWESOME ARE WHAT YOU SHOULD BE SHOOTING FOR."

The graduating seniors should pay attention to their résumé; it reflects design sensitivity, and it's our first impression of them and their work. Your first job is usually the most important job you'll ever have—it sets you on a path that is difficult to change, so choose wisely. Try to choose a job in a place that is design driven and will push you to further develop your creative abilities. Try to work at a place with highly talented and driven people. Immerse yourself in the world of design—books, magazines, web, stores, museums, new technologies, software, whatever is relevant to design. Eventually you will find that everything is relevant to design.

It's not a job, it's a lifestyle.

As for the general skills you should try to develop when in school, I'd say understand how to use visual language to express a brand. Create desire. Stay relevant—understand what is currently considered "good design." Design has never been more complicated that it is today. Great design isn't just form, it's the integration and understanding of function, form, manufacturing, branding, innovation, user interface, engineering, and costing. We are the only people who can combine all of the above and create a great product. Try to understand as many of these things as you can. Understanding them and being able to use them will make you valuable. Take things apart and understand how things work, and how they're made. A brand is "a promise of a compelling experience." You are a brand; develop your brand to potential employers—offer them a compelling experience if they hire you. Network.

Finally, on your first job it is important to note that the more you understand business, the more you will understand your clients, and what they are looking for. The more you understand manufacturing and business, the more your design philosophy will change. Design has the power to move people, and to move brands, so a project is what you make of it. Find the challenge in everyday things. There are no boring projects, only boring solutions, so motivate yourself. Understand the mechanics and manufacturing of a product; you'll need it when you go up against engineering. Understand the brand values and how the product expresses the brand; you'll need it to convince marketing. Understand how to keep the costs of a product under control, without compromising the design; you'll need it to maintain your sanity.

Our job is to create success. Have fun.

Where do you see the future of industrial design going as it evolves further in the 21st century?

Industrial design is an ever-changing field. How we design a product today is very different than how we designed it 25 years ago. At its highest level, it's much more complicated, as it is now a combination of research, strategy, aesthetics, branding, marketing, manufacturing, costing, UX, and UI. Designers are the only ones who can bring this all together. I believe that more companies now understand the strategic importance design plays in business, and our roles will be continually expanding.

Anything we didn't cover that you would like to add? Any final words of wisdom?

I think I've gone on too long already. ▣

To see Myk Lum's work, please visit http://breaking.in

STUART MACEY
SENIOR STUDIO ENGINEER
HYUNDAI DESIGN AMERICA
IRVINE, CALIFORNIA &
PART-TIME FACULTY
ART CENTER COLLEGE OF DESIGN
PASADENA, CALIFORNIA &
AUTHOR OF *H POINT: THE FUNDAMENTALS OF CAR DESIGN AND PACKAGING*

You open your book *H-Point: The Fundamentals of Car Design & Packaging* with the following quote from Sir Alec Issigonis: "Fashion dates, but logic is timeless." How has his statement guided your own work?

My main role in a studio is to support the design team by creating the vehicle architecture or package, based on sound logic: from product planning, legislation, and technology. This frees up the designers to focus on form and proportion development, without getting bogged down with too many details. Sometimes the package forces the design to be compromised, so it's often seen as the enemy, but it's always worth remembering that it's usually the logic behind a product that defines its appearance. I always try to communicate the logic as clearly as possible and remind the designers that history is littered with iconic, timeless designs that look very cool because of their architecture. I don't think Sir Alec's statement is meant to put down styling, just help to define its purpose in the product development process.

How did you break into the industry?

Through the back door actually. In the '70s not many people knew how to start a career in the car business, and there were no car companies near to where I grew up. I wanted to be an illustrator and just draw cars for a living, but my parents couldn't afford to send me to art college, so I took a sheet metal work apprenticeship in a shipyard instead. (Are you crying yet?) During my training I used a lot of geometry, spent some time in the drawing offices working on Hovercraft Structures and went to college to study engineering. When my apprenticeship finished, British Leyland—England's largest car company at the time—was looking for trainee body engineers and my training qualified me for the position. Body engineers often become studio engineers because they understand more about the issues that affect a clay model than engineers from other areas, i.e. chassis or powertrain. So after about 10 years of designing body structures, I transitioned into studio engineering and design.

What characteristics or qualities are necessary to be a successful industrial designer?

A tough question. Creativity, imagination, innovation, great communication skills—visual and oral—a diverse knowledge base and the right computer skills are all important. Having a friendly personality and working well with teams is also really appreciated by employers. You'll need to take criticism well and get used to having your heart broken when your favorite design is not chosen, or is highly modified by the project leaders. A good designer should be flexible, open minded, and a good listener.

What kinds of portfolios get attention?

I'm primarily an engineer, so my opinion about portfolios may not be worth too much. I think for sure, it should be focused on the products that are developed at the studio you send the portfolio to. My role at Art Center is to help the students develop an understanding of vehicle architecture, so I always emphasize the inclusion of architecture sketches in the ideation pages along with the exterior, interior designs. I also encourage my students to add a package logic drawing to each project. These help the reader understand the designer's process and knowledge.

What are some common mistakes you see students or junior designers make in their portfolios?

Not understanding what the client is looking for and not including work that makes it stand out from the crowd. Designers are paid to generate ideas, so there should be lots of ideation work.

Knowing the tensions that tend to exist between design and engineering, what does a designer need to do to navigate successfully between the two disciplines and see their design through to production?

Tension usually exists when there is a lack of respect. Many engineers simply don't respect the role that design plays in the success of a product and designers don't always appreciate the responsibility that engineers have meeting extremely complex criteria before they finally sign off on a component or system. Because manufacturing cars and trucks is so complex, designers have a much wider set of responsibilities than in the past.

"YOU'LL NEED TO TAKE CRITICISM WELL AND GET USED TO HAVING YOUR HEART BROKEN WHEN YOUR FAVORITE DESIGN IS NOT CHOSEN, OR IS HIGHLY MODIFIED BY THE PROJECT LEADERS.

This change is reflected in the curriculum at most good design schools, where vehicle engineering and packaging classes have been added to complement the regular design classes. Studio engineers help to create a bridge between disciplines, getting everyone on the same page. Embrace diversity and the tension should vanish.

What do you think is a good way for people to improve their skills?

Get good training and put lots of practice time in. In Malcolm Gladwell's book Outliers, he suggests it takes about 10,000 hours to become truly great at anything if you get good information from day one.

Moving around the industry can be very helpful for growth, knowing when to change jobs, and working with people who want you to succeed can help accelerate growth.

If you were just starting out now, what advice would you give yourself?

Find some good mentors and the right college. Make lots of friends, work hard, stay passionate and inspired. Find out your strengths and weaknesses, then focus on developing your strengths and avoid situations that expose your weaknesses. Don't let anyone hold you back.

Where do you see the future of transportation design going?

Over the past 30 years auto design has become more complex, diverse, and competitive. I think we can expect more of the same in the future. The lines between various types of transportation and products will continue to blur and it seems that almost anything is possible. Design has become so critical to the success of any vehicle, companies simply can't risk investing in products without getting the image right, so design just keeps getting more important. Apple has done a great job to help everyone understand the link between design and profit.

Can you elaborate a bit more on how Apple has done this and how a student or an aspiring designer can apply that type of process or thinking to further their success in developing their own ideas?

Apple has done so much to demonstrate the designer's value to industry as it grew to the most valuable company in the USA, with essentially a designer at the helm. In the '80s and '90s, most people opted for PCs and didn't understand why some people would pay more to own a Mac. Steve Jobs visualized how people could relate to the products they owned, and enriched that relationship by insisting on great design. He understood that adding value by design not only increases profitability, but also creates customer loyalty, a bond which endures through good and bad economic times.

Jobs understood that the essence of good design

is simplicity, especially critical with emerging technology. His ability to distill every creation to the bare essential elements and get every line, surface, and graphic interface perfect, was simply unmatched in his industry. Couple this to his vision, understanding of emerging technology and new retail experience opportunities, and no other company could even come close. They couldn't even do a good job of copying.

Many companies will have designers on the board, but few have an autocratic design-driven leader, and without this type of leadership, design budgets are often compromised. Many people have criticized the way Jobs conducted his business, but it's difficult to argue against the success of his design philosophy.[BI]

To see Stuart Macey's work, please visit http://breaking.in

JEROME MAGE
FOUNDER
MAGE DESIGN
LOS ANGELES

What kinds of portfolios get your attention these days? What brings in an industrial designer for an interview?

Number one, they should be short. Everyone is very busy these days. I'd like to see a lot of hand sketching and things that are a bit different, whatever different means. Could be the project the person has worked on, the way it's presented, something that shows a personal conviction. At the end of the day, there are more and more designers, more and more design schools and I don't think they do a good job at filtering people that are going through. I think it's fairly easy to get in and fairly easy to get out. People in general seem to feel inclined to give good grades and are hesitant to say: "You know what, you should forget about design, this may not be the best thing for you. You may not have what it takes to be a designer." There are so many kids with the same skills; what I'm really looking for is a point of view. In general, portfolios that show personal, stylistic, or aesthetic vision make it more interesting.

Have you seen a portfolio recently that resonated with you, and what about it stood out?

There was a guy who came in a few days ago. He was a really interesting kid in terms of his portfolio, which showed a unique design style but also a real maturity that showed that he understands the end result of a design. Not in terms of creative language, but in terms that there was a client at the end of the road. It showed a rare ability to understand how to solve a problem, the economics of the design process and a cool, unique vision.

What do you expect to learn from the designer during an interview?

In general, I would say we are a very team-driven place. I am looking for personality. I want to see that the person I bring in will be able to work with the rest of the team and the personalities that we have here. I would say again, in general, have a defined sense of self and your work. For example, on the product design side, so many kids are showing up with projects that have to do with recycling or saving the Earth, but it's a common thing across each portfolio. This has little impact on me; it means they're just another person coming out of a design school. If a kid would come up and show me a gun design instead, I would be more interested. Everyone is working on recycling and he'd work on something opposite.

I'm looking for kids that can show a personal point of view. It's very simple, but so hard to find. Especially after seeing the same projects as a result of the same school assignments. Most of these projects have nothing to do with what we have to do in professional life, and are very token. That's great when you're in school, it should be a time to work on things you may not necessarily be able to work on later on, when you're actually in a professional field. At the same time, you can be at the complete opposite of what's going on in the studios, and still make a living as a designer.

It sounds like there's a disconnect between what the students are being taught these days and what's necessary for them to succeed in the industry.

Yes, completely, I would say 100%. There are a couple of schools that prepare the kids better, but I think, in general, when you're a design student—it was the same for me—there's a strong emphasis on the creative process and some sort of clichéd ideology that is taught, and it's not the reality at all. There's nothing utopian about running a design studio, it's very matter of fact. The client is looking for results, for problems to be solved. There are things that need to be understood about the culture that you work in and live in. It's very factual.

> *"ONE OF THE THINGS THAT PUT ME IN THE GOOD SITUATION WAS ALL THE INTERNSHIPS I DID AT THE BEGINNING, WHEN I WAS IN SCHOOL. I'D GET AS MANY FOR AS LONG AS I COULD, FOR NO PAY."*

Obviously, maybe three or four designers are able to sell their name with some sort of a marketing twist to it but that's five, 10 guys worldwide. The rest work as designers; it's a very real thing. It's great to be creative, but sometimes the word "creative" is a bit mismanaged in a way the schools are presenting it to the students. Schools should prepare students a little bit [for the fact] that, not everyone is going to be the next Philippe Starck. It seems like everyone's pitched to be the next Philippe Starck at school and that's a big mistake.

What characteristics or qualities are necessary to be a successful industrial designer?

It's hard to say. One of the things that put me in the good situation was all the internships I did at the beginning, when I was in school. I'd get as many for as long as I could, for no pay. I think what I learned during those internships gave me an edge over some students to get a better position quicker.

How did you break into this business?

Once again, it was internships. I think the projects were esoteric, they were tangible enough. I spent six months interning in the US and made a lot of connections working with different companies. Also, one of the things that maybe helped me was that I was willing to work extremely hard. I would never leave the office before my boss in the evening, little details like that that showed that I really wanted it. Although in design schools students work a lot, they expect when they're out of school that they'll have a high-paying 9 to 5 job, but that's not necessarily the case. A lot of them don't really display the go-getter attitude, or try to improve themselves. For me those were the big things. So I broke in through internships and a strong work ethic.

If you were just starting out now, what advice would you give yourself?

Work harder than anyone else. I'd definitely use multimedia in a way to reach out to more people and get my portfolio out there in a different and memorable way. When I studied in the mid-90s this was not available to us, and now it's pretty incredible what you can do. I would also encourage myself to show diversity and be multidisciplinary, which I think was a key to my success—not to get stuck in a rut. Go do an internship in China, Japan, the US, or Italy. Travel and show a broad interest in disciplines and cultures. I'd study all sorts of methods and styles that would give me an edge to thinking things through and finding solutions.

The more diverse the experience, the more advantageous for the designer.

Yes, definitely. Especially now when you develop a product and it's being sold in Asia, in Europe, in the US and a lot of it comes down to understanding the culture, sociology, trends, and fashion forecasting. I think you've got to show some broad experience and go and get it.

Where do you see the future of industrial design going as it evolves further in the 21st century?

It's difficult to say. A lot of times when you try to predict the future, all the people that do, don't really do a good job at it, right? They thought we were going to be driving flying cars by now. I think we can only think in the short term. For me, in the short term, it seems that design is becoming more and more about corporate experience rather than just product. In a weird way it can be the exact opposite. I guess it depends on the client. I don't know about the future, I don't have a crystal ball. I wish I did because I would use it every day. I just hope that industrial design doesn't lose its creativity and that it doesn't get lost with all the new tools available.

Anything we didn't cover that you would like to add? Any final words of wisdom?

I think product design is a great field. I think there are still a lot of bad products that are being designed, so there are a lot of opportunities. With all the tools and social media I can imagine it's a great time to be a student and also, in a weird way, a difficult time, with so many choices. I would encourage any kid who wants to pursue this as a career to strike a balance between expressing yourself while also confronting the reality of life, the economy, and the culture. I look forward to working with the next generation of designers continuing to create great products. [BI]

To see Jerome Mage's work, please visit http://breaking.in

LEONARDO MASSARELLI
FOUNDER
QUESTTO|NO
SÃO PAULO

What kinds of portfolios get your attention these days? What brings in an industrial designer for an interview?

It's been awhile since I've seen a portfolio that captured our attention. But, I'd say that the first impression is the general layout of the portfolio, which denotes the aesthetic quality the candidate has towards design. Typography, colors, care with the images and composition. After the first layout impression, I search for the quality of the products presented. Sketch, 3D, and rendering ability are very important to provide a good impact and impression.

Finally, the most important thing is the relevance of the candidate's design ideas. What is the product intended to do? For whom? What's its context? The holistic thought in the development of a product is important in our evaluation.

What do you expect to learn from a designer during an interview?

I expect the candidate to have, not only good professional references, but also to know the history of design and to be up-to-date with design trends, technology, methods, and so forth.

What characteristics or qualities would you say make a successful designer?

General knowledge. I believe a good designer must have accumulated diverse knowledge. They must be a generalist by nature. Being able to see context with a different point-of-view is one of the differentiators we bring to projects we participate in, and this view depends on our accumulated knowledge and experiences. In our company we call this ability "creative pollination." Working in several market segments keeps our repertoire always full with new information.

How do you personally feed your own inner-generalist outside the work context?

Through natural curiosity. I think it is an inner, primitive habit. I consume a lot of information through blogs, magazines, and through my diverse group of friends.

How did you break into this business?

There are several ways to break into this business. The most coherent one is finding a job in one of the agencies already established in the market, where a young designer can learn a lot. There are

other significant ways. Nowadays, I see many newcomers producing concept designs and posting them to their blogs or other Internet-based platforms. This is a very good way to get their work seen. When we were first beginning our business careers, we had our work seen in magazines by someone interested in producing our concepts.

If you were just starting out now, what advice would you give yourself?

First of all, I'd tell myself to work for other agencies and, if possible, travel abroad for work or study. Learning from other cultures is extremely necessary nowadays. I started the studio right after I finished college when I was 21 years old.

"THE FIRST IMPRESSION IS THE GENERAL LAYOUT OF THE PORTFOLIO, WHICH DENOTES THE AESTHETIC QUALITY THE CANDIDATE HAS TOWARDS DESIGN."

Having very little experience in design and business, I feel I lost precious time trying to understand some obvious lessons. On the other hand, we had the chance to learn by creating our very own way to get things done. This brought us great confidence and lots of personality to our projects.

It's amazing to learn you boldly started your own agency at just 21. Can you tell me more about that experience? What motivated you? What were some tough lessons you learned? What propelled you to keep going forward?

On one hand it was terrible, but on the other it was terrific. Many years went by where my partner and I lived with almost no money. All of our friends had some income, either through working in the industry or landing a job in a studio. But, we had nothing, except a lot of worry. We found liberty in having the ability to create our own way of thinking and designing, however. This created a possibility for us to see design without boundaries. We think creatively through challenges. We did so from the beginning—and it worked for us.

There were difficult moments, but I really believed, and still believe in our work and our mission. This helped me to move forward, even through hard times. I simply love creating things. I believe I can make things better. The bottom line is when you're only 21, you don't know much about the world and this is a fertile ground for creativity, for starting new things, because you're open to trying things out and failing.

Where do you see the future of industrial design going as it evolves further in the 21st century?

I see design becoming a boundless activity. Of course there are multiple and very specific design specializations, but I believe the macro knowledge of design can manifest in the most diverse areas. Designers will, little by little, play an interchanging role amongst these areas. We will be like orchestra conductors. Product designers, most specifically, will face a very different dynamic in the coming years. In this near future it will be possible and cheap to manufacture low-scale products using quick prototyping technology. This will be a very fun scenario.

Any final words of wisdom for the young, budding product designers?

Think about design and do design. There are too many people out there today just talking about design, and very few doing design. [BI]

To see Leonardo Massarelli's work, please visit http://breaking.in

TOM MATANO
EXECUTIVE DIRECTOR
SCHOOL OF INDUSTRIAL
DESIGN
ACADEMY OF ART
UNIVERSITY
SAN FRANCISCO

You have had quite a long and illustrious career, so I'm curious: what would you say has been a trademark of a stellar or successful industrial design portfolio? What is the common thread?

Over and above strong basic skills such as drawing, graphic sensitivity and digital skills in 2D and 3D are important. Thinking process needs to be visually explained. They also need to have good observation and analytical skills and show personality, not the school color.

"THE STORY SHOULD UNFOLD IN A NATURAL FLOW FROM PAGE TO PAGE. NO HOLES. NO GAPS. VIEWER SHOULD NOT HAVE TO GO BACK TO PREVIOUS PAGES OR REVISIT PRIOR PAGES TO MAKE THE CONNECTIONS."

Thinking process can be visually displayed by showing ideation sketches, thumbnail sketches, or diagrams. Observation can be displayed in a storyboard style. Analytical skills can be shown via positioning maps or other visual aids, such as infographics. Personality can come through in the style of sketches, the graphic layout of the portfolio, the color sensitivity of the product, and the overall story building.

Have you seen an industrial design portfolio recently that resonated with you? What about it stood out?

There was a broad range of design vocabularies within, alongside creative and innovative solutions with well thought-out design. Essentially, there was a completeness of story, told visually. The story should unfold in a natural flow from page to page. No holes. No gaps. Viewer should not have to go back to previous pages or revisit prior pages to make the connections.

If an industrial design student came to you looking for advice on how to prepare their portfolio to get an internship or a job, what would you tell them to do? What should be in their portfolio?

Portfolios for an internship and for a job requires two different things. A portfolio for a job requires more diversity and maturity in design, versus an internship portfolio. You become an art director or conductor of the orchestra when you are making a portfolio, so exhibit the best of all skills you have through various projects. Show process. State the problem statement, show research and analysis, set the criteria for the design solution. Explore many ideas, and then reflect back on the criteria to select a final design direction.

What has been the most common mistake that students (or junior designers) make in how they present their work or their portfolios?

They don't prepare the portfolio from the reviewer's point of view.

What advice would you have to someone preparing for an interview at a design studio?

Listen to comments that reviewers make. Pay special attention to constructive criticisms. Don't just listen to what you want to hear, as you will miss out on many good points. Consider an interview as yet another learning opportunity.

What characteristics or qualities are necessary to be a successful industrial designer in the long term?

Be interested in nature and human nature that surrounds you. Be curious.

How did you break into this business?

Through a sponsorship project at the school. I found out who was coming to see our final presentation ahead of time. I studied his work and added one rendering that would suit his sense of design. It sealed the deal. Essentially, I got to know my "customer" really well.

If you were just starting out now, what advice would you give yourself?

Set a goal and develop your own measurement tools to gauge your progress.

Where do you see the future of industrial design going as it evolves further in the 21st century?

I believe that industrial design is a study of mankind, human nature, and nature. This basic principle won't change. Industrial design will shift more to the user experience-based realm. At the Academy, we added UX contents to the list of deliverables in applicable courses to prepare the students for this expanding role. Emerging technologies will demand, and open, doors to this new way of thinking. BI

To see Tom Matano's work, please visit http://breaking.in

JASON MAYDEN
VP OF DESIGN,
MARK ONE,
SAN FRANCISCO

What kinds of portfolios get your attention these days? What brings in an industrial designer for an interview?

The best portfolios are by people who are able to demonstrate their aptitude for learning and also demonstrate their capacity for maintaining a high level of curiosity. I never actually get caught up in the skill set; I get caught up in mindset. When you come into a corporation, we'll train you on the principles that define how we look at design and the product—the consumer engagement stuff and all that—but what we can't train is the pure hunger to learn. That isn't something that's taught.

I love portfolios that are diverse, those that present research and process rather than just the finished product. I love people who are multidisciplinary, who take classes in crafts, fine arts, and any other discipline that surrounds design. I'm looking for people who are creative, analytical, and critical thinkers who can think beyond the context of just the product.

How do you decipher that skill by just looking at a portfolio? What about their portfolios tells you that they have those qualities?

Well, it's the portfolios that aren't heavily related to product but to the process of getting to the product. People who clearly package their steps, their approach, how they address assumptions or opportunities. If I see a whole bunch of pretty sketches, obviously a person is celebrating the end result and not the steps he or she took to get to that end result. It's really clear. Sometimes people think that research and all of that stuff is something that needs to be articulated with words on a page. It can be articulated with photos, ethnography, the basic principles of studying user behavior, and mapping out your consumer's journey. For me, this is the most important part, so I'll look for that at the front of every project that they have.

I look for people who segment their projects by discussing what the mission or the intent was before they got into the design cycle. People who front-load their portfolio with little mini-briefs or problems that they're trying to address, or areas of interest. Folks that normally get ahead in an organization show more of the process than the end result.

What do you expect to learn from a designer during an interview?

By that time it's about the cultural fit more than anything. It has less to do with skills at that point—

we are really trying to decipher this person's ability to communicate, to have confidence in the way they speak and so forth. We understand that in today's global society there are some cultural barriers around comfort levels and how people view authority and how people express their opinion. But in person, you always can tell if someone's a cultural fit for your company.

At Nike, you don't have to love sports, but do you love play? Do you consider yourself a person who is a positive play advocate? What things do you do to play? How do you keep yourself inspired and encouraged? That's how we frame up the prototypical Nike employee: always curious, always remaining playful. So if I get a person in the room and we're talking about play and they have this straight face—they don't believe in play and they just want to focus—they may not be a good cultural fit for our company. This is not a culture of a certain race or gender, but of a certain attitude.

What characteristics or qualities are necessary to be a successful designer?

First, empathy. That's the most important thing to have to be successful. You have to be willing to look at the problem from the perspective of the user. Secondly, you need to have a huge appetite for curiosity—I can't stress that enough. For me, being super, super, super curious is critical to being successful over time. Also, being a little bit flexible about what the word "designer" means—we hold onto the word through the lens of the product but it can be strategy, business, all of it. All of these areas can benefit from the process of design. It can open up a host of possibilities for a creative mind if one is able to not be so resistant to change in what design means.

There's a fascination now with design thinking and how we work. Having gone to a traditional design school and then to business school at Stanford, I'm able to understand what the fascination is about from both ends of the spectrum. But what's happening is that the classically trained designers may say that they don't believe in design thinking because they are design doers—so we have to allow ourselves to evolve as designers, and include more people in the conversation of design. Open it up and democratize what the word "design" means.

How did you break into this business?

I would say that the design broke into me. I wasn't headed to design as my first choice, I was headed to engineering school at Georgia Tech to study industrial engineering. I wanted to play football and was set on designing shoes—I thought you had to be an engineer to do that. Until one of my track and field coaches said, "Wait, hold on...engineers don't design shoes in the way you want to design shoes. Designers design shoes." So I had to research what he meant because I had no clue about industrial design, graphic design.

"I LOVE PORTFOLIOS THAT ARE DIVERSE, THOSE THAT PRESENT RESEARCH AND PROCESS RATHER THAN JUST THE FINISHED PRODUCT."

Growing up in Chicago, the only artistic career you hear about is architecture. If you have art talent, you go and become an architect—but I had no interest in buildings. It was really about someone bringing it up to me and then searching for more information. Then I realized everything I wanted to be, I could become through industrial design. So I say it kind of found me. I was running towards it and it was running towards me, and then we ran into each other and had a baby, and that baby is my career.

I basically landed my first job by repeatedly harassing Nike. I wrote a letter to them as a kid, but got really serious about it when I was at CCS [College for Creative Studies] and heard about this magical word called internship. I didn't even know what an internship was; nobody had explained it to me other than the importance of it, until I met some of the transportation design students. That's all they talked about; they obsessed over it. There must be something about this internship thing that I need to learn. That's when I realized that that's how you get into the company, that's how you show them you can do it. It's a long-term strategy. I called and did everything I could to get

in front of Nike. I got rejected two times but then on my third attempt, I got my internship and from there it was just about being persistent. During my senior year, I showed my projects to the company to express my interest. Thankfully, I was presented with an offer upon graduation and have been here ever since.

If you were just starting out now, what advice would you give yourself?

I would tell myself to be patient. I would tell myself to be tremendously, tremendously patient. Design is a lifelong sport.

The only sport I can correlate design to is golf. Over years of experience, the more patient you become, the better golf player you'll be. It's the same with design. If you become more patient, you will become more introspective and you'll learn about yourself and your boundaries, and you'll get better as a designer. Just be patient. Just pace, pace, pace yourself. So many designers will hit the ground running and get the Red Dot award or go to the big consultancy, the big agency, or the big corporation, but what really makes you successful are all those little, small projects that you didn't think were important. They give you a foundational base to draw from when you have those big, hairy, complex problems that you need to solve.

I would tell myself to not be afraid to tell people what I'm really interested in. I remember starting out at CCS, I was so afraid of telling people I wanted to do shoes because I thought I was going to be banished to some dark corner of the school because everyone else wanted to do cars. I just trusted my own gut, my own intuition, and started to dream out loud and let people know that I wanted to design shoes, and that I'm proud of it. It's not something that means that I'm any different from anybody else; it's what brings me joy, it's where I want to go. I would tell myself to have confidence to speak out sooner about what I was passionate about, rather than have other people tell me what I should be passionate about.

Where do you see the future of industrial design going?

I see that word, industrial design, going away. The word itself is born out of industrial revolution and mass manufacturing, so I see that word dropping off and becoming more about service, interaction, and experience rather than industry. Localization—meaning manufacturing, business models, approach, messaging—all of that is going to be nuanced by culture. What works for Brazil is going to be made in Brazil; what works for the US will be made in the US. So I think when people think industry, it's going to be too big to describe the things we are going to be doing, and it's really going to be about the service. We are going to be more strategists rather than people who just design.

How do you see industrial designers as being equipped to handle that kind of a task?

The good thing about industrial design is that we're able to visually communicate what we're trying to do. There is a desperate need for industrial designers to really, really, really, really, really take advantage of the foundational work, the design philosophy, design history, and strategy. Those are the core skills that desperately need to be developed. When kids come out of school, all they have is a bunch of beautiful drawings. They have no foundational research capability, no communication skills, and no appetite to dig deeper into an insight. That's going to hurt them.

Industrial design is almost three-quarters of the way there; we just have to make sure we're open to process—not just the materials and manufacturing process—but things like need-finding and insights process. The same time and attention we put in figuring out how to make something, we should put into the insight that leads us to what we're going to make.

Is there anything you'd like to add that we haven't talked about? Any final words of wisdom?

I wish that design schools around the world would get together, hold hands, and make an agreement that there should be one universal way to teach the foundational principles of design. There are so many different ways to describe the same thing, and if everyone can agree on the important foundational curriculum for designers that would make things that much better. I mean they have it for medicine, they have it for finance, they have it for all these other industries that are structured, except for design

because design is subjective. Yes, the outcome is subjective but the process doesn't have to be.

Once we get on the same page around what the common language is, then we can stop looking around for who comes up with the most quotable phrase for the year. We can then just get down to the core of what we want these kids to do so they can be prepared to take our jobs and take the industry to the next level. We would see a radical shift in ability and in quality of what's being produced. We would see more and more kids who come from families who may not be affluent or have parents as designers embracing the field.

It breaks my heart that I don't see more women and minorities in leadership positions in design. It starts with education and having access to that education at an early enough stage. One way to do that is by having a universal agreement on what we should be teaching so that people can prepare themselves. [BI]

To see Jason Mayden's work, please visit http://breaking.in

SIGI MOESLINGER & MASAMICHI UDAGAWA FOUNDING PARTNERS ANTENNA DESIGN NEW YORK CITY

What sparked your interest in design?

MU: In my early teen years, I was fascinated by weapons: especially how different approaches can be taken by competing countries in shaping the hardware: battleships, fighter planes, tanks, etc. There, I learned about the interesting relationship between function and form as well as various production techniques and forms. More importantly, I learned that seemingly rational weapon design is heavily influenced by different cultures and design philosophies.

"EDIT YOUR WORK. IT IS NOT ABOUT QUANTITY, BUT QUALITY."

SM: Growing up I was surrounded by lots of old—or pretending to be old—things in our home. My parents didn't like anything that wasn't at least 80 years old, or looked the part. To me that didn't make sense. I wanted to live with objects of my time and I wanted to make things and make them better. I became quite interested in contemporary furniture, appliances, and cars. I didn't even know about industrial design, and when I found out about it, I knew this was what I wanted to do.

What motivated you open your own design studio?

SM: We had both been working for a while, corporate and consultancy, and felt ready for a change. There wasn't a specific company at the time we wanted to work for. Also we liked the idea of being more personally in charge of what we do. We had savings that would sustain us for about half a year, so we thought we should just give it a try.

How do you manage the non-design aspects of running a studio?

SM: There are lots of those, and we wear multiple hats, taking care of administrative tasks, client relationships, new business, staff, equipment, etc. It consumes quite a bit of time, but at the same time, we are not big enough to have special staff for those tasks.

Antenna frequently engages in creating conceptual design explorations outside of the commercial context. How have such projects informed your other, more commercial work?

SM: Those projects function a bit like a lab: we have some topic we are interested in, some material, some technology we want to try out, etc. We do the project and we get immediate learning and feedback. Sometimes this can have a direct influence on a client project, like using the same material, or more indirectly, like expanding our experience on how people behave in certain situations, which helps on other projects.

In your opinion, what does it take to be a successful industrial designer?

SM: Hard work, curiosity, persistence, good skills and thinking, a personal point of view and drive, and a portion of luck.

If you were hiring additional industrial designers to your studio, what kinds of portfolios would get your attention? What would bring a potential candidate in for an interview?

SM: We love to see a nice portfolio from which we can imagine the person's sensitivity, compatible personality, and good work ethic. A good portfolio makes us interested in meeting with the person behind it and learning more about this person.

Has there been a student or junior-level industrial design portfolio that you've seen recently that really stood out? What made this particular portfolio successful in your eyes?

SM: Yes. The student sent us a link to his portfolio website, which had a simple and clean design and that put an overview of his work right upfront. The work was diverse and instantly communicated a technical proficiency and an aesthetic sensibility that resonated with us. It made us want to see more.

If an industrial design student came to you looking for advice on how to prepare their portfolio to get an internship or a job, what would you tell them to do? What should be in their portfolio?

SM: Edit your work. It is not about quantity, but quality. We don't need to see all the projects you have ever done; we want to see the good ones. Showing the project process is good to demonstrate how you went about to achieve the final result, but not necessary for each project. Then, the portfolio should have a clean layout and design, well organized that communicates the projects in a concise manner. Very often we see product design portfolios with bad graphic design. That really hurts the work.

What are some common mistakes you see students or junior designers make in their portfolios?

SM: Sometimes students think they have to do something "special" with their portfolio to stand out. They elaborately "package" their portfolio and most often it gets in the way of the work itself or requires us to make an extra effort to look through the portfolio. That can be a real turnoff. Good work should speak for itself, no need for gimmicks.

Where do you see the future of industrial design going as it evolves further in the 21st century?

SM: Personally, we'd like to see fewer, but better products—better made, better looking, more sustainable, more meaningful and enduring. Else, we see ever more shifts to automation and self-service through the use of technology. Thus focus on interface, both physical and digital, and design of systems consisting of multiple touch points will become ever stronger.

Anything we didn't cover that you would like to add? Any final words of wisdom?

SM: Be open-minded and see every project as an opportunity to practice, learn, and do something great—even if at first it doesn't seem that exciting. BI

To see the work of Antenna Design, please visit http://breaking.in

IMRE MOLNAR
FORMER DEAN & PROVOST
COLLEGE FOR CREATIVE
STUDIES
DETROIT

Sadly, Mr. Molnar passed in December 2012. He was a dear friend and mentor, and his inspiring and creative mind is sincerely missed.

What kinds of portfolios get attention these days? Which ones are employers gravitating to?

This has always been the case, but increasingly the employers want to be able to glean a narrative that basically describes not only the solution, but also the rationale for a design and the thinking process that led to it. The notion that a portfolio is an album of pretty pictures of completed work is totally misguided. Rather a portfolio needs to be a pictorial narrative describing how various projects evolved, how each piece featured came to be. Telling the story of the project is tremendously important.

The other things people look for is evidence of teamwork, particularly working with and interacting with other disciplines. Evidence of having interdisciplinary team experience is tremendously important. Also important is project work that demonstrates that a student has had some international and/or diverse cultural experience and that he has a curiosity about social and lifestyle issues outside of those specific to the United States.

Have you seen an industrial design portfolio recently that resonated with you, and what about it stood out?

I attend the portfolio events here at the college and just last week we had about 200 companies here looking at product design portfolios. The students put together a display—a little gallery exhibition of what was, in fact, their portfolio. Here again, the students whose work attracted most attention were those who had worked on projects that touched on other cultures.

Recently, we had a project with Motorola where the class was divided up into teams, and each team was given a different emerging market around the world to research and analyze. Each team worked hard to probe their assigned region's specific market issues, focusing on the target customer's lifestyle. They then researched Motorola's current and emerging technologies and were required to extrapolate how these technologies could be configured into products that could serve the needs of emerging third-world markets. The students who worked on this project attracted a tremendous amount of attention.

The other thing of course, is that the standard of visual presentation has to be very, very high. Here I am not only referring to the skill demonstrated by a beautifully rendered design proposal. Rather the work, indeed the portfolio itself, has to exude a certain brand identity. Students are expected to present the work in the context of a company's branding position. They are expected to have a point of view on the branding and the presentation of a product's positioning within a predetermined market. The branding issues and the related graphic design are tremendously important and established baseline standards are very high. To compete, student portfolio graphics need to be superb.

So it's a combination of understanding both the market and the company you're designing for?

Absolutely. In our world, the anthropological context and user experience issues as they relate to the market are tremendously important. At many other schools, industrial design programs focus on technology, engineering, and functionality. Whereas at CCS, our focus is from a more humanistic point of view in terms of the user, the user's life experience, the user's context, the market context, and the related aesthetic issues. We are very proud of the high level of aesthetic refinement and beauty in our students' work. We see that the challenge for us is to engage our students to have a genuine curiosity for what is aesthetically pleasing for a given, predetermined market segment or customer demographic. In other words, we need for our students to take an interest in other people and not just design stuff that is pleasing to them.

Design for the end user, not for yourself.

Yeah, exactly. The daily choice of the beauty is in the eyes of the beholder. If you want to turn on or motivate a particular market segment to respond positively to a product or a service offering, you have got to understand what the aesthetic sensibilities of a particular market segment are. What has made the industrial design business interesting is the reality that manufacturing technologies have become so very flexible. It is now possible to make a business case for short, low-volume runs. As a consequence, there's a great fragmentation of the market because you can design-specific products in relatively small volumes to target a very specific demographic.

A designer can now create an item that really best suits the sensibilities and user patterns of a very specific market segment. It used to be you'd design one product, and it would be a world product, they'd make gazillion units of it. While that still exists, the trend now is to design products on a common engineering and technology architecture but with the interface—aesthetic and functionality—tweaked in a manner to best suit the lifestyles and user patterns of much smaller user tribes. This phenomenon requires that designers have to be much more cognizant of the nuances of the marketplace.

How did you break into this business?

I had very strong drafting skills, I drew really well from a very young age, and I also had a strong understanding of engineering stuff. I used to race motorcycles and cars and basically I could build and repair anything. Also, I was very interested in art and aesthetic issues. So my high school teachers basically said, "With your engineering abilities and building skills and your high level of drafting and aesthetic interests, you ought to pursue industrial design." They presented industrial design to me as an applied art. And I think you can empathize with this, my parents were émigrés and they couldn't speak English. I initially had a lot of pressure at school to pursue fine arts—to go to an art school, but my parents were skeptical about a fine artist's ability to make a living. So I took what I thought was a rational compromise by becoming an applied artist in the industrial arena. I reconciled that it would be fun because I really like engineering and manufacturing stuff and I thought it was a good balance of my skills, aptitudes, and interests.

To be frank, once I got into it, I found my way relatively easily. The whole process of going through design school and getting a job came easily because I drew really well and understood engineering, so I could talk my way into jobs. So I had a very smooth transition through college and into commercial life. Though, in actual fact, I didn't particularly like the profession at the time because I learned that my interest was really in people and the environment. In the early '70s the product design profession wasn't really people-centric or environmentally conscious.

What characteristics or qualities are necessary to be a successful industrial designer?

Another evolving trend in product design is a movement away from just a product in isolation but rather, the product being part a system and context. As a consequence, designers are expected to still create products but they have to be considered in the context of a much larger dynamic system.

> *"THE NOTION THAT A PORTFOLIO IS AN ALBUM OF PRETTY PICTURES OF COMPLETED WORK IS TOTALLY MISGUIDED. RATHER, A PORTFOLIO NEEDS TO BE A PICTORIAL NARRATIVE DESCRIBING HOW VARIOUS PROJECTS EVOLVED, HOW EACH PIECE FEATURED CAME TO BE."*

Designers still have to have strong 3D spatial perception, of course, they need to be able to imagine things, and with that they still need to be able to draw really well and to be able to sketch really well and translate their thinking into 3D digital media. Designers have to have a strong level of computing skill—the ability to creatively manipulate software.

In addition to these core skills, a designer has to be interested in people and have the curiosity to get to understand people's behavior. An outgoing persona is also useful, in addition to an openness to travel and going into places that are somewhat foreign in order to understand the way people live, behave, and so forth. It becomes tremendously important, once you master your skills, to have an attitudinal mindset where you are perpetually learning and willing to put yourself in areas, physically, where you are not necessarily comfortable so you can empathize with others and design for environments that are not your own. A designer will hit a glass ceiling early, and hard, if they can only design for their own tastes and lifestyle.

You've been in design education for a bit now. How do you see it evolving over the years, and how should it change to address the needs of the future?

Well, I think firstly you have to forgive me for stating the obvious but we're still grappling with the integration of new and constantly evolving technologies. It's a really big issue. There's finite time to develop the requisite skills. We need to provide students access to this very expensive and forever-evolving software and then address the constant challenge of developing teaching methods to keep up, including finding the time to teach teachers to teach students all the constantly evolving new stuff.

Then there's the previously discussed movement away from the object and I wonder how long it will be before the product design title ceases to exist. In order to design what we currently call products, you need to really design it in the context of a system, and the system is complicated. It's the way people use it on one hand, but it's also the way it's marketed, how is it presented to the marketplace, how people are exposed to it and then ultimately purchase it. The designer has to be cognizant of all of these phases within the system to various degrees.

Additionally, the designer still needs to be cognizant of manufacturing issues related in producing a product. Then, when manufacturing issues are factored in, the designer can no longer ignore the environmental issues involved in manufacturing, distribution, and sales.

Returning to portfolio, there are two tenets looked for in each design portfolio: the story and evidence of design thinking. A designer needs to tell a story in their portfolio—tell a story through their work. The story should talk about the problem and describe the process that led to the proposed solution through a process of design thinking.

What is design thinking? As industrial design educators, we have been teaching design thinking for a long time but we just didn't call it that. The processes industrial designers use to arrive at a solution are applicable to many things including developing systems and environments. Design is about solving problems. A portfolio needs to pictorially convey the story, describe the problem, reveal the proposed solution and the process that led the designer to arrive at their solution.

It's a fun business, but it's very, very dynamic. There's tremendous opportunity. The designers right now are extraordinarily sought after.

Where do you see the future of industrial design going as it evolves further in the 21st century?

There are various scenarios that are quite plausible. On one hand there will be a need for more and more design because of the fragmentation of the marketplace. Also what's tremendously exciting is the development of material sciences—the new materials: hard materials and soft materials—and the wealth of opportunities that will require a lot of design thinking to determine how these technological advances can be applied to products. So I think we are entering an unprecedented period of growth for design. But on the other hand, we are also entering a period of a "commodification" of design. Superficial styling work—the model "refresh," the styling of the box housing components—that stuff is going to move out of the province of true design. You will soon see software coming down the pike where anyone with a PC and a bunch of software can do quite credible styling work. What we're approaching with rapid prototyping and other digital technologies will allow untrained laymen to create credible packaging around your technology box. The software will probably offer you a menu of generic aesthetic directions and you can cut and paste and create a product design just by manipulating a palette on an interactive menu. Whereas the people who will be doing real design work, and who will be paid, in the Western context,

significant salaries will be designers who can really solve problems in the context of a sophisticated matrix that needs to consider sociological, anthropological, technological, and environmental contexts.

Designers who will be able to handle a higher level of intellectual complexity will be the only designers who can survive. Design as it has been—that is, packaging a beautiful box around underpinnings of a technology—will just phase out because any clown will be able to do it manipulating simple and intuitive software.

If you were just starting out now, what advice would you give yourself?

First of all, the ability to draw and sketch as a way to communicate to people and feed your 3D spatial perception remains key. I would do tons of drawing and sketching, particularly running a sketchbook. I'd run a sketchbook on everything that interested me, to get practice on a visual narrative, storyboarding, and so on. I would learn and focus on communicating through storyboards. On the other hand, I would travel even more. I would take every opportunity for internships, to travel abroad, to go to emerging markets. As a young designer I would avoid common, well-trodden destinations like Paris or London for example. Instead, I'd want to go to Zimbabwe or Paraguay or Rio or the Soviet bloc just to be exposed to different lifestyles. I would be taking lots of photographs, developing a visual archive of lifestyle patterns, aesthetic issues, rhythms, gestures, and features from nature.

Nature still constitutes the major aesthetic driver for the human species, so being cognizant of the aesthetic issues as they evolve from nature and how they might be applied, using contemporary technologies, to products and visual cues in the created environment is still very important. Being cognizant of patinas that exist in nature and that occur in the deterioration of manufactured items, as these changes in hue and texture warrant close attention.

Of course, experimentation and fluency in digital media as they apply to very different disciplines is also very useful knowledge. Mess around with animation, mess around with Photoshop, mess around with 3D digital tools. I can't overstate the importance of exposure to a broad range of human experiences rather than relying on the web to get information about people's lives. Be comfortable with talking to and interacting with people. Having confidence is a tremendous key.

In closing, you asked me what are the key features necessary in a portfolio today and what employers want to see: thoughtful research-driven problem solving and experience with interacting with other disciplines and cultures, all superbly presented and woven together as a coherent story.

Anything we didn't cover that you would like to add? Any final words of wisdom?

Sketch. Sketch and travel. ⬛

To see Imre Molnar's work, please visit http://breaking.in

MUGENDI M'RITHAA INDUSTRIAL DESIGNER, EDUCATOR & RESEARCHER CAPE PENINSULA UNIVERSITY OF TECHNOLOGY CAPE TOWN

We rarely hear from industrial designers from anywhere in Africa, and I'm curious what has inspired you to pursue industrial design and where your interest in industrial design came about?

I was in the United States at some point in my early childhood for four years, and during that time design in America was arguably the most technologically advanced anywhere and a stimulating environment to be in. My dad was doing his doctorate in pharmacy there at the time— so that was my first real exposure to technology and the world of manufactured products. I remember as a child wondering how someone,

somewhere sat down and actually conceived the equipment, and the products that actually made the lunar mission possible—that is really where my fascination with design really began. Consequently, when we returned to Kenya, I eventually ended up opting to undertake an undergraduate degree program in design at the University of Nairobi.

My lifelong fascination with products comes from a rather different background. Over time, I developed a knack of somehow reassembling and repairing various household mechanical and electronic items. Seven out of 10 times, I would get it right and I think that's where I developed confidence and expertise in actually disassembling and reassembling products. I was able to extend the lifecycle of a number of consumer items in our home. So after my first degree, I realized that the sub-discipline that most reflected my interests was industrial design, which brought together the synthesis of manufactured products and people whilst being cognizant of how the context of where the product fits in influences such diverse issues. Whilst working at the Kenya Building Research Centre, I was fortunate to be awarded a Commonwealth Scholarship that enabled me to study industrial design at the Industrial Design Centre at the Indian Institute of Technology in Mumbai. Upon completion of the two-year master's program, I went back to Kenya and re-joined my alma mater where I helped start the industrial design and interior design programs there.

Eventually, in 1999, I visited South Africa and made contact with Ms. Adrienne Viljoen who was the manager of the Design Institute of the South Africa Bureau of Standards in Pretoria, South Africa. I first met Adrienne when she visited the University of Nairobi in 1994—the year I formally began teaching design. Ever since this initial contact, Adrienne has consistently been one of my most influential mentors in articulating the potential of design as a change agent on our continent, and through her I got exposed to a program they ran called Design for Development. Design for Development focused on how we could harness design skills and didactic tools to address pressing "wicked" problems in Africa. I was also a participant at the 1999 InterDesign Workshop on Water hosted by the SABS Design Institute in Pretoria. That's when it became evident to me that this was indeed the basis of my philosophical leanings—towards more socially conscious or socially responsible design expressions. In 2001, I joined the University of Botswana where I joined efforts to establish a progressive industrial design program there, before finally moving to the Cape Peninsula University of Technology in Cape Town in 2005, where I have been since. During this same year, I participated in the 2005 InterDesign Workshop on Sustainable Rural Transport held in Rustenburg, South Africa.

Obviously it sounds like the industrial design community might be a little bit different in South Africa than in the rest of the world. Would you say that's a true statement?

The developments are very similar. In fact I'm associated with a design consultancy called ...XYZ Design (http://dddxyz.com) and you can see from their portfolio of products that they are a world-class design firm. ...XYZ Design is run by three very competent and respected partners who happen to also be really good friends. Within the "expanded field" of design thinking, we offer consultancy in industrial design, universal design, interaction design, service design, and sustainable design, among others. Yet at the same time I think our unique context offers challenges to our role as designers in the developing countries, or more precisely, majority world contexts.

I argue that designers in our part of the world risk becoming irrelevant to the aspirations of our people, if we fail to demonstrate the value of our profession in a tangible manner. You could say that we need to almost justify the existence of our profession in a sense. There have been engagements with socially conscious design projects. I'd say almost by default industrial designers in Africa must be socially conscious in their design endeavors. If they are conscious or sensitive to the environments they operate within, then they will most likely end up with the significant portion of their work being towards social design.

You started Design With Africa, a coalition with your colleagues. Could you tell me more about that initiative?

Yes, the same three directors I mentioned of ...XYZ Design: Byron Qually, Richard Perez, and Roelf Mulder, as well as Hugo Van Vuuren, who's an associate at Harvard, and myself—we're the five co-founders of Design With Africa (DWA). What motivated the formation of DWA was the realization that for the most part, when people think of design in Africa they were typically not from the continent and as such inadvertently retold our stories with a different slant. It wasn't really a reaction, it was more of a positive and proactive vision informed by a deep desire to encourage people to benefit from a more authentic voice coming from the continent. That was the main inspiration for beginning DWA with the emphasis being on a participatory design ethos. That's why it's design with—it's not by and it's not for—by means it's only done by Africans, while for is rather prescriptive. When you say with there's a philosophical underpinning there—a call for participation. DWA is a call to participate. Designers on our continent, and friends of Africa elsewhere, are invited to engage through this platform that we provide to discourse and demonstrate how design can actually be leveraged to help address pressing issues within the socio-technical paradigm across our continent.

Where would you see design making the most impact in resolving these unique problems that the continent has?

I have a doctorate in universal design, which is synonymous with inclusive design or design for all. In a sense, universal design is motivated more or less by human rights. Further, I have an equal passion—maybe even more so—for design for sustainability. I see our ways of being and doing here in Africa really making a unique contribution to the global agenda of sustainable design. I feel Africans live sustainably by default, but not necessarily by design. I think design could help sustain that kind of a level of responsible consumption and production, provided that people on our continent appreciate these realities.

The rather pressing challenge is to see to it that Africa willfully opts not to consume as wastefully as other parts of the world, whilst respecting the right for people to express themselves as consumers. I think that this challenge simultaneously represents an opportunity. We in Africa can contribute towards the global agenda on sustainability, and some of the practices that have been associated with a number of our customs and traditions, which offer really rich inspiration for the "wicked" problems we're grappling with presently as a human family. This is particularly pertinent in view of the current global recession and socio-economic uncertainty that the world is experiencing as we speak.

With that being said, what advice would you give to an industrial designer who wants to expand their knowledge of creating these sustainable design solutions without necessarily being in Africa or communicating with the locals? Is it even possible to design without experiencing the environment you're designing for in the first place?

I think any designer who does not allow themselves to be informed by the society, the community, is in a sense denying the reality that exists and in so doing is that much poorer from missing out on potentially enriching interactions. I don't think the challenges and experiences in Africa are peculiar in any sense. The fact is that technology now allows people to achieve ideas across boundaries effortlessly. There's growing evidence of social innovation where grassroots communities have created innovative social solutions for themselves, like urban vegetable gardens, carpooling or talent exchanges and so on, where money is not the only form of exchange. I'm not speaking of bartering, which is something we've moved away from historically, but a new way for people to connect to their fellow community members. I think research done through the UNEP-endorsed Creative Communities for Sustainable Lifestyles (http://www.sustainable-everyday.net) project in places like Brazil, China, India, Europe, the USA, and Africa demonstrates this reality beyond any doubt.

Globally, people are starting to create their own solutions and I think a socially conscious designer just needs to be aware of and help co-develop appropriate solutions within their communities. There's something exciting happening. Designers could facilitate the development of service design

systems to enhance the ability to effectively communicate one's activity with the rest of their community. For example, a large number of people do group vegetable purchases or manage urban gardens. Design can facilitate such transactions by helping to create a communication platform and tools that allow people to do those exchanges more efficiently whilst simultaneously promoting conviviality within the said community. I think what we're saying is that if we participate in these kinds of projects as designers, we become "part of the solution," in the sense that we start to promote social equity and cohesion through benign design intervention.

> *"I THINK ANY DESIGNER WHO DOES NOT ALLOW THEMSELVES TO BE INFORMED BY THE SOCIETY, THE COMMUNITY, IS IN A SENSE DENYING THE REALITY THAT EXISTS AND IN SO DOING IS THAT MUCH POORER FROM MISSING OUT ON POTENTIALLY ENRICHING INTERACTIONS."*

I think as the world becomes increasingly aware of alternative models for consumption and production, we will need to re-engage with our local community. My challenge to young designers is that they become aware of the myriad exciting activities happening right in their neighborhood irrespective of whether one is in Boston, Curitiba, London, Chennai, Brisbane, or Cape Town. It would be wise for young designers to just open their eyes and engage in this kind of design intervention: do something with your local community and prepare to be enriched through the resulting interactions.

So almost use design to solve more meaningful social problems rather than just creating more stuff for the marketplace?

Exactly. I think there's a shift of consciousness amongst the world's designers. The traditional sense in which we only responded to the limits of the brief that the client presented, the realization that we have a lot of different clients one-on-one that end up using our products, that our products, services or systems, or that whatever you design ends up impacting upon the lives of people, sometimes in a negative manner. We need to break the traditional mold of industrial design practice, and to say for example, how can we engage our representative communities—whether it's through focus groups, or through more communal projects which allow for more specificity and contribute to our design process? I think this realization points towards a more enlightened and more progressive kind of designer.

With that said, what characteristics or qualities are necessary to be a successful industrial designer?

I think a designer will need the traditional set of skills that all the designers have—they need to be people that are fascinated by products, they need to be people who are curious about how things are made, they need to have a good understanding of materials, and they need to understand the capability of manufacturing technology that's available. But the emerging designer will need an additional skill set that was previously viewed to be of peripheral importance. Such additional skills include the need to be incredibly aware of complex human factors, and by this I mean going beyond ergonomics or human factors engineering to more holistic, social, developmental, and cultural sensitivity such as the way different subgroups of consumers behave—whether they're young people in college or older consumers who've retired. Their understanding of these diverse milieus and their impact on design thinking is required of future designers. Also, designers may want to spend some of their time on a project that has an explicit community focus. Not to be too prescriptive, but to say every community is unique and there must be a lot of different opportunities for designers to contribute, not necessarily as experts but also as active participants in their specific community.

Some would say they may be extremely interested in such social projects and creating solutions for their community, but that there's no money in it, there's no investment. What would you say to designers that do want to pursue this more meaningful approach to creating solutions to encourage them to keep pursuing it despite possible hindrances that may stand in their way?

I would say that every designer obviously has responsibility for their own personal existence, has to take care of their needs, pay rent, eat. But I would like to suggest that there are other professions, like the legal profession where lawyers that do work on pro-bono basis, where some portion of their time is given to cases—or causes—that they feel merit attention, and may not necessarily be paid for by clients for a host of reasons.

Then there's the 80/20 principle, where 80% of one's time could be invested in one's day job, and 20%—whether it's done over weekend or after hours—could be towards designing for problems of collective concern. I know a lot of humanitarian organizations that would welcome design volunteers to help design for, and with, the other 90%—or for the majority of the world's context. I concede that there may not be sufficient numbers of openings to provide sustainable employment for everyone, but I still feel rather strongly that a designer can give some of their time to do something that is humanity-enriching, because they're doing something that is for the greater good.

How would you see the future of industrial design evolving in the 21st century, especially as it pertains to South Africa? How do you see it either changing or making an impact?

I have already been privileged to see the shift in that consciousness, where designers are showing growing interest in what is happening around their communities. The educational institutions are opening themselves to engage with local communities, sometimes sponsored by government and sometimes by private sector interest. There's a shift happening for designing toward greater social inclusion. If that trend continues, particularly in this increasing awareness or consciousness of the value of community, then the future is in good hands. We need to be kind to others and yet, at the same time, make a decent living. We can promote conscientious design interventions, which will certainly be beneficial to all parties involved.

I have spoken about the philosophy of being conscious of the interrelationships that happen with other people, that awareness needs to be characterized by a code of ethics that honors human life, that respects our planet, and that allows for innovations that demonstrably sustain businesses. Here in Africa we have a philosophy called Ubuntu, which celebrates our common humanity: "I am, because we are," and "I participate, therefore I am." So, I think Africa provides this enlightened form of "humanity-centeredness" in all that we seek to do. It initially appears challenging to embrace such an expansive view of fellow humanity, but once you realize it's actually an opportunity it becomes very exciting. I've seen it happen with a large organization like IDEO that's developing a good focus on human-centered design and offers simple, practical tools to effect such understanding. I'd like to invite designers from other continents to engage with challenges in their own communities, or join our efforts to do likewise with communities in our part of the world. There are lot of opportunities for benevolent design intervention.

This is what Design With Africa actually stands for and we encourage this kind of design mediation. We are quite happy to work with those who are interested in developing products, services, or systems that could—potentially—benefit communities on our continent.

That's very inspiring and motivating to hear. Anything you wanted to say that we haven't covered?

What I was going to say is that at the beginning of one's career there's an impassioned sense of idealism; one enters the professional world with these bold ideas. Sometimes your client is not as open nor willing to invest in that philosophy, nor in that new paradigm that one proposes. What I

usually encourage—and this is something I learned through reading the work of Victor Papanek—[is that] the conscientious or socially responsible designer could add more sustainable or more enriching elements to their design practice for free and work with the client to demonstrate that such thinking will not cost the client extra. Ultimately, this enlightened philosophy or paradigm makes sense. Eventually, the client sees the value inherent in adopting the designer's proposals and becomes the champion for the change you propose. So, for designers who are interested in that kind of thinking, they should go ahead and infuse their work with something that they believe is of lasting value—whether the client pays them extra or not.

There's a 20th-century philosopher-poet's quote that I like very much. Kahlil Gibran from Lebanon said: "Work is love made visible." My challenge usually to my students, particularly the ones that are about to graduate, is that everything that one does should be an expression of love, that is: the love that you have for what you do, and the love that you have for yourself. That if you're happy with who you are, and you're at peace with yourself, then your work becomes an expression from the deepest part of your being. That work, that portfolio, that body of work eventually attracts the kind of client whose philosophy and practice aligns with your own. In the final analysis, one should simply exercise patience, and be true to oneself.

It sounds like the change in the world starts with the change in design.

Exactly. I think you're making reference to Mahatma Gandhi: if designers want to see the change in the world, we need to become that change, so that the world may change. I agree totally. ⊞

To see Mugendi M'Rithaa's work, please visit http://breaking.in

KEN MUSGRAVE
EXECUTIVE DIRECTOR:
EXPERIENCE DESIGN &
PRODUCT DEVELOPMENT
DELL
AUSTIN

What kinds of portfolios get your attention these days? What brings in an industrial designer for an interview?

The caliber of the portfolio has gotten better and more sophisticated in the last eight to 10 years. It's truly remarkable how much progress has been made. Most people need to understand that when they are doing their schoolwork, much of the work that they are doing is not just to satisfy the requirements of their university, but also to be able to compete in a global marketplace. Probably 20 years ago you only needed to demonstrate a couple of skills to get your first entry-level job. In fact, back then it was about sketching and, in some sense, about form development. Now we are looking for a lot more demonstrable capabilities in these portfolios, and one of the reasons why we rarely hire someone straight out of school is because we are looking for diversity and experience. Diversity can be solving design problems for a variety of different types of user needs, maybe a variety of different industries, and in a variety of different manufacturing processes. They need to demonstrate that they have experiences that are broad enough to be able to bear the challenges that we have.

We are looking for something beyond that. We're looking for demonstration of critical thinking: the ability to take insights learned from the user's needs and the technical challenges, and find an opportunity space––tying that to how the company is going to see value. And bring the whole line of critical thinking together into a compelling story that really supports a design outcome—a design solution. This concept of translation from the insights of the designer, or wherever the insights are coming from, into a compelling design solution that can be understood not just by other designers, but by their colleagues in business. It's a far more abstract

concept but is also the one that is more and more critical. At Dell we have a fairly global organization with global customers. We have complex products with some pretty sophisticated customers. We need designers that actually understand how to address all of the different variables and be compelling and effective in a global organization.

Having a great sense of design, a command of design form, materials, and material uses...that's just the entry-level starting point. After that we're looking for those extra intangibles that we need to help influence within an organization, to help translate sophisticated user needs, and express compelling final solutions.

Have you seen a portfolio recently that stood out, and what about it caught your eye?

I have seen a couple that were close but I have yet to see a portfolio that puts it all together. I think that the concept of a portfolio has to change to a certain extent. Portfolios have historically been about a collection of cool things they've done in history, and about the object and the artifact. I think the portfolio needs to be unburdened and be more of an inventory of capabilities, proved with artifacts, insights or communication, and a demonstration of skills and reasoning. I've just begun to see portfolios that are doing that. Instead of having the collection of all the things they've worked on, they're actually talking about what these combined experiences have done for them professionally. As such, they are creating a collection of capabilities and new tools in their own toolbox.

A person can bring in a portfolio that has really thoughtful design in it, and extend that into the reasoning behind it. I've seen folks try to do this and then they get overburdened with methodology. They are confusing methodology with technique. All of these things need to be emphasized: to demonstrate, to think, and have an ability to distill an essence of an idea, the root of its insides and how it was clearly and cleanly connected to an outcome.

I'm thinking beyond product, and what we're looking for is this ability to take a lot of complexity and bring clarity to it. What we see too often is the ability to take a lot of complexity and translate it into complexity. So the inverse problem is that we'll see people who have gone to the opposite guardrail, where you almost get no sense of the final product and they're just completely dense with magnets. It's not the methods that matter as much as what conclusions were drawn from the methods. Understanding the difference between the methods and content is sort of like blowing bubbles. You're making a lot of thoughts and it looks like there's a lot going on, versus actually making some deductions or conclusions from it and consolidating a thought into a clear idea.

When you find a designer and bring them in for an interview, what do you expect to learn from them at that one-on-one meeting?

I expect them to demonstrate that they have a command of their design skills and competencies. I would hope that they can clearly and succinctly explain how they were able to bring order where there was chaos. It's really interesting, especially with more junior designers: they're trying to translate what they've learned in an institution to application in their first professional opportunity. Very often they're not really sure what to emphasize and I always tell everybody to make sure to put their conclusions into the context of what's happening to that business. In most cases, product designers end up working in business—that's why it's called industrial design.

The industry has invested in design for a reason: they're expecting an outcome. Having an ability to bridge what you're advocating to be a priority of that business and where that business is going and what it's facing—not made too far-out or too abstract—is a powerful ability. It's one that's very, very difficult for industrial designers coming out of school to grasp, as they don't have the context. So one of the things that I recommend is that they try and go get their first job with a consultancy. What I hope that they would get out of that is to not only hone their design skills and tools but to actually work with clients, understand what their challenges are, and learn about the different industries. To also learn the different dynamics, and how different clients are expecting to find abstract value out of their own work. I think there's more to be learned there in the long-run that will make them more valuable to future employers and corporations.

What would you say are the characteristics or qualities necessary to be a successful designer?

The ability to take complexity into simplicity and clarity. What continues to be critical is curiosity and imagination—the curiosity I cannot emphasize enough. Most successful folks are the ones that want to understand more, the why behind the why. They want to understand the root of an opportunity or a reason as to why something exists and maybe challenge some of those conventions. They look for inspiration from unexpected places. To have imagination to bring ideas and thoughts from other industries and have the ability to create something that has not existed in a new space. The overarching theme is simplification: how do we take a complex world and complex life, technologies, situations, and continue to distill them down to their simplest form? That quality and the ability to do that elegantly and efficiently is going to be one of the most critical attributes.

How did you break into this business?

When I was in college, I started thinking about what sort of profile of experiences the companies would see as being valuable. From as long as I remember, I started creating an inventory of different corporate design groups and different consultancies, and the type of people they seem to hire, the types of experiences they value. I talked to as many of those folks as possible at conferences, or when they came to visit the university. I would try to do industry projects in the university, even if such projects weren't available to me or the school. I would actually go and seek out a design challenge to bring to a classroom. This approach would help me demonstrate my design skills and interests, while showcasing my full creative expression. That gave me a good understanding of what companies were looking for and gave me my own conclusion that what I really needed to do was to work in a diverse consulting environment.

The other thing I realized is that, in order to set myself apart and have a compelling portfolio, I needed to have some work experience. I interned for two different companies and I made sure they were very different. I worked for a furniture manufacturer and it was fantastic. It was a "pure form" opportunity. I learned a bit about ergonomics and about a lot of different manufacturing technologies. Then I looked for something to the tune of higher technology, and more strategic and corporate design. From there I consolidated that experience into a portfolio and coming out of school I looked for a consultancy opportunity. I wanted to hone skills. I wanted to understand how a consultancy ran projects. I knew that one of the things that I love about consultancies was how efficient they were in structuring a project and making it compelling to a client. It gave me exposure to a spectrum of industries.

"WE'RE LOOKING FOR DEMONSTRATION OF CRITICAL THINKING: THE ABILITY TO TAKE INSIGHTS LEARNED FROM THE USER'S NEEDS AND THE TECHNICAL CHALLENGES, AND FIND AN OPPORTUNITY SPACE— TYING THAT TO HOW THE COMPANY IS GOING TO SEE VALUE."

One of the things I also did was continue my education. Even though I got my first job, I did not stop going to school for another eight years. I got my first job and started in March and started my graduate degree that fall. Then I did further education in research, in communications design, and I started pursuing an MBA. For 10 years I continued to study.

If you were starting out now what advice would you give yourself?

Understand design and the business of design beyond just the physical products. I would learn much more about experience design earlier and how experience design can be translated from physical products, from software experiences, through visual identities and brand experiences. Instead of doing a master's degree in product design, I probably would've gone back and done a degree in communications design or user experience and interaction design to be able to extend product experiences beyond the physical to what's wrapped around them, which is where we spend most of our time now. Look at not just the physical device, but what happens to make that device a relevant object— relevant to life. It doesn't have to be within a computer context, it can be applied to any type of project.

Where do you see the future of industrial design going?

I think that industrial design will always be relevant. I believe that the center of attention is going to go beyond where it has been historically, which has been in Western Europe and the United States. I believe that, with the sheer scale of what's occurring in countries such as India and China, much of that competency will be well rooted to the manufacturing base. I believe that design as it's practiced in the United States will be much more around experiential design and that will be inclusive of bringing software experiences to life, branded experiences to life. If you just look at some of the work that's being done around mobile devices, looking at the entire customer journey, the branded experience, and defining that, and the richness of that experience...I think that will be the area of distinction for the design profession.

It sounds like industrial design will definitely broaden and include more of these systems-based solutions as well.

I think it will and it will expand with various facets of this emerging experience design. We're already seeing that. We're seeing people doing a great job in these branded experiences and bringing traditional hardware design and marrying it with other designed elements such as software, or packaging. Think very holistically around every touch point that a customer or user might have, or a certain brand, or certain technology of a company—ensure that all of the touch points resonate with a single design vision.

Anything you'd like to add that we haven't talked about? Any final words of wisdom?

I don't think I have any wisdom, just a point of view. I do believe that, especially the Western designers need to realize that the world is global and that, as they think about who they're designing for and where the future growth and demand for design is going to come from, it may not be in the areas that they thought. They always need to take a global point of view when they are thinking of their design solutions.

They also need to realize that, as they go to break into the design profession, that they're not competing with people nearby them but that they are competing with a global marketplace. They need to think about what the intangibles are that these global designers bring from a cultural perspective, including language skills. What are the experiences that Western designers don't have and how are Western designers going to show that they are relevant to their potential employers? ⊞

To see Ken Musgrave's work, please visit http://breaking.in

GARY NATSUME HEAD OF DESIGN & USER INTERFACE MAGIC LEAP BROOKLYN & FORT LAUDERDALE

Interviewed while Mr. Natsume was the Director of Design and Research at ECCO Design in New York City.

What kinds of portfolios get your attention these days? What brings in an industrial designer for an interview?

The design industry has changed; there are a lot of traditional design schools whose focus is solely on form development; however the industry is looking for something beyond that. Basic skills of model-making, form development, and problem solving are essential––but the students need to come in with something more than that, with skills like ethnographic research or background studies. They need to talk to consumers and understand the problem, frame the issues and identify the design challenge by themselves. That whole skill set is something that is more important than the actual implementation of design.

The other aspect is that design is not just about the physical or tangible object. It's no longer static; it's constantly changing. Every object has interactions, whether it's on-screen interactions or physical interactions. The ability to think beyond static objects, this is something that design students need to be aware of. I think the schools face this challenge of how to accommodate these new aspects into their programs, so when they exit the schools the students are well prepared.

How do you see this impacting the actual content of portfolios? What do you expect to see?

I'd definitely like to see strong storytelling: not only the final result, but the process of where they started and how they identified the challenge and how they solved the problem. Also in terms of output, instead of just simple renderings or models they need to show us different stages of products with the users. If there were any interactions on the screen or a physical aspect, they need to demonstrate that. I welcome them to come in with more multimedia presentations.

When you say multimedia presentations, you mean...

It can be online, it can be a video, a webpage, an animation. There are so many rich tools available that weren't around a few years ago. I finished school about 20 years ago now, and back then we had to bring in a printed portfolio, but at this stage you can connect to a network anywhere and when you send a portfolio you can send a link to your website. There is so much one can do beyond just a static image. What else can you demonstrate? What rich storytelling can you demonstrate? How can you demonstrate what else you can do beyond the actual project?

Have you seen a portfolio recently that embodied these qualities, and what about it stood out?

I do see students approaching us with their online portfolios and sending us links. Instead of seeing a physical flier or a PDF of their portfolio, we're able to go to their site, click through and see their dynamic thinking behind the project. I teach a class at Pratt and the students are very capable in using new media. I think students are becoming much more creative in finding ways of incorporating this. Still, there are students coming in with a more traditional view of design, with photographs of hand models and traditional hand renderings. These are basic skills, which is good, but I want them to know that the world went beyond that.

What do you expect to learn from a designer once they come in for an interview?

It comes down to their personality. All of the good work is necessary, but what makes it special is if, in the meeting, they can present their work in front of a potential employer. It shows confidence and communication skills. We are interested in people. The portfolio is important, but how that individual can carry himself is more important than anything else. Does he have a clear mind, strong confidence? Does he have clear objectives as to what he wants to accomplish? Does he communicate this skill clearly to us? Does he have the ability to work with others? Design is a team game so we need someone who knows how to work with others. Eventually, we want them to be a leader, we want them to cooperate not only with people in our organization but beyond, from the vendors to model makers, even interns who may come in temporarily. We are looking for the overall package of that personality.

What would you say are the characteristics or qualities necessary to be a successful designer?

I think the designer is an interesting hybrid between a creative artist and a skilled businessman. To be a businessman, you need to have a really logical mind. How can you make a smart decision at the right moment? Versus the artistic side where it is this very unique personality. This fine balance is what makes a good designer. It's difficult to find. You often find people who are smart but overly process

oriented, and then you find others who are too much by themselves, too much about their own creative identity, and not about the project. How do you find this fine balance that is creative-led and, at the same time, understands the organizational structure and the process?

How did you break into this industry?

I'm originally from Japan, from Nagoya. It's the Detroit of Japan, center of the automobile industry. I was inspired to be an architect. I wanted to be someone who is hands-on, creative, and does large-scale installations and landscapes. I came to the US to study at Parsons at the environmental design department and that's where I discovered Cranbrook. It's a very conceptual school that teaches design but on a high, philosophical level. The school is known for architecture and crafts, but also it has a strong history in product design. After Cranbrook, I felt very confident in my conceptual ability, but I really wanted to practice my skill in a very practical and highly reputable firm so I could understand the actual, practical aspects of design.

"BASIC SKILLS OF MODEL-MAKING, FORM DEVELOPMENT, AND PROBLEM SOLVING ARE ESSENTIAL––BUT THE STUDENTS NEED TO COME IN WITH SOMETHING MORE THAN THAT, WITH SKILLS LIKE ETHNOGRAPHIC RESEARCH OR BACKGROUND STUDIES."

I was very fortunate to get into frog design and within five and a half years there, I was able to work in Silicon Valley, New York, Germany, with not only product designers but engineers, interaction designers, and so on.

If you were starting out now, what advice would you give yourself?

I always try to make whatever I do relevant to the world. If I start seeing something that I'm repeating, I need to warn myself. If I feel that then I'm overly comfortable with what I am doing and I feel like my work or my contribution is not relevant to this very fast-changing world. I feel like something is not right. I want to be on top of this very fast-changing world and I need to be a part of it. We are no longer repeating the "form follows function" type of design in this modern age.

Where do you see the future of industrial design going?

I think the whole definition of industrial design is changing. I often refer to the Industrial Revolution when product was still about producing mass volumes—that's when industrial design started. It was based on the mass market, mass production, and mass transportation. Ironically, all of these three aspects have been transformed. We are in a market where we can customize each product to each individual. If I order a car, I can make it tailored to my preference. When it comes to user interface, even more so. UI can be uniquely mine. At IKEA, we can buy design for a very inexpensive cost; however, by selecting combinations, we create our own unique environments that are tailored very much to each one of us. So thinking about what design used to be and what it accomplished, and now what design is trying to do to us, is very different. I think all of us who claim to be industrial designers need to be aware of, and we need to think about, what is our new role.

Anything you'd like to add that we didn't cover? Any final words of wisdom?

The studios looking to hire young designers are looking for two things. One is whether this person can come in and be able to contribute to our business—tomorrow. Meaning they need to come in with skill sets. Being in school is the best time to learn tools. There are many tools, and we encourage students to take their time and learn them—to equip themselves with tools so they can come in from day one and can be part of our production and contribute to our everyday business. However, a year later,

those skills will be obsolete. So what you really need to move forward from there is to be a thinker and a leader.

So the answer is that the students need to prepare for both while they are in school. They have to learn the tools and also they have to train themselves to be leaders and thinkers.

To see Gary Natsume's work, please visit http://breaking.in

RHYS NEWMAN
VP ADVANCED DESIGN
HERE/NOKIA
CALABASAS, CALIFORNIA

What kinds of portfolios get your attention these days? What brings in a product designer for an interview?

A lot depends on which school or company the designers are coming from. The work that catches our attention is of a designer who thinks about the context in which their product lives, the consequences of their design, and the behaviors and experiences that emerge around their products. Designers who think more broadly, beyond their chosen discipline, that blur the boundaries between hardware and software, digital and physical, intrigue us. The best portfolios are the ones that start a good discussion, and show the designer as a designer, but also a prototyper, an entrepreneur, a strategist, a visionary, and a bloody great storyteller.

Have you seen a portfolio recently that really stood out? What about it caught your eye?

Last summer we had an intern who presented his Kickstarter project. He had an idea, a vision of what it could be, and he translated that idea into a tangible and fully working prototype. It was incredible. He made it work from a mechanical point of view and from a software point of view. He also had that entrepreneurial spirit to get an interest and investment. Somebody with that level of ambition, and competence to make things work with an entrepreneurial edge, got him the internship. He was so good to have in the studio, really nice, really clever, and provocative. Thanks, Jeff!

What do you expect to learn from a designer during an interview?

Our studio is a creative and happy place to be, and I believe it's like this because of a shared ambition and culture that is relatively simple: "We collectively make our projects better"––which means "no dickheads." I expect and respect an open and collaborative culture, one where there is a collective responsibility, and a mutual respect for each other's strong opinions. What we look for is someone who shares this vision and these values. Obviously, you want someone who has the skills, you want them to be someone with a drive, with an attention to detail, with an ability to communicate, but above all a point of view. I believe it is important to like the people you're working with. Brilliant things are made by brilliant teams, not individuals.

How did you break into this business?

I'm not sure what "in" is. I never felt like I had to break in as such. I've never done anything else but art and design. During high school I wanted to go to an art college, as all I wanted to do was draw and paint—I still do. This passion was a little odd in my high school. Arriving at the art college and realizing there were other people like me was, I suppose, a form of breaking in. Since then, I've been very fortunate, as everything else has felt like a natural progression.

If you were just starting out now, what advice would you give yourself?

I should've been more diligent in cataloguing the work I've done. I should've traveled more, taken more risks, and trusted my intuition. Oh, and should've done a second degree in something completely different. Still time for that one.

Where do you see the future of industrial design going?

I find it difficult to think about industrial design in isolation from designing as a whole. However, specifically, I hope ID continues as it has: which is striving to make beautiful, relevant, meaningful, and responsible products for people. To harness and utilize the very latest materials and processes, but retain the craft and "spirit" of objects made by hand.

"THE BEST PORTFOLIOS ARE THE ONES THAT START A GOOD DISCUSSION, AND SHOW THE DESIGNER AS A DESIGNER, BUT ALSO A PROTOTYPER, AN ENTREPRENEUR, A STRATEGIST, A VISIONARY, AND A BLOODY GREAT STORYTELLER."

For design with a capital D, I'm excited at the prospect of a generation of designers emerging as entrepreneurs, educators, CEOs, and heads of NGOs. I believe some of the greatest opportunities and challenges in the future will require a huge amount of creativity. Why not have a few designers shaping decision-making at the heart of business, economics, and society through design?

Anything you'd like to add that we haven't talked about? Any final words of wisdom?

Draw more. Laugh more. Put your work up on a wall and talk about it. Collaborate. Be ambitious. Project first, career second. Oh, and don't be a dickhead.   BI

To see Rhys Newman's work, please visit http://breaking.in

DON NORMAN
CO-FOUNDER & PRINCIPAL
NIELSEN NORMAN GROUP
PALO ALTO, CALIFORNIA

Where does your passion for design come from? Why is design so important in your life?

That's a complex question because I came upon the field of design, in some sense, by accident. My original training was as an engineer: I have two degrees in electrical engineering and then I switched to psychology for my doctorate. I thought I was doing the same thing in psychology as I was as an engineer, which is studying intelligent machines. I wanted to build them as an engineer, and as a psychologist I wanted to study the human machine—so I used the same mathematics, the same tools. For many years, I was quite content as a satisfied academic researcher in psychology, first at University of Pennsylvania, then at Harvard, then University of California San Diego. Towards the end of that period, I started to get interested in how people make interactions and make mistakes, and started studying human error. I got called in to investigate the major nuclear power plant accident on the Three-Mile Island, to see why these operators were so stupid. Our team realized it wasn't the operators—they were doing a great job—it was the design of the plant. Couldn't have done a better job if you wanted to cause errors. That caused me to realize that the knowledge I had of engineering and of psychology were actually perfect for the modern world.

So, I became very much interested in how do we design things that people can actually use and can understand. That led me to do work on aviation safety, and then eventually to the book The Design of Everyday Things. Actually, a prior book was called User Centered System Design; the initials UCSD were of the university I was at, but that was also the introduction of the term user-centered design to the design field. My emphasis there was on making things understandable, so when

The Design of Everyday Things came out, I was asked to give some talks to design conferences and designers. I don't think I did a very good job; I truly didn't understand what design was all about. What happened then though is that I found that I was reading technology magazines before I read the academic journals. I realized that my heart was in making things that impacted people, things that people really used.

I left the University of California and came up to Apple, where eventually I became the vice president of the Advanced Technology Group, and it was at Apple that I discovered design. I discovered the design group there, and I became friends with two major designers. First with Bob Brunner, who was in charge of the design group, and second was this young guy, struggling, his name was Jony Ive. It was interesting, it really did change my mind about the importance of the aesthetic side of design, not just making something usable, but something that was pleasurable, delightful. That's where my education really began, at Apple.

But that was over 20 years ago, and since then I've been self-taught as a designer. I've worked with designers, I had taught design, I've traveled around the world and visited design schools and designed the design components of major companies around the world. Although I'm not really a great designer in the sense of being able to sketch beautiful objects, I do consider myself a designer.

You get asked frequently how to break into industrial design or design in general by people who don't have a background in design. You yourself have managed to do that successfully. How would you answer that question for them?

Well the road that I followed isn't going to work for most people. I was here at the very beginning of the home computer revolution, and also helped establish interaction design. I was also a company executive. So, yeah, start off by becoming a vice president of Apple, that's a good start. What I mainly do is give strategic advice to companies. I do not design their products. I tell them that they need to hire designers and I recommend design firms, or individuals. I look at their companies and say: "You have really good people here, but they're not structured properly so you can most effectively make use of them." I give the kind of strategic advice that an executive consultant gives. The major difference between me and most executive consultants is that I'm focused on the product, on giving pleasure, enjoyment, and satisfaction to the customers.

It is hard to break into the design field. There are many, many design schools and not as many jobs. This is true of any discipline. What you have to do is hone your skills, try to find a job as close to what you are interested in as possible. Develop your portfolio and figure out what you're good at, and not so good at. Now, many people develop portfolios that all look the same. Here's what I tell people: use human-centered design to design your portfolio. Put yourself in the place of a busy hiring manager who has no time to do this, who's busy with three other projects, and is actually understaffed—that's why they're hiring. Now suddenly, somebody comes in and says: "Hey, here are the latest portfolios," and plunks 20 down, as they're late for a meeting, having all sorts of crises...and so what do they do? They thumb through them, they give each one five to 10 seconds and they cull a set of a couple that just look interesting. Now, how do they choose the interesting ones from the non-interesting ones? There has to be something unique.

When I see portfolios, they all look the same: beautiful renderings, student projects, this, that, and the other. So I tell people: find out what you are really good at and emphasize that and make sure that stands out first. Don't write one that's in historical order, choose that one project that you're the most excited about and make that the front piece of your portfolio. You do want to be different, and if you don't have certain skills, don't hide it—you can even state it. If that says: "I won't be hired at this company," well that's okay. If you don't have the right skills, you probably don't want to work there anyway. You want the one company that's a good match for what you do, what you're good at, and what you most enjoy. If you don't enjoy it, you're not gonna be good at it. What hiring managers like is some excitement and enthusiasm.

Next, suppose you don't have training in traditional design, then what? What I recommend if you can't go back to school—maybe you can't afford

it in either time or money—is to use your existing education and experience to land a job in a design company. For example, let's say that you're trained in business or in marketing, or in finance or engineering—well, actually design companies need these people. Try to find where you play a role in a design company. The way any design company that I know works is once you're there, they want to find your talents and use you. You may be hired as an engineer, and you may end up designing, or you may decide you really love engineering and support the product that's coming out.

What characteristics or qualities are necessary to be a successful industrial designer? What do industrial designers need to know in order to succeed?

There are two parts to this question: one is what makes a person succeed in any job and the other is what is special in the design field. In any job you want someone who is dedicated, enthusiastic, creative. If you're doing a job because it's a job, or because you think you're supposed to, you're not going to be very good at it. The first thing is, you have to find a match to your talents and things that excite you. Sometimes that means changing companies, or within a company it might mean trying to find the correct projects and somehow talk yourself into them. It's amazing how many people do things or take jobs because they think they're supposed to.

Now, what makes a designer special? We train people in specialties. In engineering, you can't say, "I'm an engineer." You have to say what kind of an engineer, and you can't even say I'm a computer scientist, or an electrical engineer or mechanical engineer—that's too broad. You have to say what you do: fluid dynamics, nano-technology, programming. Even programming isn't specific enough. What kind of programming? Is it kernel, is it operating system, input/output, is it mobile phones? So they become very great specialists. Designers are not specialists. Designers are generalists. To make a product means you have to take specialty knowledge from all across. Building a medical product, you have to understand the situation of medicine, who's going to be using it—is it the physicians, is it nurses, is it technicians, is it patients? What's the setting? Is it the home, is it the clinic, is it in-service, out-service? In-patient, out-patient? And you have to figure out all the different technologies that are involved, which today are microprocessors, and actuators and sensors, and communication networks, and the materials, and the size requirements and somehow make it all come together into a wonderful system. Not an isolated product, but a thing that works well in the system.

It requires very special general skills, and that's what's so unique in design. That the specialists can't do this. The specialists are essential to your success, but you're the one who puts them together, who figures out what specialties are required and brings them together. You also have to be a quick study, because one day you're working on a medical product, the next day you're working on an airplane, the next day some consumer product and with each product you have to become an authority on the issue. That's the challenge of design, and to me, that's actually the excitement, what's so fascinating about it.

In Emotional Design you wrote: "If you want a successful product, test and revise. If you want a great product, one that can change the world, let it be driven by someone with a clear vision. The latter presents a more financial risk but it's the only path to greatness." Obviously, the late Mr. Jobs was a visionary who led Apple to create products that changed the world, yet the majority of the business world today is still perfectly alright with the status quo and very much risk averse. What are your thoughts on how designers can bridge this barrier and communicate these ideas clearly to individuals holding the purse strings?

This is a dangerous topic.

There are only a few great designers in the world. The great designers can break the rules and push and take risks. The average designer can't. Moreover, great designers have great successes and also great failures. So, first of all, Steve Jobs wasn't a designer. He was an orchestra leader—somebody else did the design, the composition, the engineering, the marketing and the industrial design, interaction design, but he stood over it. What he did have was a clear, sharp vision of what this product

should be, and he forced people to create it, even when they said: "No, no that's not possible," he said "do it anyway."

In his career he had a number of great failures. You could argue the original Apple company he failed in and was fired from. He then went to Pixar and NeXT. NeXT was a great failure. Pixar stumbled along for a while until it had its great success. When he came back to Apple he had a couple of great failures; the Apple Cube is probably the best known. To remind readers what it was, it was this wonderful transparent cube that was beautiful and sat on your desk, and was quiet, no fan. Every design company bought one, and MoMA bought one, and it was beautiful—but it failed. It failed because it didn't meet the marketplace. Just like NeXT computer was wonderful but didn't meet marketplace needs. So, it's dangerous to have expensive failures like that.

"...USE HUMAN-CENTERED DESIGN TO DESIGN YOUR PORTFOLIO."

What I talk about in my design work, the methods of human-centered design that I teach and help develop, require understanding the customers, empathy, creativity, but then a period of iterative testing: prototype, test, refine, prototype, test, refine. Testing ensures that people actually understand it, that it works well for them. I'd argue this prevents failures and creates good design. It is a pretty effective method to teach people to be good designers.

The great designers don't want good design, they want great design and my method will guarantee good design. You're always testing with people that use it, who will reject anything that's unusual or different, but the great design is almost always unusual and different and takes a while to get used to—so it will be rejected. Should everybody forget human-centered design? No. I think it's a mistake to forget it. I think that great designers need to learn human-centered design and know how to go beyond it. Know when to trust their instincts and be willing to fail periodically.

So, why don't companies do great, innovative products? Well, of course they do every so often, but I want to remind you that great innovations and radical changes don't come about very often. Every design student wants to do radical innovation—that's what they're taught to do in schools, that's what you're happy to do. Look at the design portfolios and outputs of these studios and prizes that designers get from the contests—do you ever see any of those as products? No. Very few ever make it into product world. If they're so great, why didn't they become successful products? The world can only take a few major innovations. You're gonna live through maybe a hundred major innovations in your entire life. That's not very many, and in any given field there's going to be just a few. So, I think it's a mistake to focus on these great, innovative things.

A company needs to have that every so often, but you're right, companies are risk averse. Companies in some sense do human-centered design—that is, they get feedback from their stockholders—and that's the problem. The stockholders are interested in how a company does in every three months, every quarter of the year. Very few companies can take a long-term view and say: "This is not going to succeed now, but if we're patient, it will be big." Amazon is a company that did this. They were badly treated by the press and by the investors for their first five or six years: "What are you doing? You're losing money. When will you ever make money?" It's very hard to stick to it. I think for most work that we do, human-centered design is essential. It's only when there's a real need to break out that we vary it.

One more story.

Human-centered design is what in the technical field is called hill climbing. That is, imagine you're on a hill in deep fog, you can't see anything in front of you and you want to get to the top of the hill. So what you do is, you sort of feel in every direction and you move in the direction that's up. Then you feel again, and you keep doing this, and eventually you will get to the top of the hill, and that's what human-centered design is. You don't know what the terrain looks like, but you want to be better, better, and better. This will guarantee you will get to the top of the hill, but it may not be the tallest hill. How do you get to the top of the tallest hill? Remember,

you can't see anything, and that's where the innovation comes: the inspired guess, which gets you to a new hill.

Almost always, when you have this new innovation, you get to a new hill at a position that's lower than where you started from. How do you know that this is actually a taller hill and all you need to do is climb it, versus it's actually a small hill and this is a bad thing? There's no way of knowing. No way. The only way is you have to keep trying, which means using your resources: time, people, and money, and that's the hard part. It's easy to think of crazy ideas, it's hard to know when it's gonna catch on.

Mind you, great ideas can fail. I'm fond of my failures. When I first joined Apple, one of the first products released was a failure. Completely failed in the marketplace. Was it a bad idea? It was a digital camera. It was too early, the market wasn't ready. We couldn't print in color. The camera didn't have a display because they were too expensive, it could only hold a few pictures, and not of great quality. So we were very low on the hill. Should we have persisted? Yes, I think we should have, but actually Apple quit: "No, fail. Stop." Again, it's really hard to know, but if you decide to stick with it, that's where human-centered design is essential, that's how you climb your hill.

That's a complex answer because this is a very complex topic, the subject of innovation.

What is the designer's role in business these days?

Designers are essential to business. But before I discuss that, what is design? Design is not just making a product, and is certainly not just making the product attractive. Design is trying to solve the problem that people may not even realize that there's a problem. One of the rules I have in my own consulting is: do not solve the problem that I'm asked to solve—and I try to teach this to my students. The first thing you do when you're given a problem is say: "What's the real problem?" This is what the emphasis on design thinking is about. When we're given a problem we have to back off and think: "Well, why do people think this is a problem?" Really, the underlying issues—what can we do to address the fundamental issue, the root cause, the root problem? If we can do that, that may actually lead to whole new businesses and whole new ways of thinking, and along the way the original problem will turn out to either be solved, or will turn out to not even be an issue.

One example: a long time ago we used to record television programs with something called the VCR, video cassette recorder, which you had to program. First of all, you had to set the time on it, so it knew what time of day it was. Then you had to tell it what channel you wanted to watch, starting at what time and ending at what time. You had to remember to put the tape in and set it up properly, and people tried to make this easier and easier to use, and tried to make it easier to set the time, easier to program. The correct solution was to make it unnecessary to set the time, and unnecessary to program. Today's video data recorders, the best one out is today's TiVo, do just that. You never set the time, you just simply look at the programs that are coming out in the next week or so, and you say: "That one, record it for me." You don't even know what day of the week it's going to be on, what channel, because you don't care. So that's design thinking to solve the real problem. I don't want to watch channel 32, I want to watch this particular show.

That's the real thing that the designers can do, and that's the real value they give to business. So whether you work in product design or strategy, or product management, or in marketing, stepping back and saying what is the real issue, what are we really trying to solve, that's the contribution designers can make.

If you were just starting out now, what advice would you give yourself?

When I think I really understand a topic, I tell myself: "Okay, time to move on." I like to learn a new topic every year, I like to enter a new field, I like to do different things. If I really knew everything that I needed to know I would say: "Okay, what else can I explore?" You can often make the biggest contribution when you are knowledgeable in one field, and you move to a completely different one. You bring to this new field the knowledge, and the point of view of the old field and now you see in the new field that people in the field don't see. I

recommend that to people, and I recommend that to myself. Go elsewhere and see what new things you can determine.

What you do when you enter a new field is you ask stupid questions. The most insightful and most important of all questions are what are often called stupid questions. When someone says: "I have a stupid question, but..." I always listen with great intensity because that's where great insights come from. That means somebody who doesn't have any background thinks this doesn't make any sense. Quite often that person is right, it doesn't make sense. But we were so close to the issue, we never noticed. So maybe the advice I give is: don't be afraid to ask stupid questions.

How have you seen industrial design evolve over your career? Where do you see the future of industrial design going as it evolves further in the 21st century?

Well, I started not knowing anything about industrial design, not knowing what it was, and finding my own experiences in interactions with designers. Later on I discovered industrial design and said: "That's industrial design? That's far too limited." I started looking at how industrial designers were trained and thought it was horrible.

The word design is a bad word because it means so many things: I design food, I design clothing, I design fashion, I'm an interior designer, I'm an industrial designer, I'm an engineering designer, I design nano particles, I design structures, I design molecules. It's too general, and industrial design is a relic from the late 1800s, early 1900s. Industry? Industrial? What does industrial mean? I think it's time to change the design curriculum and maybe get rid of industrial design. We may have product design, service design, large-machinery design, factory design, interaction design, experience design, on and on and on, strategic design, design strategy, design planning, design thinking.

The traditional design education today, especially in industrial design, originally came from art schools. Many, many schools of industrial design are inside the schools of art or architecture, and I think that's unfortunate. I would like to see more of them in schools of engineering because the emphasis at schools of art and architecture is on art, and industrial design is not art. The fact that you spend years learning how to draw and do two-dimensional sketching and three-dimensional sketching, and building models—that's craftsmanship. It's important that we have good craftspeople, but I want people who think. The one thing that's not taught in design is thinking. We're proud of design thinking, yet we don't teach thinking, and designers don't know much about the world. They don't read literature, they don't read history, they don't read sciences, they don't know mathematics, they don't know new technology, yet they're supposed to be building things that rely on this new technology, that require some knowledge of mathematics and science, that require tremendous amounts of knowledge about people because we're designing things for people—to change people's behavior, or society's behavior.

The result is that I've heard designers make the most outrageous statements about how their ideas will transform education, or transform business, or transform medicine, or whatever. They don't have a real clue about the complexities of these problems and also, they have no idea about how to verify these claims. I consider that modern design is a form of applied social sciences. After all, we are using our design skills to take technology and solve social issues, whether for an individual, or a group, or society, or a company, or a country. I think the training today is bad, and that the design field is ill served. Design today has become a very powerful influence. Designers need to have a much broader education in the world, maybe less education in technique.

What would you say to those that would argue against your statement, noting the success of designers like Philippe Starck or Karim Rashid, who focus strictly on aesthetics of product design and have managed to build quite a career around it?

The great designers have built simple things. Take Philippe Starck; there's a Philippe Starck—I'm pointing at Juicy Salif, his orange juice squeezer. Notice it's in my living room, not in my kitchen. I've only used it to squeeze an orange once, and that was because I wanted to see if it could be done. I consider it art, I don't consider it function. But if you look at what people like Starck do, they do chairs, wristwatch design—not the interior, just the shell of the watch—hotel interiors, they don't design anything with complexity that modern life requires. They don't design educational systems, they don't design the innards of an airplane, they don't design automobile interiors. If they did it would be maybe beautiful, but I have a feeling it wouldn't work very well. They don't design, they don't understand interaction design, or the feedback that's so essential for people to understand what's going on. So these great designers are trained as craftspeople and they produce great crafts.

We need people like that, we need the Philippe Starcks of the world, but don't confuse them with the sort of products frog works on, or the sort of products any of the major design companies work on. They're simple in comparison to this complex interaction of multiple technologies, invisible microprocessors inside, and the tasks that people are trying to accomplish. ☒

To see Don Norman's work, please visit http://breaking.in

HOWARD NUK HEAD OF INDUSTRIAL DESIGN SAMSUNG DESIGN AMERICA SAN FRANCISCO

Interviewed while Mr. Nuk was Vice President, Industrial Design Studio at Ammunition in San Francisco.

What kinds of portfolios get your attention these days? What brings in a product designer for an interview?

Each month we receive hundreds of applicants and I personally review every ID portfolio, so if someone's work doesn't immediately stand out, it can get easily lost in the abyss. In order to capture my attention, the portfolio must have all the right visual ingredients: organized layout, clean graphic design, and most importantly, the work itself must be celebrated. I am immediately turned off by over-designed graphic filigree and mismatched fonts. Designers should have the instinctual ability to tell a compelling story through imagery, whether it's a single descriptive full-bleed, in-use photo, or a collection of sketches or storyboards. Applicants typically get no more than a couple of seconds to convey their intent and make an impression, so clarity is key.

Know your audience. Many designers build their case studies in sequential order, revealing their research findings and design concepts as a build toward the final design. This approach makes a lot of sense when presenting work in-person since you can read your audience's body language and have relative control of your physical environment. That control is immediately lost once your portfolio goes over the wall into an inbox with hundreds of competing applicants. Knowing that you may only have seconds to impress the hiring manager, shifting your content around is necessary. Always lead and end with your juiciest hero images—you never get a second chance to make a first impression.

It sounds like a combination of having a good aesthetic eye and solid storytelling ability.

Yes. Storytelling itself is an art—knowing what to emphasize, when to reveal, and how your content is displayed. Quality of imagery is more important than quantity, and can dramatically affect the ease of consumption and overall perception of one's work. Make each curated moment in your portfolio count. Don't just add every asset you have for the sake of being thorough. Also invest in the right tools to help elevate the professionalism of your work. For instance, benchmark the latest rendering software packages and buy a DSLR with a range of lenses. Include a minimum of five successful projects. Try to diversify your work to show range of thinking and exploration. When building or rounding out my design teams, I always look for unique points of view.

Think about including assets from other creative talents you might possess: sketches, photography, sculpture, music, anything. Though the quality of

your ID projects will always be the barometer and focus, what may set you apart from another equally talented applicant are your extra-curricular activities. Amina, your portfolio was very memorable due to your exceptional fine art photography skills. Another designer named Francois Nguyen showed off his diverse creative talents through his music, sharing his amazing Spanish guitar album.

What do you expect to learn from the designer once they come in for an interview? How do you know that they'll fit your culture?

Every company has a distinct character, and it is usually driven top-down. My experiences at frog and Ammunition varied tremendously in business, process, and culture. And corporate design environments differ significantly from consultancies.

"MAKE EACH CURATED MOMENT IN YOUR PORTFOLIO COUNT. DON'T JUST ADD EVERY ASSET YOU HAVE FOR THE SAKE OF BEING THOROUGH."

In an interview, I want to discover who they are, both as a person and as a design professional, to better understand whether and how well they will mesh with existing team dynamics. Do they have an optimistic nature? Are they curious? Are they open to new ideas? Do they have a collaborative spirit? Based on the answers to these types of questions, I am able to gain a pretty decent sense of fit and potential. It's like putting the pieces of a puzzle together: each hire must strengthen the existing team and fulfill the required skill set.

What characteristics or qualities are necessary for the designer to have in order to succeed?

You have to have passion. If you're not passionate about design, you're not going to succeed in this field. One shouldn't pursue design as a get-rich-quick plan. We design because of a burning passion inside to create wonderful objects—objects for everyone. I truly believe that the best designers are those who cannot quench their thirst to improve the world. It's something we are born with.

A great designer must also have impeccable communication skills. Communication manifests in multiple forms: verbal, visual, and physical. As industrial designers, we have the unique opportunity to leverage an array of communication skills to express our ideas. As a designer you must have the keen ability to express market opportunities, business goals, user needs, technological innovations, aesthetic trends, materials and construction, et cetera. Communication is the key to achieving consensus and success.

How did you break into this business?

I always knew I wanted to be a creator of things. From a young age, I was obsessed with LEGO blocks. I would build cityscapes, vehicles, robot contraptions, and would rarely follow the given instructions for the set. I loved the free exploration of mechanisms and articulation. Clay was another favorite media, and with it I began developing a love for form, surface, and texture. This love for physical media was equally matched by my love for sketching. One of my favorite activities was drawing cartoons, caricatures, and even superhero comics. I have always been fascinated with the human figure, musculature, and proportion. I knew that design was in my future, only how it manifested itself was still in flux. Since childhood, I have been fanatical about both automotive design and architecture. In high school, I was certain I was going to become an architect. However, after an eye-opening internship at an architecture studio, fate steered me to the profession of industrial design. After the first day of ID Studio 101, I was hooked. I truly found my calling in life.

Over the course of my school career, my passion for the craft grew exponentially. I broke into the profession through the co-op program at Carleton University in Ottawa, Canada. They had multiple connections with local firms and corporate studios. I joined DW Product Canada as an intern, and began designing products for companies like Black & Decker and Brookstone. Over a nearly two-year period, I designed and shipped a variety of simple

consumer electronic products. This portfolio enabled me to land my dream job at frog design in California. The investment of time in an extended internship or co-op program is the best way to give students the real-world experiences necessary to help them find a prosperous full-time job after graduation.

If you were just starting out now, what advice would you give yourself?

The first few years of design studio life are a formative growth period in a designer's career. Having the freedom to explore, travel, bond with peers (peers you will likely stay in touch with your entire career) is invaluable. If I could do it all over, I would have pursued a series of six-month internships in different countries around the world, working within different types of industries. This exploration of self, culture, and area of expertise would have been an extremely inspiring adventure.

The first decade of your career should be focused on discovery. Let your curiosity guide you. My experiences have made me who I am today, and if I were to give one simple piece of advice, I'd recommend traveling as much as possible. Live simple and light, relieving yourself of too many possessions, and do whatever it takes to get the widest range of experiences possible. It's much easier to do that when you are young, single, and with very little financial burden. Be free.

Where do you see the future of industrial design going as it evolves further in the 21st century?

Industrial design has been an evolving practice since the invention of mass production. With the Industrial Revolution came sustained growth and manufacturing efficiencies never seen previously. With an ever-increasing population, the overabundance of mass-produced goods has had a detrimental effect on our environment. Driving sustainable design from cradle to cradle is more important than ever. Each day, designers are playing an increasingly important role in this change of mindset and application.

With the Digital Revolution upon us, the practice of industrial design continues to evolve. The most successful product brands take the entire physical and digital ecosystem of their products into consideration. Product complexity continues to grow as consumers come to expect more personalized functionality. With growing complexity, product designers are only beginning to scratch the surface of what it really means to simplify a product user experience. As the products around us become more seamlessly connected, packed with features and functions, and able to predict our individual habits and desires, the task of simplifying the object itself becomes a much more interesting effort.

So to those who say that product design is dying, you'd say?

Absolutely not. Product design will always be a part of human creation; after all, we are physical beings. Industrial designers will continue to evolve the craft and further integrate with digital products and services. It is not enough to simply create a beautiful object and expect market acceptance. Today's consumers have more information at their fingertips and higher expectations than ever before. The products that thrive in tomorrow's marketplace are those based on a core idea that runs deeper than a pretty shell, useful app, or catchy tagline. The success stories of tomorrow will be the products born from a truly authentic point of view that provide a unique and useful service to people, and realized with a consistent focus across industrial design, digital design and service, and marketing. More than ever before, an industrial designer's contribution has an enormous impact on the world's economics, environment, and evolution.

Anything you'd like to add that we haven't talked about? Any final words of wisdom?

For anyone with the passion to create beautiful and useful things, I would encourage you to explore industrial design. Like artists who create masterpieces to be appreciated from afar, industrial designers have the unique opportunity to create art for everyone to touch, smell, hear, and engage with. There are few prouder moments than seeing someone enjoy the product you helped shape and create, knowing it all started from your imagination, on a paper napkin sketch. [BI]

To see Howard Nuk's work, please visit http://breaking.in

PAM NYBERG
DIRECTOR OF EXPERIENCE
DESIGN
HUMANA
CHICAGO

Interviewed while Ms. Nyberg was the Director of Strategy at Thrive, in Atlanta.

What kinds of portfolios get your attention these days? What brings in an industrial designer for an interview?

The portfolios that attract the most attention demonstrate solid design skills throughout the design process and an ability to inform their work with human-centered design research. Being at a consultancy, we never know who the next client will be so we need folks who have a range of skills, everything from masterful sketching skills to knowledge of commonly used CAD programs. We also like to see people who can specifically demonstrate form intelligence, an understanding of materials, and knowledge of manufacturing processes, all of which are difficult to find in more junior candidates. Added candidate bonuses include experience with other cultures and basic business knowledge, even if it's just based on taking several marketing classes. This exposure to business enables them to have conversations in the language of business, and it sensitizes them to the challenges their business-focused colleagues must address.

One of the biggest shortcomings I've seen in student portfolios is a thorough demonstration of their design process. Many times, students show several initial sketches and then they reveal the end result, thinking that they should prioritize a short story over details. However, since we're hiring them for their thought process, in addition to their skills, we want to see that they've sought to understand user, technology, and market requirements, explored multiple options in sketches and various levels of prototypes, and made clearly articulated tradeoffs in shaping their final solution. We also like to see how the front-end user and market learnings are reflected in their final concept.

Students should plan to include at least one detailed project in their portfolio that demonstrates their entire design process. Each project should be chosen to highlight specific skills or knowledge. In addition, I recommend that students bring separate process books to show sketch development, renderings, and CAD, if they feel they need to keep a really tight portfolio. Potential employers oftentimes request to see more evidence of sketching, rendering, or CAD abilities.

What do you expect to learn from the designer during an interview?

If we're sent a portfolio that looks promising, we'll conduct an initial phone interview to learn about their project work, design process, and the way they speak about themselves. If the discussion goes smoothly, we'll bring them in for a visit. Personally, I'm most eager to see what they're like in person: do they have a great personality, a sense of humor, are they upbeat, internally motivated, confident but not egotistic, etc.? How do they engage with others? Will they mesh with the rest of the folks in our office? It's hard to downplay the importance of this chemistry test since they'll be representing the company to clients and spending lots of time with the team every day. During the actual interview, we'll discuss their portfolio in more detail to better understand their design process, project work, range of skills, and their ability to present to others.

What characteristics or qualities are necessary to be a successful industrial designer?

Designers are integrators, which requires them to interact and empathize with different types of people to develop an informed point of view about a project. As such, clients and project stakeholders—users, retailers, client support staff, etc.—appreciate working with people who are personable, humble, open-minded, and inquisitive.

Back in the studio, the most important qualities a designer can demonstrate are: respect for others, a willingness to help team members, being openly receptive to great ideas from any source, being curious about the world in general, and continually working to improve both knowledge and skills.

How did you break into this business?

In undergrad, I was searching for a product design program without knowing it. I was fascinated by physics, psychology, and art but couldn't find a major that integrated all three disciplines at my university. After numerous major changes, I graduated with a bachelor's in mathematics, only to stumble upon the Stanford Product Design Program several years later. Their master's-level program exposed me to IDEO and their human-centered design approach, which inspired me to earn a master's from the University of Michigan in human factors engineering. Upon graduation, I joined Whirlpool. Shortly thereafter, Chuck Jones arrived. I joined Chuck's human factors group and had a front-row seat as he began integrating Whirlpool's human factors and design groups into a world-class design organization. That was my big break into the working world of design, and I was very fortunate that my role allowed me to leverage my visualization skills, in combination with my background in human factors and design research.

If you were just starting out now, what advice would you give yourself?

If I were starting university now, I'd make myself aware of the industrial design major instead of taking a four-year academic walkabout. But if I could give advice to other students, I'd tell them not to settle for just getting a degree. I've looked through a number of portfolios, and the sad news is that more than a few students are graduating without strong enough design skills to get a job. In conversations with professors, they've told me that students are more concerned about grades than doing good work. Unfortunately, grades aren't going to land them a job, a killer portfolio will. Given the huge investment they've made in their education, this is tragic. Students need to look at the best work being done, in class and on online portfolio sites like Coroflot. Focus on strengthening skills that need attention and set a high bar. Do work outside of school—participate in design competitions—just to develop work that you would be proud to show. The design field is becoming increasingly more competitive, so just getting by isn't going to be enough, even in the short term.

Having spoken to other creative directors, it unfortunately feels like this is a trend that's going on these days.

Sadly yes, but the situation isn't irreparable. Design is a profession, just like medicine and engineering. Therefore, professors must hold students to high standards, for their own good, and to help those who aren't suited for the field to find another major where they can truly excel. Given the price they're paying for their education, students deserve this level of guidance. From an employer's perspective, it's not uncommon for us to view student portfolios before looking at their résumés. If the portfolio doesn't suggest that they have the potential to be a talented professional designer, the résumé matters very little.

Where do you see the future of industrial design going as it evolves further in the 21st century?

Given the advent of forums like Kickstarter, I think we'll see significant growth in the number of individual designers and consultancies who solicit project funding from communities, as opposed to clients. The best work could be licensed to companies for increased distribution through leading channels or sold through online and social networking channels for maximum profit.

I've always believed that people need to manage their own career. They need to view themselves as a brand and make each career decision very consciously. Always think about the job after the job you're preparing to accept, to ensure it's moving you along the path toward your ultimate career destination. Decisions aren't limited to a job title though. If you have the luxury of choices, consider the people you'll meet in a particular role, the knowledge and skills you'll gain, the reputation of potential employers, impressions given by your choice of topics when sharing ideas through social media, etc. In making these choices, you're crafting an identity that distinguishes you from others. Leave space for surprising opportunities though. Despite every effort to plan carefully, details and timing never align neatly. And set your sights high. You're working on the most important design project you'll ever have—your own destiny. [BI]

To see Pam Nyberg's work, please visit http://breaking.in

"THE PORTFOLIOS THAT ATTRACT THE MOST ATTENTION DEMONSTRATE SOLID DESIGN SKILLS THROUGHOUT THE DESIGN PROCESS AND AN ABILITY TO INFORM THEIR WORK WITH HUMAN-CENTERED DESIGN RESEARCH."

It's also safe to assume that the fields of interaction design and industrial design will become even more closely integrated, given the intelligence that's being supported by devices.

Anything we didn't cover that you would like to add? Any final words of wisdom?

MATTHEW PAPROCKI
FOUNDER & CEO
GOODHATCH
LOS ANGELES

What kinds of portfolios get your attention these days? What brings in an industrial designer for an interview?

My first impression is always based on what I see visually. How do their final designs look? If it catches my eye, then I look deeper for innovative and appropriate features and functionality. How smart are their designs? How will people use the products? How will the designs communicate their value at retail and through marketing? I look to see if a designer can tell a story with their designs and demonstrate how they could live in the real world.

What impresses me most is when a student can tell a convincing story and that it's evident they thoroughly thought through all the different aspects of the design, as well as the context that the product will live in. Who will use it? How will they use it? Where will it be used? How will users learn about it? How will users purchase it? How will it be made?

In my opinion, the portfolio is always more important than the résumé. I look at résumés to get a sense of a designer's professional experience, but I don't pay much attention to where they went to school or how they did in the classroom. If they learned what they needed to in the classroom, the grade doesn't matter in creative disciplines. The proof is in their designs.

Has there been a portfolio that you've seen recently that resonated with you? What about it stood out?

Not one that comes readily to mind. I'll say that the portfolios that stand out the most are from students who were able to take an idea they were passionate about and cultivate it into a great design that is viable in the real world. I'm impressed with students that can stay steadfast to the spirit behind their designs, but can also adapt the design's expression as they learn and explore. The best designs develop organically and adapt. As layers of reality are added to the designer's consideration, they need to be willing to re-conceive the design. For example, if they thought their design was going to be a box, but as they began developing it, realized that a circle really made sense, they need to be willing to make that shift. That is one of the most important skills for a designer––to be able to have perspective on their work and have the willingness to reinvent their design.

I used to teach the industrial design thesis class at CCAC (California College of the Arts). It's impressive when industrial design students are able to evaluate and explore their designs from different perspectives. I've seen student projects that take it way beyond the product's façade. They looked at manufacturing, business models, packaging, and retail. They talked to people outside of the ID world, from consumers and businesses to retailers and engineers, to hear different perspectives. They were able to synthesize it all into their design—that's impressive.

Another important quality is when a student's portfolio demonstrates that they can work with others. I've seen students who have done the industrial design work and then teamed up with an engineering student to work with them on their design. I have seen others work with a graphic design student to create packaging and marketing materials around their idea. Students that proactively engage with creatives from other disciplines have a more holistic understanding of product development.

What do you expect to learn from a designer during an interview?

Designers have to be intuitive in their work, and so naturally I use my intuition about people that I'd like to work with. I want to learn about their personality. I want to get a sense of what drives them, how they relate to other people and how they conduct themselves.

I want to work with designers who are internally driven, but externally focused on creating products and experiences that are engaging and valuable to others. I look for designers who are driven to learn, collaborate, and adapt to different situations. It's important that designers are able to connect to users like themselves, and even more important that they are inquisitive and empathetic to others with different needs and perspectives.

What characteristics or qualities would you say make a successful designer?

A good designer is optimistic. They can face the realities of the world, while imagining how people and objects can live, work, and play better together in it. While artists and designers often share some of the same skills and talents, the fundamental difference is that an artist creates to express themselves to the world and a designer creates to serve the world.

The world is a messy place and the best designers are ready to get dirty and work in the chaos. Even when it's overwhelming, the best designers I've worked with jump right into the deep end and start paddling. They embrace the complexity and chaos of product development. They don't sit on the sidelines and don't over-analyze their choices. They aren't afraid of the unknown. They trust their intuition and ability to create.

How did you break into this business? What motivated you to open your own design studio?

I grew up in a small steel town in Ohio. Manufacturing surrounded me, but I had no idea what industrial design was. But from a young age I was enamored by the material world and as I grew up I knew I wanted to be a product designer. I worked in my grandfather's machine shop, re-tooling parts for industrial presses for making dog food cans. I was able to see how science, physics, and engineering were fundamental to creating objects. I studied mechanical engineering at The Ohio State University and set up a rigorous internship program with Fitch Design, who, at the time, was one of the world's largest and most successful multidisciplinary design firms. I spent six years in school, splitting my time between studying engineering in the classroom and product development at Fitch.

"THE BEST DESIGNS DEVELOP ORGANICALLY AND ADAPT. AS LAYERS OF REALITY ARE ADDED TO THE DESIGNER'S CONSIDERATION, THEY NEED TO BE WILLING TO RE-CONCEIVE THE DESIGN."

When I first interviewed at Fitch, I didn't have a portfolio or a résumé. I was a freshman in college and basically walked in and said, "I want to be a product designer and I'll do anything you need help with so I can work here and learn how you create new products." They ended up putting me to work sweeping the floors in the model shop, packing up FedEx boxes, and taking out the trash. It was a very creative, dynamic environment and just being in it taught me so much about design. Over time, I was able to use my machine shop experience to start working in the model shop at Fitch. If a designer needed a quick breadboard model or mock-up built, I would go and make it for them in the model shop. Things progressed from there and, by the time I graduated, I was fortunate enough to be running small projects at Fitch.

Tylor Garland, my partner at Boombang, and I left Fitch Design and went to work at frog design before starting our own studio. Fitch and frog were polar opposites. Fitch was very structured and research and process driven, while frog was filled with creative chaos. I learned a lot working in both cultures that I've integrated into my own approach to design and development. Boombang is a very entrepreneurial design firm. Even on client jobs, the approach is to create within the context of the whole business.

I've had the opportunity to work with many consumer electronics companies. In 2010, I took that experience and partnered with some former clients and manufacturers to launch three new CE audio brands: Soundfreaq, G-Project, and Capello. To focus on these businesses, I've spun them out from Boombang and into a new company: Goodhatch.

If you were just starting out now, what advice would you give yourself?

Trust your intuition and instincts. There are always opportunities around you. As a creative, you're instinctually optimistic about trying to make things work. One thing I've become better at is being more discerning about the opportunities I focus on and putting myself in better situations to succeed.

Where do you see the future of industrial design going as it evolves further in the 21st century?

Product design continues to become more integrated with business and culture. Everything is interconnected. Traditional development was a linear process from research to industrial design, to engineering and manufacturing, and then to marketing and sales. The challenge of modern product development is the concurrent synthesis of all these different disciplines and the modern industrial designer leads the charge.

Anything you'd like to add that we didn't cover? Any final words of wisdom?

Design is about having a vision. When you try to make the vision a reality, there are going to be some hiccups along the way. You have two choices: either grasp tightly to your original idea while reality forces changes that compromise your design or embrace the change, evolve, and re-create your design.

Optimism drives your creativity. The magic and fun of creation happens when you embrace the way the world is today and create within it to make it a better place. 🄱🄸

To see Matthew Paprocki's work, please visit http://breaking.in

ALEXANDER PELIKAN
FOUNDER
PELIDESIGN
EINDHOVEN, NETHERLANDS

What motivated you to open up your own design studio?

It all came about really naturally. It wasn't really planned. I was finishing my third year and I wanted to work for a designer to pay for my cost of living, so I approached Maarten Baas because he had a studio next to mine and I asked him if I could build some furniture for him. He said "Yes, okay but you need to have your own studio, so you can write your own bills." So I opened up my studio while I was still studying. I have always, since I was 15 or 16, worked independently. I was used to working relatively independently and it was really natural that I started this studio. It became really handy because it allowed me to do my own design. It worked out well, not only working for other designers, but also promoting my own stuff. There was no huge plan behind it. It's kind of scary, actually.

You learned as you went?

Yeah, exactly. That's what I'm still doing.

How do you manage the non-design aspects of running your own studio?

I have a very good accountant. The marketing and such belongs to the design. It's a part of being a designer, being creative about marketing, having good relations and things like that.

"YOU HAVE TO PUT 1000% INTO WHAT YOU'RE DOING, TO BE IN LOVE WITH YOUR STUFF, TO HAVE THE DRIVE AND PASSION. THAT PASSION FOR WHAT YOU'RE DOING, THE CLIENTS WILL SEE IT. THEY INVEST MORE IN YOUR PASSION THAN IN YOUR PRODUCT."

It can be difficult, but if you approach it in a creative way, as you would approach an assignment, then it's more fruitful. That's how I do it.

What advice would you give to somebody who would like to open up their own studio like you did, straight out of school?

Basically, find out what you're good at and try to make it happen. Speak with gallery owners and companies. Do what you love, what you're good at. Try to find that magic formula. The most interesting things I did came unplanned.

When promoting your work have you found that one approach works better than others?

My theory is "don't be annoying." Be professional and get your stuff known; it's really important to not overdo it.

What characteristics or qualities would you say make a successful designer?

Be original. There are so many chairs out, so many of whatever that's been done, it's very difficult to sell things, to get an assignment. You have to put 1000% into what you're doing, to be in love with your stuff, to have the drive and passion. That passion for what you're doing, the clients will see it. They invest more in your passion than in your product. They may be triggered by your product, but what really makes a difference to them is your passion, your drive. They can see that and feel that, and it's easier to convince them that you can do the job, that you can develop a product. They can feel your passion.

How could a designer manifest this passion to a client?

Details. Details are very important. Stay in touch with your base, your suppliers. That goes for all levels. Truth, honesty, and respect. It's not easy work.

Your work at times blurs the line between art and design. Can you discuss your approach and share some examples of challenges you face in designing for a specific market?

When I design for a gallery, or when I design a limited-edition piece, it's not really an approach. It's, again, the passion. I love to make the things I make. You have to be serious about your work. As for the assignments for industrial design, there's more decision makers involved, whereas for a gallery commission, there's only one person.

Essentially understanding who your client is and how you deliver the project based on that.

Yeah.

If you were just starting out now, what advice would you give yourself?

Do more things that you love. Be more deliberate with the possibilities. You cannot do it enough if you're passionate about your work. Play around. Work hard.

Where do you see the future of industrial design going as it evolves further in the 21st century?

It's going to be more differentiated. There are a lot of opportunities for design as societies are differentiating more and more. Lots of different worldviews, so there are a lot of things to be developed. It's hard to say. It's not going in one direction, it's going in lots of directions. So it's important to be original because there is no general market anymore. To be original, you need to be strong about what you're doing, that's the thing. If you're original, you'll start discussions. The market is also so scared that you have to be smart about how to communicate about yourself and your product.

What suggestions would you have on being and staying original?

Don't do what other designers are doing. Get your inspiration from other fields. Do what you really like, what you're interested in. What makes you special? Draw inspiration from your daily life. Be your own person in general. How to do that, I don't know. You can just feel it.

Where do you get your inspiration from?

From all over the place. From nature: I really love to be in nature and see nature's structures. And also from philosophy. I'm interested in the old Chinese philosophy. From everyday objects: from trash cans and their hinges, anything, simple things, engineering solutions, industrial things. And other fields: I try to bring ideas in from other fields into design.

Anything we didn't cover that you'd like to add? Any final words of wisdom?

Buy potatoes; they are cheap and nutritious. They are great for a starving designer. Invest in yourself. Have fun. Just keep on, keep going. Eventually you will succeed.

And buy potatoes. ▣

To see Alexander Pelikan's work, please visit http://breaking.in

DICK POWELL
CO-FOUNDER & DIRECTOR OF
GLOBAL DESIGN
SEYMOURPOWELL
LONDON

What kinds of portfolios get your attention these days? What brings in an industrial designer for an interview?

In our business we tend to look for different kinds of people. We find it very hard to find the kind of polymath who can do everything really brilliantly, and when they do walk in the door we take them on. We are often looking within the portfolios for people who we think have the kind of skills and the right kind of thinking to fill this or that gap. One of the things I tell students who ask me, "Well, how can I get a job?", is be really, really good at one thing. That one thing these days might be being a really good Alias jockey, for example. Being really, really good at one thing makes you employable.

One of the key things we are looking for is, of course, more creativity. One of the great hallmarks of the creative mind is the ability to draw, it's something we at Seymourpowell have always been passionate about. There is a specific link between the ability to express yourself and the ability to communicate with others by the medium of drawing—in itself it's a great sign of a creative mind. We are constantly on the lookout for people who can think fluidly with a pencil in front of them, generating and expressing ideas. If I had to choose one ability out of all of them, it would be this ability to draw what you think.

Even in this day and age that focuses heavily on the digital, you find the ability to draw very important for a designer. Why?

The computer is a completely different kind of pencil. The creative mind thinks and executes simultaneously—the hand is an extension of the brain where the feedback loop is immediate. As you and I speak, most of the applications that we use on computers are too slow for the kind of creative interaction that we often need in the world of innovation, where designers iteratively conceive and express ideas constantly and quickly. This still isn't something you can easily do on a computer. Of course we expect that graduates who come see us are already equipped with a whole suite of the basic computer skills around the key applications that we need. That's always a given these days. So we are looking for things which are more exceptional than that, and good drawing ability is the rarest and hardest of skills to find.

Has there been a portfolio that you've seen recently that resonated with you? What about it stood out?

I haven't seen a portfolio like that in a very long time. It's really interesting that both Richard Seymour and I feel very strongly about this: about someone who can look at a human figure and draw it. That process of inquiry and perception is a part of the conception process. People who can look at the form of something like the human body and draw and capture it, understand how it is built and what the surfaces are doing and how the movements and mechanics work, things like that. That's why drawing is so very, very critical to a creative mind. If you draw, you understand things because you look at them in a different way from other people. We feel very strongly about that. Unfortunately, these days it's something that's not even enforced in most design courses, so when you find someone who has that ability you pretty much grab them.

What do you expect to learn from a designer during an interview?

First of all you have to get over the hurdle of competency. Is this person competent? Can they do the things that we are going to need them to do? There's kind of a baseline beyond which the conversation isn't even worth carrying on. You see that quickly in the level of quality and finish in the book. Then the next thing you're looking for is really startling ideas. You're looking for engaging ideas and, if you see them, you say to yourself: "I wish I thought of that," or "Isn't that a beautiful thing?" You're looking for things that startle and engage, that get your attention. Every once in a blue moon we'll get a portfolio where every page takes several minutes to explain. Something that students often fail to grasp is that they need to make an impact with a level of understanding that will happen in nanoseconds, not in minutes. The beautiful object, or whatever it is that they may have created, is startling—it gets your attention straight away. It doesn't need to be explained. Yes, you're interested in hearing about it thereafter, but you don't really want to be persuaded into it. You want to have it hit you in between the eyes.

"IF I HAD TO CHOOSE ONE ABILITY OUT OF ALL OF THEM, IT WOULD BE THIS ABILITY TO DRAW WHAT YOU THINK."

We are looking for good thinkers. People who can articulate easily what they are doing and why. People who don't only reach for a pencil, but think first. The ability to articulate what you're about and why you are doing it, is a critical part of being a designer. The successful designers are the ones who can simply and easily capture, or simplify, something complex and render it credible and understandable. A great skill of a designer is taking something which is inherently extremely complicated, from a manufacturing, usability, or mechanical standpoint, and synthesizing it and simplifying it into those few things which are really important. That takes a different kind of mind; it's the kind of mind that designers have. It's why designers and creative people are often good at innovation: they are able to take a helicopter view of different and often competing factors, and resolve them in a way which individual disciplines find difficult.

If I can illustrate that for a moment, an engineer will look at the solution from an engineering perspective and that will affect his view. The CEO will look at return on investment, the marketing director will have a campaign in mind and these views are rarely sympathetic to one another. They are always competing for mindspace. But the designer, because he's used to dealing with these kinds of complicated systems, can instinctively see through the complexity to the really, really important things which need to be captured. We are looking for people who can do that.

How did you break into the industry?

I'm afraid I have to take you back to my childhood because, when I was growing up, I was fascinated by the mechanical world, the physical world, and the structural world. I grew up with a construction set here in the UK, which is called Meccano (I think in the United States it was called an Erector Set) and I loved making these sorts of things. I loved taking engines apart and figuring out how they worked—all of those sorts of things. My other love was art and drawing, so I suppose in modern terminology I have almost equally balanced my left and right brain. On the one hand, quite logical, linear, and objective thinking, and on the other, quite intuitive, emotional, and subjective. How many careers are there that blend those two things? And I didn't discover design until I was about 17 at school and came across a magazine published by the Design Council called Design. I opened its pages and thought, "Oh my goodness, this is for me."

So there I was studying for four A-levels to study architecture at Cambridge, and all they needed in the industrial design courses was, what we call here, five O-levels. I already had 10, so I was already over the first hurdle. I did an arts foundation course, which gave me a grounding in all different art and design disciplines...and there was a lot of drawing. From there, I took industrial design courses in Manchester and then to Royal College of Arts to do a post-graduate. The making of me was there at RCA, which still is a formidable institution and its graduates fill the world's design studios. That was a very formative experience for me, and having been a student for seven years, I was so poor that I figured I had nothing to lose by starting my business straight away. If I had gone into work and had a salary, a wife and children, it would've been difficult to have my own business later, so I did it straight away and formed a business with two colleagues. We fell out after three years. I picked myself up and started again with Rich and off we went.

I think, when I started my first business, we were very much about designing products; we were an industrial design studio, or a consultancy if you want to call it that. After that fell through, I turned to my own resources for a while and met Richard while motorcycling together. He was in advertising, and the two of us had a lot in common, but also came from different backgrounds. Rich was a graphic designer by training, but had come through advertising, but not just ordinary advertising—a very different kind of advertising at the time. He's a very different kind of a thinker; he's a true polymath. The two of us were very congruent in what we were able to offer our clients. We weren't just about making things nice, or making them functionally better. Our thinking went much further upstream of product conception than most of the people at that time were doing. We were able to move upstream in the process, to do a lot more research, get involved with positioning, marketing, branding—everything ahead of the brief, if you want. This was at a time when few in our industry were doing that.

If you were just starting out now, what advice would you give yourself?

You're kind of asking what did we do wrong, in a sense? I think we did so many things right. To start with, we never got into this for money. I wouldn't tell anyone to go into this business to make money. There are easier ways to make money. You don't make a lot of money in this business. You do this because you're passionate about it and you love it. That's a key point. And the things we both did wrong? I suppose both of us had experiences before in start-up businesses that had gone wrong for various reasons, but we learned huge lessons from that—like choose your partners very carefully. Partnership in a business is like a marriage, and you need to treat it like that. You actually will spend more time with your business partner than you will with your wife. That means all of the famous things from marriage guidance count in business. Talk to each other, keep talking, don't keep secrets, be open. All of those things are very, very important.

Really what we learned was that we were doing things, and thinking in ways which industry needed but which nobody was doing, so we

dived in there. Of course there were hundreds of design businesses of one kind or another, all fundamentally doing the same thing, but we tried to give ourselves an edge over our competition. We tried to spin ourselves into a different space and that little tiny difference is the thing that creates your reputation. I think starting a design company now, of this kind, is much more difficult than it was when we did it in 1976. Much more difficult.

What makes you say that?

The first reason is the cost of entry is much higher. All we needed to get going then was a drawing board, a stack of markers, few pencils, and some pens. Nowadays you need computers, servers, and CAD systems, expensive photocopiers, scanners, and so on. I mean there's an investment cost to get you going which is quite high. The field is much fuller than it was then too. There are many more people engaged in it and you become just another small company in an ocean of small companies. You've got to be fiercely ambitious, really.

When we started in business, in one of our early meetings we talked about objectives: what did we want out of this? I said to Rich, "We will know we've been successful when Sony is looking to employ an outside design company, and we are one of the three names they might consider." That's how I categorized it. You've got to be very, very ambitious to want to do that. You've got to be prepared. This is not just me saying this; I think it's true for any start-up. You've got to be prepared to work your ass off. There's no easy route through this, and people imagine that there is, but there isn't. But the rewards are great and well worth having.

Where do you see the future of industrial design going as it evolves further in the 21st century?

We've seen a fairly consistent movement back in-house. The big brands are increasingly building their internal capability. When they reach outside, they reach outside for different reasons than they do when we started. When we started, we had a lot of work in Asia, because Asian companies wanted to learn from Western experiences and how things were done here, what contexts there were, and why people bought products. They were on a learning curve. Those times are past. They are now as good as the rest of the world and they have been for a long time.

If you think of businesses like Samsung, they're hugely competent and capable. They've gone from being a follower to a leader. So the climate is completely different. For people who work for outside design consultancies, it's getting increasingly difficult to work for big brands, unless they have specific requirements that they can't deal with in-house. We all know that Einstein famously said that "problems can't be solved by thinking within the environment in which those problems were created." You need an outside view, and very often businesses engage with us because they want an outside view, unencumbered by the thinking within the business, particularly in innovation.

Nobody comes to us asking, "I need a new, more contemporary this or that." It's all about innovation, the difference, the functional improvement, and the brand. The days where they just wanted a nice product from us are diminishing. I don't mean to say it's not there. We do get it and we love it when we get it, but usually the degree of knowledge that we need about the product, the brand, and its domain is huge and all of the upfront work we need to do to inform our design process is very large. It's difficult for a small design company to handle. Not that there's any particular merit in size, I should say. I mean we are small compared to IDEO, but we're big compared to most product-based design businesses.

It sounds like industrial design is broadening even more as a field.

Absolutely. We don't call ourselves an industrial design business and haven't for years. In our office we have a big team of people who do brand research, positioning, strategy, user research, and things like that. Then we've got product and transport design, structural packaging, branding, graphics, model shop, and prototyping. We have people who are dedicated CAD and animation people. The kind of work we have to do embraces many, many different aspects of the product: its communication, how it's researched, the interaction, the user experience, the interface, all kinds of stuff that has tended to become more discipline specific.

If you have someone who is an absolutely brilliant animator, for example, they tend to stay doing just that. People who are good at programming interactions have a palette of knowledge and experience, which makes it easier for them to do it––they quickly become specialists. What people ask us to do, and you're absolutely right about this, is much broader even than it was 20 years ago. So yes, absolutely.

It's encompassing the entire ecosystem of product development, and not just the product itself.

Exactly. Ecosystem is a good word and it's a word we use all the time. It's not just about a great idea, it's about every touch point for that idea. A lot of businesses now are trying to escape from the old retail stranglehold. Any way they can get to consumers, other than through traditional retail channels, becomes important. I suppose if I try to clarify what it is that we do, it's to answer three fundamental questions, which are: What should we make? Why should we make it? How do we do it? Twenty-five years ago it was all about the how—about the design, the feel, the manufacture of those things. But actually, most of it now is deciding what is the right thing to do and really, really, really understanding why that is the right thing to do. Not just because you want to ensure it's successful in the market, but also to make sure that the company is completely engaged in understanding why that's important.

A lot of these companies and clients are really good at making stuff. They really know how to make mind-bendingly complex things, which are, let's say, three millimeters thick and magically put together, and which deliver engaging experiences. What they often struggle with though is figuring out what people are going to want and why. They've got no one else to turn to except people like us. That's where the opportunity in the future lies: in helping determine what is it that people will want and why.

Is there anything that we didn't cover that you'd like to add? Any final words of wisdom?

I think that, for graduating students, breaking in is the most difficult moment of their career because they are emerging into an ocean that is overstocked with graduate designers. The number one thing is to be very realistic about your capabilities. Be real; how good are you? "Are you good enough to cut it?" is the key question students should ask themselves.

Number two is to get experience at whatever cost. Get into a business, even if it's not the business you ultimately want to end up in. Get into a small design business or help out a designer. Throw yourself on the rails, prostrate yourself, and get in there in order to get under the skin of business. It's so difficult to walk into a job these days without some sort of experience.

"'ARE YOU GOOD ENOUGH TO CUT IT?' IS THE KEY QUESTION STUDENTS SHOULD ASK THEMSELVES."

And number three is, as I said, be really good at one thing. The chances are the business you're looking to get into is looking for someone who can do that one thing, in addition to everything else of course. When I was leaving college, I made myself really, really good at what we used to call rendering—it opened loads of doors within the industry.

Practice makes perfect.

Yeah. It was Gary Player, a professional golfer, who, when he won this competition had a journalist come up to him and say, "Hey Gary, you got a bit lucky there" and he replied, "You know what? The more I practice, the luckier I seem to get." BI

To see the work of Dick Powell and Seymourpowell, please visit http://breaking.in

ERNESTO QUINTEROS CHIEF DESIGN OFFICER JOHNSON & JOHNSON NEW BRUNSWICK, NEW JERSEY

Interviewed while Mr. Quinteros was Chief Brand Officer at Belkin in Los Angeles.

What kinds of portfolios get your attention these days? What brings in an industrial designer for an interview?

I'm always on the lookout for people who will challenge or complement the team. We tend to think about the studio as an organism. When we look at portfolios, we ask ourselves: "What does this individual bring to the table that will push our thinking?" or "Do they possess skills that we lack?" Additionally, we look for results. Often, a portfolio will come in that has some interesting research, good conceptual thinking, or a strong design aesthetic. But if their projects can't bring it together as a cohesive solution, that portfolio may not get the attention and enthusiasm to bring them in for an interview.

Since we are very busy with projects, we never bring in a design candidate without first reviewing their work. We simply don't have the time to meet with everyone who submits a portfolio. It usually only takes us a few minutes to review a digital portfolio to get a quick sense of a candidate's strengths and weaknesses. If we see thinking that will help us evolve the studio, or special skills that may be a clear fit for a specific program, we will bring them in right away for an in-person conversation.

We are also very interested in designers that come from international offices or schools. Since we design products for global markets and specific regions, it's critical to have diverse cultural perspectives in the studio. We also look for those who have interests in emerging markets and technologies.

Other questions we often ask ourselves are: Have they developed products that integrate hardware and software? Do they have category knowledge or interests that we know we will need in the future? Have they worked in different categories and have portfolio samples to showcase this? For example: sporting goods, healthcare, transportation, environmental design, etc. We encourage applicants to bring as many physical examples of their work as possible. Prototypes are even more desirable than finished products; nothing is better at fostering conversations than seeing people's work in three dimensions.

I have found that if a designer has experience from only one industry, their ability to solve problems may be limited. We tend to hire designers from consultancies rather than corporations because usually they have been exposed to diverse product categories. Consultant studio experience is a lot like cross-training: you can bring unique knowledge from one category to another, and this really helps to shake up the thinking. This contributes to a strong, lively studio organism.

What are the elements of a portfolio that you've deemed successful?

There are many elements that we specifically look for when reviewing a portfolio, and depending on the project or role we're hiring for, we may dial up or down those expectations. If they can demonstrate a level of extraordinary ability in the following, then we usually consider their portfolio successful.

How did they go about setting up the front-end of their projects? Was the designer or design team provided a detailed objective statement or creative brief? Was formal research provided or did the designer take the initiative to learn about the people he was designing for? We like to see portfolio projects where the designer(s) spend time with real people in real-world environments. It's impossible to sit in a room to design a product and expect to understand what truly takes place in a hospital room, an airline seat, or in another culture. Designers need to spend time with people who live and work in those environments, to capture the essence of what matters to them, not just what matters to the designer.

What is the designer's development process? Do they follow a methodology that is rigid or do they tailor their approach for a specific problem or objective? Is their process iterative? Depending on where they went to school or where they worked, it's important for us to understand if our processes align or not.

Then, there's the matter of conceptual thinking. Are they able to bring fresh thinking to basic projects? Can they re-invent the everyday? Are they thinking about the total experience and how to simplify or make it more enjoyable? When we review portfolios, this is probably the most important thing we look for. We can find people to make something look attractive, but it's finding those individuals who create simple, elegant solutions to improve people's experiences that get our attention. Those are the individuals we want to hire.

"WE CAN FIND PEOPLE TO MAKE SOMETHING LOOK ATTRACTIVE, BUT IT'S FINDING THOSE INDIVIDUALS THAT CREATE SIMPLE, ELEGANT SOLUTIONS THAT IMPROVE PEOPLE'S EXPERIENCES THAT GET OUR ATTENTION. THOSE ARE THE INDIVIDUALS WE WANT TO HIRE."

As for the sketching and visual communication skills, in our studio, we aren't overly impressed with portfolios of highly polished renderings. Although basic sketching is a necessary skill for any product designer, we rely on it more for efficient communication. It's critical that our designers can express their thinking, solve problems, as well as work through the evolution of form language and detail refinement with simple sketches. A range of sketching styles is expected at

Belkin. In basic idea generation, we expect to see lots of ideas, usually one idea per page. We don't want them to show us every sketch generated during their project, but it's nice to see a raw sketchbook to show the amount of ideas that were explored and their level of thinking during the process. Community sketching is where two or more people might take turns communicating their ideas back and forth in real time. This might happen on a single piece of paper or on a whiteboard. Sometimes we see portfolios that include these sketches as part of the designer's process. We like to see this because it showcases the purest form of two-dimensional problem-solving and rapid dialogue. We also like to see designers embrace new digital tools and software. A lot of designers are creating sketches on iPads and Wacom tablets where they can easily edit, share, or archive their drawings—that is a great way to communicate ideas.

Next, we look at their prototyping skills—are they comfortable developing ideas in the physical world? We like to see mock-ups created as part of their process. It doesn't get any more efficient than this to quickly understand things like ergonomics, range of motion, scale, weight, and the effects of gravity. It's impossible to arrive at a great design by simply relying on sketches or 3D CAD models. Physical models tend not to lie.

Everyone in our studio has to have a level of proficiency in one of the primary 3D modeling packages. We don't do a product design and then throw it over a wall to engineering. Since there is a lot of back-and-forth between design and engineering teams, we need to see that a designer has basic 3D skills so they can fluently articulate their design with a degree of manufacturing feasibility. The designers we interview need to have these skills, and the ability to convince the team that they won't require a ton of hand-holding.

Finally, we look if the project presented was a success. Did they solve a problem that needed to be solved? Was it an incremental improvement or a paradigm-shifting leap? Many designers can have beautiful portfolios, but did their skills and efforts lead to something memorable, something that the designers in the studio will talk about weeks after the interview?

What do you expect to learn from a designer during an interview?

I'm always eager to learn three basic things: What is their passion and commitment for design? Where do they place the value of problem solving in relation to visual design (aesthetics)? And, of course, what are their personal interests?

If they're truly passionate about design and its role in improving things, they will usually have a strong work ethic. Some designers believe they can achieve something great with a minimal investment of time. I disagree. I'm partial to the 10,000 hours concept, and I especially think it's true for industrial design. I spent a lot of hours in design school, in internships, and my first few jobs listening to people with more experience, trying out new things, practicing ideas I gathered along the way. I'm still learning new things today. If I can get a sense of a designer's commitment to their craft during an interview, it's helpful to understand how they will fit in the studio and contribute to the team. It will also highlight their level of care and willingness to put in the time, to get it right. We don't want to be slave drivers but we want to work with people who are passionate and have a strong work ethic to arrive at great design. A degree of curiosity and an appetite to continuously learn is critical to becoming a top-level designer.

I also want to know what importance they place on true problem-solving. Not just making something incrementally better, but their passion for digging into root issues to find breakthrough solutions. This is the only way to really set our products, and our brand, apart. Beauty is important, but we wouldn't place this above addressing the critical issues. Are the pieces in their portfolio really improving things, or are they merely exercises to demonstrate they can design beautiful objects? The aesthetics of a product or interface design should come naturally as an extension of the solution to a problem. When you get the front-end right, it leads to the right visual design that is intuitive and communicates purpose.

What personal interests do they have? People in general get excited talking about the things they care about. It's no different with designers. If they're into topics that align with the types of projects we have in the studio, great. If they're into active sports and we're designing products for the outdoors, for example, it may lead to a dialogue that helps us understand them on a different level—one that a portfolio may not reveal. These aligned interests—the connection on an interpersonal level—can lead to extremely successful collaborations.

You touched upon this a little bit, but I'm curious to hear what characteristics or qualities are necessary to be a successful designer?

In the studio, we talk a lot about empathy. Some designers think about what they'd like to own, what's a reflection of their personality or their personal design aesthetic. If you're a rock star designer and people align with what matters to you, it works and that's great. But a lot of design roles are not that. They're focused on the challenges and problems normal people face every day.

The empathy piece is really key because you need to be able to get inside the head of the person you're designing for. I'm not a doctor or a nurse, but I might have to understand what will help them in their tasks or daily routine. It's a skill that's hard to learn but you can definitely develop it over time. You must truly listen to people, and pick up on what matters to them.

Another important characteristic we look for is a genuine desire to work with others and share ideas. Collaboration is really important for us. If you read about some of the more successful corporate and consultant design teams, they talk a lot about teamwork and idea exchange. The solutions always get better with more brains on it. You'll get to a more positive conclusion by linking more ideas and personal experiences. It also makes for a much more gratifying studio environment. The studio becomes "sticky" and evolves everyone to a level of mutual trust, which, in itself, propels the team to come up with even better ideas and designs.

Those are the two most important things we look for in our face-to-face interviews after we like their work. We also like to ask questions about what motivated their design decisions. How were they briefed? Did they spend time with end-users? Who did they work with to arrive here? We listen to their responses, and you can usually hear it in their voice or see it in their face how well they took these people into consideration. Are they striving to make people's lives better, richer, and more enjoyable? That sounds pretty obvious, but I'm often surprised to hear people say,

"Oh, I just liked the way that looked." That's not going to fly with us.

We don't have huge egos in the studio. The collective team wants to get to the best solutions and experiences possible—it's not about an individual's portfolio piece. If you do good, thoughtful work, you're going to end up with a strong portfolio.

How did you break into this industry?

Like many people in industrial design, I really didn't know much about this industry until I stumbled upon it in college. I noticed a product design display while attending classes in illustration. It was a memorable day, everything became so clear. I transferred into the design department right away and began taking classes despite a setback to my graduation date. One day a senior student who worked for a local design consultancy approached me. He suggested that I apply for their summer internship position, so I went in for an interview and they offered me a position that same day.

It was a huge break for me and hard to imagine that I could earn money for doing something I enjoyed, and a chance to learn new skills that I could apply back at school. That summer internship turned into a part-time job that helped me with tuition and gave me tons of experience over the next two years.

So I highly recommend one or two internships to students before graduation. Even if it means working for a lower wage, it will pay off later when interviewing for your first full-time design job. It can give you a big edge. Design employers have a business to run, and they need to be certain that the people they bring in the door can plug-in and do the work. You have to be bankable.

If you were just starting out now, what advice would you give yourself?

Make sure you pay attention to future trends in culture and society. Know what's going on in business, technology, and design-related fields. Have a genuine interest in the news.

If you're going in for an interview, do your homework on the company and the people interviewing you. Who are they? What do they do? Understand the history of that company and what might help them be successful in the future. Read up on the products they designed. How did those products fare in Amazon customer reviews? It will make you sharper in the conversation.

Where do you see the future of industrial design going as it evolves further in the 21st century?

Industrial design is transitioning beyond individual products and single point solutions to multi-connected branded experiences. The designer of the future will need to be comfortable with developing products that connect with other products, ecosystems, and brands.

Products coming to market today have a higher level of intelligence than they did even five years ago. They have firmware that can be updated wirelessly or by a wired connection (e.g., USB port). This allows for products to stay relevant as users' needs evolve. It also means that product companies can learn about people's behaviors and preferences to help guide the development of their next-generation product. This new world of updatable products, information exchange, and customer feedback loops will require an even higher level of software and hardware integration. The next generation of products will be able to sense your emotions or intent, determine what action is appropriate, and take care of things without you even knowing.

User experience (UX) and user interface (UI) design will continue to be an increasing requirement as these products become even more sophisticated. Since display interfaces will be the primary connections between people and everything else, these designers will have an important role to play as the translators between the physical world (people/object) and the hyper-connected digital world (cloud). Additionally, all designers will require a willingness to collaborate with many other disciplines in cross-functional teams. If a design student were to approach me today and ask what should be their primary area of focus in design school, I would say it's UX. It transcends product, software, services, and environments, and this type of design thinking will be in even greater demand.

As this relationship between people and products evolves, so will the need for unique and branded experiences. Designers need to understand their opportunity to design the total experience, and to help companies become respected brands—brands that people will follow, fall in love with, and even defend when they make mistakes.

It sounds like industrial design is broadening as a field.

Yes, it continues to broaden as companies recognize that design thinking can also be applied to environments and services. It's taking the methodical approach of understanding usage scenarios around a product and expanding that thinking to scenarios that encompass an entire visit to a hospital or a sporting venue. It's introducing efficiency and positive emotional benefits that can go way beyond a single product. It's connecting momentary experiences into larger multifaceted ones.

So you need to pay attention to how different business and development teams function and how they connect to each other. This will put you in a better position to collaborate and help the combined teams arrive at better decisions. It's becoming a lot more generalist.

Anything you'd like to add that we haven't talked about? Any final words of wisdom?

I think the most important thing I can share is to make sure that your portfolio work, the internships you apply for, or the future employers that you seek tie back to your personal interests. If you can land a job where you're really excited to go to work every day, and get to work on stuff that interests you, your life will be richer and more fulfilling. Your personal output will be greater and more gratifying. This will benefit you and your future employer. There's this interesting concept I discovered along the way that says, "The work you do begets the work you get." So really be true to yourself and pursue what you're interested in, and filter career choices with that in mind. Be authentic to yourself. BI

To see the work of Ernesto Quinteros and Belkin, please visit http:// breaking.in

MARY REID
VICE PRESIDENT OF
INDUSTRIAL DESIGN
KOHLER
SHEBOYGAN, WISCONSIN

What kinds of portfolios get your attention these days? What brings in an industrial designer for an interview?

Initially, we require a fairly comprehensive portfolio to be shared before we bring them in for an interview. We even do a phone interview prior and, if we get beyond that, we will bring them in. We maybe have a more in-depth process than others and we do a couple of rounds of tests. The first one is called "The Caliper" and it gives us insight into more of the natural tendencies of the individual, relative to how they work, interact with people, how they think and process. It's just another data point we use to understand a little bit more about the potential and the personality of the person we're talking to. We are a big company and we do a lot of work in teams and collaboration so getting people that will work well together is important.

What we're really looking for in the individuals is that they have passion for their career choice. It's in their blood that they're doing what they're doing. There are a lot of abilities, natural abilities, in terms of skill. Then it goes into how they present themselves and their flexibility and things like that that are beyond their talent. Do they have the ability to sell their ideas and their thinking, to talk about their process and how they got to where they did?

Has there been a portfolio that you've seen recently that resonated with you, and what about it stood out?

It's becoming challenging. I think there might be something going on within schools right now that makes it harder to find people who are exposed to what's going on in the business and have the bigger

picture in their thinking. I prefer to see people who have that ability to see beyond a product or idea and put it in the context of where it's going, how it's going to market—an understanding of business.

I really require that someone can sketch really well because it is a communication tool and, while CAD is wonderful, it's a step in the process. CAD is a tool for thinking through ideas—a tool that makes you think about how to build something. Once you're in that frame of mind it moves you beyond "what is the idea?"

If you had an opportunity to guide a student on how to create an industrial design portfolio, what would you tell them?

Show the work that you alone did. It's good to get a feeling for what it's like to work in a team and to be able to talk to that, but when it comes to a potential employer wanting to know what kind of talent they are hiring, you need to show your talent. Great sketching is still a key sign of potential talent. It shows thinking, communication of ideas, ability to demonstrate creativity, and diversity of ideas. Have a project—more is better—that is different than anyone else's. Schools are doing too many class projects where everyone shows the same thing. It's always a pleasure to see someone who has tried something that's not been done. Take risks, invent opportunities, create solutions that change perceptions, or raise awareness and improve quality of living. Having mechanical solutions among your work is a great attribute; just know you will be challenged about your understanding of them. You are a problem solver, so show your logic and be able to explain it. Showing an authentic passion and creativity in all you do says you have an innate desire for the profession. This is important.

When you bring in a designer for an interview, how do you know they'll work well with your team?

We do bring a lot of our team into that interviewing process and then we discuss it to see how everybody feels and where they might fit in. Lots of times we see the people doing the interviewing liking the people who are like them, and that can be both good and bad. But I think designers have a little bit more flexibility than the engineers or marketers. We spend a lot of time with candidates, going out to lunch and/or dinner. We chat, not only about the job, but what their interests are. Our designers tend to enjoy socializing together outside of work.

From your experience, what characteristics or qualities are necessary to be a successful designer?

Depends on what you mean by successful, I guess. If it's a motivation to grow in terms of responsibility and into management-type roles, it's very important to have a vision, to understand the business, what the products are, and the industry. You can see where the business might go, where the industry might go, what projects might evolve into, the next place we should be looking. We put a lot of focus on developing people so they do have a place to go within the organization. We have a lot of infrastructure to train and develop individuals.

"GREAT SKETCHING IS STILL A KEY SIGN OF POTENTIAL TALENT. IT SHOWS THINKING, COMMUNICATION OF IDEAS, ABILITY TO DEMONSTRATE CREATIVITY, AND DIVERSITY OF IDEAS."

Then from the other side, for a designer who is more motivated to be a designer and succeed as an individual contributor, we try to find ways for them to succeed doing what they love to do. You have to be extremely talented and work well with the team, including people from other disciplines. Those who move up at a faster pace than others are great with communication and interaction and are able to persuade and sell their ideas. They understand the ins and outs of the business. They navigate in a productive way.

How did you break into this business?

I was actually one of the two people who were hired to build an internal design organization and that was 29 years ago almost. I started as an entry-level designer and we were able to build from within. It was perseverance and having a passion about what I do. I was determined to show that we had more to offer than just styling.

As I've been doing these interviews, I've only found a handful of women that are in leadership positions in industrial design. Do you have any words of advice for budding female designers out there right now?

That's a great question because I've always been very turned off by women who make a big deal about being the only ones in a field where there aren't very many. It's almost like they deserve something. It's all about having talent, knowing what you want, and being strong enough to keep driving for it. I don't think that standing out as being a woman is a benefit, in terms of growing your career. It's about having the talent and demonstrating it. People will see, and if there are people who don't see it then maybe that's not where one needs to be. I've never wanted to belong to any women's organizations; I just get turned off by that. That's not a way to demonstrate ability and character. You just have to prove what you have and what you can do.

You've been in this field for almost 30 years now. Looking back, if you were starting off right now, what advice would you give yourself?

That's a tough one. I've had my challenges along the way. I've been frustrated to the point of being unhappy because I couldn't convince others to reach the level of change that I felt we could. In hindsight, it's not healthy. One probably shouldn't take themselves so seriously as sometimes we designers do. You've got to have a life, and enjoy that life. Work is important in order to enjoy it, but don't let it consume you.

Where do you think the future of industrial design is going as it evolves further in the 21st century?

I've been concerned along the way because, for a while, everyone from Calvin Klein to Martha Stewart was doing design and weakening our credibility in a way. I think it will be a struggle holding on to the identity of industrial design as a profession because it's getting easier to create stuff. I'm not a fan of stuff. It's interesting because I'd imagine there are quite a few of us in the design profession who believe in sustainability and the damage that people are doing to the environment. It's kind of a funny pickle to be in because I think there are a lot of us who don't believe that the world needs more stuff.

On the other hand, we enjoy beautiful things that make people's lives better. I think it could become a challenging time because there's a lot of conflict between business, commerce, and progress. And design is in a funny place within that whole scheme. We can help make things better, but it's a dichotomy that we're in the business of making things. That's what we decided to do, and it goes against quality of life in a lot of ways.

How would you advise students to consider these aspects you've just mentioned as they're creating solutions?

It's hard for a student to present cases where they can prove that it's a money-making opportunity as much as it's an environmental benefit. I think they can demonstrate or show interest in social needs and they can learn about what materials do and what the benefits are. They can demonstrate they have interest in wanting to travel down those roads and can stick to their guns and search out the companies that have sincere motivations to drive in that direction. That's a long, slow road to make real impact from a business point of view.

Is there anything you'd like to add that we haven't talked about? Any final words of wisdom?

There's a lack of creativity in the types of projects kids are pursuing for their portfolios. There is a lot going on in schools where they are trying to drive toward teamwork, and demonstrating, for some reason, the ability for people to work within teams. While it's important, right now, demonstrating creativity and real progressive thinking, applying

new ideas to new places, breaking out of prescriptive portfolios where everyone has to have a power tool and a shoe, is more valuable. It used to be you could invent your own project and be knee-deep in it and make your own discoveries and break into new territories. You don't see that in portfolios right now. They're very prescriptive. Maybe it has to do with corporate sponsorships going on in the schools. I don't know but there's a lot of redundancy in portfolios. Then it's hard to pull someone out of that and see the real talent. I'd rather see people who are demonstrating their individual contributions; I don't want to hear what they did with four other people. I want to hear what they did themselves. They need to be able to demonstrate some progressive thinking within that. ⬚

To see the work of Mary Reid and Kohler, please visit http://breaking.in

BRAD RICHARDS EXTERIOR DESIGN MANAGER FORD MOTOR COMPANY DEARBORN, MICHIGAN

What kinds of portfolios get your attention these days? What brings in an industrial designer for an interview?

First of all, the quality of the work has got to be there, especially for the line of work that I'm in. There's a certain amount of fundamentals that need to be represented, so if that's all there, in terms of a portfolio that catches the eye, it's usually something that has been built on content not flash. Having said that, there have been some unique ways people have submitted their work that creates a little buzz within the studio. So, along with the quality of work, we also may react to a unique way someone may present their work as well. But there have been a few portfolios that I've reviewed in the past that have relied solely on the portfolio itself instead of the content of the work within it. That never flies.

What we are really looking for is a certain amount of design maturity, original ideas, realistic proportions, a designer who can create a clear, concise explanation of surfaces and forms in a variety of mediums. Once you have the imagery nailed down, you must also make sure that that the writing in the portfolio works as well. If the subject has not used spell check or thoughts are not communicated clearly, or do not make sense, that tells me something about the candidate as well.

You mentioned a few portfolios that created a buzz in the studio. Can you tell me about them?

A lot of times we see work that's pretty much finalized renderings and models, with little empathic sketching. We reviewed a portfolio recently that was kind of the opposite. It was almost a refined sketchpad. They took the best pages of their sketchpad and created about a dozen pages of just empathic sketching. It was enlightening because it's such a fundamental thing. It should not have been this exciting for us, but we haven't seen anything like that in a while, so it really connected.

Empathic sketching not only communicates your design skills but also your thought process. It allows us to see inside your head a little. I've also seen portfolios sent in hand-carved wood cases—that's interesting too. But if the quality of the work itself isn't there it becomes forgettable—other than the fact that the portfolio itself was displayed in a unique fashion.

Once you bring in a designer for an interview, what do you expect to learn from them during that one-on-one meeting?

I want to get a feel for the candidate's personality. Once we have established that the designer meets our creative benchmarks, then we need to make sure we have the right chemistry—the right person. I'm always looking for the right fit, and this is very obvious stuff, but we try to find designers from all walks of life who will fit into our family, if you will. A lot of that is about personality. Within Ford, we put specific teams together for projects and I think that's something that's really important. I don't know if other design managers think about it as

much as I do, but I've always had really solid teams. People get along really well and we spend a lot of time outside of the studio together and I don't mean within some team-building exercise. Most of us hang out with each other after work hours, which I think speaks volumes.

What characteristics or qualities are necessary to be a successful designer these days?

I always look for the maverick streak in a designer—creative fearlessness. Also, a certain quality within your DNA that is never happy with the way something has already been done—this is a very valuable characteristic to have. You certainly need to have strong problem-solving skills and the ability to approach and solve problems from acute angles that others overlook. There's a certain amount of hard work that's involved as well. We like people who obviously are very passionate about what they do and are willing to put in the time and effort to realize their goals. Obviously, a sense of fresh aesthetics has got to be there. They have to be able to have something fresh to say, something new to say.

I like to find people who don't follow the trends, people who have created their own sense of aesthetic. We see a lot of redundancy in the way shapes and forms are communicated, especially in transportation design because a lot of it is unfortunately just flash. You can find a lot of people who can execute a beautiful rendering of a car, but you can't find a lot of people who can really create something new, or exciting, or something original—something that will change someone's life for the better.

How did you break into the business?

I've always loved vehicles—the cliché story. I was mesmerized by anything with wheels from day one. I also took everything apart I could get my hands on as a child. My parents realized I loved creating things so they pushed me into a lot of fine arts in high school. Like most kids back then I didn't even realize how cars were designed, didn't realize that they were designed by "designers." I thought the engineers did that but I certainly did not feel like an engineer. Thanks to a high school summer scholarship at CCS for painting, I discovered all the studios with car sketches pinned to the walls and

I finally put the whole thing together in my head and absolutely fell in love with it. And not just car design, but also product design; it really captured my curiosity. There are all these products that I've been using my whole entire life, that are actually designed by somebody. It was an epiphany to me. "Wow, someone had to do all this stuff—why can't it be me?" So I made a transition from fine art to product design before I left high school. Once I graduated, I enrolled at CCS and studied product design, furniture design, and even fine arts, so I was kind of doing it all. I have to mention that I had some really great teachers who pushed me along and showed me how to nurture what I was born with. I can't say enough about them. They were heroes to me then and now.

"WHAT WE ARE REALLY LOOKING FOR IS A CERTAIN AMOUNT OF DESIGN MATURITY, ORIGINAL IDEAS, REALISTIC PROPORTIONS, A DESIGNER WHO CAN CREATE A CLEAR, CONCISE EXPLANATION OF SURFACES AND FORMS IN A VARIETY OF MEDIUMS."

Once at CCS I went through a really tough time trying to decide whether to focus on transportation or product, and went into product because it felt like it had a higher ceiling. I was having a hard time choosing between designing a product someone may use in a hospital to save someone's life versus shaping sheet metal for an automotive manufacturer. I was pretty idealistic. So I went with product design, but the whole time I still had a passion for transportation. After graduating, I did a few years of furniture and product design at a blossoming company that was doing automotive design as well. In order to learn more about automotive design, I

went back to CCS at night just to sharpen up my skills. Eventually my main instructor, who was a very talented design manager at Ford, asked me to teach his class. After I proved I could do that for a semester or two, he asked me if I'd be interested in working in the studios at Ford. Again, thanks to a great teacher I got my break into the business. Coming from product back into automotive at that time was not that easy.

But in reality I discovered my product design background gave me a real edge as my portfolio was interesting to a jury of people at Ford who mainly only reviewed images of cars. I think at that time this was unique but now is much more accepted—in some cases even expected.

If you were just staring out now, what advice would you give yourself?

Follow your heart no matter what. Work as hard as you can. If it feels like work to you, then ask yourself if this is really what you want to do because if you really love it, the hard work will exhilarate you. It's not the person who is the most talented that always wins; it's the person who puts in the most time and effort, the person who makes the most of their mistakes and gets back up to try it again. Hard work always pays off. If you take a little bit of talent and a lot of hard work, you can do just about anything. Invert that model and it doesn't always work.

Where do you see the future of industrial design going?

The most exciting aspect of the future for me right now is the potential of the tools. The power that the designers will have at their fingertips and what they can accomplish on one computer will be staggering. From exploring the Internet for inspiration and ideas, to creating the first initial sketch, to doing full-blown two-dimensional images that completely realize the design then building what you've designed in 3D, growing physical parts at your desk, figuring out how to put it together and ultimately handing it off to somebody who can start creating the tools to produce it. Then there will be the whole marketing side of the idea that can be created, realized, then optimized and implemented on a global scale all on a designer's smartphone. It's amazing how far we've come in that respect. The power that the average designer has at this moment is amazing. Just imagine what's to come.

Anything you'd like to add that we haven't talked about? Any final words of wisdom?

Always stick to your guns, even if you're hopelessly outnumbered. If your gut is telling you you're right, you usually are. [BI]

To see Brad Richards's work, please visit http://breaking.in

DEMETRIUS ROMANOS
DIRECTOR OF DESIGN
TARGUS
LOS ANGELES

Interviewed while Mr. Romanos was Executive Creative Director at Kaleidoscope in Cincinnati, Ohio.

What kinds of portfolios get your attention these days? What brings in an industrial designer for an interview?

It depends on the level we are looking for, but ultimately, you want people who are well rounded and people who stand out. We want someone who has a good sense of aesthetic, good overall technical skills, especially at the base level of sketching. If we are talking about entry-level designers, that's the bulk of the stuff they'll be doing: sketching and initial concept development, participating in as many projects as possible just to build up their skill sets. They also might be skilled at things that are more in the technology kind of area. Anything that would make somebody

stand apart and perhaps bring something new to the team, to not only be able to demonstrate a high sense of aesthetic but how they arrived at that. Some sort of grounding and understanding of consumer brand and overall usage experience. I'm not saying that they fully have to be professionals at this point, but the more that the people can back up a good looking idea, rendering, or photograph with some substance, I think that would make somebody stand out the most.

Was there a product design portfolio that you saw recently that really caught your eye, and can you talk a bit about it?

Somebody who is presenting a portfolio would show not only good content in projects, but navigation of how you see and experience their work [which] just shows another level of consideration. I've been getting some portfolios that are more along those lines. I think people recognize when they're sending portfolios or applying for positions that they are taking time out of someone's day. You're getting only so much time to engage with them, so you better be pretty quick at it. If I have to click a link and that's going to take me to somebody's Coroflot page, and then I have to hit their profile or portfolios...if you bury your content too deep, you've sort of lost the portfolio reviewer or hiring manager. Nowadays, we are being inundated with a lot of portfolios, as there are a lot of people out of work. I think being as engaging as possible and being quick with your message is really critical. Any portfolio that does that is really what stands out. Good content, delivered quickly.

Once a product designer is in for an interview, what do you expect to learn from them during that meeting?

I want to learn how they're wired, what really gets them up in the morning, and if they would be a cultural fit. If we take the time to actually bring somebody in for an interview, that means that we've already deduced that their skill set is good: they can sketch well, have good sense of aesthetic, and know how to present that work. That would be a given. After that is how well they would fit into our company. Why do they want to work here and what else are they bringing to the table? You get a sense for somebody's personality and see what that's adding to your team. Chemistry is really important.

With that said, what characteristics or qualities do you think are necessary to be a successful designer?

I'd say diversity in skill set and willingness to learn and grow. As ID has evolved and you see more interaction and more graphic design come into the mix, somebody that's willing to learn those or can adapt to those fields is really important. We always say that industrial designers are educated to be problem solvers and I think we have focused so much on the aesthetic form that sometimes we lose sight of the problem-solving capabilities. With projects getting more complex and there being a lot more demands from the client side to validate and prove out that there's going to be some sort of return on the investment—and quantification of the quality and appropriateness of design—systems thinking, paired on top of good aesthetics, is really important to have and to be able to somehow demonstrate.

How did you break into this business?

It seems that most industrial designers, at least from when I was in school, went to school to do either furniture or car design. My parents were professors in a design school in urban planning at the University of Cincinnati. At the end of the year there's a senior show where the students from architecture, design: graphic, industrial, and interior, and fashion all start showing their work. I started going to that as a teenager and always sort of gravitated towards industrial design, but was also interested in fashion design and graphic design. As I got closer to graduating high school I knew I was going to go into something design focused. I couldn't really decide between the three of those, but I thought industrial design was going to give me the most opportunity to touch on all three of the things I'm interested in. My plan going through industrial design school was to try to be as diverse as possible and think about things beyond just a beautiful artifact. I wanted to think about how it might come to life and how many different ways somebody could experience your brand or your product. To make it more comprehensive, to create

this insatiable desire to have it, or be a part of what it is you're selling. An entire experience.

"NOWADAYS, WE ARE BEING INUNDATED WITH A LOT OF PORTFOLIOS, AS THERE ARE A LOT OF PEOPLE OUT OF WORK. I THINK BEING AS ENGAGING AS POSSIBLE AND BEING QUICK WITH YOUR MESSAGE IS REALLY CRITICAL."

People really need to get out of the mindset of thinking of a design project as just "Here, make this thing for me." It's actually really difficult for clients to understand when they give you a task to "design a new bottle" that the bottle just as a shape is really not anything without the brand or the graphic it's communicating. One needs to understand—how much is it used and what part of the store is it in? How do people find out about it? What other products exist that need to be used in conjunction with it? Unless you think about the whole ecosystem, both on the brand side and the usability side, then you're not really solving a problem. You're looking at the incremental changes and I think that's a dangerous thing.

Where do you see the future of industrial design going as it evolves further in the 21st century?

I see it continuing to merge and evolve with other things, interaction design being the obvious one. I think design has changed over the last few years. The business has embraced design and they're also looking for ways to quantify it. Unfortunately, it's not like engineering where you got the laws of physics and mathematics on your side to know when an answer is right or when it's wrong. With design it's still a little bit subjective, but I think that's forcing designers, whether for good or bad, to get really process-oriented. I think there's going to be more of that. There may be a way to prove out that industrial design can still be this feeling-based discipline that interweaves with more structured and process-based disciplines to make them that much better. Again, not just looking at artifacts; it's already been evolving from that, but as it continues to move into interactivity and what that does to physical spaces and complete retail experience, education systems, transport. Those items that were designed used to be a lot more in the territory of industrial designers; you're just seeing more collaboration now that's making products and experiences that much better.

If you were starting out now, what advice would you give yourself?

I would definitely learn how to process information so you get interaction design. That is sort of where everything is moving and merging. It used to be just web design, and it's obviously so much more than that right now. I think really understanding how interfaces work on products and making those cohesive stories is key. I suppose I would say focus on design but understand interaction, both in a static sense and in a digital sense.

Anything you'd like to add that we haven't talked about? Any final words of wisdom?

The biggest part of how I got both my career started and how it seems to continue perpetuating was to really leverage all the relationships and network I built slowly over time. I get that at some universities it's easier to do because you have co-ops and internships, so you get into the professional sphere a little bit earlier than perhaps other students, but anything you can do to engage with professionals early on will really pay off down the road. It's a small community that's pretty close-knit. We all care about one another. There's healthy competition amongst us, but, at the end of the day, we all want each other to succeed. As a professional, I really gravitate towards passionate energy that a student brings, especially at a time like this when the market is down and there are not as many job opportunities. I always try and help the students and find them ways to get professional experience and show them there are a

lot more options than just a typical job at a consulting firm or at a corporation. Meet people and know that professionals invest in designers and design students and are willing to help. ☐BI

To see Demetrius Romanos's work, please visit http://breaking.in

KLAUS ROSBURG
PRESIDENT
SONIC DESIGN
NEW YORK CITY

How did you get into industrial design? What motivated you to open up your own design studio?

So, as you can tell by my accent, I come from Germany where I was educated and trained in industrial design. After graduating I worked for five years at a pretty renowned design firm. I did quite well over there and when my boss started to think about his retirement, he offered me to take over the company. While that seemed like a great opportunity, I was rather concerned that my first job was going to be my last one. I took six months of unpaid vacation to think this through, went to New York and as you can tell, I decided to stay. After another five years as an employed designer in the United States, I felt I was ready to start my own company and to fulfill my vision.

For a couple of years I worked out of a large loft I rented in an old knitting mill in Williamsburg, Brooklyn—an industrial and, at that time, neglected neighborhood favored by many artists. I did a lot of contracting for larger agencies, until I finally finished a couple of projects under my own name that got a lot of press. Today, I feel quite lucky to have worked with large companies like Microsoft, Method, Epson, Target, and some others. We're a small studio in Brooklyn with some large clients.

What kinds of portfolios get your attention these days? What brings in an industrial designer for an interview?

The most important thing for me is a good attitude. If you work with somebody, especially on a small team, and the chemistry is not quite there, you feel it right away. It also has to be somebody who is diverse and flexible because we do so many different things. If someone just wants to do consumer electronic products, that's just not happening in a small agency. One day the team might work on a packaging program, like a simple cardboard box, the next day on a lighting project or a toothbrush, so there's a lot of shifting around. If designers are interested in just one specific category, they can get unhappy quite fast. A few times I preferred a designer who might have not had the best portfolio, but had the best attitude and was motivated and willing to learn.

If a portfolio gets sent to my office, it will most certainly catch my eye, because over the last year I have not seen many arrive by mail. It will be on my desk and as a tangible item it will be a reminder to review the work and to respond to the application.

Today, pretty much all applications come by email and quite a few every week. While I try to respond to most of them, I am sometimes just too overwhelmed or reluctant to answer, because they were sent as thoughtless bulk mails. Typically these emails start with "Hi," or "Dear Hiring Manager," have some generic content, and attached is a résumé or samples of work in PDF format. Most likely it has been sent to 50 design firms simultaneously. If someone bothers to figure out my name, however, and writes "Mr. Rosburg, I really love the work you do, it's diverse and creative, I like that pill bottle you did...", it means that someone did the homework and deserves my attention. I will write a response, say thank you for the interest in SONIC Design, whether it works out or not. If you really want the job, you need to learn about the company and communicate it in the application. It will make a difference.

What about the content itself, of the portfolios? What stands out? Have you seen a portfolio recently that resonated with you, and what about it stood out?

I just looked at one today, which was exceptional. It was not only very professional, but also diverse. The candidate had not only worked in various countries and companies, but also successfully in different disciplines. She had worked in ceramics, tableware, and high-tech products in Shanghai, Germany, and New York. The portfolio certainly stood out, but not everyone will have such background, nor need one to land a design job.

The initial samples of work sent by email should stand out, but keep in mind, it is just the teaser. It only has to get my attention and open the door for a potential interview. It is important not to use all of your bullets at once and to keep some exciting things for the interview to talk about. The teaser should be a good selection of your best work illustrating your skills and creative style. It's also very important that the selection of work you send really aligns with the company. I do a little bit of contemporary furniture design, but sometimes people send me résumés with crafted woodwork and we really don't do much of that. Whatever you send out has to fit and complement the design studio where you intend to work.

"IT IS IMPORTANT NOT TO USE ALL OF YOUR BULLETS AT ONCE AND TO KEEP SOME EXCITING THINGS FOR THE INTERVIEW TO TALK ABOUT."

A couple of weeks ago I received a portfolio in a PDF format that I quite liked. The graduate student was extremely creative and diverse, but what caught my attention were his amazing sketches and hand renderings. In a time of computer-generated renderings you don't find too many who master this craft and many schools neglect to teach it. In addition, the portfolio was just right in size, in terms of content. Well edited, it illustrated that the candidate had exposure and experience in all aspects of the design process.

What are some reasons you have rejected a candidate?

I had people coming into the interview with chewing gum in their mouth or a cup of coffee in their hand. You always wonder: "Okay, if they're already so unprofessional in the interview, how professional will they be at work?" You would think it's a basic thing, but it happened quite a few times. Some students are so convinced and full of themselves that they think they own the world, but the climate has changed. You have to be professional from the get-go. I also had students come in and they didn't even bring their work. When I asked them about it, they told me to check out their website. This is a missed opportunity because I like to hear firsthand about the work and also see a designer's presentation skills.

If candidates show me work, which they have done at school or with another company and it's not aligned with our overall design philosophy or it is just simply bad, it will also result in a rejection. SONIC Design is known for a specific style and design philosophy that is influenced to a certain degree by my German heritage. I don't like to over-style or complicate products. Simple is good and I like to keep it that way.

Naturally, of course, I'd reject someone because they don't have the right skill set. If I interview candidates for a potential program and see that they have absolutely no experience in a specific category or do not know the software packages we are utilizing at all, that means that I would have to invest and train them from scratch.

Overall, I feel that most students who come to an interview are quite motivated to get started, but it's a very competitive field right now. That's why a book like yours is successful and helpful. Everyone is trying to grab any little straw and have the information at hand to walk out of the interview with a job offer. Many more graduates are looking for jobs than there are openings. You will have to be pretty much flawless and stand out.

What characteristics or qualities are necessary to be a successful industrial designer?

The first quality it takes to produce creative and innovative products is the skill to visualize an idea in your head. Not everyone can do it. To design a phone and to put it onto paper or a computer, you need to imagine a shape or mechanism first.

I have taught at an American design school for a short while and was surprised to see many students, who were very smart, but lacked that capability. Because education is free in Germany, applicants have to go through a tough selection process to study industrial design. American schools however, do not hesitate to train anyone, whether they have the talent or not, as long as tuition is being paid. I have reviewed portfolios of students, who went through a full program, and thought that they never should've studied industrial design in the first place. They completely wasted their time and money.

Then of course, there are technical skills. Today it's quite critical to know the CAD software packages very well, so that a designer is not limited by a design tool.

If you were just starting out now, what advice would you give yourself?

The first and most important thing for me was that I always believed in what I was doing, I loved it. I've been doing design now for almost 25 years, and I still enjoy it every day. While we all have to live, money was never a key factor in my career. I was always more in it for the experience, and for the fun at work. I feel I made, for the most part, the right decisions and if I had to start out today, I would approach things quite similar.

Obviously technology has evolved quite a bit. When I graduated, I had not touched a computer. Back then we sketched, made blueprints, and carved foam models by hand in our shop. That's all different. It is not only crucial these days to stay fully tuned with trends, but also with a quickly evolving technology, like CAD, rapid prototyping and manufacturing processes. You need to understand what kinds of tools are available and how to utilize them.

Where do you see the future of industrial design going as it evolves further in the 21st century?

I don't think design is evolving for the better. When I started in Germany, industrial design was a well-respected profession and often a product was known for its designer. Today, the lifecycles of consumer products, such as a cell phone, have become so short that no one really cares who designed them. With an ocean of products, design has become almost a commodity, something you throw away and quickly forget. I wish it would be like back in the day, when products would stay in the market for 10 years plus before they would be replaced. But we live in a consumer culture; trends are short lived and technology is evolving fast. If something only lasts for six months or a year, why even bother spending money developing it? It doesn't make much sense.

There are still many companies who truly invest in design and do great work, but I think 90% of the design industry is doing it quick and dirty with little thought and no positive impact on our world. Today, a telephone service provider like Verizon, AT&T, or Sprint can go to a manufacturing company with an in-house design staff and pick from a large selection of phones. They will present 20, more or less, fashionable design variations in a suitcase and say: "These are our designs, pick one." It will get the company's logo, a catchy name, and will be on our landfill two years later. How can that be satisfying?

Do you think designers have power to change that?

Not really. I think our profession today is pretty much driven by the economy. I don't think designers have much of a choice and for the most part they even welcome the rapid development of new products. It's our business. When I started as a designer, we would work a very long time on designing just one product, but this one product would also stay in the market for a very long time. These days clients come to me, and say: "Klaus, we need this fast, in two weeks, two months, a sketch will do." Sure, no problem, but do you really think any designer can develop good products like this?

Maybe when we're running out of oil, and people really start to worry about the resources we have left, we will start to hang onto our products a little longer again, and we will be also a little more thoughtful designing them. Engineers would have to improve the functional aspects of a product and designers would have to create an aesthetic which can withstand trendy winds. If the technology is built to last 10 years, like a coffeemaker, then the aesthetics should last for 10 years, too.

As for now, many people will look down on you if you hang onto certain consumer products for too long. With the constant introduction of new designs and better technology many people are highly motivated to buy new products to be part of the in-crowd or to show off their social status. What is more gratifying for the early adopter than to put their latest gizmo onto the table and to wow their peers?

With that notion, what would be your advice to students that are graduating now?

I think students have to make the best out of their specific skills and be flexible. I'm a trained product designer, but I also do a lot of structural packaging. To be perfectly honest, in the beginning I wasn't super excited about it because packaging in general just feels wasteful. Now that I have worked in this field for many years and understand the specific issues and challenges, I feel that I can make a difference and create better packaging.

Overall I like to advise students to keep an open mind, stay positive, and be patient. It might take awhile to land the dream job, but if you have the creative spark, you will succeed. ⊞

To see the work of Klaus Rosburg and SONIC Design, please visit http://breaking.in

**RAVI SAWHNEY
FOUNDER & CEO
RKS DESIGN
THOUSAND OAKS,
CALIFORNIA**

What kinds of portfolios get your attention these days? What brings in an industrial designer for an interview?

The portfolio needs to be presented in kind of a magazine format, very well composed, a very quick read, with some deep dives into seeing how insights tickled your curiosity to know more about the person behind it. It's really a promotional piece, almost as if you're selling a service. The quality of the presentation we see are these beautifully balanced, well-constructed, well-designed books and the presentation alone says something about their ability to work within a professional design environment. It's really that quality of presentation combined with a depth that brings them in for an interview. So they need to have a quality of presentation to see the sense of freshness, a sense of understanding all of the dynamics of designing today. It's not just pretty pictures without substance. You have to have some substance to want to talk to this person and understand their process and how they got there.

Doing a portfolio today...it's got to be a semester project. Just to build a high-quality portfolio that's going to open the right doors—it's got to be a semester project.

So then what do we expect from a designer during the interview? What we expect to learn from the designer is the understanding of this person's ability to insight and strategize how they design. What they feed their heads with to create the design, the actual design exploration, the testing of the design, the ergonomics, touching all the bases. How it will be marketed, what the value is. You look to see any group projects and this leads into conversations. The conversations tell us about the work. How people answer, how they think, and how they communicate tells us about the caliber of the person and tells us about their ability to fit into an organization.

Luckily all the barriers I faced 30 years ago are gone. Now you can focus on the value the person brings to an organization. Another thing that's really important is that if you're going to be a designer, you need to know your subject matter before you design. If you go to an interview, you really should know everything about the design firm. You should be able to speak with depth and authenticity. One of the weaknesses we see is people coming in for an interview without knowing anything about our

firm. It's scary how superficial people can be; they're just checking boxes. Designers need to be much more analytical, much deeper in their thinking.

So if an industrial design student came up to you and asked, "What should my portfolio be like? What do I need to show you in order to work with you?", what would you tell them?

I would say it needs to have at least one complete project that goes from research to synthesis, to creation and exploration, developing it into a finished design and a pitch of what it is and why it's so brilliantly done. Design teams see many portfolios. A designer's challenge is to break through and break out as much as anyone.

What characteristics or qualities are necessary to be a successful designer?

It's the basics: integrity, the ability to collaborate, the gift of design sense. There's a certain hunger in a certain designer's eye that really attracts people. That's probably the silver bullet. The passion and hunger in each and every project and each and every challenge. They're not worried about their own egos, their own portfolios, they're just so deep into taking it to another level. Those people are the ones who stay in the business the longest time, because they have that passion—they love the process. They're not living for the portfolio piece. They're living because they love the process. Those are the things that really helped me.

Another characteristic is that they have to have a great sense of empathy. Empathy for the ultimate consumer, or user. That's a huge one for us.

You mentioned earlier how 30 years ago you faced obstacles in breaking into this field. I'd love to hear your story and how you got to where you are.

When I was in college I wanted to work in the design field, to see what it was really like. I started looking in the ads as to who was hiring designers. I contacted a firm who was looking to hire model-makers and I said that I was a student with good model-making skills, and if they'd interview me. They looked at my work and gave me a job. I worked there off and on for a while, and then I got a full-time job during the summer at a design firm in Beverly Hills doing model-making. They moved me into design. I worked there until I got recruited by a firm I was hoping to work at. My senior year of college, I worked at a local design firm called Hauser and I worked there until I graduated. Then I got a call from guys at another job telling me that Xerox was interviewing for a position. I went to an interview and got hired.

"THEY'RE NOT WORRIED ABOUT THEIR OWN EGOS, THEIR OWN PORTFOLIOS, THEY'RE JUST SO DEEP INTO TAKING IT TO ANOTHER LEVEL. THOSE PEOPLE ARE THE ONES WHO STAY IN THE BUSINESS THE LONGEST TIME, BECAUSE THEY HAVE THAT PASSION— THEY LOVE THE PROCESS."

When I went out and first was looking for work, I was very open. I said, "I'm willing to sweep the floors for free, I just want to be in a design environment." I had no barriers to getting work. I wanted experience; I didn't care about money or what I did. When I started taking on projects, when I went out on my own I had the same philosophy. I'd take crappy projects and every project I touched I made it twice as good as it was supposed to be. It was an ongoing work ethic. I just loved the design process and I loved designing. You see that as a culture and in our work.

If you were starting out now, what advice would you give yourself?

I would give myself the same advice. Pick a firm, a small firm, one where you won't get lost in the sauce and find out what you can do. Intern any way you can. You gotta do anything and everything you can to get in the door. Once you do get your foot in the door, then make it happen. Design is never-ending learning. We are not a design team where design is a job for us. Design defines who we are, not what we do.

Where do you see the future of industrial design going as it evolves further in the 21st century?

It's gone upstream already. When I graduated in the late '70s, design was primarily a professional practice. Today it's more about insights, thought leadership, helping businesses finding the right things to do. Taking it from "What should I do?" all the way to "Here's the it"—the product, the service, the business model. It's really expanded to a much, much larger field today than it was then. It's tied into research and strategy, the C-Level is paying attention. It's going to a higher level of credibility and a higher level of contribution. It's a great place to be.

The Internet and services haven't really started to utilize design on a high, high, high level. There's a huge platform of unique values and interactions offered on the Internet that's going to explode the demand for design. Consumers today would much rather pay for fewer but better products. They buy fewer products but better products. This forces design, and rightfully so, to perfect the designed product to a higher level. It increases the demand for design and reduces the amount of waste. It teaches consumers that they need to get continual value and not use disposable products.

Anything you'd like to add that we haven't talked about? Any final words of wisdom?

I would just say to the students to pick their options. They can start their business today, they can go work for a corporation, they can work for a consulting firm, they can work for a manufacturing firm, they can go into a family business, they can do so many things. Graduating as a designer today really gives you an opportunity to go a different way. My path worked for me, but who knows, if I graduated today maybe I would put objects up on Kickstarter. Or maybe I would be doing something for charities.

Design is being applied everywhere. Just because you're talented doesn't mean you have to take the traditional path. You can design your own path. [BI]

To see the work of Ravi Sawhney and RKS Design, please visit http://breaking.in

RAJAT SHAIL
GLOBAL DIRECTOR OF
INDUSTRIAL DESIGN
HONEYWELL
MINNEAPOLIS

Interviewed while Mr. Shail was Advance Design Principal at Whirlpool in Benton Harbor, Michigan.

What kinds of portfolios get your attention these days? What brings in an industrial designer for an interview?

Typically, there are two ways to look at a candidate: you look at a résumé or you look at their portfolio. I think a level of creativity is also how people present themselves, how they pitch themselves. I think that's very valuable because the essence of industrial design is to try and stand out from the other products. It's your ability to enable the customer to understand the value of your product, the face value as well as the assumed value. The same philosophy needs to be used by candidates to get the attention of prospective employers. It works well, this notion of approaching a job as a design problem, the way they present their portfolios.

A good portfolio is one which is empathetic to the user, the user in this case being the prospective employer. A good designer knows their audience and has a sense of how much information needs to be projected, using the right amount of detail to get attention. Once you have the hook, you can lead the audience through your project. It's almost whimsical and audacious at the same time. Design

is the hook to provoke me to ask, "How did you come up with that amazing solution?"

It's about visual communication and at the end of the day, it's about design. I don't get completely blinded by the beauty of the presentation, the glossiness of the renderings or the sketches. I start to see the meaning in how the person thinks through their sketches and design. This doesn't go to say that beautiful renderings aren't good, but that there needs to be a balance with a lot of substance and style.

What do you expect to learn from a designer during an interview?

Usually when we invite a designer over to interview, it means we are impressed by their work. Then we look for the signs: "What gives them that extra quality which makes them stand out over the other candidates?" The design field, particularly in corporations, is still quite young. One has to do a lot of presentations and sell one's design ideas to diverse groups, so we would look for someone who has storytelling ability, for someone who is persuasive enough to engage others in believing their dreams.

What characteristics or qualities are necessary to be a successful designer?

That's a loaded question because success in design can come very quickly, but sustained success is very critical. It's like photography; anyone can buy a good SLR camera these days and take pictures. Investment in taking pictures is not heavy so you can keep taking 200 pictures, and you'll come across one picture that looks fantastic. That doesn't make a person a good photographer. Annie Leibovitz said that what makes a good photographer is when a person can take a good picture every time they take a picture. That's part of a sustainable design skill, the one where you consistently give results. Your process is so solid and robust. I'm going to quote Matt Damon here; he said, "There are no small roles or big roles, there are only small actors and big actors." I feel that about design also. What makes a successful designer is a designer that can pick up anything and find its full potential.

Everyone is looking for the best product to design, but sometimes the best design solution comes from something benign, that it makes you wonder why you didn't think of that. That's what makes a really skilled designer.

How did you break into this business?

My wife had moved to the States early in our relationship. Even though I enjoyed the design scene in Asia, in India, for personal reasons I decided to move as well.

"A GOOD DESIGNER KNOWS THEIR AUDIENCE AND HAS A SENSE OF HOW MUCH INFORMATION NEEDS TO BE PROJECTED, USING THE RIGHT AMOUNT OF DETAIL TO GET ATTENTION."

I came here for my second master's degree in design methods at IIT in Chicago. Many of my professors were also professionals in companies like Motorola, so I started to work on sponsored projects with them. I started to develop connections to really understand how professional design develops in America, which is very different than in India. It becomes a chain reaction at that point because once you get a foot in the door you have the opportunity to meet other people. The one thing I learned in grad school was the ability to work in teams, the ability to get to know people and learn things from people who are completely different from you. The ability to connect with people.

If you were just starting out now, what advice would you give yourself?

At the end of the day, it's never a bad day. Whether you have success or a loss, you're still getting paid for doing work you enjoy. I have never wanted to do anything else. The advice I'd give myself is: everyone wants to be a coach, but it's better to be a player and lead by example.

It sounds like a designer needs to always stay curious and keep learning.

Designers sometimes take themselves way too seriously. We need to have fun. We need to become child-like and really enjoy. The more I design, and the more I read about designers, I've realized that if you're not honest, you can't do honest work. If you're trying to do smoke and mirrors, your design starts to be very superficial also. I don't claim I've reached that level; we all have levels of superficiality, there's a lot of noise in our minds. So it's a constant pursuit of simplifying my thinking so I can start to do simplified design.

Where do you see the future of industrial design going as it evolves further in the 21st century?

When the Apple revolution started to happen, I thought industrial design will be taken over by interaction design. I don't think that anymore. I feel that the future of industrial design will be beautiful products, but fewer products. I think the overall aesthetic, understanding of people is maturing—just like people mature over centuries.

My undergrad was in architecture. One of our family friends was a very successful architect and he said something very interesting to me: "The first job of an architect is not to build, but to get rid of stuff which is ugly." I think the future of industrial design is less stuff. There is so much noise and so much rubbish out there right now that people will start to look at their core values, and live longer with their products. This consumption-based society, getting rid of products after using them for a short time, will start to wear off. People love their cars, they name their cars and I see that as a core value in enjoying a product. That value is going to grow over time.

Apple as a company has started to show how you can simplify a lot of that experience, which is really basic and customizable, so that you want to keep it for as long as possible.

Is there anything you'd like to add that we haven't talked about? Any final words of wisdom?

I don't think I've reached a place to share any wisdom. You need to keep striving; the journey is better than the destination. Yes, we want to live in a world where things are clean and beautiful, and consumption is low—but it's good to be where we are right now so we can make the change, rather than live in a world where the change has already happened. ⊞

To see Rajat Shail's work, please visit http://breaking.in

NASAHN SHEPPARD DIVISIONAL VICE PRESIDENT PRODUCT DESIGN & DEVELOPMENT REI SEATTLE

Interviewed while Mr. Sheppard was the Vice President of Industrial Design at Smart Design in San Francisco.

What kinds of portfolios get your attention these days? What brings in an industrial designer for an interview?

The portfolios that really catch my attention are the ones that tell really interesting and compelling stories. I'm looking for portfolios from people who can demonstrate in a succinct manner that they understand and can frame the challenge, how they approached and solved that challenge, and what their solution was. Design is so often about good storytelling. I think that young designers forget this.

Has there been a portfolio that you've seen recently that resonated with you? What about it stood out?

There was a portfolio I saw not too long ago. What they did really well was that, in a couple of pages, they explained who they were, what their

philosophy was, where they had come from, and their journey to become a designer. It gave a little bit of a context and it made me feel like I understood this person even though I had never met them. When they showed a project, it was very clear what the challenge was they were trying to solve for, from the problem statement to some of the key steps they took to answer that particular problem. Then they showed a thoughtful solution. The best part was they did all this in just a few clear and focused pages. I didn't have to read volumes of information. Ultimately, it gave me everything I needed to know that they actually understood what the challenge was and created a solution that fit that challenge.

What do you expect to learn from them during an interview?

By the time I invite a candidate for an in-person interview, I will have already vetted that they can do work at a certain quality and level. When we meet, it's less about their actual output and more about how they think and communicate their approach. Also, how they would fit with our team and our culture. Every team is different and every company has a different culture. I like hiring for the long term, so it's really important for me that they will fit with Smart Design, our team and culture. The quality of people, individually and as a collective team, is number one.

I believe an interview is a two-way conversation, and I am always looking at how they're interviewing us as much as how we're interviewing them. One of the questions that I always ask is why Smart Design? Why us? Why are you here? If the answer is simply because they needed a job, the interview is pretty much over at that point. I'm looking for someone who understands who we are, what we do, and why they think they would be a good fit for us. This shows me that they've done their homework and they're coming to us because they feel like they have something to contribute.

What qualities or characteristics are necessary for a designer to be successful and maintain their career?

That's a really interesting question because I think this is constantly changing. Some of the baseline qualities that are really important are inquisitiveness, empathy, passion, and flexibility. Design challenges are forever changing and the nature of our business is changing in really interesting and exciting ways. Ultimately, to be successful regardless of the challenge someone needs to be able to break down complex challenges into smaller parts, and then rebuild those parts into a clear and focused solution that is meaningful to people and our clients' business. Those kinds of characteristics have longevity regardless of what happens in the industry.

How did you break into this industry?

If you think about the modern world we live in, somebody designed almost everything in it, but interestingly, there are just not that many people who are designers. Most people take the things and experiences in their life for granted or simply don't see it until someone points out that that thing they love was carefully designed by someone, somewhere.

"THE PORTFOLIOS THAT REALLY CATCH MY ATTENTION ARE THE ONES THAT TELL REALLY INTERESTING AND COMPELLING STORIES."

Personally, I was born into it. Both of my parents are designers. For a while I was trying to break out and do other things. I had to find my way back into design. It started with furniture design. I created a little furniture company with a partner and we sold some furniture, then I wanted to learn more about the craft of design. I went to California College of the Arts and then I transferred to Art Center College of Design and what I realized there—as much as I thought I understood design coming from a design background—was I really didn't understand the craft of design. I was surrounded by people who absolutely just blew me away at every single level. I realized really early that I was going to have to work harder and smarter than ever before. I asked myself every day, is there something more that I could be

doing, is there something more I could be learning? I continually pushed myself.

I still like to surround myself with the most talented people and I still ask myself those questions every day. It's constant learning and striving to be better. That feeling has never gone away and I don't want it to.

If you were just starting out now, what advice would you give yourself?

Today, there are many paths to success and they don't all go to the traditional, well-known consultancies. From internships to creating your own ideas and putting them out there through social networks and media, there are so many different avenues that are open for young designers waiting to start out. Never in history have designers had more ways to share their point of view. It's a really fantastic opportunity for them. To sum it up, believe in yourself, in your craft, and know that you'll get there.

There's a brilliant quote from Judy Garland I've always taken to heart, which is, "Always be the first-rate version of yourself, instead of a second-rate version of somebody else."

Where do you see the future of industrial design going?

When I think about industrial design at the dawn of the last century and look at some of the most famous industrial designers like Loewy, Eames, and Teague, they designed entire experiences. Over time industrial design has unfortunately become focused on physical products. I think now, more than ever, people desire complete and holistic experiences where the brand, product, UI, and ecosystem work together harmoniously.

This shift is enabling designers to go back to their roots and consider the entire experience, service, and ecosystems someone will have will have. As a designer moving forward, we need to think more about the greater context of the world this product or service or experience will live in.

Is it safe to say that industrial design is definitely expanding to be more than just the physical manifestation of the product?

I think that's absolutely safe to say. The lines between product design and interaction design, brand, and experience design are getting very blurry. Some of the best examples of products in the marketplace today consider all of these and create a holistic experience that somebody can interact with. People aren't looking for just one aspect of it. They're really looking for it to work seamlessly and for the whole experience to be simple, relevant, and meaningful for them. So, absolutely industrial design is expanding.

Anything else you'd like to add that we haven't talked about? Any final words of wisdom?

It seems like most design schools have developed towards creating individual superstars, making them feel like invincible stand-outs—even within a team context. That changes the day you get into the professional world. It's really not about you anymore. It's about the team, solution, and client's needs and about the greater context of what you're doing. I think it would be really helpful for people to understand that as early as possible. The sooner young designers stop using terms of "I" and "me" and more of "us" and "we" the better. It's not about your ego, it's about the work you're producing. Whatever gets to the right answer is the right path. It may not be your path, but that's the right path. ⊞

To see Nasahn Sheppard's work, please visit www.breaking.in

Industrial design is such a broad field. How have you seen it evolve over the years?

The democratization of access to computers gave a tremendous boost to designers' confidence to explore the unknown and push the limits of their capabilities or potential spheres of influence.

Today design has its own rules, its own history, traditions, processes, and adjacencies. Ways of thinking and methodologies that originated in industrial design are now seen as key to achieving breakthrough innovation across industries. Design has become an integral part of the ecosystem of people's lives because it has infiltrated analog and digital products, communications, environments, experiences, and services—the broad swath of commerce. Design can focus on discovering opportunities that will provide for the needs, desires, and unforeseen circumstances in people's lives. Industrial design has no set boundaries, and nothing lies outside of its gaze. Every type of organization in the United States is aware of the value of design and wants it. This is how industrial design has evolved.

Most recently, industrial design expertise has been extended to the realm of digital interface and interaction design not only for entertainment, but for visualizing data and abstract concepts often combined with motion and animation to deliver information in ways more people can understand. Oftentimes, it's embedded in products to improve people's ability to control or use them. After years of being castigated by bottom-line folks, some design deliverables can be measured by performance criteria or standards other than profit, market share, or sales, such as time, range of motion, usability, comprehension, efficiency, energy consumption, and other aspects of sustainability and efficacy. Achieving broader objectives and providing deeper, richer meaning through design is accomplished by designers collaborating with other specialists—not only chemists, anthropologists, or software engineers, but also design researchers, planners, and strategists.

In an economy that is not providing growth in the number of jobs, more designers than ever are being led by their entrepreneurial instincts. Risk taking is encouraged even when 95% of new graduates have gone into sometimes paralyzing debt to pay for their education. I am confident that out of this chaos will emerge new ways of doing design, new ways to reduce the cost of getting a good education, and new ways of earning income to get out of debt at the same time. That's what designers have always done, they figure it out. In addition, every start-up in new product development, financial services, technology, gaming, social media, and so on, employs at least one designer.

Our culture's ambition for design will always continue to change, stretch, and grow. Design cannot be static and be useful at the same time. Building on what we learned from our consulting and recruiting engagements with HP, here's an easy framework to use to talk about the evolution: "Design to simplify, design to differentiate, design to innovate, design to dominate, design to understand."

What characteristics or qualities are necessary to be a successful industrial designer?

Over the last 10 years they have been the following: the ability to collaborate and accomplish things with and through others. Being capable of combining analytical, intuitive, and strategic thinking. Having the ability to persuade and communicate both verbally and visually the value proposition contained in the recommendation of a path or design direction in terms that non-designers—who make the go or no-go and investment decisions which lead to implementation of the recommendation—can understand and will be moved by.

It is more important than ever to develop oneself as a person people will want to work with and help. Make no mistake, this does not mean strong opinions and beliefs are verboten. If you don't believe in your ideas, why should anyone else? Nobody does anything by themselves anymore. You

can't accomplish anything important, in my opinion, without engaging with other people. The best way to do that is to understand or learn how to collaborate. Listen carefully for and encourage feedback. Develop authentic behaviors through learning and practice. I think this is one of the most important things about designers that nobody talks about—that the best designers are the best collaborators. They care passionately about the success of the organization, people they work with, the project or program at hand, and the people who are the ultimate recipients of the benefits of what they are designing.

Then there are the skills. There will always be a demand for extraordinary sketching, form development, graphics, color, and computer skills. The hands-on skills are the hardest to master, but they are table stakes for some employers when looking for designers coming out of school.

Would you say you've noticed a different trend developing over the years in regards to what employers are looking for in industrial designers?

Yes. I think they're looking for fully functioning human beings who are intelligent, caring, able to write and communicate clearly, with confidence and eagerness to learn. They have to be inspired by and literate in the issues that affect their work. They also need to be aware of the global and local economy, technology, trends, science, art, human factors, and the convergence of digital media, etc. They have to have a great antennae.

It sounds like from your perspective that a combination of being humble and curious is almost an ideal trait for a designer to have in order to succeed.

Absolutely. They also have to be good presenters. They have to understand what media to use to best convey the content of their presentation. They should be very curious, willing to do their own research if necessary, and be skilled in extrapolating information from research others have done to inform their thinking. A doctor will not be successful if they can't communicate. They have to convince a patient to follow prescribed therapy in order to get well. If the doctor does not, the doctor has failed and the patient may die.

Anybody who is going to be successful at anything has to be able to communicate, understand, anticipate, and remove the barriers between them and the people they need to develop an understanding with. People who are responsible for the health and growth of their organizations may think they must be logical, rational, sequential, analytical, focused on the details, and objective when listening to the presentation of a recommendation. Designers think strategically, but they also welcome the influence of their intuition—creativity and a holistic way of observing their work and synthesizing ideas. They value aesthetics and their ability to design to arouse emotion and make connections with the people who sell or use whatever it is they are designing, and will admit to being subjective.

It appears it's getting harder and harder to get into the industrial design business these days. What would you say it takes to stand out?

It takes a portfolio designed for digital browsing, filled with inspiring or beautiful content. Or, as Massimo Vignelli would say, "Magic." The content can be research about discoveries of opportunities, or airport seating, but the presentation needs to be outstanding. Include video, show your process, and use language that is easy to understand. Errors in spelling and grammar are distracting.

It is difficult to find a good industrial design entry-level job today. For that reason, my advice is to stay in a perpetual job-hunting mode until circumstances change, and continue to do freelance work. Imagine the widest possible application of industrial designers' skills and take risks on entrepreneurial ventures alone or with friends, or explore different design environments through internships in order to understand what it takes to be successful.

What are the most common mistakes you've seen students or junior-level applicants make in how they present their work or their portfolios?

They need to rehearse their presentations to lose their fear, and they need coaching. They need to have the story of each project practically memorized and talk about the work context, their action, and the result. There will often be more than one person in the interview so they may have to use a projector and present standing up. Instead of saying you did research, present the research as part of your portfolio. Show the process and if you sketch well by hand, show that too.

The biggest mistake is that they don't read the job posting and requirements. They are either lazy or fantasize that the person posting the job will be able to intuit that they can do what the job requires, although neither the résumé or the digital samples are customized to point out the relevance of their experience or interests to the requirements. Second, their résumé does not come to the point: "this is where I worked," "this is the role I played," "these are some of the actions I took," and "these were the results." Basically, "this is why I am interested in the position and this is how my background relates to what you are looking for." Short sentences and bullet points are allowed, all on one page, especially for a new graduate. Finally, they don't invest the time required to design a great portfolio. If a designer is presenting suggestions about how to improve K-12 education to the governor of Kuala Lumpur, the governor won't "get it" if the data is not beautifully presented, visually and verbally. The better the design of the presentation, the more likely it is that the communication will be successful. I wouldn't bet on selling a good idea or myself with a lousy presentation.

What would be the one piece of advice you would give to an aspiring industrial designer or somebody that has just graduated and is trying to break into the industry?

First decide what areas of design interest you, like medical or transportation, or if you want to specialize in one aspect of the design process. Make sure that when you tell the story of what you've done on your résumé, you mention some of those things. Make sure that when you put your portfolio together that you have some of that stuff in there. If you're really interested in medical design but are presenting how you tackled an automobile or transportation problem, then try to relate the two somehow. You can do that. Anybody that's smart can do that. Investigate companies that do the work you're interested in and see the vocabulary that they use, see if they're advertising any jobs and how they talk about those jobs.

Then, I think you have to put together a list of companies that are in your areas of interest and email every single one of them with your résumé and a link to digital samples. Don't send a three-paragraph cover letter saying, "I just graduated." Give them the true story: "I'm really interested in your company and I'd like to be involved. I want to use what I have learned about design, observing people doing research to become a part of the advances in the medical industry." Email a résumé that captures everybody's attention with its direct relevance. You must understand when somebody opens it, and they have just read 10 others, you can really bore them to death with a very long summary. Just include some short sentences, bullet-pointed, that feature work experiences you've had and what you've accomplished. Do things in bullet-points because with everybody you write to, or every job you respond to, there are hundreds of people responding and writing. So think about how you're going to set yourself apart and get somebody's attention.

"BOTTOM LINE IS THAT DESIGN IS A CALLING. IF YOU DON'T PRACTICE IT THAT WAY, YOU'RE NOT GOING TO BE VERY IMPORTANT IN IT.
YOU CAN'T DO ANYTHING IN DESIGN HALF WAY."

You should also speak to anyone you know who might know somebody in these companies, because getting an introduction where you can make a personal connection helps. This is the reason why, when you're at school, you should begin to build your network and for your entire life, continue to build your network. You should always know somebody that will get you to somebody you need to get to. Find out who the hiring manager or creative director at the firm is and send your materials to them directly. Bypass the screener.

How would you suggest they do that?

The Internet, your network, your friends' networks, your parents' network. One of the ways is to look up design competitions because some of them will list the names of the judges, who are oftentimes lead designers in the companies they work for. There are many sites you can search for the information, and if you can't find it, call the company and ask for it. Ask everybody. Ask your parents, perhaps they know somebody who works at Microsoft, for example. Because you're a new graduate, you can call a place of interest and say something like, "I'm a student, and I'm graduating soon and am very interested in working for your organization. I'd like to know who is the recruiter in charge of industrial design or the name of a product design creative director." You can also get to people through LinkedIn groups. Just do it. I'd just do whatever is necessary to get the information I want. As long as you're not annoying or insulting anybody, "please" and "thank you" will get you a million miles.

As you are one of the rare women in the industry, what are your thoughts on women entering the field, and how has the industry changed around that, if at all?

There have always been women industrial designers, and in the last 20-plus years, women are about 50% of all design graduates. The industry is very welcoming to women and not just because women make so many of the buying decisions, and use the digital or analog artifacts designers create, but also because a diverse workplace is healthier and more interesting than one that isn't. There is no simple answer to the question of why there aren't more women designers in senior design management positions. I get asked all the time. My simple answer, with which you may not agree, is that maybe that's not everyone's priority. This is a very complex subject and I have not done any formal research, so this is just my opinion.

Both women and men may be very ambitious and want to take on more responsibility in order to get design leadership jobs in management. If a man or a woman is motivated and dedicated to achieving such a goal—and has whatever else is required—they have an equal chance of getting it. Everywhere I go, there are more women in marketing than ever before, and based on the searches we have done in the last three years, I have no doubt that the population of women designers is increasing. I want there to be more women in the design business, and I purposely try to find and encourage them.

There are women who want to make $500,000 a year plus bonus as a senior director of design, VP, or chief creative officer, or as a partner in a top design firm. Like men with the same aspirations, they are willing to make the sacrifices of frequent travel, developing and implementing a strategic vision that leverages the power of design to propel business growth, hiring and managing people, and being responsible for the design function's profits and losses. Fewer women than men in the past have wanted to make the sacrifices of their personal lives to reach such a pinnacle, but this is changing. This also reflects the priorities of women in law, banking, and consulting, not just design.

Bottom line is that design is a calling. If you don't practice it that way, you're not going to be very important in it. You can't do anything in design half way. If you want to accomplish anything of significance and if you want to help other people, your job in design has to be what you build your life around.

Anything we didn't cover that you would like to add? Any final words of wisdom?

The importance of travel. Just go. Usually it's easiest to travel early in your career. If you plan it properly and make contacts in advance, you can go around the world with very little expense. Visit designers and design educators and the families of international students who were in your class. People are very welcoming and if you work it right, will offer you a place to stay and a meal or two. Develop a familiarity firsthand with the needs, concerns, and interests of people all over the world. Eat food you have never seen before. Learn other languages. Keep a journal and take lots of photos. Most organizations highly value employees who become citizens of the world. They have a broader perspective on what "global" means and bring with them insights others don't have. [BI]

To see RitaSue Siegel's work, please visit http://breaking.in

MIKE SIMONIAN
PARTNER
MIKE & MAAIKE
SAN FRANCISCO

Interviewed before Mike and Maaike was acquired by Google.

What motivated you to open your own design studio?

We wanted to create an independent and experimental design studio that works on a broad range of subjects. Prior to starting Mike & Maaike, we had both worked for industrial design firms and gained a lot of experience. We were excited to combine this experience with an optimism and energy that we had both maintained through our careers.

We also wanted the studio to be very personal. We didn't want to just churn out as many projects as possible and do whatever we were asked. For this reason, we named the studio Mike & Maaike. Having your name attached to your work makes you think differently about the work you produce and makes everything more authentic. Practicing industrial design in the US is typically quite commercial and service-oriented. For us, working on both independent and client projects was very important and we had to create a different business model in order to maintain this independence.

How do you manage the non-design aspects of running a studio?

Every aspect of our work and lives is mixed together in one big pot. Everything can be approached in a creative way. I would argue that there are no non-design aspects. Even paperwork and contracts can set the tone for design projects and establish the possibilities for the design work. Sometimes, though, I wish I was an intern here.

Speaking of interns, who qualifies for an internship at Mike & Maaike? What do you look for in prospective industrial design intern portfolios?

We look for people that have an eye for design, an interesting point of view, and the technical skills to express their great ideas in a compelling way. We have been lucky to work with, and learn from, many talented and optimistic people over the past few years.

If you were just starting out now, what advice would you give yourself?

Accelerate!

Accelerate! In what respect?

Don't hesitate. The future will no doubt include successes and failures. The faster you can turn your future into your past, the more successes you will have experienced and the more failures you will have learned from. We tend to think the future is directly related to time, and therefore out of our control, when in fact, we are in control of how often we take risks, try new things, and put ourselves in the position to fail or succeed.

> *"THE FASTER YOU CAN TURN YOUR FUTURE INTO YOUR PAST, THE MORE SUCCESSES YOU WILL HAVE EXPERIENCED AND THE MORE FAILURES YOU WILL HAVE LEARNED FROM."*

In your opinion, what does it take to be a practicing industrial designer?

You have to have depth and a voice. By depth, I mean that you have to put yourself into lots of new situations, tried and failed, experimented and learned. This can/should happen in life, in design school, and in your career. With this experience, you can have a voice and feel confident that you are bringing your unique approach to your work.

With the current economy and the ever-expanding pool of global talent, it seems that it's getting harder and harder to get into the business these days. What does it take to stand out and break in?

I think it is easier than ever to break in. There are fewer barriers than ever thanks to technology, new business/funding structures, and availability of knowledge. I think focusing on doing great work and doing it in your unique way is what it takes.

Where do you see the future of industrial design going as it evolves further in the 21st century?

I see it going in all crazy different directions. If industrial designers in the past were more cookie-cutter in their approach and skill sets, industrial designers in the future will be a diverse group with all kinds of other skill sets. It may become harder to avoid specialization because the complexities involved in creating something truly new are not skin-deep, but require dedication and experience.

Anything we didn't cover that you would like to add? Any final words of wisdom?

When Maaike and I started our studio, we decided to have no clients for one full year. In this way, it was clear we were starting a design studio, not just a business. Our studio's success was not to be confused with our bottom line. This allowed us to find our voice and to experiment in areas that we were excited about. The independent projects we started that year have led to all of the commercial opportunities and experiences we have enjoyed ever since. BI

To see the work of Mike Simonian and Mike & Maaike, please visit http://breaking.in

BODO SPERLEIN
FOUNDER
BODO SPERLEIN
LONDON

What kinds of portfolios get your attention these days? What brings in an industrial designer for an interview?

I'm actually quite surprised how bad the portfolios are, and it has nothing to do with the students but how designers are trained these days. I definitely feel like the students are being trained to literally design products based off of what's happening now. I always look for innovation and ideas, and it can be pretty raw. A designer who has a vision or an idea that can be put in a product is far more valuable than a sleek presentation. These days it feels like students go to design stores for research and all they're doing is copying what's already out there. It's happening more and more; there's definitely a lack of innovation.

It's not a good sign. My professor in college was always saying, "If you want to design a cup, don't go into a shop or a museum, or anything where you look at other cups—what you should be doing is going into a forest or going to the cinema—get your inspiration somewhere else." The reason why is to train your eye.

From your perspective, what would an ideal industrial design portfolio entail?

It's about the raw idea—the innovative, creative idea. I don't expect fantastic or producible products, but ideas. I find it much more important from our point of view that there is good ID, good ideation, use of challenging materials, techniques. Combining traditional craft with modern high-tech applications.

If an industrial design student came to you looking for advice on how to prepare their portfolio for an internship or a job, what would you tell them to do? What should be in their portfolio?

It is important that they show their thought process and really show their skills and abilities. The most common mistake I've seen students or junior designers make in their portfolios is not showing the process they have gone through to reach the final product.

What do you expect to learn from a designer during an interview?

I expect them to be intelligent, to have good research skills—that's really important these days—and interest in marketing as well. Right now, a lot of the manufacturers in the big industries employ designers to be just a designer. If the company is to be successful, they should look for designers who have a much more multi-layered skill base. Someone who can help change a brand or enter a new market, who knows how to showcase things, someone who is not just a pure designer anymore, but an advisor.

Sounds like product design is wearing a lot of different hats these days.

Absolutely, yes. However, you also need to have knowledge and experience, that's really important. Another important thing is to encourage students to do a lot more work placements during their studies; it will make them far more employable. An employer will find it hard to hire them straight out of college without any actual work experience. They'll be so far detached from reality. So I highly recommend getting a work placement or an internship during school.

How did you break into the business?

I was a little bit more mature when I started, which I highly recommend in design, as you have to have a library of experiences and troubles. All of those help in creating your own style. I also find it quite difficult to believe that someone at 18, going into college, can come out with good design knowledge. I recommend taking two or three years off, doing something else, and then going to university. You'll have a little bit more experience, a library of resources: it can be design, art, politics, anything that plays a crucial role in designing products. In order to design products for this century, you need to understand the history. I strongly believe in that.

What inspired you to start your own studio?

I had success right during college and was thrown in the deep end. I had to start working basically straight away. Once the boat leaves early, you've got to go with it. It's what happened, and I was very fortunate in that aspect. I got commissions, I got projects, and I started working straight away.

If you were staring now, what advice would you give yourself?

Now it's somewhat more difficult, as it's a far more competitive marketplace. Luckily, I was in the position of setting up my own studio and that gave me confidence and a knowledge base, which is now needed to be a successful designer. We worked on projects where we would come up with our own concept, the art direction, the branding, everything. It's important, if you're attaching your name to a project, to make sure it looks the way you want it to be, as you don't want to be associated with a very crappy project.

"IT'S ABOUT THE RAW IDEA— THE INNOVATIVE, CREATIVE IDEA. I DON'T EXPECT FANTASTIC OR PRODUCIBLE PRODUCTS, BUT IDEAS."

It's about market value. What is your market value and market worth? In terms of design, do you have a name? Not a lot of companies these days are investing in no-name designers because it's a marketing tool. If you take on a no-name designer then you not only have to build up your own brand, but also of that designer, and why you're working with them. It makes it much more difficult.

Where do you see the future of industrial design going?

On one hand we have a recession going on and, on the other we have consumers who are becoming a lot more savvy. They don't want to go to a supermarket to buy bread anymore, they want to go to an artisanal bakery, or artisan cheese shop and know where that cheese is coming from, and what breed of cow, or where the milk is coming from. There's definitely a curiosity and people are really interested in products. A lot of heritage will come back in again.

Similar trends are popping up here in the States as well.

Absolutely, and you can see it. People are saying, "Hold on a minute, I was working for a large corporation and now I'm laid off, so what I'm going to do is something out of my own personal interest." If I love chocolate, I'm going to open a chocolate business. It's happening all over the place and I think that's where design is going as well. Less global thinking, more local. We use global networking but we are getting far more localized in terms of business. It makes it far more interesting in the global marketplace as well. It's just more entrepreneurial and a lot more interesting to me as a customer.

So this will impact industrial designers as well as they become design-makers and utilize local manufacturing. We are a little bit like that as well; we make one-off pieces and we also work for big companies to design collections. So, don't be disarmed as a young student if you can't get a job at a big company, why not go and make your ideas? Once you have a name, you can go to the next level.

Is there anything we haven't talked about that you'd like to add?

A lot of designers are finding the importance of design history; it's teaching you how to design research properly. Also writing essays is a great exercise to communicate your own work and talk about it. A lot of designers are not able to talk about their own work and I think it's a basic skill they should have. It's overlooked a lot of the time, even at universities. It's a really important tool to have. It's not just ideas—you have to be able to sell yourself, and talk about yourself. It's not just visual communication skills. You need to be able to explain why you designed something, or what's the inspiration for something, the whole package. I find this so utterly important. BI

To see Bodo Sperlein's work, please visit http://breaking.in

BRIAN STEPHENS
FOUNDING DESIGNER & CEO
DESIGN PARTNERS
DUBLIN

What kinds of portfolios get your attention these days? What brings in an industrial designer for an interview?

We get relatively few and maybe that's partially because our main office is in Dublin, Ireland. What gets our attention is somebody who has a clear proposition from the beginning, and a clear point of view. Somebody who's confident, somebody who knows what they're about. Somebody who makes a sustained effort to connect with us.

When it comes to technical skills what do you expect to see in an actual portfolio?

Some visual acuity, a sense of judgment, a clear understanding of the design process, a clear demonstration of intelligence and vision, and obviously a sense of excitement, passion, and creativity.

Has there been a portfolio that you've seen recently that resonated with you? What about it stood out?

Yes, one was a post-graduate employee and what impressed me about him was his passion, his sense of energy, and his clarity about what he was presenting. In this particular case, it was his creative ways of using digital media and videos to communicate how he solves a problem. Also, he bridged mechanical engineering, innovation, and

industrial design. Finally what impressed me about him was that he was working in the medical area and had the ability to understand the language of science and to communicate that both through his portfolio and his face-to-face presentation.

"YOU REALLY WANT TO HAVE CHAPTERS IN A PORTFOLIO, EACH THAT IS TRYING TO MAKE A DIFFERENT POINT. THEN HAVE SOME JUDGMENT ON THE DAY OF THE INTERVIEW TO GO BACK AND FORTH BETWEEN THE STORIES."

If I may, I'd like to share what I don't like in a portfolio: badly selected work, clichés, both visual and otherwise, and noise—stuff that's there to superficially impress but it doesn't have any reason behind it. You really want to have chapters in a portfolio, each that is trying to make a different point. Then have some judgment on the day of the interview to go back and forth between the stories. I'd say portfolio presentation is 50% work and 50% the ability to engage the audience. The other thing that disappoints me, and it disappoints all of my colleagues here, is when applicants, especially young applicants, come in and don't have any models with them. Also, when people send in poor résumés. Résumés are useful when you're assessing candidates. Just because you're going in for a face-to-face interview, doesn't mean you shouldn't have a résumé with you. I would argue that the current generation of young designers has a big advantage over their predecessors in that they are pretty fluent in digital media and it's easy for them to produce relatively high-quality résumés that can be illustrated. There's no reason for not having a good-looking presentation or a résumé.

When you say cliché and noise in the portfolio, what are you referring to?

Sometimes it's easy for people to pick up idioms and stylistic references and to incorporate them into a product. It results in work that's a little bit derivative. It's better for the work to be a little planar with some solid thinking behind it. I'm also thinking of presentation styles. Sometimes you see students who hide behind presentation techniques. It takes a while to read through the presentation stuff and actually look at the design behind it. Sometimes it's cliché, and sometimes it's noise, and it makes the presentation visually confusing rather that visually clear. Design is all about clarity and being propositional, and putting an idea in front of an audience. So sometimes design students and young designers hide in technology, rather than trying to express something that's related directly to design. It's partly an educational problem, and partly it depends on the college.

You mention bringing in actual, physical models to the interview. Can you share more about that, and why is that important for your team to see and experience?

It's part of our own philosophy that you've got to work in a three-dimensional world. If you live in the 2D CAD world, you're not embracing the opportunities of designing a product. We look for people with an understanding of that and with a relatively high level of craft skills, who can express themselves well in model form. Not just in CAD or sketching, but in three dimensions. Therefore, the quality of models and of experimentation in three dimensions is key. Often people show photos of models that have been retouched so you don't know if they made the models themselves. You don't know what level of hands-on experience they've got.

What else do you expect to learn from designers when they come in for an interview?

That they can listen and have good social skills. That they have the right balance of being confident but not arrogant, and that they're potentially good team players.

What characteristics or qualities would you say make a successful designer?

I would say an ability to apply objective thought. To have some analytical skills, to have some fluency in the creative process, to have a strong willingness to learn and a strong work ethic. To understand how to apply creativity. To be able to express themselves clearly and to understand that the industrial design process is a collaborative process. To be ambitious. I think we look for people who have emotional intelligence.

How did you break into this business? What motivated you to start Design Partners back in 1984?

I think I'm the classic case of one of those people who like making things. Even as a child, I knew I was creative and was encouraged by my parents and siblings. Industrial design was relatively rare in Ireland at the time, but I kind of understood that I wanted to be the sort of architect who designed all the little things that were going to be inside the building. That was my introduction to industrial design. So when I heard it was a job, and you could get paid for it, I couldn't believe it.

I trained in the UK, and worked in England, Ireland, and Japan. When I came back in 1983 with my business partner, I pretty much set up Design Partners so I could have a job and I've been doing that since. It's as simple as that.

If you were just starting out now, what advice would you give yourself?

Be ambitious and take the long view. Don't try to do everything yourself. Trust your instincts.

Where do you see the future of industrial design going as it evolves further in the 21st century?

I think it will become more integrated into the entrepreneurial and start-up sides. In big corporations, I see it becoming an essential part of normal business activity. I think, at the moment, it's an interesting time because people are looking at design and creativity as a new, potentially useful, business methodology—a way in which corporations can solve problems and build their own strategy. What this reflects is a recognition that design is one of those disciplines that really just links the normal practice of making things with properly and deeply understanding the end-user or the consumer and respecting their needs. Traditionally, it has sometimes been seen as a bolt-on service, not central to the company's return business. I see it evolving more to becoming more central to business activity and less external—more integrated. It's no longer about the object, it's more about the experience. Products need to become deeper and more fundamental. There were many aspects of design in the past that were very superficial, and that's not good enough anymore. Everybody understands that you're designing an entire experience. From subconsciously connecting with the brand right through to disposal of the product at the end, and all of the stages in between. It's a much more holistic experience.

I believe industrial design is still one of the best professions for applying creativity within industry. It's kind of the cohesive glue between many other disciplines, right through to usability, interface design, and all of those things that are happening on the screen. Various industrial designers think it's the paramount profession for connecting a lot of disciplines that are essential to making something.

What makes you say that?

Pride in the profession, I suppose. I think there's something good that happens in industrial design training where students realize that they are generalists, creative generalists. That they need to be fluent in a number of different media, that they need to be able to cross disciplines, and that they need to be incredibly inquisitive and adaptable. I must give credit to recent graduates and recent generations of young designers. They get that. They understand that and they've got the confidence, education, and understanding of technology. I think that's good news. They're quite powerful, and they're connected culturally.

Is there anything we didn't cover that you'd like to add? Any final words of wisdom?

I have a strong sense of confidence in the people that are up-and-coming and joining the profession. I'm significantly impressed by the quality of graduates and their optimism, enthusiasm, savvy, and confidence. I think they're a generation that's going to make a big difference to the world.　BI

To see the work of Brian Stephens and Design Partners, please visit http://breaking.in

DONALD STRUM
PRINCIPAL OF THE PRODUCT DESIGN GROUP
MICHAEL GRAVES DESIGN GROUP
PRINCETON, NEW JERSEY

What kinds of product design portfolios get your attention these days? What brings in an industrial designer for an interview?

For a portfolio to capture our attention there has to be something engaging, something beautifully functional popping off the page. My tendency is formal beauty. Exemplary functionality and exquisite proportions garner my attention first, whether it is entry or senior level. We carry a high aesthetic acumen here, fused with intuitive functionality. Next, I peruse for well-rounded skill sets. For the manner in which we work, we are not looking for a designer to come into our office and revolutionize the way we are going to design. Evolution perhaps, but we have an established, tried-and-true methodology. Plus, it happens to say "Michael Graves" on the door, so one can generally figure that there is a design vocabulary at work here. We are looking for designers to come and learn the intrinsic way we design, first and foremost. It takes a little while, usually 16–24 months for a designer to have the foundation of the aesthetic, and that's for someone right out of school. We need a designer to carry the strong, basic skill sets of computer drawing, computer rendering, sketching, and model building. They need to be very computer savvy; they have to be tuned into the programs we are using. They need to understand orthographic projections—being able to visualize and draw a product from all viewpoints. If they have decent form-factors, aesthetic judgment, and taste, I'd recognize that as a perk.

Has there been a portfolio you've seen recently that caught your eye? What about it stood out?

There has been a portfolio that caught our attention recently, and yes, we actually hired her. The work in the portfolio was very well rounded and there was a systematic approach that worked well to showcase every project. Again, this was looking at a portfolio for an entry-level person; my requirements are different for someone at a higher level, such as a senior designer or design director. For her, there was an understanding, a way of thinking, and a balance to all of her projects. It wasn't heavily laden with research. Remember, I'm looking through these portfolios very quickly, so I want to get to the essence of the design brief, what they set out to do, what captured their attention, what inspired them, where the research piece informed the design, and if there was any ethnographic work done. Then I want to get right to the sketches and renderings because I want to see whatever they deduced. It's okay if it isn't always feasible or practical. That's what design school is for at times—to explore the "what ifs." This design candidate did all that. I mean on every project, whether it was something environmental or whether it was something as small a toothpick dispenser. Everything carried a reliable, balanced narrative. She told a persuasive, creative story. It was a methodology that served this designer well and held our interest.

If you had an opportunity to guide an industrial design student in how to create a portfolio that would resonate for you, what would you tell them?

I would tell them exactly what I described about the candidate we hired in the last question. Tell me three to five well-rounded problem-solving design stories, utilizing all of those skill sets. Design every aspect of it and make it clear and visually exciting. Show me you are well rounded and can sit down on day one at our office and be able to contribute in all the ways I described above and below.

What do you expect to learn from a designer during the interview?

I expect to learn that they are able to communicate and that we have made a connection. We've had young designers come in who've had beautiful portfolios, but they lack social competence, so they can't communicate properly, or be comfortable around people.

Again, we take a really balanced approach. One needs to have socialization skills—some level of character and personality—which is evident through their work. We operate in a team environment, so one must be able to express and present their thoughts in a way where they don't take themselves too seriously. Also, we are a small, efficiently run team, so it is impossible to hide out.

This might sound crazy, but one thing that always gets our attention right off the bat—and this is business 101—is having the ability to shake someone's hand firmly and look them in the eye. I'm known for taking new people aside and demonstrating this first impression technique. My business partner is of the same mindset. We discount a candidate's eligibility based on their handshake and if they are unable to hold eye contact. We understand people are nervous when they come in the door but to be able to leave a positive impression—the "I'm going to be able to work with you, day in and day out"—is extremely important. Design is not about being shy, it's about being in the world. Our office is all about humanism and carrying a narrative. It all starts with the handshake. You have to present yourself the same way you present your work. To me, it's seamless. It's one in the same.

> "DESIGN IS NOT ABOUT BEING SHY, IT'S ABOUT BEING IN THE WORLD. OUR OFFICE IS ALL ABOUT HUMANISM AND CARRYING A NARRATIVE. IT ALL STARTS WITH THE HANDSHAKE."

One last comment: I mentioned the importance of the visualization of projects. Every one of our team members is part of the design presentation. One must be "on" and able to get themselves fired up and prepared to do this. We want to witness that a candidate really wants to be a part of our design family. This is not business-as-usual where mom and dad are going to love you regardless of what happens.

What characteristics or qualities are necessary to be a successful designer these days?

You have to present a range of poignant ideas. You have to tune in to what the client wants and you have to design and present it in a new and compelling way. You're hitting all the tenets that they have openly discussed or documented, so there must be a level of familiarity with what the client has stated. Then you interpret it back to them in some really exciting approach that they would never have considered. That's the role of the designer: to be fresh, original, contextual, and transformative in a believable format. Ultimately, for our clients, the design has to be tangible and imbued with feasibility. There has to be an essence of "I've seen this before, but never like that."

In years of working with dozens of clients, I know that every client wants to be delighted. They want to be surprised and pushed a few degrees out of their comfort zone. The undeniable nature of the design is what forges the trust. Our clients must feel the desire to execute the project without compromise. We have done our job when there are smiles on their faces after the presentation and the product launch.

I've read that you were one of the first product designers to be hired at Michael Graves, so I'd love to hear your story. How did you break into this industry?

I was one of the first product designers hired here. It happened by way of nepotism, timing, and luck. My timing was impeccable. It was the fall of 1983, and I was still in my senior year of college at the Parsons School of Design, majoring in environmental and product design. My sister, Suzanne, who is an architect, was working in Michael Graves' studio. At the time, it was a real atelier atmosphere. They had three or four full-time colorists, meaning they studied and explored the color relationships for the architecture and the interiors and worked directly on blueprints in oil and latex paint. They were all trained as fine artists and illustrators. Michael's palette was about an interpretation of rich Tuscan colors and his architecture always reflected an intense application of color, so we had highly trained people to fill that role. My sister was one of the architectural, artful ones who knew how to

paint murals—she had a BFA in fine art as well as a master's in architecture. Everyone wore many hats here. Suzanne heard that they were looking for a gofer—someone to run errands, make blueprints, sweep the floors, pick up a crate from the airport, or help build a model. She told me about the job and I said, "Sure, I'd love to be exposed to a professional studio," so I worked here during my off hours during my senior year at school. It was a vibrant and highly influential atmosphere. I began to feel I was a part of something larger than myself. There was a movement going on around here and it was receiving attention on a global scale.

In the spring of 1984 I was called down to Michael's office with one of the senior partners of the firm. They stated that they just received this letter from Alberto Alessi and he was inviting Michael to design a new kind of tea kettle for the American market. They asked me if I would like to stay for the summer to work on that tea kettle, knowing that I was just finishing my degree in industrial design. It was an easy decision to make. I graduated, and the Whistling Bird tea kettle was my first project right out of college.

After that, Michael's international recognition just exploded. We spent quite a bit of time working on that project during the summer of '84 and then it came out early in the summer of '85. I remember dropping to my knee when they unveiled the prototype at our offices that winter. It was so iconic and shiny, the ultimate hood ornament for your kitchen stove. Alberto Alessi already realized there was something going on here, and that Michael had a way of tuning into the public's taste. From that came another hundred projects with Alessi over the next 15 years. It was the perfect wave to ride. The range and diversification of commissions were an industrial designer's dream, and this was an architectural firm.

Wow, what an amazing story! So then, looking back, if you were just starting out now, what advice would you give yourself?

At Parsons I had an excellent art and architectural history professor and a good design studio department that played really well with how Michael works and his utilization and knowledge of design history. I knew how to draw, draft, make models, be crafty—all skills that are needed here. I would say I wasn't as well-versed or confident in my design conceptualization, but by working here I was able to improve. Working in this office during my early, formative design years really helped complete and complement my Parsons education. I actually needed to be here during those years to get what I call my "MG masters degree." After all, Michael is an educator and was a Princeton University professor of architecture for 39 years. I was really lucky to have direct access to Michael Graves and he loved the product design projects. He loved—and still does love—working at this scale. I was able to become very friendly with him and learn from him directly. How wonderful it is that I am still able to learn from my mentor.

Michael draws exquisitely and when he draws a line or a product, there is a conveyance that emanates from his pencil. For me, a line was just a line, but for him, it was an expression. We would take his drawings, because they were just perfect, and would scale them up on a Xerox machine and draft over them. He nailed the proportions every time. Michael has a way of drawing such that everything is captured and resolved in that sketch. You don't get that in a corporate environment. You sort of have to be immersed in it for a while, let it permeate you, and be with those types of people to whom design is the summation of everything. Design is not to be reduced to an afterthought. Design is first and foremost in everything you do, time and time again. Design is an embedded spiritual practice performed on a daily basis. Michael is "design" and it is intense and moving.

Where do you see the future of industrial design going as it evolves further in the 21st century?

I would always say that good industrial design will continue to expand our daily lives. It is an enhancement that makes a positive difference to people. It's not just adding a decal or color to something—it's a lot more. Design is going to be there, expanding upon how we relate to each other. It's only going to get more and more important, and people are going to appreciate it more and more, especially in this country. Our years of success with our ongoing product collections at Target stores prove this, and

soon our new collections will be moving to JCP where we will have our own shop in the spring of 2013.

Years before, in Europe and Japan, there was always an appreciative notion about design. People take care of well-made objects and use them for years. I think there's been an explosive awareness over the last 10 years in this country and people are beginning to look at and pay attention to design and what makes them happy, and what attracts them. They want more of it. The only problem is that sometimes people need to appreciate what they have now, not just appreciate what's coming.

There's always a sense of timelessness in really great design and that is something we look to instill in our work. It's not trend driven. It's going to stand the test of time. We have a series of quality products that are 10, 15, and some over 25 years old that are still selling well. That is meaningful and hopeful. Talk about "sustainability." Design shouldn't be viewed as transient. It should be viewed as something that belongs with us and works for decades. That is true timelessness.

It's more difficult in electronics, as there tends to always be something new being developed. It's ever-changing. Tech products always seem to be revised, but there are still good tenets of design that should be incorporated into any product: symmetry, rounded forms over sharper forms, and the ideas of proportion and golden ratio. Good designers carry those moves in everything they do.

Anything you'd like to add that we didn't cover? Any final words of wisdom?

I wish to stress the importance of developing environments, products, or experiences that are beautifully integrated. Beauty goes hand-in-hand with functionality. It goes hand-in-hand with the research and innovation. I've seen a lot of products that don't take that into consideration. It's just not stressed or taught enough. Having an understanding of classic disciplines—golden sections, formal beauty, function, and composition—inform what one can do. I know people have moved away from hand drafting and understanding orthographic projections, and they are designing on the computer. But designers must carry through their early influences of understanding the basics. That is what I'm looking for.

I want to be swept away by the form of an object and really get to understand how someone was able to capture that and experience it in plastic, wood, glass, fabric, ceramic, and metal. Those moments are what really attract me. I'm saying these bits about beauty, functionality, composition, and proportion because I think that's what makes us human. That's what people are viscerally attracted to first and I think they intuitively choose those types of designs. They may not know why, but that is my job. ⊞

To see the work of Donald Strum and Michael Graves Design Group, please visit http://breaking.in

KYLE SWEN
PARTNER & EXECUTIVE VICE PRESIDENT OF DESIGN
ASTRO STUDIOS
SAN FRANCISCO

What kinds of portfolios get your attention these days? What brings in an industrial designer for an interview?

First and foremost, we are looking for dynamic work, but we're also looking for clever ideas and insightful solutions. Did the candidate think about the overall user experience in regard to their projects? Oftentimes a portfolio gets more attention if it's easy to go through, organized well, and is graphically stimulating. We are still a sketch-heavy studio, and look for how a candidate uses a sketch to communicate ideas and evoke emotion.

Have you seen a portfolio recently that resonated with you, and can you share what about it stood out?

We're always looking for talent, but recently I've been looking at more experienced designers—designers with five years or more under their belt. For the more experienced candidates, I look for a range of concept ideas, and the variety of products that they've worked on. It's not just about the object, it's about the overall experience and how they consider that. I'm looking at how the person solves a problem and offers a solution to see how much depth is there.

For people fresh out of school, we look more at the skills and a confident attitude. We also look for people who would fit in well and add to our culture.

Can you talk a bit more about the importance of sketching in industrial design?

If you go straight to CAD you might get to a solution faster, and it's going to look "real" quicker, but often the emotional content won't be there. You could end up with just another polished rock.

Sketching allows designers to communicate ideas quickly and effectively. A sketch or doodle usually has more emotion and feeling than a CAD rendering. It's quick and spontaneous. When you start building in CAD you become committed to an idea before you have had a chance to really figure out a solution or had a chance to see if there was a better one. Sketching allows you to get a lot of ideas out quickly without a big commitment. You can also sketch emotional movement in the drawing that you may want to try and capture in the refined 3D world.

What do you expect to learn from a designer during the interview?

Usually when we call them in for an interview, we're already excited about their work. When they come in, we're looking to see how they fit culturally with our studio. Because every studio is a little different, the cultural dynamic is important to us. Even though they might not have all the answers, we want them to be well prepared. Depending on the experience level, we want to see how they present their work and what they present. We might ask some questions to see how they respond to those. Because we believe what a designer does outside of work influences how they design, we ask about interests and hobbies outside of design as well.

What characteristics and qualities are necessary to be a successful designer?

Motivation and a humble confidence. Charisma and being a self-starter are definite pluses.

How did you break into this business?

I didn't even know about industrial design as I was approaching my college years, so I was taking a career course at the junior college at the time and I typed in my skills and attributes and industrial designer came up. I researched ID and thought, "Wow, this really fits who I am." From that point forward, I attended college and looked at the top three firms at the time and started to emulate work they were doing.

"OFTENTIMES A PORTFOLIO GETS MORE ATTENTION IF IT'S EASY TO GO THROUGH, ORGANIZED WELL, AND IS GRAPHICALLY STIMULATING."

I also think it's really important to get an internship right away for a couple of reasons. Even if you start off as a model-maker, as I did for the first couple of years, you get real-world experience. You learn all kinds of different skills that you may not learn in school. It's a real-world experience. The networking is important as well. If you have a couple of stamps on your résumé, we pay attention to that. Real design experience puts you way ahead of anyone else who's never had an internship. I can't stress how important that is in helping you break in.

If you were just starting out now, what advice would you give yourself?

Fortunately, it worked out for me, but nowadays there are so many skill sets to learn and it's easier to learn from other professionals. Try to get real-world experience any way you can.

Where do you see industrial design going as it evolves further in the 21st century?

That's a difficult question. It's always changing and it's not as much about the artifact as it is about the overall experience these days. Many of our design programs consider the moment you first see the object, purchase it, open it, interact with it, and recycle it. A lot of the projects we are getting today are focused on the experience before we design any physical artifacts. There are also a lot of cultural considerations and demographics. The world is a smaller place now too and there are new types of problems to solve. We're in a throw-away society, so what do we do about that?

What will not change are the problem solving and the building of an emotional connection with people and consumers to the products and brands. That will always be there with whatever we design. There's certainly a bigger UI component involved in our daily lives. Many of things we're designing these days have screens or electronics. It's still solving problems and making things better, it's just moving from artifacts to overall experiences. It's going to be quite different in that sense. ID will continue to evolve over many facets. As designers we are always blending lifestyle with technology. There is always going to be a need for beautiful objects that interact with us.

We're so used to things being a certain way, feeling a certain way, and the overall quality of products has gotten better. Now people expect a product to last longer, especially if you're paying a premium for an iPhone or something similar. Manufacturing and materials have progressed and things can last longer, unless they're meant to be disposed of. We are always making greater demands for things to work better and faster. The world has higher expectations of what an object can do. The world's a smaller place; the Internet makes us all closer for the most part.

Is there anything else you'd like to add that we haven't talked about? Any final words of wisdom?

Design is a great career choice, and there are a lot of different avenues you can take. It is fast-paced and you'll learn something new every day, which is quite important to me. We can make the world a better place. It's a lot of effort, but at the end of the day, it's a very rewarding career. BI

To see the work of Kyle Swen and Astro Studios, please visit http://breaking.in

DANIEL TOMICIC
PRINCIPAL
SCUDERIA ZAGREB
ZAGREB, CROATIA

As an art historian with a penchant for automobiles and transportation design, what trends have you noticed over the years as the industry evolves to meet new challenges?

Latest trend is a car designed by an online community. Automotive industry follows potential buyers online and gets them involved in creation process of the new product. Instead of doing research of what people would like to get out of a car and then trying to create a product to suit them, potential buyers today get involved in the very process of creation. We already saw this in the fashion industry and now Local Motors and Marussia are offering cars created in this way. Big manufacturers have to follow this trend soon. On stylistic level, there are a lot of trends like smaller headlights, "bell-bottoms," in-car timepieces, horizontal "lip-chin creases," etc.

From your experience in organizing design events such as Auto(r), what does it take to be a successful industrial designer?

To be successful in any job you must work hard, get a good education, and be modest. You have to be hyper productive. Level of presentation has to be excellent. Work has to be purpose driven and you must avoid endless perfectionism. Good educational institution will give you a level of

knowledge, gain employer trust, and provide good connections. Employers neither have the will, nor the time, to get you introduced into work. You must fit in a workplace environment perfectly from day one. Personality is extremely important, because after all we are humans and like to be surrounded with positive personalities. Modesty is a universal value and all great designers are simple and accessible.

You are based in Croatia. Have you noticed any regional differences in design approach and solutions between the Eastern and Western European designers?

Eastern European designers grow and work without a system, basically everybody is on his own. You can say the same is in the West, but in the East the scale of chaos is exhausting and often paralyzing. When Iceland went into bankruptcy, they still had a much higher standard of life than the rest of the world. Governments in Eastern Europe don't support a domestic industry, but instead import goods, and consequently there is no need for designers.

"...LEARN FROM THE BEST BY BROWSING THEIR ONLINE PORTFOLIOS AND READING THEIR INTERVIEWS, USE THE SAME PLATFORMS TO PROMOTE YOUR OWN WORK. START A BLOG."

There is no conscience about importance of design. There are no good or bad schools, they are all the same. You don't get practical knowledge, so after graduation you don't know what to do, where to go, and how to behave. For instance, a lot of designers don't have a portfolio or a personal website. They don't know what the rates are, so they either overprice or undervalue their work.

Level of output is very low. Designers create one or two designs and then they spend years promoting it. They are like a child who plays life.

So, what would you recommend a prospective industrial designer from the region do in order to break into in the field?

The most efficient way is to graduate from an excellent university. That will lead to good internships and connections. Living and working in some of the cities where world trends are created is crucial to gain experience—that saves self-development time, but unfortunately requires more money than majority of people in the region can afford. Alternatively, one should use resources one has already: learn from the best by browsing their online portfolios and reading their interviews, use the same platforms to promote your own work. Start a blog. Send your best project to as many design media outlets as you can and some of them will publish it. Use the resources in the area where you live: go to events and meet new people. It is crucial not to give up and to have a good balance. You have to balance between self-confidence and self-awareness, ambition and realistic goals. Step by step you can achieve whatever you desire.

What's the one piece of advice you would give to an aspiring industrial designer or somebody who just graduated and is trying to break into the industry?

Use the Internet to promote yourself and your work. Everybody is online and people do read messages. If you are good, you'll find clients sooner or later.

How would you suggest one find these contacts, and how should the designers approach introducing themselves?

Use social networks and blogs to find people you would like to get in touch with. Send them a very short and sincere message with clear intention. Don't ask for a six-figure salary; just be happy to get advice. Include a link to your online portfolio that will give them an impression of how good you are. If you develop a nice relationship, they will open new doors for you. If you don't get a

reply in several weeks, try once more with a short reminder. After all, they are all very busy people. Be persistent.

Where do you see the future of industrial design going as it evolves further in the 21st century?

For some time design has been democratizing, thankfully due to digitalization. With easy-to-use software, you can create products ready for production. Next step is the same level of simplicity in production phase. This is possible thankfully to CNC and 3D printing. This will further democratize and demystify industrial design.

Anything we didn't cover that you would like to add?

Cars are the most recognizable products in the world and yet virtually no one knows their designers. Why is Chris Bangle not as famous as Philippe Starck? [BI]

To see Daniel Tomičić's work, please visit http://breaking.in

PIP TOMPKIN
FOUNDER
PIP TOMPKIN DESIGN
LOS ANGELES

What kinds of portfolios get your attention these days? What brings in an industrial designer for an interview?

I am looking for a portfolio that puts a smile on my face. This comes from originality, personality, and someone who goes above and beyond. Students need to be original and innovative to compete today. Their portfolio needs something that stands out to get to an interview. As a reflection of how competitive the design job market is, we are a small studio and, when we post a position, we receive in excess of a thousand portfolios from around the world. We ask for digital portfolios to be submitted through our website. Every portfolio is reviewed in its entirety by myself and the team, but over time we have come to recognize that a portfolio's quality and originality can usually be accurately assessed simply from the first introduction page. The point of this remark is that every detail of a portfolio needs to be designed to be able to sell your story. First impressions count and an obsession with the details is a sign of someone who goes above and beyond.

Have you seen a portfolio recently that resonated with you? What about it stood out?

It's rare for me to come across portfolios that truly resonate. I sometimes think this problem is in education, with schools guiding students to do projects that don't show well or don't allow a student to express themselves. I do look for a balance of skills in a portfolio, but primarily I am looking for someone who shows depth in their thinking, innovation, and quirkiness. Portfolios that include a quirky project stand out as these always put a smile on my face.

So if an industrial design student came up to you and asked, "What should my portfolio be like? What do I need to show you in order to work with you?", what would you tell them?

There are three elements I look for in a portfolio. I am primarily looking for signs of original thinking and creativity. This, to me, is by far the most important element in a portfolio. As a result I would suggest that a student, when considering what to work on at college, should select a project or topic that allows them to express their philosophy and make bold statements. The second element I look for is evidence that the student has "considered" how to bring an idea to market. Please note my emphasis on the word "considered," for I understand that a student is at the start of their career and there is a lot to be learned. All I am looking for is that someone has purely given this area some thought. The final element is communication. The presentation should primarily be digital and should tell a great story.

What do you expect to learn from a designer during an interview?

We have two rounds of interviews. The first round is on the phone with between four to six applicants. In the phone interview we ask the applicant to present their work. Through the presentation we look for depth-of-thinking, an unhealthy enthusiasm for design, and good communication skills. The second interview will be with the final two applicants. This interview is, to quote an old boss of mine, "to simply establish who I would not mind working next to at four in the morning."

"I AM LOOKING FOR A PORTFOLIO THAT PUTS A SMILE ON MY FACE. THIS COMES FROM ORIGINALITY, PERSONALITY, AND SOMEONE WHO GOES ABOVE AND BEYOND."

I would also like to add that interview etiquette is important as it represents the applicant's ability to represent the company. Attributes we look for are punctuality to the interview, personal hygiene and smart appearance, enthusiasm towards the position, and an interest in world affairs. It is always appreciated when an applicant writes to us within 24 hours to thank us for our time. This all may seem obvious, but it has amazed me how many applicants we have had that have shown very poor etiquette and dignity.

What advice would you give to the students then on how to interview well?

Designers are truly great creative problem solvers, but they need to apply that kind of thinking when preparing for an interview. The problem is: I need to go into this interview and convince this person that I'm the right person for the job. Design interviews tend to be more informal than normal, but the interviewee should show a level of reserve. Designers need to be able to display their creative side when needed, but also show dignity in business when called upon.

I would also recommend being yourself. A lot of times studios are looking for designers that fit well with the studio dynamic. Being yourself allows the interviewer to place the new designer in the right position. Therefore relax, look sharp, clean your nails, and smell good. Read the news, speak with confidence and pride, and sell your story to the best of your ability—and you will get what you want. That's what it comes down to at the end of the day: getting what you want.

What characteristics or qualities are necessary to be a successful designer these days?

There are more products in the world today than there have ever been and competition has never been greater. As a result a successful designer needs to innovate, alter paradigms, and create products that truly connect with the user. Being a designer today also requires exceptional communication skills. The right product will never reach the market without the designer's ability to convince investors and strategically protect the product's vision through to production. Another quality is a considerate, open-minded view of the world with a sensitivity to different cultures. For this reason every designer in our studio has either worked or studied in another country. I also think that a successful designer is someone who pushes a personal belief or philosophy. There are a lot of people out there who can design, but not a lot who know why they design and this is always evident in their work.

How did you break into this business?

I wish I could tell a great story about how I broke into the business but I feel like I was naturally "gravitated" in this direction. From the age of four I always thought I would be either a sculptor or architect. Great education then helped guide me. Firstly, I was very lucky to attend Trent College, a private high school in Nottingham, which had an A-level in product design. I then attended an undergraduate degree in industrial design in Newcastle followed by a master's at the Royal College of Art (RCA). At each educational step I was fortunate to be surrounded by great educators and progressive peers.

What motivated you to open your own design studio?

There were a number of reasons why I created this studio. I was interested in exploring new design methods. I wanted to understand business as only a business owner knows and I wanted to set up a studio in Los Angeles. I am aware that as designers we are always challenging others to push what they believe in, move in new directions, and take a chance. I believe that we should also practice what we preach and apply these values to our own lives. I had in the past worked for a design and production company, several design consultancies around the world, and a couple of major corporations. In the spirit of continually learning and reinventing myself, I felt that founding a new studio would provide the next chapter.

If you were starting out now, what advice would you give yourself?

One of the most remarkable things about design as a profession is that you can pretty much work anywhere in the world. The skills you learn as a designer can be applied anywhere. This was important in my career as I have worked in a variety of countries including the UK, Norway, Holland, Sweden, Finland, Germany, and finally the US. So, the advice I would've given myself is to have done that a little bit sooner than later, maybe even studying in another country. It would be nice if it were mandated to spend some time studying overseas. Designers really truly grow when they are able to work in different environments and observe different cultures. Through travel, designers are able to see a lot of the same problems solved in different ways. Travel also allows the designer to become more sensitive to different cultures, an important attribute when designing products with a global reach.

Where do you see the future of industrial design going as it evolves further in the 21st century?

The last 10 years have been great in industrial design history due to advancements in manufacturing. Manufacturing has become more flexible, accessible, approachable, and cost effective. It's truly been a phenomenal and liberating period to live through as an industrial designer. Unfortunately, there is a dark side, which is that product manufacturing has almost become accessible to anyone. This has resulted in products that are being developed by people who do not have the education or skills to create high-quality designs. This results in a lot of poor products, resulting in unnecessary waste. It upsets me as a designer when I consider the environmental cost of poorly designed products.

I am also concerned about the personal human cost. I am not comfortable that there are people around the world working in squalid conditions just to make cheap products for the developed countries. So my answer to this question is more along the lines of "how I would like to see the industry evolve further in the 21st century." As a profession, it would be nice to mandate the use of well-educated industrial designers in the development of products so we can control how we spend the world's resources and reduce unwanted waste.

Anything else you'd like to add that we didn't talk about? Any final words of wisdom?

When I graduated from the RCA, I thought after seven years of higher education that I was at the top of my game and that I knew everything. This was the first and last time I would ever think this. One year later I remember reflecting on how much I had learned working in the industry and how little I really knew upon graduating. The same happened one year later when I reflected again on how little I knew after working in the industry for one year and how much I had learned in my second year. It has been the same every year since. So, as an insight to a student I would say this: consider that when we employ a student designer, we understand there is a lot to be learned. On average in our studio, it takes between six to 12 months for the best graduate to become profitable. Hiring designers straight out of college is, in my experience, a long-term investment. My expectations are that we will teach new designers how we work and the tools we use. Original thinking, a strong design philosophy, enthusiasm, and the ability to learn are not skills we can teach. So, I would discourage student designers from trying to teach themselves every CAD package or design tool and ask them to spend the time developing their creative skills. BI

To see Pip Tompkin's work, please visit http://breaking.in

KLAUS TRITSCHLER
VP DESIGN
ICON AIRCRAFT
LOS ANGELES

What kinds of portfolios get your attention these days? What brings in an industrial designer for an interview?

First, it takes one or two very strong, exciting projects that relate to what I'm looking for to catch my interest. Once I'm interested, I review for a good volume of varied work samples showing appropriate, well-targeted design solutions, plus skillful use of design tools: manual, 2D, and 3D digital. Those are my top-level requirements that bring in a candidate for an interview.

Beyond that, the best portfolio makes me feel that hiring this person will not only get the job done well, but will move us forward and bring a unique, desirable quality or character to our product. I review portfolios first for skills, then for experience and then personality. For a junior position the candidate's interests—are they into power sports or airplanes?— and the unique character in his/her work can be more important than specific experience.

As for specific skills I look at their competence in design skills, design process, use of creative tools. Do they have targeted, fresh, unique, intelligent solutions? How is their craftsmanship in sketching, rendering, 3D modeling, graphics, etc., as well as their communication? Is it clear, to the point, and graphically interesting? I also look for specific experience/qualifications that match our needs and their personality, their affinities, interests that match our needs and/or our brand. Do they have a unique personality/character that is visible through their design and presentation?

What do you think of showing work that's not industrial design in a portfolio? Things like art, photography, hobbies, etc.?

In addition to showing great design and excellent craft that's directly relevant to the position, seeing samples of past-time projects such as photography, sculpting or—for example—your hand-built custom motorcycle is a big plus. This often shows passion and interests in a very direct, unfiltered way and tells me that the person has a natural drive and enthusiasm to create. However, if the design-portfolio section is not convincing, showing past-time projects won't help much.

What do you expect to learn from the designer during an interview?

Are they excited about design? How does it come across? I ask a lot of questions about the candidate's designs, such as why did you choose this sketch as your final design direction? What in your design communicates the brand? Ultimately this is to discover what drove the designs and learn how conscious the creative process was, if solid design goals were established, and if they can communicate them clearly and concisely. And then, is this thinking visible in the design solution? Did they succeed in meeting the design goals?

Beyond that, I look to see if there is any deeper thinking behind the design. Do the design goals come from critical observations or a new way of looking at things? Is there a unique perspective or an expression of the designer's personality? I don't spend much time reading detailed design briefs or explanations when reviewing portfolios, unless they are very short and to the point. Typically I try to dig deeper in the interview. In regards to personality and fit with the team, I look for energy level, drive, enthusiasm, and a balance between being humble and confident. I'm also interested in finding out how an applicant manages criticism. Does the candidate react defensively or do they take an interest in suggestions, reflect on them, learn from them.

What characteristics or qualities are necessary to be a successful industrial designer?

Interest and openness, natural inquisitiveness, ability to observe and take in what's happening on a deeper level. Innate confidence that they can come up with a strong solution and a willingness

to experiment and iterate without giving up. A strong connection to your core, to your gut feeling. Creativity starts in the gut, not in the head.

What are some reasons you have rejected a candidate?

Work samples were not relevant for the position or they had higher interest in other areas than the area of job focus. The obvious, such as lack of craft (ability to draw, etc.), or lack of 3D (Alias, Rhino, etc.). Too much styling and too little thought or the opposite, lots of thinking, but no/few visually attractive solutions. Weak work samples—even if there were also good ones in the portfolio. And finally, a personality that did not fit well for the team.

How did you break into this business?

I enjoyed a solid industrial design education and worked on a number of vehicle design projects at school. I think it was the combination of a strong grasp of the design process and design-thinking coupled with the emotional component of car and motorcycle design that made for a good launching platform. My internship at BMW Motorcycle and my thesis project at Opel were also key. I learned a lot at both companies, and the projects and brand names gave a lot of credibility to my work.

If you were just starting out now, what advice would you give yourself?

Focus on what you are most passionate about and find the best teachers to learn from, and the best teams to work in.

Where do you see the future of industrial design going as it evolves further in the 21st century?

Industries across the board are using ID in their development process and the product landscape has become extremely competitive. Simply "styling" a product is no longer enough to give it an edge. The years of low-hanging fruit are over. Most products are developed with experienced industrial designers on staff who are charged with the task to drive commercial success. "Good design" is the new norm, and we have arrived at a kind of "mass mediocrity."

To develop products that differentiate themselves further, we need to dig deeper and that, in my mind, set the tone for the future of industrial design. For our schools this means that design educators need to teach design process at a new level and provide strong mentorship. Digging deeper requires a stronger focus on the entire user experience, which broadens the scope of the design process to include a larger spectrum of disciplines and technologies. Collaboration in all stages of development will become ever more important and designers have to expand their knowledge base to collaborate effectively.

Designers are creating more and more niche products, designed for very small markets with very specific design requirements. The Internet allows us to reach long tail/niche customers and to do international business from our home design office. Innovative processes make low-volume tooling more and more affordable. This is a huge opportunity for the entrepreneurial spirit in many of us. We can launch our own product or brand much easier and turn it into a viable business. This is not only an expanding business avenue, but perhaps more importantly a chance to do what we love, express ourselves, and fulfill our dreams. ▣

To see Klaus Tritschler's work, please visit http://breaking.in

"...THE BEST PORTFOLIO MAKES ME FEEL THAT HIRING THIS PERSON WILL NOT ONLY GET THE JOB DONE WELL, BUT WILL MOVE US FORWARD AND BRING A UNIQUE, DESIRABLE QUALITY OR CHARACTER TO OUR PRODUCT."

TJEERD VEENHOVEN
FOUNDER
STUDIO TJEERD VEENHOVEN
GRONINGEN, NETHERLANDS

In this collaborative process, designers are ambassadors for the user, and this perspective can serve as the North Star for development. This will earn designers leadership opportunities at the intersections to areas outside their traditional areas of expertise. The playing field becomes bigger and designers who are willing to branch out will be able to enjoy previously unknown career paths.

Anything we didn't cover that you would like to add? Any final words of wisdom?

Another factor that will start driving ID is that consumers are starting to look for the meaning in a product: TOMS shoes, Patagonia apparel, and Tesla for example appeal to this notion.

What kinds of portfolios get your attention these days? What brings in an industrial designer for an interview?

Designers should try to develop their unique selling points, especially now in times of financial crisis. You are still a little bit of a luxury item to many companies. Design is still a very small element of the product design process in general. Of course, designers would like to change this but sometimes it's too difficult and too expensive to do so. What I'm doing right now with our studio is making sure that throughout different projects we clearly state what our benefit is. Our studio is so eclectic in the things we do that it's sometimes very difficult for companies to assess how we would be of any value to them. We try to work towards establishing proper descriptions on our web page. In the last few months, as we have been working with a lot of bigger companies, we noticed that for them design is just not as easy to understand as we may think.

Also I'm Dutch, and we're more into content and conceptual-based design, and sometimes I think there's a bit too much of that out there. We try to tell the clients we are specialists in design thinking, in design process. We like to be involved at the earliest stage possible so we can first assess what is in place before we start designing. We finally met some companies that are willing to give us this space to roam, before we call out a design solution or even a concept.

How many designers work with you?

Right now we work with freelancers as it's too difficult to work with full-time employees in Holland. We have a team of about three designers, one in India and two in Holland and several junior assistants.

How did select your designers? What about their portfolios stood out and said to you, "Yes, these are the people I want on my team"?

In my studio I'm not too involved with the business aspect, so I have an associate in place to handle the business side. When hiring staff, it was important to bridge the gap between my point of view and my associate's point of view by hiring people who would fill up this gap. We have a very style- and aesthetics-oriented designer, and we have a designer who is very good with content. I knew them from before and they were both designers who wanted to get their own career started. They saw our studio as an opportunity to learn a lot, especially how to get a project from concept to business, which is always difficult.

What would you say are the characteristics or qualities necessary to be a successful designer these days?

I can only tell you about the elements that should be successful and will be successful in the future. I think it's very important right now for a designer to get a place in the entire process of design of the product. Not only to think about the consumer experience or what's already on the shelves or what's going to be the next trend. Right now, as

a designer, you should really get more involved. Where does the sourcing come from? The raw materials? The production techniques? The energy consumption? The afterlife of a product? All of those things are key for designers to focus on to become successful. Many of the big companies, this is what they're going to look for. They know that the material source of their production is at stake at the moment—all the plastics and all the synthetics. They are going to look for innovative solutions in design.

"RIGHT NOW, AS A DESIGNER, YOU SHOULD REALLY GET MORE INVOLVED. WHERE DOES THE SOURCING COME FROM? THE RAW MATERIALS? THE PRODUCTION TECHNIQUES?... ALL OF THOSE THINGS ARE KEY FOR DESIGNERS TO FOCUS ON TO BECOME SUCCESSFUL."

So many people can just make a nice 3D rendering, but what's your unique selling point? When everyone is tight on budget you have to make sure you know a lot.

If you were just starting off now, what advice would you give yourself?

The danger is that, over time, you become more of a project manager than a designer. For me designing is about curiosity and wandering. Stay pleasantly surprised by your surroundings, pay attention to small things and—I know it sounds corny and cliché—but be curious. Keep that in mind. Be aware.

I was talking to my colleague who is an architect and has been in this business 10 years longer than me.

I asked her how does she ensure she maintains her own quality and integrity when she runs a studio? She said, "You have to reinvent yourself. You have to make sure that you're right there where you should be, at the forefront of design. It's complicated and scary."

Where do you see the future of industrial design going as it evolves further in the 21st century?

We had a lot of meetings in the last few weeks and I'm very interested in the base of the pyramid target group. There are two billion people who are waiting to become the part of our world, of our wealth. In general, there is no design for these people, just lower-end products based on higher-end products, or there's just a lot of crap. In India we are trying to collaborate with big companies on designing for this segment and it's quite complicated. It's extremely complicated, but very interesting, because you have to start designing from scratch. You cannot just take some knowledge that you know and just put it in place and say, "Presto, I'm done." You really have to think about all the aspects of design—every single aspect from water usage to afterlife, to consumer experience. A lot of people think that if you're poor that you don't have the same wishes, but one can have the exact same wishes and the exact same crappy habits. It's exactly the same consumer but with less money to spend. I think design should bring and will bring a lot of solutions to the problems at hand.

Is there anything you'd like to add that we haven't talked about? Any final words of wisdom?

I would like to get the whole perspective on bio-friendly design, on socially responsible design, moving and change its perception. Often the feedback from people is that they think you're doing all of this to serve a better purpose, to be nice to the world and everything around you. In fact, it's not even so much about that. Instead, it's a very interesting business model and opportunity. Why would you not try to invest a bit more of your company's time into the largest segment of the global population? I'm getting a little bit fed up with some of my colleagues because they still think we're trying to change the world. Of course we are, but again, we're basically doing our job in an environment that's different than what it used to be. It's a very good business opportunity, it's not just hippie talk.

We have plenty of that in San Francisco.

I'm sure. I am out here in India now and I've spent some time in the field today preparing my material with a local company and yesterday I went to the slums of Mumbai to check out how people live. It's a horrible sight sometimes, but the solutions are creative and people are good. Don't patronize them. ⒷⒾ

To see Tjeerd Veenhoven's work, please visit http://breaking.in

ALBERTO VILLARREAL SENIOR INDUSTRIAL DESIGNER GOOGLE MOUNTAIN VIEW, CALIFORNIA

Interviewed while Mr. Villarreal was Director of Product Design at AGENT in Mexico City.

What kinds of portfolios get your attention these days? What brings in an industrial designer for an interview?

I have seen tons of portfolios, and actually have been teaching some short courses on portfolio creation to students, and probably less than 5% of the portfolios that I review attract my attention. There is an incredible amount of portfolios that are not really attractive. It depends really on what I'm looking for, the specific skills. It depends if it's more of a senior profile or junior, if it's specialized or a generalist type of person. Usually, with junior designers, what I look for is more diversity in their portfolio and process.

Basically I want to find out how they work, how they think while they're working, what are their methodologies, how they make decisions. I also like to see a wide range of skills. Some portfolios are very oriented towards one specific skill, like 3D modeling or sketching, but I think the portfolios that are more interesting are those ones that cover a wide range of methods. A person who can do research, but can also sketch and can make quick foam or cardboard mockups, and then jump into 3D and jump into CMF [Color, Material, Finish] specs—that, to me, is a really strong junior designer. The one who can really tackle a whole project from start to end. Then again, there are some portfolios that are very strong in one particular skill, and those ones also attract my attention because I immediately stop flipping through the pages when I see something amazingly executed.

I dedicate a small percent of my time to reviewing portfolios. When we have positions open, we get hundreds of portfolios coming through, and then sometimes even if we're not looking for a designer, we get portfolios randomly. I usually spend very little time browsing through them because my busy schedule is filled up with tons of other activities [that are] equally important, like that of any other design director. I spend more time when I see something interesting. As I said, I open a PDF and flip through the pages. I don't read the text—I don't think anybody does—so I always suggest to my students not to have a lot of text in their portfolios. Whenever I see something attractive visually, then I stop and I dedicate more time.

Obviously, presentation skills and style are very important. I've seen portfolios that have very small pictures on the page—those are not attractive. If you blow up a picture all the way to cover the entire page, you immediately have more impact. These types of details I think are very important to get the first attraction from the audience. I think visually, the first impact is very important, then obviously the content—but nobody will find great content if the presentation style does not call attention.

On the other hand, I see portfolios that are very strong visually, but which have no content at all, or they have process or taste or design language that are not aligned with what I'm looking for—so I'm not attracted to those even if they are very interesting visually. As a side note, usually when

I want to hire someone I have a very clear idea of the type of profile I need for my team. In general, I look for a profile that is different than those of other team members, or sometimes someone with a very strong skill or a lot of experience in a particular field.

Coming back to content versus presentation, I think there's a balance between content and presentation skills that is important. There might be some people who have really interesting ways of designing or they may be great out-of-the-box thinkers, but if their portfolio is not strong enough visually, they're not going to get attention from anyone. I think the first characteristic I'm looking for is strong visual impact, and then I look into content. As I said, process is what I'm more interested in when looking for a junior designer. In a senior designer I probably won't look much at how they solve a problem as long as the problem is solved and the result is stunning. In senior designers I look more for results: is the product in the market, whether the product gotten any recognition (awards, articles, etc.), or whether they solved any unique problems. Of course, if I'm looking for a specialist—someone who's really strong in ergonomics or user interface—I look for strong emphasis on that in their portfolio.

I think both junior and senior designers should craft their portfolios according to their audience. If you're looking for a job at, let's say Adidas, for a shoe designer position, I would expect to see several shoe projects. If you're looking for a job at Philips Healthcare, you probably should demonstrate that you're interested in health care and have experience in it, and so on, and so on. Making your portfolio is a tailor-made project. You can't make one portfolio and send it to everybody. I think every time you send a portfolio you have to know who you're sending it to and try to craft it toward what they're looking for. I've seen applicants who've copied a ton of people on their email and sent a portfolio over. I think that's the worst thing you can do, but I've seen it happen.

Another important aspect is to really transmit your personality in your portfolio. Portfolios are something very intimate, very personal. I once heard Carole Guevin from Netdiver say that nobody sees color the way you see it, nobody sees typography the way you see it, because we are all different and we don't perceive the world in the same way. Maybe someone has a really interesting color palette that's their personality. It's very important that you immediately read someone's personality when you browse through their portfolio. I think people should do this consciously and try to really imprint and communicate their style and particular persona through their portfolio. This goes from the typography you choose, to format, to the amount of projects you show, to the details. Some people write on their CVs: "I'm a detail-oriented person," but when you look at their portfolios you find some pixels that are not in the right position and then the whole "attention to detail" goes away. The personality and how it's expressed in a portfolio through every single detail and the impression you get when you review it as a whole is important to me.

Have you seen a portfolio recently that resonated with you? What about it stood out?

I recently received a portfolio from a Korean designer that definitely attracted my attention. The cover page was really nice graphically, and when I kept flipping through the pages all of them had a very consistent graphic style that was attractive and contemporary. I've seen portfolios that are kind of outdated in style, font-wise and color-wise, and that tells me that maybe the person isn't up-to-date. This Korean guy was a junior designer. His portfolio was very strong because he had a diverse range of products. He had everything from a wristwatch to home appliances to furniture and housewares—that was interesting. The quality of the projects was consistent. That's important. Sometimes you see portfolios that have a few really good projects, and then there are a few that are so-so, and maybe one that's not good enough. It's very important that all projects show the same level of quality and that consistency is kept along the entire portfolio (using format, grids, etc.).

Another thing that I tell my students is that you never have a deadline for a portfolio. If there are some renderings of an old project that you want to show, you can remake them. You have time to redo sketches, to take better pictures of your prototypes. There are no rules to make a portfolio, there are no deadlines, so people should definitely consider this.

The Korean designer I mentioned—aside from the fact that he showed a wide range of projects—also had a really good control of form language on each project; he understood geometry and proportions really well. I could see that in all of his projects. They may have had completely different design languages or very different target markets, but he showed that he could really design something without trying to imprint a particular style. He could deliver different solutions for different problems. After I saw his portfolio, I wrote back to him to have an interview. But he didn't get back to me, so that was kind of strange. If you send your portfolio to a company, you have to follow up.

What do you expect to learn from a designer during an interview?

I'm looking to see something new. I don't want someone to come in and show me the projects I've already seen in his portfolio. I want to find out about his or her particular personality, learn about the person behind the work. I want to find empathy and I want to find knowledge. I want to find out if he really did the projects that he's showing. I'll probably ask some questions about the projects to find out if he actually was the one making decisions. Plenty of times we do group projects and people want to show those group projects in a portfolio, when their participation was actually very minimal. So I want to find out those things.

I'd like to see a sketchbook. Things that are not necessarily included in the 10 MB PDF. I want to see the soft skills, the persona, the human being. I want to find if there's chemistry with the design team. They'll be working with us for eight hours a day or more, and I want to find out if there's a fit personality-wise. You've seen their work previously, so it's more about the person during the interview.

What are some reasons you have rejected a candidate?

When I review portfolios and find something interesting, I send it to the other members of the design team, we discuss it and decide whether to bring the person in for an interview. When we interview, we do it as a design team and we have a discussion afterwards about the candidate and the work, the way they presented, etc. If we reject someone it's probably because we already have someone with those skills on the team. Sometimes there isn't a personality fit. If someone is too arrogant about his/her work I just don't feel like that's a person I want to work with. I think those are the two main reasons.

I always try to find the people who I don't have in my team. It's like a soccer team; if you only have goalkeepers on your team then nobody's going to score goals. I always try to find different types of designers for the team. I have some people that are really strong at research, some others that are very strong at refinements, some others that are really strong at ideations. I always look to bring new skills to my team.

What characteristics or qualities are necessary to be a successful industrial designer?

I guess it depends on how you define success. If success is economic success, maybe the designer should also be very good at business, or a natural salesman. If you define success as someone who is an opinion leader or industry leader, that might require a different way of measuring success. It really depends on how the person wants to see themselves in the future. If your goal as a designer is to be an industry leader, you publish books, you write on blogs, and you give talks. You should also focus on creating a strong differentiated opinion through your work. If your goal is to be a successful businessperson, you'll probably do that through prospecting clients, PR, and finding out how the product can do in the market. It really depends on what the person wants and how they define success. Once you figure that out, you craft your career in that direction.

I never really considered success to mean economic success; maybe that's why I'm not a rich millionaire. To me success is more about how my work can influence other people: how I can inspire others, have a social impact, or make positive change. That's why I love mentoring young designers, teaching and participating in academic activities, and getting involved in social-oriented projects. I don't just get involved in any project that comes in the door for money. I look for meaning in the stuff I work on.

How did you break into this business? What motivated you to open your own design studio?

I decided to be a designer when I was nine years old, and I never changed my mind. My father is an engineer and he got a postgraduate degree in industrial design so ever since I was young I had books and magazines about ID. I immediately fell in love with the profession. My type of profile as a designer is very oriented towards the project. I'm not necessarily a manager type of designer but more of a hands-on creative person. After working for about 10 years for different companies, I decided to open my own practice because I wanted to have my own voice out there.

"YOU CAN'T MAKE ONE PORTFOLIO AND SEND IT TO EVERYBODY. I THINK EVERY TIME YOU SEND A PORTFOLIO YOU HAVE TO KNOW WHO YOU'RE SENDING IT TO AND TRY TO CRAFT IT TOWARD WHAT THEY'RE LOOKING FOR."

When you work at a bigger company you don't always get to choose the projects you're going to be working on, and I wanted to be more selective. Not because I didn't like some industries or types of projects, but because I wanted to transmit my philosophy through my work. Also because I'm more of a generalist type of a designer, I don't want to work for just one industry for 10 years; I wouldn't be happy designing cell phones for the rest of my life, for instance. I always try to find diversity. I think having my own practice gives me that opportunity to work sometimes in furniture, sometimes in interior design, sometimes in consumer electronics, and sometimes in some strategic or branding programs.

How do you manage the non-design aspects of running a studio?

That's the thing I hate. When you're young you say: "Oh, I want to be my own boss, and have my own company," but you don't really think about the administration activities you'll have to deal with. When you have a small company you have to do all sorts of stuff like paying taxes, managing employee benefits, finances, dealing with safety issues, hiring, establishing the company's long-term vision and strategy. Just the prospecting and sales job alone is a huge task. We recently hired a person just to do business development. Otherwise at the end of the day you realize you have very little time to sit and design, and you end up hiring other people to do the design work, so it's kind of absurd.

It's not easy for me to deal with all the non-design related things. I try to involve myself more in the design process and try to be really close to what's happening on the design side of the office. The other stuff is really time consuming but equally important if you want your firm to be up and running. You can't just forget about paying taxes and all those things. It's difficult. I still don't have a formula that works other than trying to hire people to do the work that you don't want to do. I have an admin department that deals with a lot of all this stuff directly. I still have to manage a huge amount of information, especially at the beginning, but then the machine starts working by itself. But even having a dedicated admin staff, you're the leader so you have to deal with leadership stuff, not just creative direction. You'll have employees asking for more vacation days, you'll have a landlord saying you have to find another space because he's selling the building, etc. You'll have all these things that you never imagined you'd have to deal with.

You opened your studio in Mexico. Can you talk a bit about the design opportunities there and why you chose Mexico after your very international career prior to it?

I spent about seven or eight years abroad and at some point just felt like I needed to come back to my home culture, settle down a bit, have family and friends close by. I also saw an opportunity because the design scene in Mexico is kind of up and coming. I wanted to be a part of that, as opposed to being in a design industry that's very well established, as it is in the Bay Area. I spent four years in San Francisco and the industry there is super solid. There are design studios everywhere and some pretty big houses like frog and IDEO. I felt like being there I was just one more, whereas here there's more opportunity to have impact because the design industry is much smaller and because there's a lot more to be done in many regards. More fertile ground, so to speak.

The problem is that the product development industry in Mexico is not as developed as in other countries. There's not a lot of connection between the design world and the manufacturing world. It's difficult to sell or to get paid for design service. Sometimes you have to sell the product with the design cost hidden. That's why a lot of people here are in the furniture business; they end up manufacturing their own furniture and that's how they make their business work. Sometimes you spend a lot of time trying to convince companies about how they can benefit with design service. Some companies get it, some companies hire outside firms to do design with them. It's not like in the US where you have this very strong and established industry with highly specialized model shops and all these other vendors. Here, you have to find and figure out all of these things on your own. In a way I feel like my generation is paving the way for the younger folks.

There are some advantages, of course. For example, prototyping certain products is so cheap and easy here. There is very high-quality craftsmanship and low labor costs, not as low as in Asia, but very low and very close by so I've been able to make some furniture with local shops. It's very nice because we're very close to them. It's not like you send your prototype to be made in China; here you can actually go to their shops and factories, see how they're cutting and folding and innovate during the process which is something that you miss when your manufacturing facilities are overseas. That's definitely an advantage, but as I said the design industry here is very oriented towards furniture and interiors because the heavy manufacturing industry doesn't pay attention to design or to local designers. There's the automotive industry for example, most of those companies are foreign so the design is made somewhere else and they just manufacture it here. So with them, the design opportunities are very limited. That's kind of the reality.

It's not been easy. It will be four years since I came back and I've had up and downs. We've had to be very flexible, intelligent, hardworking, and agile, as well as strongly adaptive to the different situations we've been facing in order to position the company to where it is now, but there's still a lot to be done.

If you were just starting out now, what advice would you give yourself?

When I finished school, it was a very difficult year. Nobody from my class got a job, and I did transportation design so we were all looking for car design jobs; it was really hard. The car industry wasn't hiring, so we all ended up doing other things. We had to use any possible tool and avenue to get our work seen by the industry. These days it's different. There is a huge opportunity to publish your work everywhere on the web, so that's definitely some advice that I would recommend to young designers. There's Coroflot, Behance, and it's really easy to make a website these days. When I left school we were kind of the pioneers on the web because if you knew how to program a website you were king. But that was 10 years ago. These days, everyone can make a website, there are some really nice templates out there, there are social networks...some people just put their work up on their Facebook profile and that attracts clients or potential employers.

So, tailor your portfolio. Publish your work. Try to be diverse. Focus on what you really want to do. Try to find areas that people haven't been interested in before. A lot of people want to be the next Karim Rashid or the next Bouroullec brothers. They want to be the next rock star, but there are a lot of design opportunities in healthcare, design for seniors and children. There are a lot of open doors in the design world that people aren't paying attention to. I would really try and focus on finding the niche opportunities, instead of trying to do what everybody else wants to do. A lot of portfolios have furniture or lighting. There are other problems out there that haven't been solved and they need design

attention. That's one opportunity to be successful—try to find something that nobody's paying attention to.

You were one of the co-creators of Lunar's Designer's Field Guide to Sustainability, which was one of the first such guides released. How have you seen the design world change since then?

I don't have an actual measure to know how people are using the field guide. I'd love to know if people are using it or downloading it. I've definitely been using it and promoting it to my students through workshops and such. I find it to be a great tool, and as you said it was one of the first ones oriented towards the design process. You have the complicated LCA tools that are oriented towards engineering and you have to have your product finished by the time you apply it. This one is oriented towards the design process, so you can make decisions about sustainability while you're creating concepts. Things like the Designer's Accord are also great to share knowledge among designers, to learn from each other. I'd love to see more people participating in this. In Mexico, it's not commonplace yet. There are a few firms doing it but it's not like everybody's thinking green design from now on. Many people, especially the young designers, are interested in it but there needs to be more dialog among designers and a lot more between manufacturing industry and designers.

As far as the future of design, I see a lot of democratization of design. I think we see more and more co-creation platforms and tools that really allow people to design and co-create without really being designers by training. There's definitely a huge trend in democratizing the creative tools, which is threatening to the design field in a way. Either we get really specialized or we get more into the strategic arena. Nowadays, a 15-year-old in his bedroom somewhere can do great 3D models and can design for a company that doesn't want to pay as much as a large consultancy would charge. We face that competition all the time. I've lost projects to very small competitors, to freelancers out there working from their living rooms because they have really good quality and very low fees. It's getting really competitive because of the democratization of tools. I think it's going to change quite a lot in the next couple of years.

Another thing is rapid prototyping applied to mass production, because it's going to decentralize all the manufacturing. These days everything is made in China, but as soon as people start to get their own 3D printers at home, you will be able to make your products at home. Instead of just going to the supermarket and buying a new toothbrush, you might as well just download it from the web and print it at home. Just like everybody has a paper printer at home today, that's going to happen to 3D printers. That will change the game quite a lot. That's where I see it: democratized.

Anything we didn't cover that you would like to add? Any final words of wisdom?

Try to find opportunities people aren't paying attention to. Don't forget about being a designer; even your CV has to be beautiful. Show your design passion in every single thing you make. BI

To see Alberto Villarreal's work, please visit http://breaking.in

CRAIG VOGEL, FIDSA ASSOCIATE DEAN FOR RESEARCH & GRADUATE STUDIES COLLEGE OF DESIGN, ARCHITECTURE, ART & PLANNING UNIVERSITY OF CINCINNATI CINCINNATI

A lot designers that I've talked to for this project have brought up University of Cincinnati and the co-op program. Can you talk a bit about the benefits of having an internship while in school?

We do not admit students by portfolio. We use the university admissions process of academic performance. In high schools today there aren't a lot of classes one can take that would necessarily be a good preparation for design. There aren't many art classes. There aren't many shop classes or architecture classes in high school. Our students have come in with a very high academic standing. We run them through a very rigorous first two years to prepare them to go out and do co-op. We make sure that they can go into a professional setting and make a contribution. That required us to accelerate the content of our foundation and second-year courses to include more than other design programs. The program takes five years to complete.

After the second year our students will work in alternating co-ops during the rest of the program. The most successful students pick a theme and companies they want to work in and get an excellent exposure to the information they need to start their career. Some students just experiment and think of every co-op as a new experience. The ones that tend to be more strategic will often get hired by their co-op employer.

With that said, what are the characteristics or qualities that make a successful industrial designer?

There are several qualities we expect a design student to have when they graduate. The first is to have a set of skills and methods that allow a designer to conduct research and translate insights into products and services. These include visualization methods from sketching to 3D modeling to desktop modeling to rapid prototyping. Students need to have excellent qualitative ethnographic consumer research skills and human factors knowledge from anthropometry to ergonomics. Designers must also be able to minimize environmental impact and design products that follow the concepts of "cradle to cradle." Successful designers work effectively in multidisciplinary teams. And designers need to understand current and emerging trends.

What's driving the designers to pursue business skills these days?

There are two major reasons for the trend to learn more about business and take courses in marketing. The first is the fact that designers interact with business functions in the development of products.

In order to be effective in consultancies or in-house design groups, designers need to be able to communicate their ideas to marketing, sales, and upper management. It is also important for designers seeking to become managers. The second is for entrepreneurial purposes. Many designers seek to start their own companies and or market their own products. Many students want to start companies right after graduation. Business courses give them the ability to better understand how to start a business and get products to market.

How do you see design education evolving over the years? How should it change to address these needs of both industrial designers and their employers or clients?

I've been a long-standing supporter of interdisciplinary education, in allowing students to work in teams with upper-level undergraduate and graduate students. Designers need to have general knowledge and a key strength. I call this "Design + What." Once you learn the core design skills, what's your unique attribute? Is it human factors? Is it manufacturing? Is it business related? Where do you want to go with the complementary ability to find your role or fit? I think the programs must be much more supportive in helping students find out how to present and understand their competitive edge. The programs have to be ready to prepare the students for a much more diverse series of opportunities than they have ever had before. The other area that is developing is the awareness of the role of service design. Products are always connected to a service and services require products to operate. The idea of service is a new way to look at the field and the service sector is the fastest growing part of the economy.

How did you break into this business?

I had an undergraduate degree in liberal arts with a focus in psychology. I had experience with several disciplines as an undergraduate but did not feel that any of them were areas I wanted to pursue after graduation. I always had an interest in drawing and making things but did not know about industrial design. It was actually my mother, a Pratt alum, who told me to look at Pratt. When I interviewed in industrial design, I could not believe people could do that type of work. I had to take a year of courses to get accepted in the MID program.

My thesis was focused on researching a unique approach to teaching 3D. After working in a variety of design jobs, including environmental graphics, I was offered an opportunity to teach in Chicago at the Institute of Design. I've been working primarily in education ever since. My career evolved from teaching foundation to working with companies and consulting on early phase innovation processes. At Carnegie Mellon, I started teaching integrated product development, working with engineering and business faculty. Most of what I do today is working on graduate research, looking at issues of collaboration, and design research for consumers age 50 and over. I was an active member of IDSA and, as an officer on the board of IDSA, I was able to connect to develop an extensive network of design colleagues in practice and education.

If you were starting off now, what advice would you give yourself?

Plan for the next five years of your life because you cannot plan for many more than that these days. Find out a unique combination of abilities that you have, that no one else has. Be prepared to morph throughout your career as shifts in trends occur and new opportunities open. Do not worry if you end up doing something that is not called industrial design.

If I look back, my career has been consistent with the idea of adapting to change. I didn't stay at one university for my whole career. I started out as a foundation teacher and now teach design history and design strategy. I've also formed a nonprofit research collaborative. I never would've predicted 30 years ago that I would be working with multinational companies.

Part of the challenge of moving is that you lose the advantage of a consistent context, but you gain an opportunity to do new things and reinvent yourself. I think most designers starting their career would be fortunate to say that after five years they are doing things they could not conceive of doing while in school.

Where do you see the future of industrial design going as it evolves further in the 21st century?

I think the tangible artifacts that we have historically called products will still be with us. Tangible things will never go away. The difference is the role they play and how products interact with systems. Most products have embedded intelligence or are supported by an intelligence network. Products today are touch points connecting consumers to each other or to service systems. The traditional focus on product aesthetics must now be complemented by a whole array of other factors that drive smart products. These issues are changing the nature of both practice and education.

"BE PREPARED TO MORPH THROUGHOUT YOUR CAREER AS SHIFTS IN TRENDS OCCUR AND NEW OPPORTUNITIES OPEN. DO NOT WORRY IF YOU END UP DOING SOMETHING THAT IS NOT CALLED INDUSTRIAL DESIGN."

There are two interesting contrasts emerging that pit globalization against working local contexts. An idea can start anywhere and finish anywhere. You may conceive of it in Detroit, send it over to Singapore, get it developed there and push it over to China or South America—wherever. Design will continually need to think about global networks of how things get done and how you learn to connect with resources and partners.

On the other side, I see a lot of designers who want to be local and regional and want to commit to using their knowledge to build a local collective. Many are using new approaches, blending new technology with traditional craft methods. Product designers seem to be splitting into two main groups. They choose to work for multinational companies or in small-scale local contexts, but both understand how to leverage digital tools and global communication networks.

Anything you'd like to add that we haven't talked about? Any final words of wisdom?

Several years ago I was at the Cooper-Hewitt Museum in New York and they had an exhibit on "Change: For Better or Worse." Change is still driving most of what's going on in the world. The fundamental role that the designers have historically played in helping to manage and humanize change is still what drives the field. The problem is change is occurring more rapidly and more dynamically all the time, increasing in complexity and requiring designers to integrate more factors to be successful in developing new products.

Each new product design program is an attempt to develop temporary clarity in a complex, changing world. Designers need to know how to read changes in the social, economic, and technical (SET) trends and translate insight into solutions, realizing that the solution may have a short life before the next SET factor change makes it obsolete. This approach to rapid change needs to be balanced with the issues of environmental responsibility. The challenge for design is how to develop an approach that embraces both. This will require a more sophisticated approach to biomimicry than we are currently employing.

I like to look both forward and back to history for answers to these issues. Every generation faces new challenges and looking at how they have responded to design challenges in the past can help us with the future. Franklin and Jefferson generated solutions to complex challenges they faced. The ideas and approach developed by Charles and Ray Eames, Henry Dreyfuss, Victor Papanek, and Buckminster Fuller are both relevant and inspirational. I am fortunate to be in a college within a research university with undergraduate and graduate students who help me to keep pace with change. BI

To see Craig Vogel's work, please visit http://breaking.in

LINDSAY WHITE FUNK
FOOTWEAR DESIGNER
VANS
CYPRESS, CALIFORNIA

What kinds of portfolios get your attention these days? What brings in an industrial designer for an interview?

I like portfolios that show the entire creative process and tell a story. I don't just want to see sketches of shoes and a pretty rendering of a final design. I want to know what is the brief, who is the consumer, what type of trend research did you do, what trends did you pick up on, and how those trends are incorporated into your design.

Having some written information is nice, but I want to see all these things represented visually. Show images of the consumer and mood boards for trend research. I also want to see any work you did with color and material stories. Mix all of these things with the standard sketches and renderings and you'll have a really nice project to show in your portfolio.

I also like when designers inject a little bit of their personality or humor into their portfolios. Nothing gimmicky or overdone, but something that will be memorable. Design should be fun and creative, so don't be afraid to have a little fun with it.

Has there been a portfolio that you've seen recently that resonated with you? What about it stood out?

One portfolio I saw a few years ago that caught my eye was by a third-year design student looking for an internship. His work was great, nice sketches and renderings, but there was one thing that made him memorable. He had done an illustrator caricature drawing of himself and put it on his résumé. Our whole design team got a kick out of it and we ended up hiring him.

What are some common mistakes you've seen junior designers make in their portfolio?

I hate when I see grammatical errors and misspelled words. I've seen new design graduates so overconfident in their design skills that they dismiss the importance of writing skills. If designers expect to own projects and be the face of the company, communicating directly with clients, they need to sound smart and professional both in person and in writing.

When it comes to content in your portfolio, have someone proofread it and remember to spellcheck everything. Sending out a portfolio with misspellings shows that you lack attention to detail. A misspelling on a huge presentation could mean losing a client. It will put doubt in a future employer's mind about what other details you will let slip through the cracks.

What do you expect to learn from a designer during an interview?

I expect to learn about their work and what makes them unique as a person. At this point I've already seen their portfolio so I'm not looking for a portfolio run through. I want to know more about their favorite project. I'll ask them to tell me about their process, any challenges they encountered along the way, and what they enjoyed most about the project.

I'm also looking to learn about them as a person, how they work, and if they participate in any applicable action sports. Most of our designers are personally connected to the categories with which they work. While being an active participant isn't always necessary, having some level of enthusiasm and familiarity is definitely a plus. It's important for us to gauge the designer's level of participation so we know their starting knowledge base.

What characteristics or qualities would you say make a successful industrial designer?

I think to be successful, you have to be a good listener. As industrial designers our job is to solve problems, problems that other people have. Instead of going in thinking that we know the right answer straightaway, a good designer will listen to the client or the user before designing. You should hear not only what they tell you, but also what they don't tell you. Observe and you will "hear" much more than what they are telling you.

To be successful, you also have to be somewhat fearless. Our whole job is to come up with new ideas and sometimes those ideas will fail, but sometimes they will be amazing. You have to accept that sometimes your ideas will crash and burn, but that's okay. As long as you are pushing limits and trying something innovative, then it's not a total failure. That idea may lead you to the winning idea. You won't have your best idea first, so don't worry if you have a few failures along the way.

How did you break into this business?

I did five internships while I was in college. I went to University of Cincinnati, where five semester-long internships are required to graduate. Those internships were more valuable than any studio class. I was able to work at five different companies, all in different disciplines of industrial design, in cities all across the country.

I received a great education at a top-ranked ID program, but it was the internships that really made me ready for the real world. By the time I graduated I had done at least five versions of my portfolio and résumé and interviewed with at least 20 companies. I had already made most of the mistakes that a new design graduate will make when applying and interviewing for their first job.

I also had something that a lot of other new graduates do not have—experience. I had worked on real projects that were produced, in real-world timelines, with real clients, and my hours had been billable. I was a more attractive candidate for a job because I would need less training and could start working right away.

Industrial design still seems to be a predominantly male-dominated field. I'm curious what advice you may have for women who are just now starting out?

As a woman in a traditionally male-dominated field, you have a real opportunity to set yourself apart and be successful. Take advantage of the fact that you are instantly memorable in a sea of male applicants. If your work is good and you are brought in for an interview, point out to the hiring manager that you will bring a new and unique perspective to the design team.

A lot of companies have finally realized that women are savvy shoppers and we can pick out products instantly that have been created using the shrink it and pink it philosophy. It simply is not acceptable to us to have smaller versions of men's products in different shades of pink. We are unique in our stature and activity and our products should be unique, too. An all-male design group will never have the instincts that you will have when designing women's products. As a female designer, you can market yourself as an expert. If this is something that interests you take advantage of the opportunity.

"I HATE WHEN I SEE GRAMMATICAL ERRORS AND MISSPELLED WORDS. I'VE SEEN NEW DESIGN GRADUATES SO OVER CONFIDENT IN THEIR DESIGN SKILLS, THAT THEY DISMISS THE IMPORTANCE OF WRITING SKILLS."

If you do run into a "boys club," you will have to decide for yourself if that is the right fit for you. At some places it might not turn out to be a big deal. However, if you find yourself isolated or passed over for promotions, and you suspect it's because you are a woman, it's probably time to start looking for a new job. Unfortunately you will not be able to change those people, and in truth, they aren't worth your time anyway. You'll be happier somewhere else.

If you were just starting out now, what advice would you give yourself?

I would tell myself to perfect the art of networking and to keep in touch with everyone. At every internship, get to know the other designers, directors, project managers, recruiters. Get connected with them on LinkedIn. Trade personal emails and phone numbers with them and check in now and then after you leave the internship. Stay updated on who works where, who has been promoted, who left and works at a different company. Update your network with new internships or jobs you have had and new skills you have developed. Send out a little teaser of a project you have just finished that you are particularly proud of. Let them know when you are ready to graduate and invite them to your senior show and then thank them if they come.

By staying connected with old coworkers and classmates, you have an instant advantage when looking for a job. You will no longer be just another portfolio that comes across their desk, if it ever gets to their desk at all. If you hear that there is a design position open with their company and you've already been in regular contact with them, it's perfectly appropriate to send a quick email inquiring about the job and to whom you should send your portfolio. Better yet, if they think that you are a good fit for an open design position that they know is coming soon, they may even contact you.

Where do you see the future of industrial design going as it evolves further in the 21st century?

I think industrial design will continue to evolve to be more than just product design. I think it will become more and more popular to have industrial designers work in more conceptual and strategic roles. Industrial designers are usually more analytic than other disciplines of designers and can be very useful in tackling problems with systems, strategy, and other big picture problems.

As more industrial designers are brought into more strategic roles, I think that design will continue to gain more respect and importance in the eyes of traditional business leaders, making CCOs—chief creative officers—a more common position in creative and noncreative-based companies. ⊞

To see Lindsay White Funk's work, please visit http://breaking.in

BOB WORRELL
FOUNDER
WORRELL, INC.
MINNEAPOLIS

You had the honor of studying under Victor Papanek, who authored the famous *Design for the Real World* back in the early '70s. I'm curious, how has it influenced and shaped your career?

That's a bittersweet deal. Victor was very engaging. I enjoyed him a lot. He was eccentric, very controversial, but at the same time he could be nurturing. But here's the dilemma: while I enjoyed my tenure studying under Victor, receiving what I believe was a good theoretical design education, he did not prepare me for the real world. Certainly having been schooled by Victor is something of a badge today in some circles and his bitter feud with IDSA has never seemed to hurt me personally in the profession, but when I graduated—which I believe was the second class out of Purdue University—I was absolutely not prepared. Now, is not being prepared for the real world by the author of *Design for the Real World* a bit of an anomaly or what?

The real world, for me, came crashing in when I graduated in 1970 and we were at the height of the Vietnam War. I got drafted. Now this was a desperate struggle for several months because my wife who had just put me through my last year of design school was pregnant, we sold what little we had and prepared for a long separation. But as fate would have it—I flunked the induction physical. I was rejected from serving. So, it was a very unsettling time because now when I needed a job, I had no portfolio. Victor did not prepare me to do any interviewing, nor did I have any possibility for interviews. There was no plan or design for that. You see, I was a happy little design student living naively in the shadow of Victor Papanek, but when it came to design for the real world, I was totally unprepared.

So, what motivated you to start your own studio in 1976?

Amina, let me back up a little bit to tell you something about me and where design started for me. I knew that I wanted to be an industrial designer when I was in 8th grade. I am convinced I was born for this. I think it is amazing that I actually realized who I was and who I wanted to become at such a young age. I knew that I had an ability to draw. I looked at it as a gift. Where I was going to take that I just didn't know, but when I entered into an elective art class in the 8th grade my art teacher, Ray Bullock, had a copy of Syd Mead's Steel Couture. I saw what a design futurist did and I thought to myself: that's what I want to do.

So from that point I started to work towards becoming an industrial designer—but realize this happened in a rural farming community school in middle Indiana where design was virtually unheard of. Certainly neither my parents nor 99% of people in my community had ever heard of such a thing.

When I went to Purdue, my parents barely had the money to pay for the first year. I chose Purdue because of in-state tuition. I could not find a school that I could afford for industrial design. I really went there thinking my dream was done. Purdue had no design curriculum. On orientation day I went to the engineering school and they told me that I might be able to squeak by in engineering but it would be very, very difficult because of my math grades. When they saw my art grades, they encouraged me to walk over to the art department and talk with them. My immediate thought was that I just can't imagine how I could make a living in fine arts. That's just not going to happen. But for lack of anything else to do that day, I did walk over.

Here's the amazing part: I found out that they had just started a design curriculum but it hadn't been published yet. I mean this was unbelievable. It hit me that this was just too much to be a coincidence. It was my first time to think that there might be some higher order of power or God who was putting this together for me. Imagine, here I am, an 18-year-old kid from rural Indiana totally having to bail on my dream because I had no means to make it happen. Then settling on Purdue University with no communication about its newly started design curriculum and I just happened to stumble into, of all people, Victor Papanek.

Coincidence? I was beginning to think not. My time with Victor was a bit tempestuous. I had my ideas of how things should be done. He flunked me one semester because of it. I thought I had it right, but was persuaded otherwise. Even with that I graduated the top of my class. You know that story, right? There were only three people in the class. Nonetheless, I was destined to be a designer.

But again, when I went into the real world I was totally unprepared. I worked in my father's travel trailer factory for two and a half years. I worked manual labor there and then worked nights to prepare a portfolio and a résumé to try to get a job somewhere, anywhere, in design. Finally, out of hundreds of résumés I sent out, a small, two-man design firm in Minneapolis responded. These two young guys came out of Art Center College in Pasadena, and they were going to take over the design world in Minneapolis. I was hired on as an intern model maker. That's how I broke into the business.

This, too, was nothing short of miraculous. My résumé was really strong because I had three entries in Victor's newly published book *Design for the Real World*. I was in the Chicago Tribune Sunday Magazine, which was a big deal at the time. My portfolio, on the other hand, was very weak. They flew me up on the strength of my résumé but when I got there and opened my portfolio it was the biggest let down. It scared me to death and I realized how woefully short I had fallen and how unprepared I was. I cursed Victor and my college. I thought back to how life seemed so great in school learning about social relevancy, social responsibility, green design, saving the world, the Whole Earth Catalog, all that stuff. But now I realized what I had learned was for naught. There was no interest in any of that. My content was weak and my presentation skills were weaker. I was really in a difficult position.

They sent me back to Indiana packing. I asked these designers for samples of their sketches and drawings because coming from Art Center they were masters. I was at the end of my ability. I had a wife, two babies, we were living under the poverty level, and yet I had this sense of destiny. But more important now, through the trials, I came to the realization of where that sense came from. I came into a personal relationship with the Master Designer of the universe, Jesus Christ.

Finally after several months, probably half a year of practicing sketching in their style I imposed on them and begged them to look at my work. I was desperate. It was a dream that was put into me, and I simply was panicked that it might not happen. Faith isn't always easy. The idea of going into some other kind of career to me was like a nightmare. So I worked day and night, and every minute I could on my sketching skills just to be able to break in. Providentially, having worked in the travel trailer factory, I actually became really good at building things. I prototyped and built an entire motor home myself. So that was a skill set that translated to model making that was useful to my prospective employers. With persistence and an amazing sell job I was finally able to break in. I got a job. That's my breaking in story.

Your passion definitely comes through, indeed.

Yes, it happened. I made it into the industry—but six months after moving my family to Minneapolis I was let go. These guys were living the high life. They were good designers but terrible businesspeople. They were buying and remodeling exotic homes in upscale neighborhoods, flying around the world, buying expensive cars, and then the bills came due. They kept the Jaguars, but they let me go. My wife and kids and I were alone and isolated in Minneapolis barely making ends meet. Despite working day and night to prove myself, the Jaguar was more important. I cried. It was really traumatic.

After some time I managed to find a small design shop where I worked for a couple of months. I hated it. I fasted for a week before finding another job as a designer in what was probably one of the two larger firms in Minneapolis with about 10 people. In that job, I dedicated myself to making my employer successful. In two and a half years I was asked to become the general manager of that design firm. Imagine, I'm only six years out of school with, at best, three years of experience and I was asked to be the general manager of this design firm. I mean, is that not totally crazy? After my boss explained that my salary would be based on profitability, and knowing they were paying out

a partner to retire, there was a big money gap. While I had no access to the books even I could see we were not profitable. I reasoned that I was going to make actually less as the general manager than I was making as a staff designer. I thought to myself: "If they are going to make me a manager, and I'm going to be paid less, do I want this job?" I quit the next day. I had no idea where I was going or what I was going to do. Yet another crisis.

So the next day, I started my business. I put on a suit, a tie, I walked out of the bedroom and into the living room and waited for the phone to ring and of course, that didn't happen. Eventually, I did start making phone calls. That's how we started our business. My wife, Judy, had more financial sense than I did, so she was responsible for our finances, billing, and bookkeeping. I removed the doors of the closet in the living room of our two-bedroom apartment and set up a desk in it. That was the first office. I did manage to convince one of the clients from my former employer to start working with me. They rejected me at first, citing the importance of their relationship with my employer. A few weeks later they found out who was really doing their work and what was going on. That's when I got the call. That went on to be a seven-year working relationship and the stability I needed. Kroy CEO Don Gustafson became my business father and mentor.

But just before that relationship started we were near destitute. I mean we had nothing, no backup and no savings. My wife was working part-time in the apartment office complex where we lived but it actually came to a point where we literally had nothing to eat. I had never been in this situation before. What happened next was miraculous. We received a check for $100 in the mail. It was a cashier's check with no return address on the envelope. This was, I believe, God intervening and His way of promising to take care of us. To this day, I have no idea where that check came from. It allowed us to buy food. Talk about humbling. We had the same experience two weeks later, another anonymous check for $100 came in the mail. I was surprised, thinking, why would God have someone send us another check when we have a payment coming from a client within the next few days? The reality is the payment didn't come. So again our needs were met a second time. The payment did eventually come but God met us at our point of total dependence and I got His message: remember what I've done for you so far. We never received any other anonymous checks. From then on, it was almost 10 years of continuous growth—that is until the next crisis. That's my breaking out story.

That's quite a story! Lots of perseverance and determination through very challenging times.

Very much so. It's been difficult and being in Minneapolis? Well, I wouldn't call it a hub of the design world, although a few years ago I read that Minneapolis was called "design city." It was a reference to Target.

What kinds of portfolios get your attention these days? What brings in an industrial designer for an interview?

To me, the portfolios that are the most impressive are the ones that display the designer's ability to think, where you can actually see their process. It's thinking that's based in the ability to sketch and communicate. I look for sketching ability and page layout that has a nice composition. My design team here agrees that the best industrial designers still exhibit those wrist skills. You can just see an individual's ability come through those simple line sketches, highlighted by color felt tips. Then what I'm looking for is a finished presentation with amazing form generation with the ability to drop the form into context with Photoshop.

I also look for CAD skills such as Alias or other programs used for surface modeling. We look at that ability to model and then—as I mentioned—for the ability to Photoshop. It's important to take those CAD images and drop them into scenarios or an environment that allows you to see the context and use of the product. It's this combination of thinking combined with these amazing new tool sets that can bring an idea to life very quickly. We are looking for the best talent we can find from all over the world. I will say it is sometimes difficult to attract people to Minneapolis. Nonetheless, we manage to do it.

Have you seen a portfolio recently that resonated with you, and what about it stood out?

On top of what I already mentioned I've seen some portfolios now where young designers are conducting their own observational or ethnographic research around a problem. When design is informed by good research, the result is compelling. Add to that excellent graphics and that is a powerful presentation.

I've read that you have invented a proprietary customer research process called CENSYS that projects customer behavior and streamlines the product to market process. Can you discuss that a bit as well as the importance of research in industrial design and its relevance in portfolios?

In 1985 I won every major national design award you can win. The product was in Time magazine as one of the 10 best designs of the year. We won graphic/packaging design awards for this product. We literally just cleaned up. I was in Washington, DC for World Design at the Daughters of the American Revolution Hall for the largest gathering of industrial designers in the world and I spoke and presented. It was amazing meeting so many top industrial designers, members of congress, various personalities—it was really a head-trip.

Shortly after my return from Washington, DC, I learned that the product was failing in the marketplace. It ultimately went nowhere. How is it that I could win all those design awards, but have the product fail in the marketplace? There was something wrong. So I determined that I needed to understand what we could do to be a better corporate servant while designing and developing products that met market needs. Design for design's sake is not good business. I think this was one of Victor's problems with the design establishment at IDSA when I was in school.

In exploring and looking for a solution I was turned on to what was called Quality Function Deployment (QFD). So I went to Detroit to explore this and was subsequently trained in the process. QFD is one tool in the total quality management system that was becoming popular in the mid-'90s. Out of that movement came Six Sigma, which almost everyone in product development has heard of. However, not everyone has heard of QFD. Yoji Akao developed this systematic, qualitative system that was influenced by the quality systems that Joseph Juran, W. Edwards Deming, and Philip Crosby used to help Japan build their manufacturing sector after the war. It was basically a system that developed customer requirements and maintained those requirements throughout the entire development process. This is actually where the term "voice of customer" originated.

Throughout much of my professional career I have experienced companies using "focus groups" to understand people's attitudes about products and services and it seems they have wide acceptance. But in my opinion and from firsthand experience, focus groups have been a disaster for product developers. In the last 15 years I've innovated on QFD to develop CENSYS: an empirical, quantitative research tool. It's been used on hundreds of projects to the point where it's now a unique systematic process for uncovering unspoken customer requirements or what is called "Customer Delights." We combine CENSYS with ethnographic tools to ensure we're designing the right product, or the right system for the market. It's also a powerful tool for business strategy.

Once you have a candidate you like and you bring them in for an interview, what do you expect to learn from them in that in-person meeting? What characteristics or qualities do you look for in an individual to fit your team?

I'm always looking for someone who is going to shift the culture of our company in a positive way. What I'm looking for beyond sheer talent is humility. Don't get me wrong, I'm not looking for a talented wallflower. What I mean by humility is the basic character and potential for leadership. I want someone who can put other people's needs first but then effectively lead them to a fresh perspective. This can be learned but the basic character foundation needs to be there. We are looking for that blend of confidence, poise, and the ability to explain ideas and tell a story. When we find such a young designer and they come on board we frequently have them presenting to clients almost out of the chute. There is a lot of on-the-job training.

If you were just starting out now, what advice would you give yourself?

I don't know that I would ever advise anybody to start a business the way I did. Let me relate this story for anyone who wants to break into his or her own design business.

A few years after I started I was thinking I needed a plan. I contacted Dan Wefler who started the Association of Professional Design Firms. Dan asked me: "Bob, what's the most important thing to a design firm?" and I told him, "Well, design—obviously." And he replied: "No, you're wrong. It's sales. Because if you can't sell design, you don't have anything to work on and you don't have a business." So I reluctantly agreed. It dawned on me that this is, in fact, what I had to do all along. If I couldn't sell I never would have survived. He then asked, "If sales is the most important thing what is the next most important thing for a design firm?" I said, okay now design. "Wrong again. It's management. If you can't manage the work you have, client expectations, and possibly other staff members, you won't last long."

"IF YOU DO DECIDE TO START ON YOUR OWN, KEEP THIS IN MIND: THE LONGER YOU STAY WORKING FOR SOMEONE ELSE, THE MORE COMFORTABLE AND MORE SECURE YOU FEEL. THE MORE SECURE YOU FEEL, THE LESS LIKELY YOU ARE TO TAKE RISKS."

These things may seem obvious but as designers we tend to let our passion and the artistic, right side of our brain dominate our thinking. If you are thinking about breaking out on your own and you can't do these things then you have to think about partnering. That's a totally different issue. When I think about starting out with only three years of experience in the business I'm still a little shocked. There are smarter ways to start. Frankly I think a designer's board life is short. Don't be too eager to start this on your own until you are ready to give up a big chunk of your actual design time. Certainly, you better have some business savvy and some ideas about how to read a balance sheet, and if you can't sell or don't like to sell, don't do it.

If you do decide to start on your own, keep this in mind: the longer you stay working for someone else, the more comfortable and more secure you feel. The more secure you feel, the less likely you are to take risks. Balance also has a lot to do with the sacrifices you will have to make. Don't sacrifice your family. Don't sacrifice your integrity and character. Breaking in or out requires dependence on others as well. You have to have faith, either in something or someone, but it will require a leap. I was not prepared to design for the real world. My story is all about the leap. Yes, I did trust in my abilities and to some extent on my very short on-the-job training but in my case it was more about "who" I trusted than "what" I trusted.

I read that Worrell is partnering with a large consumer packaged goods company to help build design as an organizational competency across all divisions of the company. You've already mentioned this shift towards system design. I'm curious then to hear, where do you see the future of industrial design going as it evolves further in the 21st century?

The second part of the question first. It's a difficult question and one that I have heard asked throughout my career. Designers have always been innovators even before it came into vogue about 10 years ago. I think industrial designers will always work on durable hard goods. In the future I don't think we will design fewer boxes, cabinets, housings, cars, tools, etc. We will, however, extend our range to other things that change our relationships with such hard goods, things like screen interfaces (GUI). I think industrial design is becoming less about the design of "objects" and more about the design of "objects in context,"

including systems, strategy, and business. Design research and tools like CENSYS that have yet to be invented will extend our range to designing more complex systems, environments, and experiences.

Technology advances will also extend our range to things we can't imagine. When I started my design career we didn't have copiers, faxes, computers, or cell phones. Who knows what designers will work on tomorrow? I think the future of design is very bright but I will reiterate: we will not only design objects in context but we may also be designing those contexts as well, including systems, environments, businesses, and experiences.

You asked about my relationship with our large packaged goods client. Here is the challenge I am having in this company that I believe is instructive for young designers, if not all designers. I was brought in under management that sees design as "tactical." It's clear to me that designers are still perceived as "box shapers" or "exotic menials" today by most industries. Design as a strategic focus inside this company is a far greater need than the tactical needs. I am working to change this but it is not an easy task. Design must become more strategic and young designers need to have this in mind to be successful. I think there is a huge risk of design becoming devalued and commodified if managed by business. An easy and frequently distasteful example of this is service or component suppliers who provide free design for the promise of production.

Conversely, design will not be commoditized if design manages business. It's a tall order but we need creativity and innovation around business itself including business models, how products are offered, how they are distributed, etc. I believe designers can help solve these problems but what will make the difference are solutions that are elegant by design and solutions that are strategically innovative, if not disruptive. As the purveyors of beauty in the manmade world we are going to have to go deeper than the surfaces of the things we design. I think Apple does this as well as anyone today. Speaking of box shapers, they are an excellent model of the value and strategic application of design. They shape boxes but they also have shaped their industry, by design.

It's interesting that you bring them up because I've done almost a dozen interviews so far, and everyone mentions Apple at some point or another.

Apple has been on my radar from the beginning because Apple disintegrated two of my biggest clients in 1985. Apple reshaped my world from its inception. That's the crisis I alluded to after 10 years of continuous growth. I lost a huge percentage of my business because of the Apple Macintosh. The technology in this computer simply usurped two entire industries along with their leaders and my clients. Regardless of my situation Apple is the poster child for design, the example of how we as designers think business should work. Apple stands out because most other companies are great examples of design mediocrity. What is sad is there are so many company executives who look at Apple and don't get what Jobs understood. Consequently they will never make the investment in design.

Jobs had an unusual appreciation for the value of design and he just didn't pay lip service to it. Not only was he maniacal about user interface and industrial design but he looked at all parts of the company through the same design grid. Did it pay off? Does there seem to be better model of the value of design in our lifetime than Apple? There may be other companies and leaders who have the financial resources to do what Jobs did but somehow it just doesn't happen.

Anything we didn't cover that you would like to add?

On my own I may not be the best example of well-planned intentionality and designing a business. On the other hand I may be the perfect example of well-intentioned designing of a business on the part of someone bigger than myself. I think we covered it. ⌷

To see the work of Bob Worrell, please visit http://breaking.in

MICHAEL YOUNG
FOUNDER
MICHAEL YOUNG LTD
HONG KONG

You have stated that, "It is design as industrial art that interests me, not in a limited edition, but in mass-production." How does this guide your design approach and design solutions?

Simply that I want all my design to have the same empathy and love that one associates with art, but in a commercial mass-market process. It means we design finely manicured industrial products which are invariably of better quality than competitors, but at a lower price. I love craft design, but I save this for galleries. Art is of course conceptual and design is not, but the empathy of art is an emotional subject that people feel and are inspired by. I wish design to be this soulful.

What motivated you to open your own design studio?

Lack of alternatives. I have never had a job and this is all I know. I made one light in 1993 and then I made another, then I made a chair, and then I made a desk, and here I am now—now, I am driven by a greater wisdom and passion to explore the industrial universe. I am driven and feel in a good place to offer large companies a good service.

How do you manage the non-design aspects of running a studio?

I have an office manager, a press and exhibitions manager, a lawyer, and an accountant but I guess within that there are a lot of decisions to be made, but we are pragmatic. I am blessed with a good team around me. We are a good studio and good things attract good things.

You have been designing for the Chinese market with the expertise of local industry and manufacturing capabilities for some time now. Can you share some of your insights or experiences that may be of benefit to budding designers?

Don't copy my mistakes, make your own. You're only going to be able to offer anyone anything by way of experience or interest in the subject, so you just need to throw yourself at it. Young designers tend to be proud and wary, but really they should be wiser than that and understand that other people can teach them a lot more than they expect, if they meet them half way—not to compromise, but to listen. Things you take for granted others may not even know exist.

What kinds of portfolios get your attention these days? What brings in an industrial designer for an interview?

I have known my staff for years, but it would I guess be fluid computer skills and a pleasant attitude. Most European designers know nothing about production, and most interns end up with a whole load of renders in their portfolios, that turns out they did not do, which gets frustrating and results in a ticket home. We actually have no interns as I speak; we do not like the mayhem they cause. We made a few mistakes in our time but now the office is peaceful. We all love it even if it does mean grabbing the milk yourself.

Have you seen a portfolio recently that resonated with you, and what about it stood out?

If you're referring to interns, I don't do the selection process; the staff selects whom they can work with. As for any additional staff, I am not looking for any at the moment. Basically, no. I don't have the time.

They should send a portfolio that takes 10 seconds to look at, a mood experience, not all this: "I like walking in the Alps in my time off and have a keen interest in teamwork."...Wow, I'm so mean.

If a product design student came to you looking for advice on how to prepare their portfolio to get an internship or a job, what would you tell them to do? What should be in their portfolio?

It should be all their own work and they should make sure if it's not, to make it known. On a personal level, they should express their life through the portfolio.

What are some common mistakes you see students or junior designers make in their portfolios?

Poor design solutions are quite common but not being concise is the most frequent mistake. A picture says a thousand words, as they say.

What characteristics or qualities are necessary to be a successful industrial designer?

You need balls of steel and a vision; there is a lot of crap to deal with in this business. That's from Eugenio Perazza [founder of Magis]. You can boil it down to talent, intuition, and passion.

How did you break into this business?

I fell into it as I failed all my exams at school. I had to make a living out of making things and selling things; it grew from there. The first five years were hell on Earth: no money, no home, no confidence. My first collections were in museums right away and I was eating in the best restaurants by invitation and then trying to find a place to sleep. I slept under cars at one point, normally Range Rovers in Notting Hill.

"YOUNG DESIGNERS TEND TO BE PROUD AND WARY, BUT REALLY THEY SHOULD BE WISER THAN THAT AND UNDERSTAND THAT OTHER PEOPLE CAN TEACH THEM A LOT MORE THAN THEY EXPECT, IF THEY MEET THEM HALF WAY—NOT TO COMPROMISE, BUT TO LISTEN."

I slept in a coal bunker once in Earls Court and ended up in a hospital with pneumonia, which was great as far as I was concerned. Food and nurses, what more do you need?

If you were just starting out now, what advice would you give yourself?

Invest in a jumper.

Where do you see the future of industrial design going as it evolves further in the 21st century?

It is not an easy question. Fifteen years ago I told Wallpaper magazine that we would send molecular formulas to factories to make things. Well, I guess we do in a way but it was pretty dumb. I don't know, everyone is a designer these days. When I started there was only a book about Memphis and a few eccentrics kicking around. Now there are Jasper Morrison replicas sitting in bars in the East End. I really don't know, I've never seen an MY [Michael Young] copy—the ingredients are safe. ◾️BI

To see Michael Young's work, please visit http://breaking.in

GIANFRANCO ZACCAI
PRESIDENT & CHIEF DESIGN
OFFICER
CONTINUUM
BOSTON

What kinds of portfolios get your attention these days? What brings in an industrial designer for an interview?

Before I answer, it's important to understand that the industrial design profession has an ongoing discussion of even its name. It was born in the '30s and '40s, when it was focused around the design of an industrial product. What

we're doing now goes way beyond that, so we're involved in everything from qualitative research to innovation in both product and services. It's much more multidisciplinary. As a result, the people that we hire are more multidisciplinary, so we look for people who have multiple degrees. What we're looking for is not just technical skills in the portfolio, but also in how they think and the way they go about analyzing a problem, conceptualizing the solution and the skill sets in terms of implementing that solution.

You mentioned designers with multiple degrees. What combinations have you seen that work the best?

There isn't just one combination that works out the best. There are a lot of them depending on the nature of the individual. The people that we have here, for example, may have a degree in engineering and a degree in industrial design, or a degree in psychology or an MBA and a design degree, or an architecture degree. It's very broad.

Would you say that's a reflection of the times these days? That it's not enough to have just a traditional industrial design background?

We do have people with traditional industrial design background but they come from programs that are much more diverse in the way they train people, training them to think about problem solving in a different way. Some programs are more skill based; they are more about styling cars for example. It's the nature of the program, the nature of the person, and sometimes the combination of the experiences that they've had in their educational background.

With all of this said, if an industrial design student came up to you and asked, "What should my portfolio be like? What do I need to show to you in order to work with you?", what would you tell them?

Show me how you think. How do you go about understanding people and their problems and aspirations? How does this understanding inform your concepts? Show me how you took such abstract insights and translated them into a practical and compelling solution. Finally, show me how your solution can make someone's life better.

What do you expect to learn from a designer when they come in for an interview?

How they handle questions, how they think of problems. We will review someone's portfolio and then we'll ask them how they went about doing a certain project in their portfolio. We will engage them in a broad conversation about things and see how they think about a variety of subjects. How they break down a problem into its component parts, how well they can collaborate with different people. We create teams and the teams are always composed of people of different backgrounds. How well can someone collaborate within a diverse team?

As they present their work what do you expect to see and hear?

First of all, there should be a problem statement and how they evaluated and perhaps re-defined the statement, and how they went beyond what was just asked of them. How did they go about gathering information that has led them to a hypothesis? How did they test that hypothesis and develop the concept? Is it something that they did from intuition or something that was informed outside of themselves? Where did they focus on this problem? Did they focus on one aspect or a more holistic understanding of the problem? How do people react or relate to an activity in which the product was supposed to provide the benefits? What's the overarching issue and how did they address it with the product, environment, or service?

Then when we look at the physical manifestation of the concept made real. Is the form appropriate for the problem? Is it the right visual language? Does it embody the right experience? Does it communicate the right things? What about the other senses? How does it feel? How do you interact with it? How do you perceive what you're supposed to do with it and what it does for you? Is there poetry in the execution? So we're trying to understand their sensibility for designing for all of the senses, and with both right and left brain. Does it make sense what they're proposing, in sort of a quantitative fashion? And does it make sense in a social, psychological, and emotional context?

What do you think are the characteristics or qualities that are necessary to be a successful designer?

A lot of it comes from trying to understand how someone thinks about a problem. [We look for] someone who thinks broadly, who doesn't just explore different aspects of a problem but also uncovers opportunities to enhance the total experience. But, just figuring out the aspects of a problem and uncovering opportunities does you no good unless you can translate that into something that's technologically feasible. The ability to integrate that knowledge and translate it into something that's not only physical, but also virtual. We need people who can see the future. What should this thing be if it doesn't exist and then how do you make it real?

What motivated you to start your own studio? How did you break into this business?

I studied industrial design at Syracuse University and the idea of having my own studio was always there. At Syracuse, I was fortunate to have been exposed to lots of different dimensions of design as well as engineering, marketing, and psychology. I came out of school with a broader understanding what Design, with a capital D, was. That Design was much more than styling; it was about making the world better. While I was in school I worked in a design office as a junior designer and I had some consulting experience, but first I wanted to work in a corporation to understand how large organizations worked. Even though I had an offer from an automotive company, I wanted to do something more meaningful than styling cars—which was the norm for design in that industry at the time. Fortunately, things have since changed in the automotive industry as well. I thought designing medical products would be a real challenge, and that it would be a tremendous learning experience while doing something more meaningful as a designer. After graduation, I had the opportunity to work for a multinational medical diagnostics company. There I understood more profoundly the importance of designing things from multiple points of view, especially when you're doing things where people's lives depend on it.

To broaden my experience, I also did some consulting in my spare time. One of my clients asked me to take on some projects that were bigger than what I could do just in my spare time. So, after many years of corporate life, I started my full-time consultancy and soon joined forces with a highly accomplished friend, Jerry Zindler, an engineer and a physicist. When we started Continuum, my years of experience in the corporate world helped me understand what worked and what didn't work in organizations. Silos in organizations of different disciplines is not what we wanted to do. The other thing that I learned during my corporate experience is that we needed a better brief to work with than what we were usually given by the client. We started doing our own primary and secondary research to better learn the context of projects. This became the core of design research and our current work on business strategy comes out of that.

Can you talk a bit more about the importance of design research in developing a product?

Very often things are designed, whether by designers or engineers, from their own perspective or their own sensibilities. We think it's really important to get out and really understand how someone lives in the world you're trying to improve. What are their values all about? What's the child's life while wearing diapers? What's it like to think of a car for the city versus the country?

"SHOW ME HOW YOU THINK. HOW DO YOU GO ABOUT UNDERSTANDING PEOPLE AND THEIR PROBLEMS AND ASPIRATIONS? HOW DOES THIS UNDERSTANDING INFORM YOUR CONCEPTS?"

A car for a young couple versus an elderly person? That kind of in-depth research into someone else's life leads you to uncover some important guidelines or objectives for the design process. It ultimately transforms design into an innovation process that can profoundly impact business success.

If you were just starting out now, what advice would you give yourself?

I think, in retrospect, I kind of stumbled into some very great things, so I guess my advice would be not to stumble so much. Do it in a more proactive, methodological sort of way, but still be open to serendipity. But I'm not sure I would change too many things in any case. I assume, if I had the resources, I would've done an additional degree earlier, and not only in architecture but something else—maybe an MBA?

I've talked to several creative directors with traditional industrial design backgrounds who went back and ended up getting their MBA. I'm curious to hear why you think that would be a good addition for a designer?

Well because ultimately, if you do design the way we do it, it's not just about the innovation of the product but the innovation of the business. You need to explain that and communicate it in a language that business can understand, and you, as a designer, need to understand the drivers of business success. You need to have a command of the metrics that business uses traditionally. We've added that capability over time, and have a number of people here who are excellent in that area, but we didn't start with it. It was always a challenge to communicate what we were showing in our concepts, so it's not just another product, but a different way of doing business. I think that's especially important now because the world is changing so fast, the competition is moving so fast, technologies come and become obsolete so fast. The ability to think about business the way a good designer thinks about a problem—in other words laterally, quickly, visually—is essential. We increasingly have clients coming to us who want us to help them innovate their business, not just their product or service.

Where do you see the future of industrial design going as it evolves further in the 21st century?

It's not about products anymore. Products are becoming the smaller parts of everything, but they're also products as a vehicle for much bigger things. Look at Apple. Apple makes products but products are a vehicle for services and those services are accessed through interfaces. That's the domain that is the future. It's physical products and services that are delivered because they are embedded in things that you carry around with you, that know where you are and what your interests are.

Is there anything that you'd like to add that we didn't cover? Any final words of wisdom?

It's no longer a domestic or a global market for anything; it's both. We're also living in a global world and we have clients in China, in Korea, in Europe, in America. They're all working globally. Their products are being sold globally, but that doesn't mean that the product or service should be the same everywhere in the world. The way people experience things is local. Understanding the way people act and behave and their aspirations in the local context may become the winning innovation for global success. This is really going to be even more important in the future. I would say that one of the important things for designers now and in the future is to get outside of our comfort zone, get outside the country that we live in and experience living elsewhere. Learn other languages and cultures to understand there are different ways of perceiving the same reality. [BI]

To see the work of Gianfranco Zaccai and Continuum, please visit http://breaking.in

CHRIS ZARLENGA
DESIGN MANAGER
HYUNDAI
IRVINE, CALIFORNIA

What kinds of portfolios get your attention these days? What brings in an industrial designer for an interview?

Everyone comes in knowing how to draw, so it's not about just knowing how to draw. The biggest thing is

seeing different ideas and a graphic breakup of your concepts. The beginning ideation sketches are the number one thing that the majority of the industry is looking for because the industry is a little bit stagnant on the design side. Everyone's looking for the next great designer, for the new great wave of thinking, for possibilities of rearranging the components to make the design more fresh.

"WE WOULD MUCH RATHER HAVE SOMEONE WHO IS WAY MORE CREATIVE, WHO WE COULD DIAL BACK INTO REALITY, THAN TRYING TO TAKE SOMEONE WHO'S GROUNDED IN REALITY AND TRY TO PUSH THEM FURTHER OUT."

Students have a lot of freedom in school. That freedom means they're not knee-deep in the production process of how to put a car together from inside out. They are experimenting and the sky's the limit on how they can assemble this thing, piece it together and look for something new. It's very hard to find somebody who can do that; it's very competitive as well in schools. So it's really funny when someone finds this something new, how all the students gravitate towards it and it becomes a norm for that school, a signature of a design philosophy. Basically, it's very hard to find that person who stands out and is different from his counterparts.

Has there been a portfolio that you've seen recently that resonated with you? What about it stood out?

I just went to Art Center to look at the student show a couple of weeks ago and we didn't hire anyone. It was a little disappointing. It was not a strong class. Sometimes schools go through that cycle— one school is up, one is down. Right now, there was nobody there who was thinking about putting something new together. There were some good people who knew how to put a car together and how to do traditional surface development, but no one really stood out.

I looked at a portfolio around Christmas and this guy had some really good problem-solving skills and good "real world" skills as well. He knew how to put a car together. The really hard thing to combine is someone who is really creative with someone who is disciplined enough to bring that passion into reality. Sometimes you have people who are too deeply rooted in reality that they can't think of anything new. Then you have people who are too far out and are able to create for the blue-sky environment but they don't know how to dial in what they're drawing into reality. We would much rather have someone who is way more creative, who we could dial back into reality, than trying to take someone who's grounded in reality and try to push them further out. That's essentially harder to do.

What do you expect to learn from the designer during an interview?

We look for how they articulate their ideas. Do they know what they're drawing? How they are showing you their vision, promoting their ideas. The main thing is personality, checking verbal communication skills, and how they articulate their design aesthetic or philosophy to you, and their own personal preference.

What characteristics or qualities would you say make a successful designer?

Being highly creative in coming up with great designs two dimensionally by drawing them, and translating sketches into three-dimensional forms. At the end of the day, that's what's being sold and how the company will make money. The companies are making money on the translation of an idea on paper to a real vehicle. That's the hardest thing to find, a person who is well rounded with great communication skills. Someone who's setting a vision, doing great work, and taking on ideas and translating them into three-dimensional models. What makes a great designer and a great leader is someone who can do all three.

How did you break into the industry?

Back in high school, I wanted to be some type of a designer and didn't know anything about product design or industrial design. I thought engineers designed cars. I was really into architecture and took a lot of those classes in high school thinking that's the field I wanted to go into, but it was just a little too restraining for me. I read in the paper about a local guy who was going to a school in Detroit, Michigan, and he was a car design student who had won an award. I found out about the field through that article. I met with him in person and he showed me his portfolio. It got me really excited because I saw these really cool car sketches and models.

So, I went to Pittsburg to do product design and did cars on the side. I did a little bit of everything because I didn't know if I wanted to do the cars all the time. One of my professors who was from Art Center showed me a bit more of the automotive design side and I did some freelance work for him. I broke into the automotive industry with him through his clients. I did my first clay model with him and I was taught by him how to do surfacing. That lead me to go full time into car design. When I graduated from Pittsburg with a BFA, I went to College for Creative Studies in Detroit. With the independent study I did with my professor, I got into the advanced standing in the transportation design department and went there for two and a half years before graduating. I had internships with Ford and Chrysler, and started my career working for General Motors.

If you were just starting out now, what advice would you give yourself?

That's a good one...don't do it? I kid. Maybe I would tell myself to pace myself a little bit, slow down a little bit. The tendency is that people will work really hard and then burn themselves out. It hurts their motivation and long-term goals a little bit. Slowing it down and pacing yourself may be better. If I could go back, I would definitely pace myself.

Where do you see the future of transportation design going as it evolves further in the 21st century?

The biggest thing is that there won't be any flying cars. There's still going to be four wheels, and you're still going to have doors, and the safety features will get even more restraining. So the biggest change we'll see with the car is the way we interface with it from the inside. That is going to be the largest change. There is going to be a lot of motion sensors, less dials, less buttons. The whole interface of the iPhone now is changing the interface between the human and the machine. Right now, when you get into a car, you have a key. You have a certain way of turning on the radio and it's usually a button. To turn the heat on, it's a button. In the future I see a lot of that going away and being way more simple.

The biggest change will be on the inside of the car, by far. I'm not talking electronically in a Tron way, but screens that look like the real thing but digital. Everything will be streamlined or combined. Your eyes won't be leaving the center of the steering wheel or looking down the road. There will be a lot more customization, your own screens, your gauges, your music, the way you might want your button layout to be.

Sounds like a much more intuitive way to experience the joy of driving.

Exactly. On the outside, I don't see much changing; maybe some lighting technologies will change. The majority of the change will be how you interact with your car.

Anything you'd like to add that we didn't cover? Any final words of wisdom?

Anything is possible for the new designers, especially the way the technology is going. The sky's the limit. It's completely wide open. I personally feel that right now car design is a little bit stagnant. Most companies have really great-looking cars but I feel that everything's on a cycle and that we're in a little bit of a lull in the industry as a whole. I think in the next decade we'll see some really creative solutions on how we live with these vehicles. We are still putting vehicles together in the same way we did 50 years ago but that's slowly changing. There's a new generation entering these companies and that's why I feel that in the next decade we'll see a huge, huge change in car design as a whole. BI

To see Chris Zarlenga's work, please visit http://breaking.in